"Bob Crossman's 'Butterfield's Overland Mail Co. use of Steamboats to Deliver Mail and Passengers Across Arkansas, 1858-1861' tells the story of this important part of the Overland Mail Company's history."
Gerald T. Ahnert, Butterfield Trail historian and author

"The new book by Bob Crossman regarding the use of steam boats by John Butterfield to transport mail across Arkansas is extremely interesting and is a treasure trove of new information."
Margaret Motley, President, Pope County Historical Foundation

"In depth study of the overland mail route across Arkansas by stagecoach and steamboat. This is a great resource not previously available."
Glendle Griggs, Ouachita County Historical Society, Camden, AR

GW00472140

Butterfield's Overland Mail Co. use of STEAMBOATS to Deliver Mail and Passengers Across Arkansas 1858-1861

by Bob Crossman

To learn about the STAGECOACH LAND ROUTE across Arkansas, see Bob Crossman's 2021 book:
"Butterfield's Overland Mail STAGECOACH Route Across Arkansas: 1858-1861"
available from your local bookseller and
walmart.com   barnesandnoble.com   amazon.com
To order signed copies, contact the author at bcrossman@arumc.org

First Printing, January 2022
Ingram Spark Press
12.10.2021

Stagecoaches were used about 324 times to carry Butterfield's Overland Mail across the country. On 81 occasions the stagecoach stations in eastern Arkansas were bypassed when John Butterfield used his steamboat *Jennie Whipple* to carry the Overland Mail and passengers between Little Rock and Memphis.

"The Stagecoach Journey"
Painting by Morgan Weistling, 17"x 28" limited to 50 prints
Image reproduced here by permission of Morgan Weistling, November 17, 2021.
Morgan Weisling's amazing art is available at
legacygallery.com/portfolio/morgan-weistling/

NOTE:
Several of the steamboat images from the files of the Corps of Engineers are faint due to their use of the Cyanotype photographic printing process that produces a cyan-blue print. Engineers used the process well into the 20th century as a simple and low-cost process to produce copies of photographs. The same process was used to produce architectural or schematic blueprints. The process uses two chemicals: ferric ammonium citrate and potassium ferricyanide.

Even though the quality is poor,
the images are included here for historic preservation reasons.

"Big Rock on the Arkansas River"
This steamboat is passing the landmark "big rock" which is two or three miles upstream
from the "little rock' on the opposite bank of the Arkansas River.
Source: Harper's Weekly, May 26, 1866, page 328

Butterfield's Overland Mail Co.
use of
STEAMBOATS
to
Deliver Mail and Passengers
Across Arkansas
1858-1861

by Bob Crossman

LITTLE ROCK, ARKANSAS.—[See Page 317.]

"Little Rock, Arkansas"
Note two wagons and pedestrians waiting for the ferry shown midstream at right.
The Butterfield stages used this same ferry over 300 times to reach Little Rock.

This 4¢ U. S. stamp, was issued in 1958 to commemorate the 100th Anniversary of Butterfield's Overland Mail Co.

This 29¢ U. S. stamp, was issued in 1994 as part of a set of 25 stamps to commemorate *Legends of the West.*

These two U. S. 25¢ stamps, were issued in 1989 as part of a set of four stamps to commemorate *"Traditional Mail Delivery Vehicles."*

John Butterfield, President, Butterfield Overland Mail Co.

ISBN: 978-0-9996578-5-0

Front Cover Art:
"Fort Smith, Arkansas, Recently Captured From the United States Secessionists,"
Source: Illustrated London News, May 20, 1861, page 499

Table of Contents

River Maps

"Whipple Steamboat"
Sketch by David Garrison, Conte Crayon, Nov. 19, 2010
Southeastern Community College, 1500 West Agency Rd., West Burlington, Iowa

Two of my grandchildren, Grayson and Blake Crossman are pictured here with the captain of the Branson Belle sternwheel showboat. Launched in 1994, she has a speed of 14 knots and can seat 700 passengers for its dinner cruse on Table Rock Lake. She is 1,250 tons, 278 ft. x 78 ft., with a 7 ft. draught, and a crew of 76. The paddle wheels are 16 ft. wide and have a diameter of 24 ft.

CHAPTER ONE
Introduction

This book greatly expands my previous book, *"Butterfield's Overland Mail Co. Stagecoach Trail Across Arkansas 1858-1861."* While my previous book had a 19 page section on Butterfield's use of steamboats, this work has 300 pages of recently discovered information on the subject. Only a small portion of chapters five and six in this current work duplicate what was included in the previous book.

While the purpose of my research of the Overland Mail was to satisfy my personal curiosity, hopefully this collection of my research will also make a contribution to the efforts of officially recognizing the route of Butterfield's Overland Mail Co. as a National Historic Trail.

Early Arkansas Trails and Watercraft

More than 10,000 years ago, Paleolithic hunters who arrived in Arkansas walked the trails that had been beaten down by herds of mastodons and then bison. These trails became the major transportation routes and continued for centuries. Today, these ancient trails lay under the asphalt or concrete highway system.

The Southwest Trail was the most significant land route extending across Arkansas Territory from the northeast corner (through Batesville) to the southwest corner (through Old Washington) south to Texas. There was also the Chickasaw Trail from Memphis connecting to the Southwest Trail. Also, there was the Chocktaw Trail across the southern part of Arkansas.

Southwest Trail Across Arkansas
Source: "Southwest Trail" Encyclopedia of Arkansas

Arkansas is blessed with significant waterways that are navigable or semi-navigable in the almost every corner of the state.

As Europeans began to explore this portion of North America, the waterways grew in importance. The Hernando de Soto expedition spent the years 1541 to 1543 in Arkansas. Henri de Tonti's created a settlement called Arkansas Post (Arkansas County) in 1686 along the river a short distance northwest of the Arkansas' River mouth.

More than thirty rivers pass through Arkansas. Including rivers and streams in Arkansas, they stretch 90,000 miles in length. Within Arkansas the longest rivers are: White 690 miles; Ouachita 500 miles; Mississippi 480 miles; Arkansas 445 miles; St. Francis 350 miles; Saline 300 miles; and the Red River at 180 miles.

Arkansas enjoys one of the largest inventories of navigable waterways in the nation with 1000 miles along five rivers including the Arkansas, Mississippi, White, Red, and Ouachita Rivers.

The mighty Mississippi River forms the eastern border of the state. This mighty river was the main trade corridor for cotton traveling from Arkansas to Memphis, St. Louis, and New Orleans.

The hazards of river travel included rapids and hidden snags, yet prior to 1850 Arkansas' rivers were the best means of transportation across this territory. Many of Arkansas cities and towns were first established on the river's banks. When the railroad came through, many of these towns relocated a mile or so from the banks to cluster around the train depot.

When paved roads were built in the 1900's, many of these towns once again relocated a mile or so to access the highway system. In many communities, this relocation process repeated itself in the 1970's with construction of the interstate system.

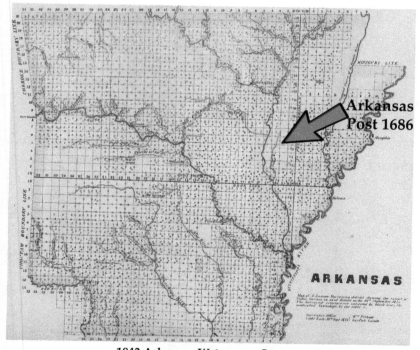

1843 Arkansas Waterways Survey
"Map of Arkansas surveying district showing the extent of public surveys in said district on the 30th September 1843. The surveyed exteriors are indicated by black lines. The subdivided Townships by the letter S.
Surveyors Office, Little Rock, 30th Sept. 1843. Wm Pelham, SurPubLands"

Prior to the 1800's early Arkansas River travelers used boats called pirogues, fashioned from a single log large enough to carry passengers and freight.

24 foot long Pirogues, commonly called a Dug-Out Canoe
This 900 year old Pirogues was found in 1999 by Charles Greene, in the Saline River. It is on display at the new River Center at Riverside Park in Benton, Arkansas.

Eventually on Arkansas Rivers, the dug-out canoes were replaced by flat-bottomed boats constructed out of wood boards.

Flat Bottom Boat on the Arkansas

The flatboat was superseded by the keelboat. A keel ran the length of the boat's underside, making it easier to steer than the flat bottom boats. Poling, pulling or sailing were more common than paddling when trying to move keelboats upstream.

Keelboats and Flatboats Once Ruled Arkansas Waterways

Keelboats and flatboats were used to carry family and personal possessions as settlers explored the new state searching for a place to homestead. Also these boats delivered products to Arkansas' mercantile stores for their shelves.

Mercantile Store Stocked by Riverboat, circa 1800

© 2022 Robert O. Crossman

In 1786, John Fitch built the first steamboat in the United States. His 45 foot steamboat successfully launched on the Delaware River on August 22, 1787, in the presence of delegates from the Constitutional Convention. Fitch later constructed a larger steamboat that carried passengers and freight between Philadelphia and Burlington, New Jersey. Fitch was ultimately awarded the first United States patent for a steamboat on August 26, 1791.

The First Steamboat With US Patent by John Fitch, Built in 1786

Beginning in the 1820's steamboat design and efficiency had reached the point that the flatboats and keelboats were slowly replaced by the more powerful steamboats with their superior speed, greater pay-load, and ease of going upriver.

A replica of Steamboat The Clermont

The Clermont, built in 1807, was the first steamboat in public service. The Clermont was designed by American engineer Robert Fulton and built in New York City by Charles Brown with the financial backing of Robert Livingston.

Snags In The River

To successfully navigate the Arkansas River, the larger and faster steamboats needed a larger clear channel than the earlier keel and flat boats did.

Snags are trees, branches and root masses that are found in our rivers.
Also known as large woody debris, snags result from trees on the river bank either falling in or dropping their branches. This can occur because of flooding, bank erosion, wind or limb shedding and is a natural process. The snag boat shown above, is a river boat, with deck-mounted cranes and hoists for removing snags and other obstructions from rivers and shallow waterways.

The U. S. Army Engineer District of Little Rock, on page 4 of their booklet, *"The Arkansas – Renaissance of a River,"* report on the initial serious attempt to remove snags and open the Arkansas River to navigation.

"Henry M. Shreve... went to work on the Arkansas River in August 1833. He removed 20 snags before he ran into another difficulty which frequently plagues the Arkansas – the river was too low for work.

He returned to the Arkansas River on January 1, 1834 and reported that by February 22 he had cleared 250 miles, up to Little Rock – removing 1,537 snags. In addition, he said '3,370 snags and logs cut from the dry sandbars, and under the banks within the bed of the river, producing together with those taken from the channel, a total of 4,907 removed from the high waster bed of the river.' That averaged a snag or hazard to navigation every 88 yards, from the mouth of the river to Little Rock. For the work, Shreve had at his command the snag boats Helepolis and Archimedes, three machine boats 'worked by hand' and the steamboat Java.

Larger machine boats were needed, Shreve reported, as some snags on the Arkansas weighed 'at least on hundred tons' or 200,000 pounds. Shreve recommended larger boats, and clearing timber along the river – at an estimated cost of $40,000...

In 1872, the Arkansas Gazette published a list of 117 steamboats which had already been lost on the Arkansas, and the list was far from complete. Although a few terrifying boiler explosions counted for some of the sinkings, the vast majority of the boats had been ripped apart by snags. Even snag boats were sunk by collision with snags and submerged wrecks, and by the 1870's the Engineers were pleading for steel-hulled snag boats."

Unloading Goods From a Steamboat at the Memphis Levee, circa 1860

What Did Steamboats Carry Aboard?

Newspapers at the time often printed the manifest of steamboats on the Arkansas River. The manifest lists reveal that they carried passengers, slaves, as well as troops. The manifest of freight aboard might include whiskey, factory goods, ceramic table wares, pianos, furniture, salt, bales of cotton, cotton seed, corn, livestock, wool, bricks, lumber, barrel staves, pecans, beeswax, poultry, gunpowder, rifles, animal hides or logs.

For example, the Friday, January 28, 1859 *Des Arc Citizen* reports in their *"River News, & c."* column on page three: *"The steamer Admiral, last evening, brought over one thousand pieces of furniture; 50 tons of merchandize, and over fifty passengers for Des Arc. Our landing is literally covered with freight."*

Also, the Wednesday, April 20, 1859 *The Memphis Daily Avalanche*, on page three, reported, *"Among other freight brought by the Jennie Whipple from Arkansas River, were 83 barrels of green apples, the product of Arkansas, 17 bales of cotton, and about 6,000 pounds of dry hides."*

Steamboat Carrying Bales of Cotton on the Mississippi River

Personal Account of Travel
by flat boat up the Arkansas in 1819

Thomas Nuttall traveled up the Arkansas to Cadron in 1819. Cadron is the site where, thirty-nine years later, the Butterfield stages would cross the Cadron Creek by ferry to reach Plummer's Station. His journey by flatboat was a gruesome 100 day trek in comparison to when, thirty-nine years later, the *Jennie Whipple* made the same trip in four days.

Thomas Nuttall records his reflections in the book he published in 1821 entitled, *"Journal of Travels into the Arkansas Territory During the Year 1819."* The following remarks are taken from that book.

January 19, 1819 *"The Arkansa (sic.) had here a very gentle current, and was scarcely more than 200 yards wide... We proceeded chiefly by means of the cordelle but at a very*

[Note: The cordelle was a strong tow rope used by persons walking through the water pulling the boat behind.]

tedious and tiresome rate, for, after the utmost exertion, with our unwieldy boat, we were this evening only six and a half miles above the outlet of the bayou... With painful exertions, after wading more than three hours in the river..."

"I was obliged to plunge into the water up to the waist, and there worked for some time, to disengage the boat from a hidden log upon which it was held; the men I had employed, being this morning scarcely willing to wet their feet, although I had to pay them exorbitant wages."

January 20, 1819 *"Towards evening, two keel boats came in sight, one of which was deeply loaded with whiskey and flour; the other, a small boat fitted out by a General Calamees and his brother, two elderly men out on a land speculation, who intend to ascend the river as far as the Cadron, [Conway, Arkansas] which is 300 miles from hence by water, to the Fort [Fort Smith] which is 350 miles further."*

January 22, 1819 *"On arriving [at Arkansas Post] I waited on Monsieur Bougie, one of the earliest settlers and principal inhabitants of the place... containing between 30 and 40 houses... This morning I again proceeded up the river*

— 16 —

with my flat boat... after a good deal of hard labor and wading... the current would not permit us to advance with the oars... water too deep for poles... dragged her along, up to our waists in water. The sand was here so moveable, as to bury our feet at every step."

February 27, 1819 *"We arrive at Cadron... From Arkansas Post to the Cadron, a distance of about 300 miles by water, I now understand there existed a considerable line of settlements along the north border of the river, and that the greatest uninhabited interval did not exceed 30 miles."*

April 1, 1819: *"About eight miles from the Cadron, we passed Mr. Marsongill's... Three miles further, we passed Mr. Fraser's... Here at the distance of 12 miles, the hills of the Petit John* [Petit Jean Mountain] *appear conspicuous and picturesque. In three miles more, seven or eight houses are seen, situated along either bank of the river, and sufficiently contiguous for an agreeable neighborhood. From the Cadron... a saw mill had been erected."*

April 3, 1819: [climbing Petit Jean Mountain] *"...I found the ascent very steep... From the summit a vast wilderness presented itself covered with trees..."*

On a return visit to Cadron in 1820, Nuttall noted several more families, three or four outlying houses, and a thriving but slovenly tavern. On February 20, 1820, a bill was introduced to move the territorial seat of government from Arkansas Post to Cadron. An amendment changed Cadron to Little Rock. On October 18, 1821 Little Rock won by a vote of six to three. By 1831, the Cadron settlement had been abandoned.

[AUTHOR'S NOTE: I happen to live a short distance from the site of the old Cadron settlement. It's close enough that two of my grandsons, Grayson and Blake Crossman, enjoy walking along the nearby wooded ridge to Cadron. To fish in the Arkansas River at the mouth of Cadron Creek, they walk past the old ferry site used by Butterfield Overland Mail. Co.

Reconstruction of the Blockhouse at Cadron Settlement
This blockhouse is near the site of the Cadron Ferry crossing used by the Butterfield's Overland Mail stagecoaches. The original Cadron blockhouse served not only for defense but also as a trading post and community center.

Personal 1859 Account of Steamboat Travel on the Arkansas River by a Butterfield Station Agent's Daughter

One of the Butterfield stations where stagecoaches stopped for a change of horses and for the axles to be greased - was called Sevier Tavern. The tavern was the first stop for Butterfield stagecoaches north of Little Rock. Below is the record of the Sevier family's travels on a steamboat up the Arkansas River and his selection of a homestead where he built the tavern where the Butterfield stopped four times a week in 1860 and 1861. This personal account was written by Sophia Sevier Mosely, daughter of Butterfield Swing Station Agent - Robert Michael Sevier and Sarah Emmeline Bayless Sevier.

"When I was eleven years old... 1859, father took a desire to go westward. With our household goods we boarded a steamboat, the Lady Walton, and came down the Mississippi

to the mouth of the Arkansas River. Here we turned and came up this river until we reached Benedict Landing, 30 miles above Little Rock. This place is now in Faulkner County, Arkansas. We unloaded our goods, and father went to look out a location. When he came back he had a yoke of oxen and a wagon, which he had borrowed from one of the settlers. He moved us to the hills about 3 miles north of the river, within a quarter of a mile of my present home. Our closest neighbor was about four miles away.

Wild animals were very numerous. From the door droves of deer could often be seen grazing. Wolves, foxes, wild cats, panthers, cottonmouths and many other animals roamed the woods...

In 1860 my father built a fine colonial house, the finest in all the surrounding country. It was on the Little Rock - Fort Smith stagecoach line and was used as a stage stand. (It is now 9 miles southwest of Conway, Arkansas.) Seven large rooms, two wide porches, and three hugh chimneys made up this two-story house.

We were living in this house when the Civil War was in full sway. My father was a Union man, but was too old to join in either army... [she goes on for several pages about experiences during the Civil War]

Since that year, when we landed at Benedict Landing, I have been in this settlement all the time. I saw it in its wilderness condition and in its gradual development... a twenty minute drive will take me to my old stagecoach home, where I can again dream of by gone days..."

Source: An eleven page handwritten letter by Sophia Sevier, daughter of Butterfield Swing Station Agent Robert Michael Sevier. This letter was provided by Lynita Langley-Ware, M.A., R.P.A. Director, Faulkner County Museum, Conway, Arkansas.

August Hartje built his tavern about 1854. About 1860, Mike Sevier built his tavern a mile and a half to the south. Some sources only list the Hartje Tavern as a Butterfield station. Other sources indicate that the Savier Tavern was the normal stop. Based on the dates of construction, it is entirely feasible that the Butterfield Swing station was at Hartje's Tavern in 1858 and 1859, and that it changed to the newer Sevier Tavern in 1860 and 1861 that was about one and a half miles closer to the Palarm Creek crossing.

**Sophia Sevier as an adult and her 1860 Childhood Home
The Butterfield Swing Station, circa 1930**
Image Source: Faulkner County Museum, Lynita Langley-Ware, Director

Did Gold Prospectors Sail to California Before Butterfield?

News of gold being discovered in California began spreading in 1848. The news resulted in desperate people seeking passage to California. When the ships arrived in San Francisco, the ship captains could not find cargo or passengers to justify a return trip to the east coast. Captains also experienced desertion by crews anxious to try their hand in the gold fields

Often a keeper was hired to guard the empty ship, but as time passed the ships began to deteriorate. Charles Hare started a business breaking up the ships, employing over 10 Chinese laborers. Taking the old ships apart, they salvaged the brass, while the bronze and lumber was recycled for building new ships.

The whaling ship, Niantic, was intentionally run aground in 1849. The empty hull was used as a warehouse, saloon, and a hotel during the two years before it burned down in a massive fire of 1851 that claimed other ships in the cove as well a Charles Hare's salvage business.

A 'forest of masts' grew in Yerba Buena Cove as abandoned ships stockpiled.

Bow of the whaling ship Niantic
The bow was discovered, containing 35 baskets of champagne,
in 1978 while excavating for the Transamerica Pyramid.

Also at San Francisco, owners paid to have their ships run aground at particular spots and intentionally sunk, so the owner could claim the land under it. The ships were filled with dirt, resulting in a prime piece of real estate. Eventually the entire Yerba Buena Cove was filled in by this process, and new piers were constructed.

Land Routes to California:
The 1824 Military Road

Few improvements were made on land routes prior to 1824. In 1824, for use of the military, the federal government made appropriations to construct a road from Memphis to Little Rock, and then on westward toward Fort Gibson in Indian Territory (now called Oklahoma). The section of the Military Road from Memphis to Little Rock was completed by August of 1828. In 1832-1840 this road served as part of the removal route, known as the 'Trail of Tears,' for the Choctaw, asaw, Creek and Cherokee Nations.

Military Road north of Forrest City, Arkansas
This 2.5 mile section is preserved in the Village Creek State Park.
Source: Photo by Bob Crossman, November 12, 2021

By 1832 this Military Road was developed enough to allow mail delivery between Little Rock and Hopefield (near Memphis), but the annual threats from floods made the roads impassible from time to time. This same flooding problem kept the railroad from being completed until after the Civil War.

This 1824 new east to west military road across Arkansas

became a major land route during the 1848 gold rush to California. Across Arkansas in 1858-1861, Butterfield's Overland Mail Co. stagecoaches route overlapped many sections of the Military Road.

1849 Road From Arkansas to California

The search for a safe and year-round route from Fort Smith to California did not begin with John Butterfield's search for a route for the Overland Mail in the spring of 1858.

Decades before Butterfield's Overland, Fort Smith newspapers aggressively promoted Arkansas as the premier launch point for immigrants bound for California. Captain Marcy returned from his 1849 survey and had shortened the trip by about 300 miles along a southern route. In 1858, Marcy's route would be adopted, in large part, by Butterfield's Overland Mail Co.

On Wednesday, July 11, 1849 the *Fort Smith Weekly Herald*, ran an article promoting what it called "THE GREAT NATIONAL ROAD FROM FORT SMITH TO CALIFORNIA." It was advertized to take wagon trains two months by pack-mules or four months by wagon. Butterfield's stages covered the same distance from Fort Smith to California in about 20 days.

The July 11, 1849 issue of the *Fort Smith Weekly Herald*, on page two, reprinted the following article from the July 6th issue of the *Arkansas State Democrat* newspaper:

"FROM THE ARKANSAS STATE DEMOCRAT, JULY 6, THE ARKANSAS ROUTE TO CALIFORNIA. – *It is desirable that all persons who may be contemplating an overland trip to California should be informed that, according to the testimony of Col. Cooke, of the U. S. Army, the route by the river Gila is A GOOD WAGON ROAD, and especially adapted for a journey during the WINTER MONTHS. The climate is mild. In the winter of '46, Col. COOKE went to California by this route AND SAW NO SNOW.*

The GREAT NATIONAL ROAD FROM FORT SMITH TO CALIFORNIA, by the way of the settlements of New Mexico along the valley of the Rio Grande, and to Col. COOKE's route, had just been surveyed, opened, and put in good order, by a corps of U. S. Topographical Engineers, and a strong force of soldiers and emigrants. By this road California can be reached from Fort Smith in about two months by pack mules, and in about four months by wagons.

Companies leaving Fort Smith, Arks., as late as October, can travel as slowly as they choose, and yet have ample time to arrive in the gold regions before the commencement of the season for digging.

The character of the country over which the Great National Road to the settlements of New Mexico is located, is such as to warrant a good supply of grass or 'range,' for the subsistence of any number of teams which may be stated on this route at the time above stated; down the valley of the Rio Grande, and over Col. Cooke's route by the Gila, any amount of supplies and forage can be readily obtained.

The Arkansas River is well supplied with good steamboats capable of reaching Fort Smith at the lowest stage of water."

"Marcy & The Gold Seekers: The Journal of Captain R. B. Marcy, with an Account of the Gold Rush Over the Southern Route"

1855 Road From Arkansas to California

In 1855, Fort Smith and Van Buren advertised that emigrants would be able to outfit themselves at reasonable prices in either city, and could arrive in California in only three months duration along what they called "the Arkansas Route."

In 1855, *The Traveller's and Tourist's Guide Through the United States of America,* by Wellington Williams, on page 181 reports:

"*Captain Marcy says, in his report, that the best season for emigrants to leave the United States for California, upon the Southern Route is about the first of June. There would then be good grass and water to the Rio Grande, and they would reach there about the last of July, and would have time to stop two or three weeks to graze and recruit their animals, and lay in additional supplies, should they require any, for the remainder of the journey. There is abundance of wood and grass at all places upon the road. From Fort Smith to the Big Spring, 513 miles, there is water at short distances along the whole route. From Big Spring to the Rio Grande, water is not so abundant, and certain points have to be made, from day to day, to get it.*"

Prior to the Butterfield Overland Mail Co. route being established in 1858, there were many previous trails to the west cost.

Pre Butterfield Trails to the West
by Frederick Smoot

Did Arkansans travel west to the California Gold fields?

The Encyclopedia of Arkansas (*"Effect of the California Gold Rush"*) reports that thousands gathered in Fort Smith and neighboring Van Buren to begin their journey to California seeking fortune. The *Baltimore Sun* on April 28, 1848 estimated that some 900 wagons with 2,000 emigrants, along with thousands of mules, horses, and oxen left for California on April 4, 1848.

Robert Brownlee of Little Rock and F. J. Thibault recorded their experience in journals that have been published, along with the letters of Alden M. Woodruff that were reprinted in the *Arkansas State Democrat* (Aug. 7, Dec. 21 of 1849 and Jan. 25th of 1850) and in the *Arkansas State Gazette* and *Democrat* (Apr. 19, 26 and Oct. 11, 1850).

James Calvin Jarnagin was one of the few lucky gold seekers from Arkansas. He left Johnson County with a company of others from Clarksville to Sonora, California. At Sonora he lived in a rough log cabin with several fellow miners. He reports that one day in 1850, he was *"digging by myself in the claim when suddenly my pick broke away part of a bank of earth and there in front of me – a piece of gold lay exposed... shaped like a common corn-doger, it was nearly pure gold!"*

As it turned out, the nugget weighed 23 pounds, 11¾ ounces, which he sold for $3,000. After several years in California Calvin Jarnagin returned to Arkansas and married Mitilda Caroline Pittman.

Kirkbride Potts, future Butterfield Station Agent at Galley Creek's Potts Station, made several trips to California with herd of cattle to sell at lucrative prices to the miners. His accumulated fortune allowed him to build a rather fabulous home that still stands in Pottsville, Arkansas. The *Weekly Arkansas Gazette* on July 25, 1857, published a letter from Kirkbride Potts:

> *"I have no doubt you will be somewhat surprised at receiving a letter from me, situated as I am, at this time almost on the confines of the State of California, herding a little over*

three hundred head of cattle. I left my home, in Pope County, on the 22nd of April, 1856, expecting to have returned last winter; but not getting an offer for my stock that I thought would justify for the time, trouble, and expense, I concluded to stay one summer with them and bring them into market this coming fall or winter. They are now in fine order, and will be very fat by November, at which time I hope to meet a good marker for them, and return to Arkansas by January, if possible. The crops are very light here this year, owing to the drought...

Beef is down to ten cents on foot, owing to the quantity of Mexican cattle pushed into market. Last winter American beef was 12 ½ to 13 ½ on foot, and I think will bear that price again this coming winter. There is not much large America beef in the country: a few thousand head have been driven in from Oregon this spring; but it is doubtful if they get to be good beef by fall. They come in as poor as cattle driven from the States across the plains; and the grass being very short, and pretty much dried up, but few of them will be fit for market the coming fall...

My post office is Red Bluffs. Hoping this may meet your eyes fully restored.   I remain yours, Kirkbride Potts."

Hand Dug 1828 Well of Kirkbride Potts
Image courtesy of Potts Inn Museum, Pottsville, Arkansas

Kirkbride Potts had this well hand dug in 1828 when he built his first home at Galla Creek. The home and well were located on the on the first of several long, relatively narrow strips of level land on the slopes of Crow Mountain. The 1828 a two story log cabin was located close to both Galla Creek and the 1826 Military Road that connected Little Rock and Fort Smith. No photos of the house exist. This well was used until 1858 when the existing Potts Inn was built one mile to the south. The 1858 home is still standing, now housing the Pope County Museum.

Kirkbride Potts returned home to Arkansas from the California Gold fields. However, there is no estimate of the total number of Arkansans who returned to Arkansas after seeking gold in California. A number of them died and were buried in graves along the trail. Some remained in California, but a likely majority returned home to Arkansas without having achieved the riches they dreamed of.

Why Was the Butterfield Overland Mail Route Needed?

The population of California tripled in size in less than a decade in large part due to the discovery of gold and the Gold Rush that resulted. The only means of communication between the miners and family back east was by letter.

Before the Butterfield, mail was transported from New York or New Orleans to California by ocean steamer. The ocean trip took up to six months. These ocean ships also carried passengers. Priscilla McArthur, in her book, *"Arkansas i the Gold Rush,"* (page 153-4) tells the story of Arkansan Thomas Parsel who chose to travel to the California gold fields by ship instead of by land. Writing to his wife on July 29, 1849, he described his trip.

"I left Panama on the 9th of May... I can give you no idea of the suffering and hardship endured upon the trip. The passage was 81 days, and the number on board the small vessel was 225. In the midst of constant rain and terrible storms, to which I was exposed, for I had to sleep on the open deck, with moldy bread to eat and foul water

to drink, you may imagine that my situation was any-thing but pleasant... But I am safely through although weak and exhausted, and will in a few days start for the mines."

"Arkansas in the Gold Rush," by Priscilla McArthur, (page 179-183) captured a woman's perspective of the gold rush in the diary of Arkansan Catherine Duval Rector, wife of Major Elias Rector of Fort Smith.

March 22: *"Oh, California, the thought of thee makes me sad. All the gold in the mines cannot prevent me from having sad forebodings. Will I ever see* [my husband] *again? Oh, what a journey and to be absent so long! It appears impossible..."*

May 22: *"How often do my thoughts turn to thee, my poor husband."*

A year later, April 3: *"I sent to the post office expecting to get a letter from him. But how sadly disappointed I was..."*

March 1857

The rush of mail attempted to and from California revealed that the United States Post Office Department had failed to prepare for such population growth that was taking place in California.

In response to that growth, on March 3, 1857, Congress authorized Aaron V. Brown, U.S. Postmaster General, to contract for delivery of the U.S. mail overland to California. The mail was to be carried over land in four-horse stagecoaches from St. Louis and Memphis to San Francisco in twenty-five days or less. The six year $600,000 per year contract was awarded to the Overland Mail Company, John Butterfield, president.

The contract was awarded to John Butterfield because, as historian Gerald T. Ahnert wrote, *"What was needed was some-one with some of the most extensive experience in the United States."* That person was John Butterfield. At the time of bidding on the contract for an *"Overland Mail Service to California,"* Butterfield owned and operated 40 stage lines in New York State. Butterfield was chosen from among the nine bids for route

#12578 on September 16, 1857. In the opinion of Postmaster General Brown, Butterfield had *"greater ability, qualification and experience than anybody else to carry out a mail service."*

The Contract Butterfield Signed

In the October 23, 1859 issue of *Frank Leslie's Illustrated Newspaper*, the following article reprinted the contract, which was signed in September 1857. The contract was for:

"Transporting the entire letter mail, agreeably to the provisions of the 11th, 12th and 13th sections of an act of Congress, approved 3rd March, 1857 (making appropriations for the service of the Post Office Department for the fiscal year ending 30th June, 1858), from the Mississippi River to San Francisco, California, as follows, viz.: From St. Louis, Mo., and from Memphis, Tenn., converging at Little Rock, Ark., thence via Preston, Texas, or as near so as may be found advisable, to the best point of crossing the Rio Grande above El Paso, and not far from Fort Fillmore; thence along the new road, being opened and constructed under the direction of the Secretary of the Interior, or near to Fort Yuma, Cal.; thence through the best passes and along the best valleys for safe and expeditious staging, to San Francisco, Cal., and back, twice a week, in good four horse post-coaches or spring-wagons, suitable for the conveyance of passengers as well as the safety and security of the mails, at $600,000 a year, for and during the term of six years, commencing the 16th day of September, in the year 1858, and ending with the 15th day of September, in the year 1864."

Up Front Expenditures

When John Butterfield formed the Overland Mail Company, it was primarily a family operation, but he also chose some of his directors from Adams Express, National Express, Well Fargo & Co., and also with American Express.

The October 23, 1859 issue of *Frank Leslie's Illustrated Newspaper* writes:

"Immense expenditure, combined with the extreme of energy and activity, have necessarily been required for

the accomplishment of this successful result. No less than $300,000, we believe, were laid out by Mr. Butterfield and his associates in the preparatory expenses, in fitting up the stations, procuring the rolling and live stock, &c., but we have no doubt that their outlay will be commensurately rewarded."

Among several possible routes, the Postmaster General chose the El Paso and Los Angeles route because it was the only route on which stagecoaches could travel every day and night, summer and winter.

Butterfield had one year to establish a route over 2,800 miles of virgin country, rugged mountains, forest, deserts, and rivers. Not only did the route have to be established, but swing stations had to be set up, and staffed with station agents, drivers, conductors, veterinarians, blacksmiths, horses, mules, hay, grain, stagecoaches, stage wagons, reliable water sources, and passenger meals. This was truly one of the greatest achievements of the 19th century.

The Overland Mail Company set up 139 stations at 15 to 20 mile intervals for a quick ten minute stop for a change of horses and to have the axles greased, with stage coaches running day and night on this 2,800 mile journey. Within a year, the number of stations increased to 175.

Every 60 miles, more substantial home stations were established for exchange of crew, and to provide a comfort stop and meals for passengers during a brief 40 minute stop.

Initially, Butterfield purchased 34 Concord stagecoaches and 66 of the lighter weight and less expensive Celerity stage wagons. The Concord stagecoaches were used in the more populated portions of the route where the roads were smoother. In the desert areas of the southwest, with sandy conditions, the heavier Concord stagecoaches were too heavy. In those sections, the lighter weight Celerity wagons were necessary. Also when the roads were extremely rough, such as the section north of Van Buren, Arkansas, the Celerity wagons were also the best choice for transportation of the Overland Mail.

The stages bore the name of the company painted on the

upper side, "Overland Mail Company," and did not include the name "Butterfield." None of the original stagecoaches or stage wagons exist today.

Reserve stagecoaches and Celerity wagons were kept at the stables behind the Fort Smith home station at John Rogers City Hotel. Reserve coaches and wagons were also scattered among the home stations all along the route to be available in case of breakdowns or accidents.

The rear 'boot' for holding mail and luggage shown here is a good representation of the style stagecoach that Butterfield used, manufactured by the Abbot-Downing company of Concord, New Hampshire.
Source: Nita Stewart Haley Memorial Library at Midland, Texas.

A copy of a photograph of a Butterfield stage (Celerity) wagon.
This copy of a 1861 daguerreotype image is courtesy of the Nita Stewart Haley Memorial Library at Midland, Texas.

The driver in the 'ten gallon hat' was David McLaughlin.

This stagecoach in the Otero Museum, La Junta, Colorado was made by the same manufacturer as the Butterfield stagecoach.

According to Gerald T. Ahnert, Butterfield authority and historian

"Wells, Fargo & Company never operated on the Southern Overland Trail. They did operate as a stage company on the Central Overland Trail only from 1867 to 1869. They ordered 40 Concords for this purpose from Abbot-Downing, Concord, NH.

Today, only two of these 1858 original stagecoaches survive and the gear of a third. No. 251 is owned by the State of California and is on loan to the Wells Fargo History Museum, Old Town, San Diego, CA. The gear of coach No. 253, on which is hung the body of No. 106 is owned by Otero Museum in La Junta, CO. Pieces of coach No. 259 are exhibited at the Gateway Museum in St. Louis, Missouri.

All others represented in museums along the overland trails, and elsewhere, are replicas. Doug Hocking supplied the close up photo of No. 253 in the Otero Museum."

*Source: "Rocking Coach Adventures:
Celebrating the 150th Anniversary of the Butterfield Overland Trail"
Aug 1, 2008, by Mike Moore, True WestMagazinecom.jpg*

Four-horse Stagecoach
Source: Image by Steve Brandon from Pixabay

Overland Mail Company.

DUPLICATE WAY-BILL

No. *106*

From *Smith's*

To *Van Buren*

Dec. *17* *1860*

The Butterfield Overland Mail Co. also carried freight. These images are the front and back of an Overland Mail Company, Duplicate Way-Bill for two boxes shipped from Smith's Station in Missouri to Van Buren, Arkansas.

Duplicate Way-Bill No. 106
From: Smith's Station
To: Van Buren
Dec. 17, 1860
Mess.: Nottingham

No. Packages: 1 Box
Check: A Jus
From Whom Received: ___
To Whom Addressed: J A Dubrell
Destination: Van Buren
Charges Advanced: 2.50
Our Charges: 1.00
Collect: 3.50

No. Packages: 1 Box
Check: do
From Whom Received: "
To Whom Addressed: Tilley Co.
Destination: "
Charges Advanced: ___
Our Charges: Dh
Collect: ___

Images by permission of
The Arkansas State Archives.

The stagecoaches travelled day and night with only moonlight and candle lamps beside the driver to guide them. According to historian Gerald T. Ahnert, the candles for the lamps by the driver and the two additional lamps inside the stage were Karch brand candles made in Switzerland. On September 20, 1858, passenger Waterman Ormsby wrote to the *New York Herald*, *"As the night was dark, the roads difficult, and the coach lamps seemed to be of little use in the dim moonlight... I must confess it was a matter of utmost astonishment to me how the driver ever found his way in the wilderness."*

The 3,000 mile route was divided into nine divisions, with each assigned a Superintendent.

Division	Route	Distance in Miles	Travel Hours
1	San Francisco to Los Angeles	462	80
2	Los Angeles to Fort Yuma, California	282	72.2
3	Fort Yuma to Tucson, Arizona	280	71.45
4	Tucson to Franklin (El Paso) Texas	360	82
5	Franklin to Fort Chadbourne, Texas	458	126.3
6	Fort Chadbourne to Colbert's Ferry, Texas	282.5	65.25
7	Colbert's Ferry to Fort Smith, Arkansas	192	38
8	Fort Smith to Tipton, Missouri	318.5	48.55
9	Tipton train depot to St. Louis	160	11.40
TOTALS		**2,795**	**596.35**

Hand hewn dovetail log construction.

The 1850 Edwards Store, near Red Oak, Oklahoma is the only Indian Territory structure remaining on Butterfield's Overland stage route. Apparently, when the stagecoaches were ahead of schedule, they stopped at the Edwards Store flag station for a very tasty 45¢ meal.

What were the official stations from San Francisco to St. Louis?

In 1858 the Postmaster General submitted his official report to Congress. The report contains information from G. Bailey, Special Agent of A. V. Brown, Postmaster General. The report included the following summary of the swing stations and distance between them:

> *Memorandum of distances between the stations on the overland mail route from San Francisco to St. Louis, and of the time made on the first trip.*

FIRST DIVISION.

San Francisco to Clark's, 12 miles; San Mateo, 9; Redwood City, 9; Mountain View, 12; San Jose, 11; Seventeen Mile House, 17; Gilroy, 13; Pacheco Pass, 18; St. Louis Ranch, 17; Lone Willow, 18; Temple's Ranch, 13; Firebaugh's Ferry, 12; Fresno City, 19; Elk Horn Spring, 22; Whitmore's Ferry, l7; Cross Creek, 12; Visalia, 12; Packwood, 12; Tule River, 14; Fountain Spring, 14; Mountain House, 12; Posey Creek, 15; Gordon's Ferry, 10; Kern River Slough, 12; Sink of Tejon, 14; Fort Tejon, 16; Reed's, 8; French John's, 14; Widow Smith's, 24; King's, 10; Hart's, 12; San Fernando Mission, 8; Cahuengo, 12; Los Angeles, 12. **Total, 462 miles. Time, 80 hours.**

SECOND DIVISION.

Los Angeles to Monte, 13 miles; San Jose, 12; Chino Ranch, 12; Temascal, 20; Laguna Grande, 10; Temecula, 21; Tejungo, 14; Oak Grove, 12; Warner's Ranch, 10; San Felipe, 16; Vallecito, 18; Palm Springs, 9; Carrizo Creek, 9; Indian Wells, 32; Alamo Mocho, 24; Cook's Wells, 22; Pilot Knob, 18; Fort Yuma, 10. **Total 282 miles. Time, 72 hours and 20 minutes.**

Note.-There is no water on this route between Carizo creek and the Colorado, except at the stations.

THIRD DIVISION.

Fort Yuma to Swiveller's Ranch, 20 miles; Fillibuster Camp, 18; Peterman's, 19; Griswell's, 12 ; Flap-Jack Ranch, 15; Oatman Flat, 20; Murderer's Grave, 20; Gila Ranch, 17; Maricopa Wells, 40; Socatoon, 22; Picacho del Tucson, 37; Pointer Mountain (Charcos de los Pimas,) 22; Tucson, 18. T otal, 280 miles. Time, 71 hours and 45 minutes.

FOURTH DIVISION.

Tucson to Seneca Springs, (Cienega de los Pimas,) 35 miles;

San Pedro River, 24; Dragoon Springs, 23; Apache Pass, (Puerto del Dado,) 40; Stein's Peak, (El Peloncillo,) 35; Soldier's Farewell, (Los Penasquitos,) 42; Ojo de la Vaca. 14; Mimbres River, 16; Cook's Spring, 18; Picacho, (opposite Dona Ana,) 52; Fort Fillmore, 14; Cottonwoods, 25 ; Franklin, (El Paso,) 22. **Total, 360 miles. Time, 82 hours.**

Note. – There is no water on this route between Tucson and the Rio Grande, except at the stations.

FIFTH DIVISION,

Franklin to Waco Tanks, 30 miles; Cornudos de los Alamos, 36; Pinery, 56; Delaware Springs, 24; Pope's Camp, (Pecos river,) 40; Emigrant Crossing, 65; Horse Head Crossing, 55; Head of Concho, 70; Camp (_____,) 30; Grape Creek, 22; Fort Chadbourne, 30.

Total, 458 miles. Time, 126 hours and 30 minutes.

Note. – There is no water on the route between Franklin and Pope's Camp, and between Horse Head Crossing and the Mustang Ponds, (near the head of Concho,) except at the stations.

SIXTH DIVISION.

Fort Chadbourne to Valley Creek, 12 miles; Mountain Pass, 16; Phantom Hill, 30; Smith's, 12; Clear Fork, (of the Brazos,) 26; Franz's, 13; Fort Belknap, 22; Murphy's, 16 ; Jackboro', 19; Earhart's, 16; Conolly's, 16; Davidson's, 24; Gainesville, 17; Diamond's, 15; Sherman, 15; Colbert's Ferry, (Red River,) 13½. **Total, 282 miles. Time, 65 hours and 25 minutes.**

SEVENTH DIVISION.

Colbert's Ferry to Fisher's, 13 miles; Nale's, 14; Boggy Depot, 17; Gary's, 16; Waddell's, 15; Blackburn's, 16; Pusley's, 17; Riddell's, 16; Holloway's, 18; Trayon's, 19; Walker's, (Choctaw Agency,) 16; Fort Smith, 15.

Total, 192 miles. Time, 38 hours.

EIGHTH DIVISION.

Fort Smith to Woosley's, 16 miles; Brodie's, 12; Park's, 20; Fayetteville, 14; Fitzgerald's, 12; Callaghan's, 22; Harburn's, 19; Couch's, 16; Smith's, 15; Ashmore's, 20; Springfield, Missouri, 13; Evans', 9; Smith's, 11; Bolivar, 11½ ; Yost's, 16; Quincy, 16; Bailey's, 10; Warsaw, 11; Burns', 15; Mulholland's, 20; Shackelsford's, 13; Tipton, 7.

Total, 318½ miles. Time, 48 hours and 55 minutes.
NINTH DIVISION.
Tipton to St. Louis, (by Pacific railroad,)
Total, 160 miles. Time, 11 hours and 45 minutes.

RECAPITULATION.

Miles		Hours
San Francisco to Los Angeles	462	80
Los Angeles to Fort Yuma	282	72.20
Fort Yuma to Tucson	280	71.45
Tucson to Franklin	360	82
Franklin to Fort Chadbourne	458	126.30
Fort Chadbourne to Colbert's Ferry	282½	65.25
Colbert's Ferry to Fort Smith	192	38
Fort Smith to Tipton	318½	48.55
Tipton to St. Louis	160	11.40
Total	**2, 795**	**596.35**

"Deducting from this two hours and nine minutes for the difference of time between San Francisco and St. Louis, and reducing it to days, there results twenty-four days eighteen hours and twenty-six minutes, as the time actually occupied in making the trip."

According to Gerald T. Ahnert, referring to the above report by G. Bailey: *"I have found his distances to be as much as 50% off. Bailey would have a difficult time trying to keep notes in a stage wagon passing over a very rough trail. This is also the reason he used some station names that were never mentioned again. He also misspelled some of the station names. Some of this may have been done from trying to transcribe his rough notes taken along the trail."* [Facebook, *Butterfield Trail Friends*, May 3, 2021]

ACCIDENT.—The California overland stage upset on Boston mountain, about twenty miles north of this place, on Sunday morning last. Nobody was hurt, and the breaking off of the top of the stage was the only damage done.—*Van Buren Press.*

Source: August 14, 1860 Memphis Daily Appeal, page two

What were the stations between
Fort Smith and Memphis?

1. John Roger's City Hotel Home Station (Fort Smith)

The Overland Stage Office at The City Hotel in Fort Smith
Source: *University of Arkansas at Little Rock Center for Arkansas History and Culture. The Roberts Library / Butler Center collection dates this photo as ca. 1870.*

St. Charles Hotel about 1870.
Photo courtesy Fort Smith Public Library.

Hiram Rumfield's letters report that when a major fire occurred at the City Hotel, the Butterfield Home Station moved across the street to the Saint Charles Hotel.

In the September 22, 1860 issue of the *Arkansas Gazette*, the financial loss caused by the fire is listed: *"September 22 – Fort Smith has the most destructive fire in its history. As reported by the Fort Smith Herald, the losses were as follows: Captain John Rogers (founder of Fort Smith), $10,000, mercantile house; J. M. McKenzie, $2,000; W. M. Bennett, $10,000; Walton & Bourse, $18,000; Bennett & Foss, $2,000; J. B. Gridley, $2,000; Wheeler & Sparks, Times office, $5,000; J. P. Spring, $3,000; N. Spring, $12,000; Sutton & Spring, $40,000; G. W. Sisson, $700; A. H. Cline, $7,000; post office, total loss; A. J. Mayers, $300. (These losses were partially covered by insurance.)"*

2. Lavaca Swing Station (on Strang or Andrews' land)
3. A. J. Singleton's Swing Station (Charleston)

Singleton's Station
showing the rear side. At the time of the Butterfield there was a kitchen addition on this side of the house.
Image Source: Charleston Express, July 9, 1976

4. Moffet's Home Station (near Paris)
– 40 –

5. Creole Swing Swing Station
6. Shoal Creek Swing Station
7. Stinnett's Swing Station

At Dardanelle, Butterfield stages crossed the Arkansas River by ferry to reach Norristown.

8. Potts Inn Home Station (present day Pottsville)

Potts Station, built by Kirkbride Potts is still standing, and in excellent condition for its age. Serves as the Pope County Museum.

Potts Station
Potts Station was built in 1858 by Kirkbride Potts, serving today as the Pope County Museum.

Source: Pope County Museum, by unknown artist.

9. Hurricane Flag Station (east of Atkins)

Hurricane Station
Hurricane is located on the east side of present day Atkins, Arkansas.

Source: Photo by Bob Crossman

10. Lewisburg Swing Station (southside of Morrilton)
11. Plummer's Swing Station (present day Plumerville)

Plummer's Station
Samuel Plummer built this structure and adjacent leather shop about 1830. It is still standing but is in great disrepair as seen in this 2020 photo.

12. Cadron Ferry (west of Conway)

It is not known who owned the Cadron Ferry during the Butterfield years. The Jan. 25, 1832 issue of the *Arkansas Gazette* reveals that in 1832 it was owned by Robert Earheart. The location of the ferry is described as: *"on the Cadron Creek, at the point where the Military Road leading from Little Rock to Cantonment Gibson crosses that creek, and where it is not fordable at any season of the year."* ['Cantonment Gibson' is referring to Fort Gibson in Oklahoma.]

According to the Encyclopedia of Arkansas, *"Periodic attempts were made to reclaim the town, mostly by aspiring ferry boat operators. In 1860, Elias Stone platted out a town to be called Cadron Burg, hoping to benefit from a stage stand on the road, but it amounted to nothing. During the Civil War, there was considerable traffic up and along the Arkansas River with ferry crossings at Cadron; however, the near vacant town was apparently of no strategic importance."*

13. Hartje's Tavern or Sevier's Tavern Swing Station

Based on dates of construction, apparently the Hartje Tavern was the station in 1858 and 1859. The Sevier Tavern, built in 1860 served until 1861 as the station.

Sevier Tavern
This station was built by Robert Michael Sevier, and it served as a Butterfield swing station from 1860-1. This photo was taken about 1930.
Image Source: Faulkner County Museum, Lynita Langley-Ware,

14. Anthony House (after crossing the ferry at Little Rock)

When the Little Rock loop was added to Butterfield's Overland Mail route in early 1859, the stage crossed on the ferry and stopped at the Anthony House on the southwest corner of Markham and Scott streets for mail and passengers.

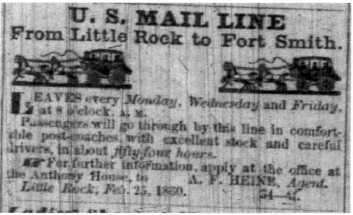

Source: Weekly Arkansas Gazette, Feb, 23, 1861, Sat. page 4

15. Otto's Greathouse Flag Station

Otto's Greathouse was dismantled in the 1960's and reassembled on the grounds of the Faulkner County Museum and Courthouse.

Otto's Greathouse
Daniel Greathouse built this house in 1830 at Otto, eight miles east of Conway. It served as a residence, inn, and stage coach stop. The house was relocated to the Faulkner County courthouse grounds in Conway in 1961.
Source: Division of Arkansas Heritage, Arkansas State Archives

16. Atlanta Hotel at Oakland Grove (present-day Austin)
Shirley McGraw and Carol Bevis, in their book, *"Lonoke County, Arkansas A Pictorial History,"* report that the Oak Grove community grew so rapidly prior to the Civil War that the thirty local households owned commercial establishments including a wool carding factory, cotton gin, sawmill, livery stable, two carriage shops, tailor shop, three doctor's offices, saddle shop, two blacksmiths, grocery store, five dry goods stores, hotel, three saloons, and the Butterfield Overland Mail Co. stage station.

"Witness Tree" ca. 1776
This tree 'witnessed' the Butterfield Stagecoach as it passed by.

This tree is ½ mile west of the Atlanta Hotel Home Station. The tree is about 250 years old and has been measured and dated by a State Forester. It is listed among the Historical Trees of Arkansas. A pioneer cemetery with about 60 graves is within sight of this tree also.

Source: R. D. Keeverm Cabot, Arkansas. He taught history for 25 years at Jacksonville High School.

Possible additional station on this 28 mile stretch

17. Jackson House at Des Arc's (by stage or steamboat)

Jackson House Hotel
The old Jackson House, later known as the Des Arc Hotel, on 4th and Main in Des Arc was demolished about 2011. Staff at the Des Arc Public Library identify this as the original structure.

Possible additional stations on this 50 mile stretch

18.   Madison (transferring from stagecoach to the train)*

19.   Hopefield (West Memphis to board a train)

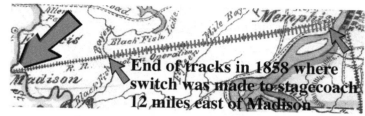

End of tracks in 1858 where switch was made to stagecoach 12 miles east of Madison

20.   Mississippi River Ferry (Hopefield to Memphis)

Early Memphis to Hopefield Ferry, perhaps the ferry "Nashoba"
When steamboats were not available, the Overland Mail crossed from Memphis to Hopefield, Arkansas by ferry, then boarded the train for a short 24 mile trip, where stagecoaches carried the mail and passengers the next 2,700 miles to San Francisco.
Image from Gene Gill, www.historic-memphis.com

21.   Memphis Commercial Hotel to Memphis Post Office
To reach Memphis, the Overland transferred from the train to the ferry to cross the Mississippi River. Mail was delivered to the Memphis Post Office. Passengers were carried to the Commercial Hotel where the Butterfield offices were located. Concerning the ferry, the Tuesday, Feb. 8, 1859 issue of the *Memphis Daily Avalanche* reported: "CHANGE OF

OWNERS - *The former proprietors of the Memphis and Hopefield ferryboat Nashoba, have sold the boat and ferry privileges for a term of years to Messrs. Richardson and Everett, who have improved the boat, and rendered the line in many respects more efficient than heretofore."*

Commercial Hotel
According to page two of the April 6, 1860 issue of the *Memphis Daily Appeal*, the Commercial Hotel housed Butterfield's Overland Mail offices in Memphis.
The hotel was built in 1848 and survived until about 1891.

21.   Memphis Post Office

After crossing the Mississippi in the Hopefield Ferry, passengers arrived at the Commercial Hotel and their journey was completed. From the he mail bags were carried to the Post Office

"1862 Memphis Post Office"
The Overland Mail began its 2,700 mile journey to San Francisco at the Memphis Post Office. The mail was carried to the wharf to board the *Jennie Whipple*, then south on the Mississippi, then up the Arkansas River. At Little Rock or Fort Smith, the mail and passengers transferred to stagecoaches for the balance of the 2,700 mile trip to San Francisco, California.
Image from Gene Gill, www.historic-memphis.com

"Memphis Wharf"
The *Jennie Whipple* would have docked here to receive Overland Mail and passengers bound for San Francisco. Traveling south on the Mississippi, then up the Arkansas River. At Little Rock or Fort Smith, the mail and passengers transferred to stagecoaches for the balance of the 2,700 mile trip to San Francisco, California.
Image from Gene Gill, www.historic-memphis.com

The Memphis and Little Rock Railroad

On the first day, September 16, 1858, only 25 miles of track has been laid. On Thursday, October 28, 1858, the Memphis Daily Appeal reported that the track had been extended and would reach from Hopefield to Madison soon:

> LITTLE ROCK RAILROAD – *Owing to the indomitable energies of the able officers of the above company, MR. ROBERTSON and MR. ROBINSON, the portion of this road terminating at Madison, is nearly completed. The train will today pass over thirty miles. A mile and a half is laid near the St. Francis river, and but five and a half miles remain to be laid. On its completion, the good citizens of Madison intend celebrating the occasion by a good barbecue. The occasion promises to be a most agreeable one. It will not be long before the importance and value of this road will become universally acknowledged.*

The train also connected with the Arkansas Stage Company to Hot Springs, Washington, Arkansas as well as Clarksville, Texas. The fare for the 36 mile train ride from the Hopefield/Memphis ferry to the end of the tracks at Madison, Arkansas was $2.

This advertisement mentions that the railroad connects at Madison
with Hanger, Rapley & Co., semi-weekly Overland Mail Co.
stagecoaches westward to Little Rock, Dardanelle, Fort Smith, with
connections to San Francisco.
Source: April 24, 1860 Memphis Daily Appeal, page one

ARKANSAS

STAGE COMPANY

AND

OVERLAND MAIL LINES,

FROM

MEMPHIS, via. LITTLE ROCK and FORT SMITH, Arkansas.

TO SAN FRANCISCO,
California,

AND ALL IMPORTANT POINTS IN

ARKANSAS AND TEXAS:

COACHES LEAVE MADISON, ARK., DAILY ON arrival of the cars from Memphis of the Memphis & Little Rock Railroad, for

SAN FRANCISCO,	CLARENDON,
PRINCETON,	FORT YUMA,
BROWNSVILLE,	SEARCY,
TUCSON,	LITTLE ROCK,
DARDANELLE,	EL PASO,
HOT SPRINGS,	BATESVILLE,
FORT CHADBOURNE,	SHERMAN,
ARKADELPHIA,	BOSTON,
WASHINGTON,	CAMDEN,
CLARKSVILLE, Ark.,	ATLANTA,
CLARKSVILLE, Tex.,	LEWISBURG,
BROWNSTOWN,	OZARK,
NORRISTOWN,	VAN BUREN,

FORT SMITH.

Extras furnished at all times when desired.

Trains leave Memphis daily (Sundays excepted) at 6 ¼ e'clock A. M.

For THROUGH TICKETS and correct information apply to the General Railroad Office, 14 Jefferson street, opposite Commercial Hotel.

S. H. SHOOK, Agent;

or to

L. S. KNOWLTON,
Union Ticket Office,

au11-1m   Reading Room, Gayoso House.

Source: August 15, 1860 Memphis Daily Avalanche, page three

On October 2, 1860 an advertisement in the *Memphis Daily Appeal* states that at Madison the train connected with the Overland Mail to Little Rock, Fort Smith and San Francisco, California:

MEMPHIS AND LITTLE ROCK RAILROAD.
Passenger Train leaves Perry Landing daily (Sundays excepted) at 6:30 A. M. Arrives at 5 P. M. Connects at Madison with Arkansas Stage Company and Overland Mail Coaches to Little Rock, Fort Smith, San Francisco, California; Hot Springs, Washington, Arkansas; Clarkville, Texas, and all principal points in Arkansas and Texas. Tickets for sale by L. S. Knowlton, sole agent for this line. Union Ticket Office, Gayoso House Reading Room.

Source: Memphis Daily Appeal, October 2, 1860, page 3

Overland Mail Bags Robbed

Butterfield's Overland Mail. Co. mailbags were cut open and the contents were robbed on their way by stagecoach to Madison, Arkansas. At Madison, they were to connect with the Memphis and Little Rock Railroad for the 25 mile trip to the Mississippi River. The August 9, 1860 issue of the *Memphis Daily Avalanche* (page three) reported:

"MAIL ROBBERS ARRESTED. — *Mr. S. H. Shock, agent in this city* [Memphis] *of the California Overland Mail route, received news, on Tuesday, that the mail bags, which reached Madison, Arkansas, last Sunday night, had been cut open and robbed of their contents. He imme-*

diately started for the above mentioned town [Madison], on hearing the intelligence, to investigate the matter and bring the parties concerned to arrest.

The circumstance of the robbing led to the suspicion that the driver of the stage coach was concerned in the act, and he took him in charge, together with two others, who turned out to be accomplices. Their names are Marselus Noles, Louis Burton, and Martin Dox. The rifled bags were in route for Memphis, but we have not ascertained what amount of money had been abstracted from their contents.

Mr. Shock brought his prisoners to this city [Memphis] and had them confined in prison to await definite orders from the head of the department, to whom Col. Gallaway telegraphed yesterday.

This makes the third instance, within the last ten days, of the imprisonment of Mail robbers in the Memphis jail; and two instances when the guilty parties were the carriers of the mail."

The August 11, 1860 issue of the *Memphis Daily Avalanche*, page three, reported:

"The three men whom Mr. Shock arrested in Arkansas, some days ago, for having rifled the bags of the California [Butterfield's] Overland Mail, and brought to the prison in this city [Memphis], have been taken back to Madison where the robbery was committed, to have their case tried. This was done in accordance with orders from the head of the department."

The August 14, 1860 issue of the *Memphis Daily Appeal*, page three, reported:

"REMOVED. – Knowlton (sic.) and Burton, two men charged with purloining letters from the mail bag sent from Little Rock and destined for Memphis, were taken to Madison, Ark., yesterday for trial. The third party arrested – Dox – was taken before a magistrate and discharged, there being no evidence sufficient to hold him."

At First, Little Rock was By-passed
by the Butterfield Overland Mail Co. Stagecoaches

In the first few months of 1858, Butterfield's Overland Mail stagecoaches travelled direct between the Cadron Ferry, Otto's Greathouse, and the Atlanta Hotel in Oakland Grove – bypassing the state capital of Little Rock. Little Rock residents wishing to catch the overland stage had to board one of Hanger & Ayliff's Daily Mail Stage Line stagecoaches to Oakland Grove. Mention of the Hanger stage line and the interconnectedness of the various regional stage lines with Butterfield's Overland Mail Co. stages is expressed in an advertisement printed in the April 29, 1861 issue of the *Daily Missouri Republican*:

> "STAGE CONNECTIONS. – *The Missouri Stage Company is now running in close connection with the* [train] *cars of this Company.*
>
> *A TRI-WEEKLY line of Mail Stages from Pilot Knob via Greenfield, Missouri, to Pocahantas and Batesville, Ark., connecting at Pocahontas with a semi-weekly steamboat mail line for Powhatan, Jacksonport, Napoleon, and all points on Black and White Rivers.*
>
> *Connecting at Batesville with Hanger & Ayliff's Daily Mail Stage Line for Little Rock, which intersects the Mail Stage line from Des Arc to Fort Smith, at a point fifty miles south of Batesville; also, intersection with the semi-weekly Overland Mail route from Memphis via Fort Smith to San Francisco, at a point fifteen miles north of Little Rock.*
>
> *At Little Rock, stages leave daily for Hot Springs and Camden, Arkansas and for Clarksville, San Antonio, and other prominent points in Texas, thus forming an entire new line to the Southwest.*
>
> *James A. Felps, Superintendent*

MEMPHIS AND LITTLE ROCK RAILROAD.— All persons wishing to attend the agricultural fair at Memphis will not be charged fare but one way over the Memphis and Little Rock railroad, during the time of the fair. Tickets from Madison to Hopefield and return two dollars.

oc2-4t

Source: Memphis Daily Appeal, October 2, 1860, page 3

Beale Street in Memphis, Tenn., ca. 1860s
Source: historic-memphis.com

1858 Butterfield's Road to California

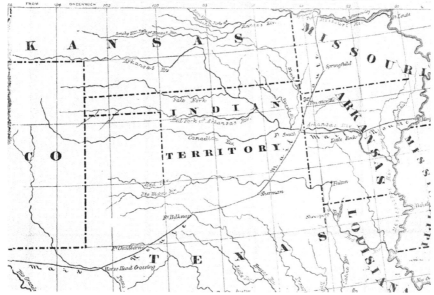

Butterfield Overland Mail Co. Stage Route - Arkansas to El Paso, drawn 1858

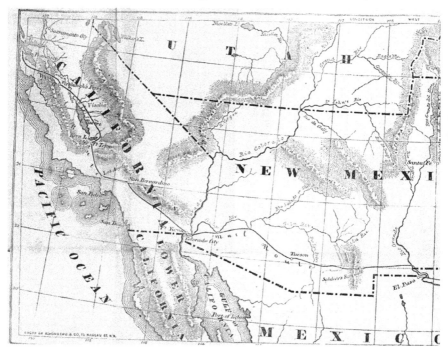

Butterfield Overland Mail Co. Stage Route - El Paso to San Francisco, 1858

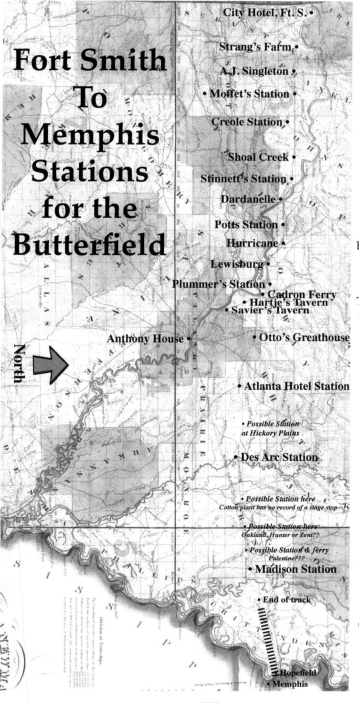

Fort Smith To Memphis Stations for the Butterfield

Stations shown on map:

City Hotel, Ft. S. •
Strang's Farm •
A.J. Singleton •
• Moffet's Station •
Creole Station •
Shoal Creek •
Stinnett's Station •
Dardanelle •
Potts Station •
Hurricane •
Lewisburg •
Plummer's Station •
• Cadron Ferry
• Hartje's Tavern
• Savier's Tavern
Anthony House •
• Otto's Greathouse

North →

• Atlanta Hotel Station

• Possible Station at Hickory Plains

• Des Arc Station

• Possible Station here
Cotton plant has no record of a stage stop

• Possible Station here
Oakland, Hunter or Zent??

• Possible Station & ferry
Palestine???

• Madison Station

• End of track

Hopefield
• Memphis

Map showing the approximate locations of the Butterfield home and swing stations set up by subcontractor John T. Chidester between Fort Smith and Memphis.

These are the stations that were used when water levels did not permit the use of the *Jennie Whipple* to carry the Overland Mail and passengers on the Arkansas River.

The author has placed the station locations and names on this 1852 map of Arkansas.

1822 Map of 'Arkansa' Territories, by Stephen Harriman Long

One of the reasons John Butterfield was interested in using steamboats between Fort Smith and Memphis was to avoid the "*Great Swamp*" that plagued road travel west of Memphis.

This 1822 map labels what would later be called Crittenden and Mississippi Counties as the "*Great Swamp.*"

This map shows all of what would be later called Indian Territory or Oklahoma as part of "*Arkansas Territory.*"

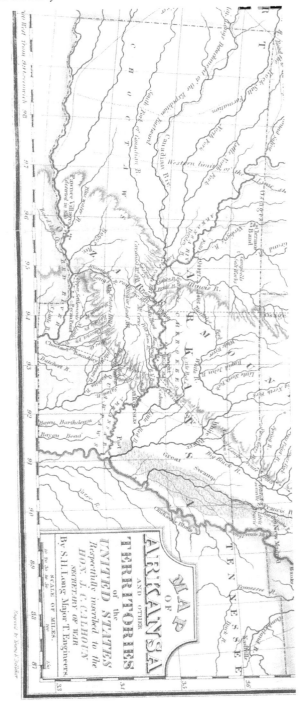

Tell Me More About The Steamboats

Butterfield's Overland Mail Company stagecoach service operated from mid-September 1858 to mid-March 1861, carrying U.S. Mail and passengers from the Mississippi River westward to California to fulfill the U.S. postal contract. Beginning September 15, 1858 at two eastern points, Memphis, Tennessee, and St. Louis, Missouri, each route began the westward journey by train.

From St. Louis the train travelled 168 miles and stopped at Tipton, Missouri. From Memphis, the train travelled 24 miles and stopped 12 miles east of Madison, Arkansas. Transferring from the trains, the two stagecoaches travelled westward from Tipton, Missouri and Madison, Arkansas.

During its time of operation, Butterfield's Overland Mail made about 324 transcontinental trips. On about 80 occasions, when Arkansas water levels were favorable, John Butterfield used his steamboat the *Jennie Whipple* to transport the Overland passengers and mail on a portion of the Arkansas River, direct to Memphis thereby avoiding many of the swing stations between Little Rock and Memphis. On 15 occasions, John T. Chidester used his steamboat, the Charm, to transport the Overland Mail and passengers between Des Arc and Clarendon on Arkansas' White River.

Were The Steamboat Passengers Comfortable?

When steamboats were used, Overland Mail passengers rode on the upper decks as **'cabin passengers.'**

When the 203 foot steamboat Katie Frisbee was used, passengers had private rooms, and were served cuisine on par with the finest hotels. Often the boats were quite ornate with wood trim, velvet, plush chairs, and gilt edging. The central hallway running down the center of the main cabin was called *"the main saloon."* At dinner time, the stewards set up long tables down the center of the main saloon where meals would be served. The cabin passengers could drink in bars with gambling tables, or lounge on the deck and watch the river.

Main Saloon of the Vevey, circa 1907

When Butterfield's smaller 135 foot ***Jennie Whipple*** was used, the accommodations were not as luxurious, yet they were far from shabby.

The Tuesday, October 25, 1859 issue of the *Memphis Daily Appeal* records the report of a woman passenger of the ***Jennie Whipple***: "*...the best passenger packet that ever visited the Rock. Her staterooms,*" she says, "*are not only well furnished, but clean and even the plates and knives and forks, at the table are clean...*"

The August 10, 1859 issue of the *Memphis Daily Appeal* observes: "*No boat of her class has better accommodations, and no boat of any class has better officers.*" On July 16th, the same paper observed: "*...the saloon of the **Jennie Whipple**... furnished the bar with the very best refreshments the market affords.*"

On February 11, 1859 the *Memphis Daily Avalanche* reported: "*The **Jennie Whipple** is one of the most pleasant modes of conveyance on the Arkansas River.*" On Friday, May 20, 1859 The *Memphis Daily Appeal* wrote: "*The fastest and finest of all the light-draught boats in our knowledge, is the **Jennie Whipple**.*"

While Butterfield passengers on the ***Jennie Whipple*** were quite comfortable, there was a second group of passengers not so fortunate. For half fare, the non-Butterfield **'deck passengers'** were crowded onto the ship alongside hot boilers, and the cargo of livestock, cotton, logs, lumber, molasses and poultry. The conditions were crowded, sweaty, dirty, smelly, with few amenities available. At night, the deck passengers slept wherever they could find a spot among the cargo. Their meals consisted of food they brought on board or purchased on shore. Deck passengers were also required to join the crew in loading wood for fuel when stops were made in route.

Separate and Unequal

The entire lifespan of the Overland Mail Company's existence took place prior to the Civil War. There is no record of John Butterfield owning slaves, but sadly slavery was part of the southern culture.

On June 22, 1860, Hiram Rumfield, assistant treasurer of Butterfield's Overland Mail Company, wrote a letter to his wife from Fort Smith. He described Fayetteville, Arkansas as follows: *"From the steps of the court house I there witnessed the sale of a slave boy—a spectacle that was indeed grating to my feelings."*

Waterman Ormsby, passenger on the first Butterfield stage leaving St. Louis, mentioned slavery several times in his record of his stagecoach experience:

"He has a large gang of slaves at work on the banks of the river, cutting away the sand, so as to make the ascent easy. His boat is simply a sort of raft, pushed across the shallow stream by the aid of poles in the hands of sturdy slaves..."

"He owns about twenty-five slaves, and says he considers them about the best stock there is, as his increase is about four per year..."

"Many of them are quite wealthy, their property consisting chiefly in cattle and Negroes. Their ownership of slaves is quite common, and many of them have large numbers..."

Like all of the steamboats in the south, John Butterfield's steamboat Jennie Whipple, from time to time transported slaves. The book, *Negro Slavery in Arkansas* by Olivia Taylor (page 64) reports:

> "*On May 29, 1859* [Nathan Bedford] *Forrest placed Dick and Edmond, two negro boys whom Sheppard had purchased in person two days earlier, on board the steamboat* **Jennie Whipple**, *bound for Pine Bluff and points above. Late the next day, after a voyage down the Mississippi and up the Arkansas, Captain James A. Gray delivered the slaves to Sheppard's overseer in Pine Bluff, who paid these charges incurred in delivery: two days board at the Forrest slave jail at forty cents each per day, board and room from Memphis to Pine Bluff, $14.*"

Van Hawkins, in *Smoke Up The River*, (page 95) in a chapter entitled '*Separate and Unequal*,' writes:

> "*Black steamboat passengers experienced many of the tensions and difficulties they faced during everyday life in the post-Civil War South. In most ways they were separated from whites and not treated as equals...*
>
> *Discrimination in accommodations for black passengers aboard steamboats eventually led to this ruling from a federal judge in Pittsburg, Pennsylvania announced in the May 28, 1878, Arkansas Gazette. The judge declared that 'colored' passengers on steamboats were 'entitled to the same treatment as white people.' However, they did not have the right to eat at the same table or sleep in the same stateroom if the vessel offered facilities equal in value to those provided for white people. The judge rules that boat captains had the right to manage their boats as they thought best.*"

Van Hawkins, (page 107) also writes, "*Though white workers sometimes performed menial tasks on steamboats, for the most part black employees filled those slots. ...In most situations black workers held jobs no one else wanted.*"

The Steamboat Crew

Duane Huddleston, in *Steamboats and Ferries on the White River*, (page 32)writes:

> "*The average crew on* [Arkansas'] *White River*

steamboats numbered from fifteen to thirty... Officers consisted of the master, the pilot, the engineer, the clerk, and the mate. In addition to these, there was usually a second pilot, second engineer, a 'mud' clerk, head fireman and his assistant, the steward, always a cook, a night watchman, cabin boys, and deckhands. Frequently, there were also chambermaids to care for the lady passengers."

Van Hawkins, in *Smoke Up The River*, (page 24) refers to comments of former White River steamboat clerk John Q. Wolf in the September 1, 1940 issue of the *Arkansas Gazette*. The duties of the crew, roughly in order of status, were as follows:

The **captain** commanded the boat, set departure schedules, controlled business matters, and was expected to idly chat with the passengers.

The **master** was the executive officer and often owned the boat.

The **pilots** stood at the wheel and controlled the course on the river.

The **clerk** checked the freight as it was loaded and unloaded off the boat to ensure it matched the manifest.

The **mud clerk**, or assistant, recorded the freight on shore, often having to wade through muddy landings.

The **engineers** were to oversee the propulsion system in the engine room, communicating with the pilot in the pilothouse by using bells.

The **firemen** fed the fuel, usually wood, into the furnace.

The **mate** managed the deckhands.

The **deckhands** and **roustabouts** were the manual laborers who loaded freight on and off the boat.

Van Hawkins, in *Smoke Up The River*, (page 107) also mentions:

The **stewards** supervised the service staff, and had to be diplomatic with finicky passengers.

The **cooks** worked 18 hour days preparing food for passengers and crew.

The **waiter**s set up dining tables for cabin passengers.

The **porters** carried luggage aboard and stowed it in the baggage room on the boiler deck.

Porters and **waiters**, wearing white coats and white shirts, tended the stoves in the heated cabins, and cleaned the main saloon.

Chambermaids, wearing long cotton dresses and aprons did the washing, ironing, and cleaning.

The lowest rank among the crew were the **cabin boys** who handled "disagreeable tasks."

In 1855 the typical monthly salaries for the crew were: captain $200, clerk $150, pilot $300, engineer $150, and mate $150.

Steamboat Whistles

In the January 18, 1941 issue of the *Batesville Daily Guardian*, John Wolf reminisced about the steamboat whistles.

"They usually had three prongs, each prong keyed to a different tone, and were very musical... they could be heard for twenty-five miles... If a boat were going to land, it gave three blasts from the whistles, while yet half or three-fourths mile away – one fairly long, one short one, and then a long drawn out blast... When it was ready to depart, two or three taps of the bell out in front warned everybody who did not belong on the boat to get off. Likewise it was a warning to passengers loafing on shore to get on board."

Dining, Entertainment and Gambling

Duane Huddleston, in *Steamboats and Ferries on the White River*, (page 23) writes:

"The main cabin of a steamer was well used as the dining area at mealtime, so it was equipped with drop leaf tables. On most of the boats, these tables were set with fine china and silverware placed on beautiful linen

cloths. [On page 45 Huddleston mentions the menu: *Those tables were loaded with delicacies of food and drink, including such tropical treats as oranges, bananas, and lemons, and such seafoods as fresh shrimp, crab and oysters. During the season, fresh venison and other regional game was sometimes featured.*]

Often, there was a piano in the room for entertainment of the travelers. Occasionally they even danced here to the strains of a live band or orchestra.

There was also a bar and poker room on each vessel and the guests could rely upon the gambler aboard to be honest. If he wasn't, he didn't last long... he was simply placed on the next river island. Other craft, seeing a lone man on one of these islands, would never pick him up because everyone knew the reason for his being there, and there he remained."

In the February 11, 1859 issue of the *Fort Smith Herald*, there is a report of a calliope aboard one of the steamboats. A calliope is a keyboard instrument resembling an organ but with the notes produced by steam whistles.

"At Pine Bluff there was a circus steamboat with a calliope aboard. Just about dark, it struck up the tune, "The Girl I Left Behind Me," and never did I hear such music! The high notes seem to mount to the very stars, and the low ones to rumble to the bowels of the earth. The performer played with great enthusiasm. He stood enveloped in the rolling clouds of steam, and kept both his ears stopped with cork... It was furious music!"

In the March 22, 1861 issue of Des Arc's *The Constitutional Union*, there is a report of a party on the steamboat the Admiral.

"Dancing, mirth, and merriment reigned supreme in the midst of 'fair women' and the rougher sex until the 'wee small hours ayant the twal.'

[NOTE: "The wee sma' 'ours ayant the twal" is a commonly quoted Irish phrase referring to dancing until the early hours awaiting twilight of sunrise.]

Accessions of the beautiful ladies and their gallant escorts were made to the party at each point 'till the boat became literally crowded with the moving numbers of the dance. The kindness and politeness of Captain Baird, Mssrs. Campbell, Wigginton, and other officers of the Admiral will long be remembered pleasantly by all who were on board..."

March, 1858

In March of 1858 a large decision still needed to be made. Would the stagecoach from St. Louis and the stagecoach from Memphis merge at Preston, Texas, Little Rock, or Fort Smith, Arkansas?

The April 16, 1858 issue of the *Arkansas Intelligencer* (page two) reprints the March 28, 1858 letter of James Glover. In the letter, Glover reports the decision of the Postmaster General:

Dear sir – I arrived here on last Monday. Mr. Butterfield came in last night – he is in fine health and spirits.

We called to see [Postmaster General] *Brown last night, and I am gratified to say, we succeeded in getting his consent to make Fort Smith the connecting point of the two arms of our great route, and we also obtained his consent to run our mail and passengers on the boats from Little Rock, to your beautiful and growing city* [Fort Smith]*. This arrangement will greatly facilitate operations, and add considerably to the convenience of our passengers, beside affording great advantages to the river people.*

A dispatch received last night, announces the arrival of Mr. Kenyon at New Orleans. He had charge of the expedition from the California side.

Letters from the party who went from St. Louis, give the most glowing description of their trip as far as Fort Chadbourne.

A letter from Kenyon, some time since, informs us that he had contracted for 400 head of mules and horses to be delivered in July.

Mr. Butterfield has contracted for a large number of

coaches, wagons and harness, part of which will be shipped to California on the 10th of April.

Mr. Croker and myself will start in a few days, to buy horses and mules, and make contracts for the delivery of grain along the route.

Thus, you see that the most active preparations are being made, for the execution of the contract.

Yours truly, James Glover

With the decision made to meet at Fort Smith, Arkansas, the two stagecoaches would merged there twice a week into a single stagecoach to continue westward out of Fort Smith. Butterfield's stages travelled through Indian Territory (Oklahoma), Texas, New Mexico, Arizona, Mexico, and California ending in San Francisco.

April, 1858

The April 4, 1858 issue of Little Rock's *Arkansas True Democrat*, (page 3) records the following letter James Glover wrote from Gallatin, Tennessee:

EDITOR OF THE TRUE DEMOCRAT, *"I have just returned from Washington, and am happy to inform you that the question of the route to be used by the contractors for the transportation of the overland mail has been settled. The contractors are satisfied with the route originally adopted by the Post Master General, and all efforts to change it have been made without their knowledge or consent.*

They have obtained the permission of the Post Master General to bring the two branches together at Fort Smith, and to carry their mails and passengers on boats from Little Rock to Fort Smith – is is a very important and valuable arrangement for your city. The Company will have BOATS built for the express purpose, which will not draw more than 16 inches when, loaded, and believe they can run them all the year. They have contracted for a large number of horses, mules, stages, harness, etc., and the most active preparations are being made to carry their contract into effect.

Yours truly, James Glover"

May, 1858

In May 1858, as routes were being set, Butterfield continued to propose carrying mail and passengers from Memphis to Fort Smith in steamboats instead of stagecoaches. When the Arkansas River levels were favorable, Butterfield believed the mail could travel from Memphis by steamboat down the Mississippi River to the mouth of the Arkansas River, navigate up that river to Little Rock and continue on the Arkansas River to Fort Smith.

The Saturday, May 1, 1858 issue of the *Weekly Arkansas Gazette* reported:

> *"Mr. Butterfield, in going down the river last January, became satisfied from observation and from the statements of pilots and others, that a class of boats could be built drawing not to exceed 12 inches, which could run up and down the river throughout the year. At any rate, he proposes, if allowed to connect at Fort Smith, to try the experiment, and he had a man employed expressly to make the necessary arrangements."*
>
> *He also felt that, "passengers from California, by the time they reached Fort Smith, would be glad to leave the stage and get on board of a boat, and moreover that if boats could make regular trips, there would be greater regularity in that mode of conveyance than by land, as high waters could not prove obstruction."*

John Butterfield produced a *"Butterfield Overland Mail Record Book"* for distribution to his conductors and station agents along the trail. He was so confident in his Little Rock to Fort Smith steamboat idea that inside the front cover, laid out as if it were a newspaper advertisement, Butterfield included the statement:

> *"Also, a SEMI-WEEKLY LINE of STEAMERS, carrying mails, freight and passengers from LITTLE ROCK to FORT SMITH, Ark."*

What Was Butterfield's Apparent Revised Plan?

On further reflection, the uncertainty of the river levels in the summer and fall of 1858 forced Butterfield to make a change in plans. Butterfield realized that his original intention of only using steamboats from Fort Smith to Memphis would not work due to low water levels on the Arkansas River.

It appears that John Butterfield's revised priorities were:

First, a sub-contract would be made with John T. Chidester's stage line to carry the Overland Mail and passengers between Memphis and Fort Smith.

Second, efforts would begin to secure one or more low draught steamboats for the Fort Smith and Memphis route.

Third, when water levels allowed, mail and passengers would travel direct by steamboat from Memphis to Fort Smith.

Fourth, when water levels were too low to make it all the way to Fort Smith, mail and passengers would travel direct by steamboat from Memphis to the Little Rock port, and then continue on to Fort Smith by stagecoach.

Fifth, if the Arkansas River levels were to fall farther, steamboats would be avoided altogether. The mail would cross the Mississippi River by ferry, then travel on the Little Rock Railroad out of the Hopefield train station (near present-day West Memphis, Arkansas). The 25 miles of track ended 12 miles east of Madison, Arkansas, on the St. Francis River. At the end of the tracks, the Overland passengers and mail would be transferred to John T. Chidester's stagecoach line for the journey to Fort Smith.

September, 1858

September 16, 1858 arrived and the Overland Mail Co. route from Memphis to Fort Smith was not carried by steamboat. Instead, the mail departed Memphis on a ferry across the Mississippi River to Hopefield, Arkansas. There it was transferred to a train for a short 25 mile trip. At the end of the tracks, the mail was transferred to one of John T. Chidester's lightweight stage wagons, for the remainder of the journey across Arkansas to Fort Smith. At Fort Smith, merging with the stage from St. Louis, a single stage would continue the journey westward to San Francisco carrying mail and passengers.

On that first day, the only passenger between Madison and Des Arc, was R. M. Brummer of the firm of Chidester, Reeside & Co.

On September 19, 1858, the *Nashville Union and American* reported on the first Overland out of Memphis:

The overland mail to California left Memphis on the 16th inst., by the Little Rock Railroad, over which it goes the distance of twenty-five miles; thence it is taken by the contractors, via Little Rock, to Fort Smith, where it connects with the mail from St. Louis, and is from that points take on through Texas to El Paso, thence to California The New York *Herald* says the rates of fare for the present will be as follows : Between the Pacific Railroad terminus and San Francisco, and between Memphis and San Francisco, either way, through tickets, $200. Local fares between Fort Smith and Fort Yuma not less than ten cents per mile for the distance traveled. Between Fort Yuma and San Francisco, and between Fort Smith and the Railroad terminus, the rates will be published by the superintendents of those divisions. The meals and provisions for passengers are at their own expense, and over and above the regular fare. It is intended, however, by the company to have suitable meals at proper places and at moderate cost prepared for passengers as soon as they can complete their arrangements. Forty pounds of baggage will be allowed to each passenger ; but the company will not at present transport any through extra baggage, freights or parcels.

Little Rock's *Weekly Arkansas Gazette* reprinted the details in their September 25 1858 issue from the *Fort Smith Times* and the *Des Arc Citizen*.

THE GREAT OVERLAND MAIL.—The Overland California United States Mail left Memphis on Thursday morning last. It is brought by the Memphis and Little Rock Rail Road to within twelve miles of Madison, on St. Francis river, thence by light vehicles to Des Arc—thence by Messrs. Chidester, Reeside & Co.'s line of four horse U. S. Mail coaches to Fort Smith, where it meets the St. Louis mail. Messrs. Chidester, Reeside & Co., are sub-contractors under Butterfield & Co., from Memphis to Fort Smith ; the whole then proceeds over the plains to El Paso and California.

R. M. Brimmer. Esq., of the firm of Chidester, Reeside & Co., who came with the California Overland Mail, early yesterday morning, has our thanks for Memphis papers of Thursday. This arrangement places Des Arc within fourteen hours of Memphis. We are now "close neighbors" to the Bluff City.

[*Des Arc Citizen.*

OVERLAND MAIL.—Thursday last was the day on which the overland mail should have left St. Louis and Memphis, and San Francisco for this place. We expect the stage in this evening, from Memphis, and the one from St. Louis on Sunday morning. We look forward to the period as one of the greatest events in our history. Our citizens will make some public demonstrations on their arrival from Memphis and St. Louis, but a general "*turn out*" is expected when they arrive from San Francisco, Cal., which will be about the 10th or 13th of October next.

Source: Weekly Arkansas Gazette, Sept 25 1858

October, 1858

A special agent of the Postmaster General, George Bailey, was a passenger on the first Butterfield stage out of San Francisco. He made a detailed five page report of his trip to St. Louis. On pages 739-744 of the December 4, 1858 *Report of the Postmaster General*, George Bailey's October 18, 1858 report is reproduced. In conclusion he writes:

> *...the Memphis branch ...the contractors on this route ...have been behind time on all their trips from Memphis to Fort Smith...*
>
> *In conclusion, I have to report that, with the exception mentioned above, the company has faithfully complied with all the conditions of the contract.*
>
> *The road is stocked with substantially-built Concord spring wagons, capable of carrying conveniently four passengers with their baggage, and from five to six hundred pounds of mail matter.*
>
> *Permanent stations have been, or are being established at all the places... and where, in consequence of the scarcity of water, these are placed far apart, relays of horses and spare driver are sent forward with the stage to insure prompt arrival.*
>
> *The various difficulties of the route, the scant supply of water, the long sand deserts, the inconvenience of keeping stations hundreds of miles from the points from which their supplies are furnished; all these, and the many minor obstacles, naturally presented to the successful management of so long a line of stage communication, have been met and overcome by the energy, the enterprise, and the determination of the contractors.*
>
> *Thus far the experiment has proved successful... but they have yet to encounter an enemy with whom they cannot successfully cope unaided. I refer of course, to the tribes of hostile Indians through whose territory they necessarily pass. Their stations in Arizona are at the mercy of the Apache, and the Comanche may, at his pleasure, bar their passage through Texas...*

What happened in Fort Smith when the FIRST Overland stage arrived from San Francisco?

On October 25, 1858, the *Commercial Advertiser*, reprinted correspondence from the *Missouri Republican*:

> *Celebration of the Arrival of the First Overland Mail from California at Fort Smith, Arkansas, on the 13th and 14th inst.*

FORT SMITH, ARK., OCTOBER 15, 1858

The celebration took place or rather commenced on the morning of the 13th, and was continued until the morning of the 15th. At 9 o'clock A.M. a national salute was fired by the U.S. troops at this place, under the command of Lieut. Stein, and shortly after the procession was formed on Washington Street, headed by two companies of U.S. Infantry, commanded by Lieut. Stein and Bell, gentlemen who have the escort for Lieut. Beall's Wagon Road Expedition, then came the Hook and Ladder Company in uniform; the Odd Fellows in full regalia; the mechanics – every department of which was represented – by platforms on wagons; with their tools & c., at work, with banners spread forth to the breeze, declaring the different occupations, and each one wearing a badge of his profession; then followed the farmers, on horseback, with an appropriate banner, and then came the orator of the day, Mr. John B. Luce, Honorable John Phelps of your state, the Town Council, and the Rev. Messrs. Pearce and Van Horne, seated in an Overland Mail Coach.

The procession reached around two or three squares, and was the largest, longest and most imposing one ever seen in any place in Arkansas. After marching through the principal streets of our young city, the procession proceeded to a grove, where preparations had been previously made for its reception, with platforms and seats. The procession was preceded by a band of music, composed of young men of the city.

The multitude being seated, the band played a very animated tune, and then the blessings of God was invoked in an appropriate manner by the Rev. Mr. Van Horne, of Fayetteville, after which the orator of the day, Mr. Luce, was introduced by our worthy Mayor, Mr. Walton, who acted throughout the day as master of ceremonies. Mr. Luce made an able speech, giving a detailed history of the progress of matters in Arkansas, the history and description of the various routes proposed for the Pacific Railroad & c. After Mr. Luce concluded, the Honorable Mr. Phelps was loudly and repeatedly called for, to address the assembly. He arose and gave a very animated and eloquent speech of an hour in length. After Mr. Phelps concluded, dinner was served by Mr. S. M. Ellis, in the form of a barbecue.

I said before, all passed off in good order, and the only drawback to the whole affair was the lack of the presence of the Old Land Admiral, John Butterfield, who had gone to your city with the first mail from San Francisco, and who was expected every moment, and all eyes were turned up the road, looking anxiously for him to make his appearance. A sight of the multitude and the procession in its movements would have made his heart leap for joy, for the old man – he will excuse me, I know, when I apply that appellation, as his head is now white, but his ardor and energy unabated – is one that can fully appreciate such a manifestation of the feelings of the people of this state upon the accomplishment of such a magnificent and stupendous enterprise – unequalled in any stage of the world – as the successful carrying of the overland mail 2,700 miles in twenty-four days, from San Francisco to St. Louis, through his instrumentality. However, he [Butterfield] *did not arrive until eight o'clock in the evening; and along with him came John Butterfield, Jr., a true scion of the old tree, full of energy and go-aheadativeness, having witnessed it fully in the first trip of the overland mail, which started from your city on the 16th ultimo* [of last month]. *He did not leave the seat of the driver from Tipton till the stage reached Springfield.*

On the morning of the 14th, the stage from San Francisco arrived, with Mr. Bates, Superintendent on the route from Red River to Fort Chadburn, having been detained a little on its time by rains and heavy roads.

These obstacles, though trifling, will soon be overcome.

All the machinery is new, and it will take some time to make all the joints work with ease. In the twinkling of an eye, almost, the stages for Memphis and St. Louis were whizzing away with the second overland mail from San Francisco. Just think of it! Two mails a week from California! It is like a dream.

I omitted to mention above that although Mr. Butterfield was not present on the 13th, yet the next man to him was here – Mr. Hugh Crooker, Superintendent of the O. & M. Company. He witnessed with great pleasure and satisfaction the procession, and listened attentively to the speeches, and was much gratified. He is a man of few words, but in his business he is in the proper place, and is capable of doing all that can possibly be required of him.

The supper was a grand affair, prepared by Mr. J. K. McKenzie, of the City Hotel. When the doors were thrown open the crowd was amazed at its appearance, so fine and so brilliant. At the head, and above the table, was a painting, executed by Mr. Syndall, of the Wagon Road Expedition, representing the Mountains of the Desert and California in the distance, with a faithful picture of the Overland Mail Stage, horses and driver, at full speed.

This was a sight that none of the company were prepared to see, and it was as pleasing as it was beautiful and unexpected. A large cake in the precise shape of the mail bags, endorsed Overland Mail, San Francisco, in gilt letters, was on the table, which when cut open had in its center a letter, post marked San Francisco, stamped in exact imitation, was taken out, directed to Mr. John Butterfield, President Overland Mail Company, Fort Smith.

**Garrison Avenue,
Upper End, Fort Smith,
Arkansas**

100

Fort Smith, Ark., Sept. 15th, 1858.

DEAR SIR:

In view of the fact that the first mail by the Overland Route from California, will arrrive at this place on the 13th of October next, the citizens of Fort Smith and the surrounding country, have determined to celebrate that event. We would, therefore, be glad to have you visit us on the occasion.

You are aware that Fort Smith is the point where the St. Louis and Memphis branches of the Overland Mail route form a junction.

Hoping that you may regard the occasion sufficiently National in its character to induce you to honor us with your presence, and that it may be both convenient and consistent with your engagements to do so,

We remain, very respectfully, your obedient servants.

J. J. WALTON, *Mayor,*	JOSEPH BENNETT,
F. WOLFE,	JOHN ROGERS,
GEORGE MORLEY,	G. S. BIRNIE,
B. T. DUVAL,	HENRY BECKEL,
M. SPARKS,	S. L. GRIFFITH,
JAMES BATERSBY,	DR. N. SPRING,
DR. J. H. T. MAIN,	THO'S VERNON,
R. P. PULLIAM,	A. G. MAYERS,

JOHN F. WHEELER, *Committee of Invitation.*

To _____

Invitation to September 15, 1858 Celebration
Source: Image courtesy of the Arkansas State Archives

C. C. Scott Papers, MS.000691, L.1956.0015, Box 1, Folder 6 "Broadsides"
The Fort Smith *"Committee of Invitation,"* consisting of seventeen leading citizens of the city, made preparations to celebrate the anticipated October 13, 1858 arrival of the first Butterfield's Overland Mail Co. stagecoach from San Francisco. The Committee printed this broadside on half of a 5 x 10 inch piece of paper, that was dated September 15, 1858. On September 19, 1858 it was folded, addressed and mailed to leading citizens across the state to invite them to be present at the celebration.

This particular copy was mailed to Arkansas Supreme Court Justice C. C. Scott.

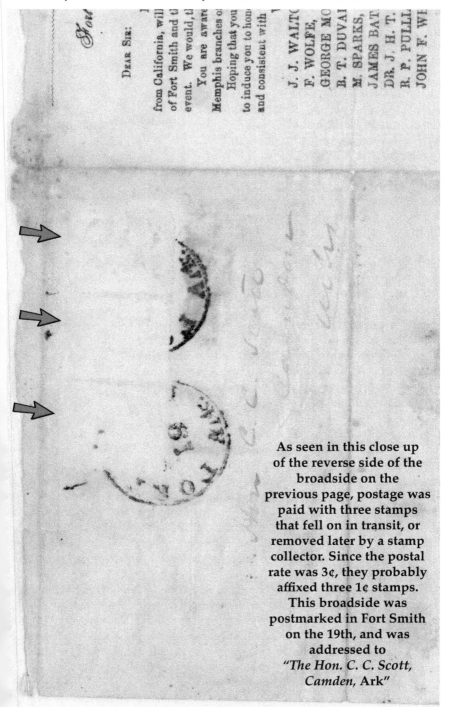

As seen in this close up of the reverse side of the broadside on the previous page, postage was paid with three stamps that fell on in transit, or removed later by a stamp collector. Since the postal rate was 3¢, they probably affixed three 1¢ stamps. This broadside was postmarked in Fort Smith on the 19th, and was addressed to *"The Hon. C. C. Scott, Camden, Ark"*

The Honorable C. C. Scott received the invitation on the previous page the year before he died.

According to the Encyclopedia of Arkansas, *"Christopher C. Scott of Camden, Ouachita County, was a circuit judge and an Associate Justice on the Arkansas Supreme Court, serving until his death in 1859, the longest tenure of any justice in the antebellum period.*

Christopher C. Scott was born in Scottsburg, Virginia, on April 22, 1807. He was the son of General John Baytop Scott, who was a prominent lawyer and Revolutionary War soldier.

Justice Christopher C. Scott painted by Guy Gilbert; circa 1850s.

In January 1859, a stagecoach came to Scott's residence in Camden to take him to Little Rock (Pulaski County) on court business. During the trip, he acquired acute pneumonia and died on January 19, 1859, in the Anthony House in Little Rock. Scott is buried in the Scott Cemetery in Camden."

In response to receiving the September 18, 1858 invitation to attend the celebration when the first Butterfield Overland Mail Co. stagecoach from San Francisco was anticipated to arrive, Arkansas Supreme Court Justice C. C. Scott wrote on September 30, 1858 his regrets:

Washita County Arkansas
September 30, 1858

Gentlemen,

Your kind invitation reached me yesterday. I regret that both my affixed engagements and the continued illness of my family render it impracticable for me to visit you. Were it otherwise, it would afford me great pleasure to do so.

The event you prepare to Celebrate, so _____ interesting to our Western border, is second less so to the Whole State, as the forerunner of the great Southern National Highway to the Pacific. That, I think, in view of our Vast Natural Concerns in that region, it is no less the duty of the Federal Government to construct at once, than her true interest as the great land proprietor of the immense intervening domain.

And when this shall have been done, an additional kind of union among the States will have been added and the Slave States bound, as with hooks of steel to an almost boundless region stretching to the South-west where destiny ____ are peaceful _____. Then, if the great principle of the Nebraska bill shall be maintained, the South may hope for equality of rights under the Federal Constitution, and then an ultimate _____ pre eminence in the Union...

Image of his letter courtesy of the Arkansas State Archives
C.C. Scott Papers, MS.000691, L.1956.0015, Box 1, Folder 3

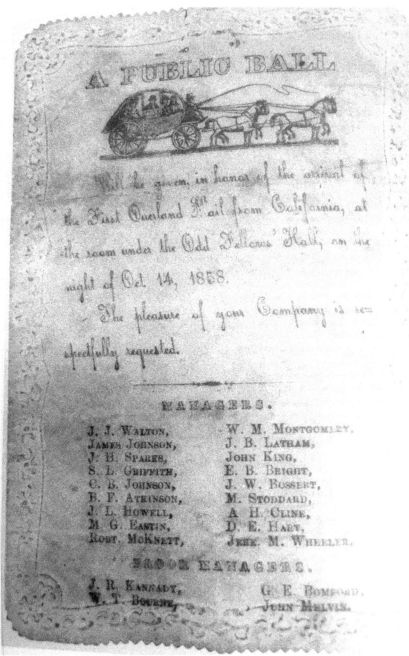

"A Public Ball will be given in honor of the arrival of the First Overland Mail from California at the room under the Odd Fellows Hall, on the night of Oct. 14, 1858. The pleasure of your Company is respectfully requested."

Tell Me More About Fort Smith's Celebration

In the Oct. 23, 1858 issue of the *Weekly Arkansas Gazette*, Little Rock Arkansas, an second eyewitness account of the events in Fort Smith is recorded:

FIRST ARRIVAL OF THE OVERLAND MAIL STAGE —
THE CELEBRATION ON THE 18TH INST. —

Hoping that some of our correspondents would have favored us with a description of the celebration, we have deferred making the attempt ourselves, until the last moment. Occupying a place in the procession ourself, it is impossible for us to do justice to all and hence if anything should be omitted, we hope no one will condemn.

The morning was bright, and beautiful, and auspicious — it seemed as if the day was made for the occasion. At daylight all the bells in the city were rung, rousing the inhabitants and reminding them of the joyful event to be celebrated. At nine o'clock the military fired a salute of 32 guns, when the procession formed in front of the City Hotel — the soldiers stationed at this post, commanded by Sts. Steen and Bell, preceded by a brass band in front, next the Odd Fellows in full regalia, the Hook and Ladder Company, the Mechanics and last though not least, the farmers of Sebastian, followed by a host of strangers and citizens.

The mechanics with praise worthy seal and energy, had platforms erected upon wagons and while the procession moved onward worked at their trades.

Upon one platform we noticed our venerable friend F. H. Wolfe, with manner, moulds &c, engaged in making work in his line of Gold and Silver Smith, and his son, Geo. Wolf, binding books. The platform was tastefully decorated with flags and banners bearing appropriate mottoes.

Following him was a blacksmith's forge with artisans at work – an incident occurred which gave them an opportunity to show their speed and skill, one of the wagons broke down which was soon mended by them.

There were carpenters and house joiners, wheel rights, wagon makers and cabinet makers all carrying on their trades during the progress of the procession. Young America was aptly illustrated by Young Pearson with his one horse wagon, containing the sign and tools of his father.

One of the most unique and striking representations was the butcher's wagon representing a market stall surmounted with a beef's and sheep's hams, and containing beef steaks and sausages.

A very large number of the farmers of the county joined in the procession carrying a banner with the inscription, 'we feed the hungry' an apt and comfortable motto, giving assurance of thrift and plenty.

After forming, the procession marching under the command of the Chief Marshal, and his assistants, to the soul stirring music of the bands through the principal streets of the city and then to a beautiful grove in the suburbs, where a stand was erected for the orator of the day. We omitted to notice in the proper place the brass band composed of our citizens, it compares favorable with any.

We regret our inability to do full justice to the procession and the various branches of art and industry represented. No town in the Union can show a greater number of intelligent and industrious mechanics than Fort Smith.

The banners and flags with their appropriate mottoes and the large concourse thronging in every street in the city showed that the general heart was alive to the greatness of the achievement which had called them together.

On arriving at the grove the Mayor accompanied by the orator of the day, J. B. Luce, Esq., and distinguished guests ascended the platform.

Mayor Walton then stated to the audience that the occasion of the assemblage was to celebrate the arrival of the first overland mail stage at this place from Califor-

nia. He announced that the first stage arrived here on the 7th last, only TWENTY ONE DAYS out from San Francisco. He, in behalf of the citizens of Fort Smith and Sebastian county, tendered a warm and cordial welcome to the strangers present and invited them to partake freely of our hospitalities. He then read the letters received by the committee on invitation — we were surprised to hear none from our delegation in Congress. Surely this is an event of sufficient importance to our State to deserve from them at least a passing notice. We cannot remember all from whom letters had been received, there was one from the Hon. J. B. Floyd, Secretary of War.

After the Mayor finished reading the letters he introduced Mr. Luce who addressed the crowd upon the various routes to the Pacific, their characteristics, &c., and congratulated the country upon the success of the Overland Mail.

He reviewed the origin and progress of rail roads in England and this country. We cannot do justice to his speech and as we understand it will be published, we will conclude by saying that the large assemblage listened with attention, and not withstanding there were no seats, good order was preserved. His speech was long and contained a large fund of useful and interesting information and will repay a careful perusal.

After Mr. Luce concluded, Mayor Walton introduced the Honorable John S. Phelps, of Missouri, who addressed the audience in an able and eloquent speech. He reviewed the merits of the various proposed routes to the Pacific and proved the immense superiority of the 35th parallel over all others. He exhorted the people of Arkansas to push forward their own internal improvements and thereby secure the main trunk through our State. He alluded to his efforts to procure the transportation of the mail on the 35th parallel, and his agency in obtaining a modification of the contract, in order that the junction should be made west of Little Rock. The interest of his constituents are identified in the establishment of this route and as a faithful representative he has devoted his best energies to its accomplishment. Mr. Phelps sustained his great reputation as an orator, and has added by his visit and speech here, a host to his long list of admirers in this State.

We trust that we may have him frequently with us. We admire him for his devotion to the interests of his constituents and will ever remember that in the discharge of his duty to them, we owe the junction of the Overland Mail at this place. Under the influence of this junction, we hope to see Fort Smith increase in wealth and population until she will be second to no city in the Mississippi valley. In our day of prosperity we will remember, with gratitude, over debt to Honorable John S. Phelps.

At the conclusion of the speaking the company partook of a sumptuous barbecue prepared for the occasion. We will add that a large number of ladies were present and enlivened the scene by their beauty. Unable to do them full justice we will dismiss the subject by challenging the world to produce a greater display of beauty than those Arkansas ladies whose presence lent a charm to the scene of Wednesday.

The number of persons present at this celebration is variously estimated at from five to seven thousand, the largest concourse ever assembled in this State, on any similar occasion.

In the complete and triumphant success of the vast enterprise of transporting the mails from the Mississippi to the Pacific, a distance of 2,700 miles, partly over an uninhabited desert, we witness another triumph of American energy and genius.

The stage is but the precursor of the car and ere long the Golden State, once so distant — involved from her sister States, will be but a few days journey from the center of the Union.

California, enthroned upon the Pacific, as a Princess

with her robes gorgeously inlaid with gold, will no longer sit in solitary grandeur, but a bevy of younger sisters will grow up to the east, under the quickening influences of the rail road, to rival her charms, and challenge her to a generous rivalry. In all this we are the finger of destiny pointing unerringly to the greatness and glory of our own State.

In conclusion we will state, that it is with pride and pleasure that we can say that no unpleasant or unbecoming incident occurred, to mar the harmony of the occasion. Every thing was conducted in good order, and all enjoyed themselves to the top of their bent.

Fort Smith Herald

What happened in St. Louis when the FIRST Overland stage arrived from San Francisco?

When the first stage from San Francisco arrived in St. Louis in October of 1858 there was a great celebration. The October 14, 1858 issue of the *New York Times* reported the events of that day.

ARRIVAL OF THE OVERLAND MAIL –
ITINERARY OF THE ROUTE

In the NEW YORK TIMES, of Monday, we have the pleasure of announcing the arrival at St. Louis of the first Overland Mail from the Pacific, through in twenty-three days from San Francisco, bringing advices ten days later. To the telegraphic outline then furnished, we now add details of the highest interest, with such items of intelligence as may be important.

Of the reception of the caravan at St. Louis, we gather the following information from the REPUBLICAN.

As a matter of course, the reception of the news by telegraph from Jefferson City, that the Overland Mail, with MR. BUTTERFIELD, who had been chiefly instrumental in putting it into successful operation, would arrive in the city by the Pacific Railroad, created very considerable feeling. It was at once determined that a fitting reception should be given to MR. BUTTERFIELD: and before 8 o'clock, a large number of our most respectable citizens had assembled for that purpose.

The procession was formed in front of the Planters' House last evening at 8 o'clock, headed by the St. Louis Silver Band, in ARNOT'S band wagon, drawn by six horses, and proceeded to the depot of the Pacific Railroad. On the arrival of the train in a little before 9 o'clock, MR. BUTTERFIELD was received, on behalf of the reception Committee and a large concourse of citizens present, by JOHN F. DARBY, ESQ., who said:

"SIR: On behalf of the Committee and the citizens of St. Louis, I extend to you a hearty congratulation on the achievement of an undertaking worthy of genius and perseverance of an American. (Applause.) You have demonstrated to the nation the practicability of bringing communications from San Francisco to the center of the Valley of the Mississippi, in the wonderfully short space of twenty-four days, and for the accomplishment of which you deserve the thanks and gratitude of the whole American people. We have experienced for years the difficulty of communicating with our brethren on the shores of the Pacific, and for ten years have been striving for means which would obviate those difficulties, and bring us in closer contact. You, Sir, have accomplished that object by your indefatigable exertions, and secured a result so desirable, and fraught with so many blessings, that you are entitled to the warmest gratitude of the American people. You, Sir, have inaugurated a system which, though yet in the incipient stages of operation, is of paramount importance in the results which it will secure in social, political, and mercantile points of view, at the same illustrative of the transcendence of American skill, enterprise and untiring perseverance. In conclusion, let me again return to you our most hearty thanks and congratulations on your noble achievement."

In reply, MR. BUTTERFIELD expressed the emotions

which filled his heart at this demonstration of the good will and approbation of his fellow citizens, and said they were not the less pleasurable by being unexpected. He regarded it as the happiest moment of his life, in view of the fact that he had accomplished an object which had so long been desired by the citizens of St. Louis, and had received their hearty approval for his labor.

Great difficulties had lain in the way, but what obstacles, he continued, cannot be surmounted by American enterprise? (Applause.) He had entered upon the work with a determination to succeed, and by the help of his assistants, (whom he complimented very highly) had succeeded. But the operations were yet imperfect, this being the first trial. For the next six years, thirty thousand miles of mail traveling will be accomplished every day. Nations had taken hold of the great works, but had not reported. An Atlantic telegraph had been laid, it was true, but the Overland Mail was ahead of the submarine lighting at last, and had reported. (Applause.) He thanked the people and the Committee for their cordial welcome, and concluded amid continued applause.

Upon leaving the depot, the carriages proceeded to their starting point, on Fourth Street, proceeded by the band-chariot, and passing around Pine, did not draw up until they reached the Post Office, when the mail was turned over to the proper officials.

Some extra bags containing the San Francisco EVE-NING BULLETIN, the special edition of the ALTA CALIFORNIA, and other papers, were retained and put out at the hotel Here they were opened and the papers handed round to the assembled spectators, who read them with great apparent interest. The ALTA CALIFORNIA was most in demand, as it sported a fine special head of "BY THE OVER-LAND MAIL" and an imposing picture of a mail coach with four horses in full gallop. It was a weekly edition, and bore evidence of the most commendable enterprise of the part of it's publishers.

THE DEMOCRAT *says: "MR. BAILEY, one of the passengers in the mail trail, was also besieged by crowds of anxious persons, to whose innumerable questions he returned willing and satisfactory answers. We are indebted to MR. BAILEY for a table of stations and distances of the route, which will be found below. The mail team started from San Francisco on the 16th ult. [of last month]. It consisted of a four-horse mail coach, six passengers and the mail. They all came through ahead of time with perfect safety, though some of the passengers were so jaded with the ride that they concluded to lay over a day or so at Springfield, in this State. They will probably reach the city today or tomorrow."*

What did President James Buchanan think?

The October 11, 1858 issue of the *Washington D. C. Evening Star* reprinted a letter President Buchanan wrote to John Butterfield. On Oct. 9, 1858 when the line was just three weeks old, the President wrote to John Butterfield:

President James Buchanan

"I cordially congratulate you upon the result. It is a glorious triumph for civilization and the Union. Settlements will soon follow the course of the road, and the East and West will be bound together by a chain of living Americans, which can never be broken..."

What happened in St. Louis when the THIRD Overland stage arrived from California?

On October 25, 1858, the *Commercial Advertiser*, reprinted an article from the St. Louis *Republican* of October 19th:

Arrival of the Overland Mail

The third Overland Mail from San Francisco, Cali-

fornia, arrived last night "on time," twenty-five days from city to city. The mail was a small one, the only papers received being from Los Angeles, of the 25th September. The mail left San Francisco on the 24th. There were five through passengers. It may be a week or two before we get our regular exchanges, but when we do we shall be able to anticipate very frequently, the news by the steamers at New York...

The five passengers... Mr. J. C. Geary, whose destination is Michigan; Virgin Oden, Missouri; Mr. Lake, Maine; Mr. Fidler, Ohio; and Louis Long, Pennsylvania.

These gentlemen, Mr. Geary informs us, left San Francisco by the second mail which took its departure on the 20th ultimo [of last month]. *Near Fort Yuma they met the first mail from St. Louis going west. It had met with no detention, kept contract time nearly the whole distance, and was sure of touching its Pacific terminus within the specified period of twenty-five days. The second St. Louis mail was met at a locality, the precise name of which was not remembered, but situated four or five days journey East of Fort Yuma. It has lost some time by detention in the Llano Estacado or eighty mile desert, where the great distance between the stations which bound it and the soft sandy soil of the Llano were sufficient to throw down the mules attached to the coach.*

For a short distance the mail was conveyed on horseback, another coach station was attained and all went on smoothly again, the mail when met being in course of recovering all its lost time. The Company everywhere keep extra stock, and have such arrangements that delays cannot be of long duration, or troublesome or inconvenient to passengers. The mules collected along that division of the line are said to be generally small, but the Company are preparing to replace them with stronger stock.

Passing the Llano and the second Westward mail as we have described, Mr. G. and his companions continued their route, sustaining, however, an interruption by the breaking of the coach. This was overcome, and the time so lost was nearly all regained.

Fort Arbuckle, near which the bloody conflict between Major Van Dorn's command and the Comanche Indians took place, lies away from the mail route, a long distance to the South. Nothing was seen, therefore, of either of the belligerent forces, and they had no knowledge of the battle, except some very partial information they acquired at Fort Belknap, or at stations East of that post.

No Indian interference was offered on any portion of the immense distance traversed between San Francisco and St. Louis. None were met in fact during the journey except some friendly Pimos, in the vicinity of Fort Yuma. The Pimos are on the best of terms with the Company, and are staunch supporters of the overland route. The Company's stables afford them a market for their grain, and the agents and employees of the mail contractors cultivate friendly intercourse and the best of relations with their red-skinned neighbors.

Pimos Indians, Arizona, circa 1875
Albumen silver print by photographers Elias A. Bonine and Isaiah West Taber
Source: Smithsonian American Art Museum

At Sherman, a station about two hundred miles beyond Fort Smith, the passengers of whom we write stopped for a resting spell, thus abandoning the second mail, on which they left San Francisco on the 20th – the same which came into this city on Saturday night last.

After remaining two days the present or third mail took them up, and enabled them to arrive securely at the St. Louis end of the route. A passenger or two on the third, stopped at Sherman to come in on the next train due, which is the fourth..."

On October 20, 1858 what did the Postmaster General write about Butterfield's Overland Mail?

Aaron Brown, Postmaster General
March 1857 – March 1859

On October 25, 1858, the *Commercial Advertiser*, reprinted a letter from the Post Master General Aaron V. Brown, addressed to John Butterfield, Esq., President of the Overland Mail Company, St. Louis, Mo.

LETTER FROM THE POSTMASTER GENERAL
POST OFFICE DEPARTMENT
WASHINGTON, OCT. 20, 1858

Sir: – on my return from Tennessee, I received your despatch announcing the arrival at St. Louis of the first great overland mail from San Francisco. Since then, the public journals have announced the safe arrival of several other mails of that line.

I rejoice in your success. It may develop not one only, but several Californias on this side the shores of the Pacific. The country cannot award too high credit to the lamented Rusk, and other members of Congress, who authorized this line to be established or to the President, who devoted his great abilities to carrying the law into execution.

Respectfully, your obedient servant,   AARON V. BROWN

November, 1858

Butterfield repeatedly made it clear that his original intention was to only use steamboats to carry Overland Mail Co. passengers and mailbags between Memphis and Fort Smith.

On Tuesday, November 6, 1858 the *Memphis Daily Appeal* reprinted a portion of the letter that John Butterfield wrote to Postmaster Carroll of Memphis.

John Butterfield wrote:

"When the contract was made, and always subsequently till just previous to September 16th, it was my expectation and intention to have given the Memphis portion of the route the best or superior service, as it is styled by the Department. That is, by steam from Little Rock to Fort Smith. I had obtained the consent of the Department, selected and partially negotiated for the necessary boats. But a sudden falling of the water prevented me carrying out my intentions. It was too late then to stock the route, and start it in No. 1 shape. My only (as I supposed at the time) available method left of performing service agreeable to the contract, was to arrange with Reeside & Co., which was done by Mr. Crocker, one of our superintendents, with the understanding that the service was to be performed according to contract."

Three weeks later, John Butterfield wrote a short letter to the postmaster at Little Rock, expressing his hope to improve service and make the route popular with the citizens of Little Rock. The letter was reprinted in the *Weekly Arkansas Gazette* issue of November 20, 1858.

New York, Nov. 3, 1858

> *T. J. Churchill, Esq.,*
> *Postmaster at Little Rock, Arkn.:*
> *Dear Sir – Your favor of Oct. 19, with a copy of your report, reached me here within a few days, and for which please receive my thanks.*
> *I had heard from other sources in regard to the service on the Memphis Branch, and have just been on to Washington City, and have arranged with Gov. Brown to have the service performed in a satisfactory manner and according to contract, as soon as it is possible for me to go there and attend to it.*
> *I hope before long to make it a popular line with the citizens of Little Rock, and of Arkansas generally.*
> *Respectfully, your obedient serv't,*
> *JOHN BUTTERFIELD, President*
> *Overland Mail Co.*

In the November 27, 1858 issue of the *Des Arc Citizen*, the editor writes:

> *"Whoever led Col. Butterfield to believe that he could carry the Overland Mail from Little Rock to Fort Smith by steam, was either a knave or a fool.*
> *The "sudden falling of the water" spoken of by the Colonel, happens so often with that stream, that it is rendered unnavigable below Little Rock, as well as above that point.*
> *The recommendation of Col. Hutton, a Civil Engineer... recommended that this Mail be conveyed from Memphis to Des Arc by steamboats, thence westward by coaches. This Mail should never have been carried via. Little Rock. That point is 27 miles south of the direct route to Fort Smith..."*

December, 1858

On December 2nd, John Butterfield wrote another letter that was printed in the January 5, 1859 issue of the *Arkansas True Democrat*. The letter was addressed to John F. Wheeler, editor of the *Fort Smith Times*. In the letter, Butterfield mentions his original intention to use steamboats, and then makes a lengthy appeal for improving the Memphis to Fort Smith road. In postscript, he reports the purchase of the **Jennie Whipple** so he can bypass the road and use the Arkansas River to transport Overland Mail Co. passengers and mail from Memphis to Fort Smith.

John Butterfield wrote:

LETTER FROM COL. BUTTERFIELD

NEW YORK, DEC. 2, 1858

DEAR SIR – *You are aware that it was my intention to put steamboat packets on the Arkansas River last summer, but was thwarted by the lowness of the water. You are also aware that the impossibility of using the river was apparent to me at too late a period to allow of my stocking the line between Memphis, Little Rock and Fort Smith in time to commence mail service on the 16th September, and was therefore compelled to make arrangements to have that service performed by others.*

The service thus unintentionally confided to others has not been of a grade nor of a speed satisfactory to me, nor to the post office department, and is entirely below the just expectations of the people of Arkansas, Texas and of the Indian country, as well as of the traveling community generally.

That route from Memphis through Little Rock to Fort Smith, and then to northeast Texas direct, is exceedingly important. I intend to put on to it fine stock and first class coaches and spring wagons without delay; I intend the route shall be as well stocked as any route in the United States.

Then if the good people of Arkansas will do their duty manfully, that route, through the centre of the state, will be one of the greatest thoroughfares in the southwest. It will be not only important to Arkansas, but to all the citizens of the south who have business in Arkansas, and the Indian country or Texas. That duty is to build a good turnpike road from Memphis to Little Rock, and then to Fort Smith. Not a railroad, which, at $30,000 per mile, would cost nine millions of dollars in money and ten years in time, but an old fashioned, well drained dirt road costing at $300 per mile, only $90,000 in money, and 60 or 90 days in time.

It was in this way that New York, Pennsylvania, Maryland, Virginia, and other states opened up to market the interior settlements – afterwards followed by canals and railroads. So in Arkansas, let the legislature pass a law, ordering turnpike road, appropriating $90,000 or $100,000 to pay for it. If the appropriation does not hold out, I doubt not, the planters, farmers, counties, villages, and merchants along the route will gladly contribute to its completion. I have seen a good many of your people, and I am not mistaken. To a practical scheme, they are as ready to contribute as any people in the world – at any rate, I intend to visit Little Rock and ask the attention of the legislature to the subject. I have no fears from what I have seen of the people of Arkansas, that their legislature will fail to give a candid hearing to a plain old-fashioned man of business, when pleading the necessity of a state thoroughfare, if, Arkansas would secure a fair portion of the trade, emigration and travel which Missouri will otherwise engross.

The distance from Fort Smith to Memphis through Little Rock ought not to exceed 300 miles, whilst the distance actually traversed by the Overland Mail Company, between Fort Smith and St. Louis, is 483 miles, and with full loads, in from one to two days quicker time. With a good turnpike and using 40 miles of railroad running west out from Memphis, we could travel the whole line in two days. When this is done, no state north or south can direct business from Arkansas, for the establishment of trade, emigration, and travel will promptly settle the country, increase values, and cause the railroad to be built at an early day.

Will you, sir, lend your influence and your aid to this enterprise? Will you explain to the people the im-

portance of constructing a good road through the centre of the state, which everybody may travel free of charge for its use, if they would promote settlements, multiply villages, increase trade and hasten the construction of a rail road?

Will you tell them through your journal, that Missouri has built 162 miles of road which will be increase by Christmas to 168 miles over which her people expect, as a just reward for their enterprise, to attract the whole of the business of western Arkansas, the Indian country lying to the west of it, and of Upper Texas, until the Central Road of Arkansas is opened? But do not misapprehend me. I do not desire to build up one state at the expense of the other. I wish to see them both prosper. If both rapidly fill up with people, our interests are promoted; if either remains stationary, we are injured, inasmuch as our stages for the long period of six years are to run entirely across both of these. Good roads, connecting our St. Louis route with the railroads north of the Ohio and our Memphis route with the railroads of the entire southern states and with Washington City, are indispensable to the attainment of the object of the government in establishing the Overland Mail stages, viz: the extension, and easy communication with settlements between the Mississippi and California.

Missouri is earnestly engaged on one route – will not Arkansas as earnestly labor, in order to develop its own great resources to perfect the other? If the subject is thoroughly considered, I have no doubt but wise and energetic action will follow. A great central road will be created before the end of June next. I feel satisfied that I can so employ and direct the necessary labor as to secure the building of a good turnpike road across Arkansas as to keep the cost within the sum of $300 per mile, including the bridging of all streams not navigable, which would establish and maintain a mail stage communication across the State, which shall please your people and satisfy the government of my country. And this with God's blessing, I intent to do.

From this purpose, I shall allow nothing to direct my attention, to carry it out; I find good roads wanting, and to obtain good roads, I appeal to the good sense, to the interests, and to the public spirit of the people of Arkansas. With the aid of the public press, to clearly explain what will be the effect upon Arkansas, if she does nothing, when Missouri is doing so much, I shall be disappointed if I am not able to drive four horse stages of the first class through central Arkansas, upon a good turnpike road within the year of 1859. I shall be disappointed if our horses and stages are left another year to slowly wallow and flounder in the oceans of mud in the alluvial bottoms of eastern Arkansas.   Most respectfully,

John Butterfield

President, Overland Mail Company

P. S. Since writing the above, I have purchased a boat, the **Jennie Whipple**, with which I shall leave in the early part of the week to establish and start the route, and hope, yet to satisfy the people that, if they will lend their aid to improve the roads, that they will reap the benefits that they desire. J. B.

Two days after John Butterfield wrote the above letter, the *Des Arc Citizen*, on December 4, 1858 reported:

"OVERLAND MAIL – Mr. Walton, agent of the California Overland Mail company, informs the editors of the Memphis Enquirer that he has just returned from a visit of inspection over the line, with a view to ascertain the cause why the route from Fort Smith to Memphis was not as well filled as that to St. Louis.

He finds that owing to other contracts of the sub-contractors, the mail is laid over about 48 hours at Fort Smith, and about 24 at Des Arc. At present this cannot be remedied; but arrangements are in progress for putting stock on the line under the direct supervision of the contractors, Messrs. Butterfield & Co. As soon as these *arrangements are completed, the same grade of work will be done between Memphis and Fort Smith, as between the latter place and St. Louis."*

Six Observations

First, it appears that the State of Arkansas did not proceed with Butterfield's proposal of Dec. 2, 1858 to build a quality turnpike from Memphis to Fort Smith.

Second, it also appears that Butterfield never personally stocked the Memphis to Fort Smith route with horses and stagecoaches. Instead he continued to sub-contract with John T. Chidester's stagecoach line. Perhaps Butterfield was still confident in his steamboat plan, and intended the sub-contract to be brief.

Third, it appears that it was Chidester who purchased ten new stagecoaches from Concord, New Hampshire, and who stocked the route with additional horses instead of John Butterfield. The Saturday, June 25, 1859 issue of the *Memphis Daily Appeal* reported:

*"The **Jennie Whipple** took on board yesterday, for Little Rock, ten coaches for Messrs. Chidester, Rapley & Co., for the California Overland Mail Service. They were all the way from Concord, N. H."*

Historian Ted R. Worley summarized the issue this way in the *Arkansas Gazette*, issue of September 21, 1958, section F, page 2:

"Butterfield's subcontractor, J. T. Chidester ... After a conference with postal authorities at Washington in December 1858, Chidester went to Memphis to straighten out the snarls in the Memphis-Fort Smith service. In less than a month he had bought about 400 horses and enough stages to supply the route."

Fourth, it appears that Butterfield bought the *Jennie Whipple* in late December 1858, hoping it would make the trip between Memphis and Fort Smith every four days, and then a return trip. At the same time, John T. Chidester would also make that round trip in the opposite direction by stagecoach, so that working in harmony like this, they would fulfill the contract with the Post Master General.

Fifth, it appears that John Butterfield intended to eventually buy a second and perhaps a third steamboat. Then, along with the *Jennie Whipple* as he originally planned, he would not have to rely on stagecoaches at all on this bifurcation of the route.

On November 6, 1858 John Butterfield wrote: *"...I had... selected and partially negotiated for the necessary BOATS."* [emphasis added]

In a March 28, 1858 letter by James Glover, he records the decision of the Post Master General: *"...we also obtained his consent to run our mail and passengers on the BOATS..."* [emphasis added]

On December 2, 1858 John Butterfield wrote, *"DEAR SIR – You are aware that it was my intention to put steam BOAT PACKETS on the Arkansas River last summer, but was thwarted by the lowness of the water."* [emphasis added]

On April 4, 1858 (page 3) James Glover wrote to the Little Rock's *Arkansas True Democrat*: *"The Company will have BOATS built for the express purpose, which will not draw more than 16 inches when, loaded..."*

Finally, sixth, it also appears, that the water levels of the Arkansas River were not reliable. Far too often the *Jennie Whipple* was not able to travel between Little Rock and Fort Smith. Frequently the *Jennie Whipple* ended up hard aground in the mud and sand bars of the Arkansas River. In fact, for most of the last fourteen months that Butterfield owned the *Jennie Whipple*, she was hard aground up the Arkansas River in Indian Territory. As the editor of the *Des Arc Citizen* wrote on November 27, 1858:

"Whoever led Col. Butterfield to believe that he could carry the Overland Mail from Little Rock to Fort Smith by steam, was either a knave or a fool."

Traveling by steamboat on the Mississippi and Arkansas

Rivers in the 1860's may seem romantic: with the sounds of the paddle wheel as it pushes the boat forward, the pulse of the engines, smokestacks billowing smoke from burning wood fuel, steam whistles, gentle flowing rivers, and watching the dramatic landscape of the shoreline slowly pass by. However, the reality of steamboat travel was not always filled with romantic imagery. In addition to low water limiting travel, the August 11, 1859 issue of the *Memphis Daily Appeal* reports:

> STATISTICAL – *It appears that more disasters have occurred on our Western waters, during the past six months, than any former period of the same length. The statistics are given as follows:*
>
> *Boats snagged, 22; boats exploded, 4; boats burned, 26; lost by collision, 13; lost by Rock Island Bridge, 1; lost by running against bank, 2; lost in storm, 1; Total number of boats lost, 74. Flatboats lost, 36. Lives lost, 327.*
>
> *Value of boats and cargoes, $1,770,520.*

Purchase of the *Jennie Whipple*

After three months of stagecoach service, December 1858 approached. The waters of the Arkansas River rose to navigable depth that month. John Butterfield purchased the steamboat *Jennie Whipple* in St. Louis on December 15, 1858. The transaction was reported in the Thursday, December 16, 1858 issue of *The Louisville Daily Courier*:

> *"The steamer **Jenny Whipple**, a very excellent light-draught stern wheel boat, was yesterday sold to Messrs. Butterfield & Co., for the sum of $8,000. She is intended to run as a packet between Little Rock and Fort Smith, in the Arkansas River, for the accommodation of the Overland Mail."*

Butterfield's purchase of the *Jennie Whipple* is recorded in a newspaper clipping from December 21, 1858 provided by Shelley Blanton, Archivist of The Pebley Center, Boreham Library, University of Arkansas-Fort Smith:

> **Messrs. Butterfield & Co.** have purchased the steamer Jennie Whipple, to run as a packet between Little Rock and Fort Smith, in the Arkansas river, for the accommodation of the overland mail.

Source: Vicksburg Daily Whig, Tuesday, December 21, 1858

The *Jennie Whipple* arrived at the Little Rock port on December 20, 1858.

However, it appears that the *Jennie Whipple* was not brand new on December 15, 1858 when it was purchased by John Butterfield. In 1857, 142 steamboats, including the *Jennie Whipple*, were constructed in the Pittsburg, Pennsylvania area according to a list printed in *Allegheny County's Hundred Years*, by George H. Thurston, A.A. Anderson & Sons, Book and Job Printers, Pittsburgh, 1888, page 157.

The *Pittsburg Commercial*, in its June 6, 1876 issue published a list of western steamboats. The list reports that the *Jennie Whipple* was built in August of 1857 at a cost of $13,000.

Way's Packet Directory, 1848-1994, by Frederick Way, Jr. records that the *Jennie Whipple* was a sternwheel packet with a wood hull, built in 1857 at Brownsville, Pennsylvania. She was 138 tons, 135 feet long, and 30 feet wide. The engines were 15 ½'s 3 ½ ft.,with three boilers. The *Jennie Whipple* was built for the Chippewa River with Capt. Charles C. Gray, but soon went to the Arkansas River from 1858 to 1859 with Capt. A. D. Storm running to Memphis. The *Jennie Whipple* went off the lists in 1866.

The August 28, 1857 issue of the *Louisville Daily Courier* reported, *"Two new boats, the Jeannie Gray and Jennie Whipple, from Pittsburg, were at Cincinnati yesterday."*

The initial commander may not have been Captain Charles C. Gray. In the *1912 Proceedings of the State Historical Society of Wisconsin*, October 26, 1911, George Byron Merrick and William R. Tibbals presented a paper entitled, Genesis of Steam Navigation on Western Rivers. In that paper they aimed to give the histories of the steam propelled vessels on the upper Mississippi – their names, tonnage, where built, description, and names of officers. They record (page 147) that Captain Charles Whipple, in April 1857 built, owned, and command-ed *"Jennie Whipple"* in the Chippewa River Trade.

Apparently Captain Charles Whipple commanded the *Jennie Whipple* from April 1857 until the spring of 1858.

In the March 31, 1858 issue of the *Weekly Davenport Demo-crat* (Davenport, Iowa), Captain Gray is listed as the master of the *Jennie Whipple* when it arrived at Davenport from St. Louis.

Shelley Blanton, Archivist of The Pebley Center, Boreham Library, University of Arkansas-Fort Smith was kind enough to provide the following newspaper clipping concerning a collision that occurred nine months before *Jennie Whipple* was purchase by John Butterfield. The *Louisville Daily Courier*, reported on March 31, 1858 that the *Jennie Whipple* was in-volved in a collision:

> COLLISION BETWEEN THE **JENNIE WHIPPLE** AND *G. H. WILSON — On Friday night, the 26th, about 12 o'clock the* **Jennie Whipple**, *bound up, and G. H. Wilson, bound down, came in collision below Rock Island, one of the barges of the latter striking the former about ten feet from her bow, and is supposed damaged her so much as to cause her to leak badly."*

More details of the collision were reported seven days lat-er in the April 6, 1858 issue of New Orlean's *Times Picayune*, when it added:... *Captain Humberstone, an old pilot, was at the time steering the Wilson, and attempted his utmost to avoid colli-sion, but was unsuccessful. He sounded his whistle, signifying his wish to pass the* **Whipple** *on the right, but the pilot of the latter misunderstood the signal."*

Concerning the location of the **Whipple's** collision: Rock Island on the Mississippi River is almost 1,000 acres in size. It is located in the river by Davenport, Iowa. It is also known as Arsenal Island, the home of the First Army headquarters. Fort Armstrong was built on Rock Island in 1816.

A month prior to John Butterfield purchasing the *Jennie Whipple*, the steamboat was sold by the U.S. Marshal. The December 9, 1858 issue of the *Vicksburg Daily Whig*, reported, "*The steamer **Jennie Whipple** was sold at St. Louis a few days since, by the U.S. Marshal, for $6,000. Captain Gray was the purchaser.*"

Apparently Captain Charlie Gray did not personally purchase the **Jennie Whipple**, but rather acted on behalf of Butterfield and Co.

A few days later, the December 21, 1858 issue of the *Vicksburg Daily Whig*, reported, "*Messrs. Butterfield & Co. have purchased the steamer **Jennie Whipple**, to run as a packet between Little Rock and Fort Smith, in the Arkansas River, for the accommodation of the Overland Mail.*"

The 135 foot **Jennie Whipple** was eight months old when purchased by John Butterfield. He relocated the **Jennie Whipple** from the Chippewa River to the Arkansas River to run as a mail packet to fulfil his Overland Mail Co. contract with the Post Master General.

Captain Charley C. Gray continued to command the **Jennie Whipple** after he sold it to John Butterfield.

The **Jennie Whipple** made it's first official run toward Fort Smith out of Memphis on January 20, 1858. The day before, the *Memphis Daily Avalanche* reported:

"*For Arkansas River – The fine regular packet **Jennie Whipple**, Captain Charley C. Gray, will leave for Little Rock, Fort Smith, and all points on the Arkansas River, at five o'clock this afternoon. The **Whipple** has embarked in a trade which is a very important one to our business community, and they should see that Captain Gray, who is a worthy man, is property encouraged. Messrs. Harmstad & Hayman, No. 17 Madison Street, are the agents.*"

Pilot Steering a Steamboat
Image courtesy Smithsonian National Museum of American History.

OVERLAND MAIL COMPANY.

THROUGH TIME SCHEDULE BETWEEN
ST. LOUIS, MO, & MEMPHIS, TENN. } & SAN FRANCISCO, CAL.

[Sep. 16th, 1858.]

GOING WEST.

LEAVE	DATE	Hour	Distance from Place to Place	Time allowed	Ave. Miles per Hour
St. Louis, Mo., & } Memphis, Tenn. } P. R. R. Terminus, -	Every Monday & Thursday,	8.00 A.M	160	10	16
Springfield, "	Monday & Thursday,	6.00 P.M	143	37½	3¾
Fayetteville, "	Wednesday & Saturday,	7.45 A.M	100	26½	3¾
Fort Smith, Ark	Thursday & Sunday,	10.15 A.M	65	17½	3¾
Sherman, Texas	Friday & Monday,	3.30 A.M	205	45	4½
Fort Belknap, "	Sunday & Wednesday,	12.30 A.M	146½	32½	4½
Fort Chadbourn, "	Monday & Thursday,	9.00 A.M	136	30½	4½
Pecos River, (Em Crossing)	Tuesday & Friday,	3.15 P.M	165	36½	4½
El Paso, "	Thursday & Sunday,	11.00 A.M	150	55½	4½
Soldier's Farewell	Saturday & Tuesday,	8.30 P.M	184½	33½	4½
Tucson, Arizona	Sunday & Wednesday,	1.30 P.M	141	41	4½
Gila River,* (Em Crossing)	Tuesday & Friday,	9.00 P.M	135	31½	4½
Fort Yuma, Cal	Friday & Monday,	3.00 A.M	200	30	4½
San Bernardino,	Saturday & Tuesday,	11.00 P.M	150	44	4½
Ft. Tejon, (Los Angeles)	Monday & Thursday,	7.30 A.M	127	32½	4½
Visalia, "	Tuesday & Friday,	11.30 A.M	82	28	4½
Firebaugh's Ferry, -	Wednesday & Saturday,	5.30 A.M	163	18	4½
(Arrive) San Francisco,	Thursday & Sunday,	8.30 A.M		27	6

GOING EAST.

LEAVE	DATE	Hour	Distance from Place to Place	Time allowed	Ave. Miles per Hour
San Francisco, Cal.	Every Monday & Thursday,	8.00 A.M	163	27	6
Firebaugh's Ferry, "	Tuesday & Friday,	11.00 A.M	82	18	4½
Visalia, "	Wednesday & Saturday,	5.00 A.M	127	28	4½
Ft. Tejon, (Los Angeles)	Thursday & Sunday,	9.00 A.M	150	32½	4½
San Bernardino, "	Friday & Monday,	5.30 P.M	200	44	4½
Fort Yuma, "	Sunday & Wednesday,	1.30 P.M	135	30	4½
Gila River,* Arizona	Monday & Thursday,	7.30 A.M	141	31½	4½
Tucson, "	Wednesday & Sunday,	3.00 A.M	184½	41	4½
Soldier's Farewell	Thursday & Sunday,	8.00 A.M	150	33½	4½
El Paso, Tex.	Saturday & Tuesday,	5.30 P.M	248½	55½	4½
Pecos River, (Em Crossing)	Monday & Thursday,	12.45 P.M	165	36½	4½
Fort Chadbourn, "	Wednesday & Saturday,	1.15 A.M	136	30½	4½
Fort Belknap, "	Thursday & Sunday,	7.30 A.M	146½	32½	4½
Sherman, "	Friday & Monday,	4.00 P.M	205	45	4½
Fort Smith, Ark	Sunday & Wednesday,	1.00 P.M	65	17½	3¾
Fayetteville, "	Monday, & Wednesday,	6.15 A.M	100	26½	3½
Springfield, Mo.	Tuesday & Friday,	8.45 A.M	143	37½	3½
P. R. R. Terminus, -	Wednesday & Saturday,	10.30 P.M	160	10	16
(Arrive) St. Louis, Mo. & } Memphis, Tenn. }	Thursday & Sunday,				

This Schedule may not be exact—Superintendents, Agents, Station-men, Conductors, Drivers and all employees are particularly directed to use every possible exertion to get the Stages through in quick time, even though they may be ahead of this time.

If they are behind this time, it will be necessary to urge the animals on to the highest speed that they can be driven without injury.

Remember that no allowance is made in the time for ferries, changing teams, &c. It is therefore necessary that each driver increase his speed over the average per hour enough to gain the necessary time for meals, changing teams, crossing ferries, &c.

Every person in the Company's employ will always bear in mind that each minute of time is of importance. If each driver on the route loses fifteen (15) minutes, it would make a total loss of sixteen and one half (16½) hours, or the best part of a day.

On the contrary, if each driver gains that amount of time, it leaves a margin of time against accidents and extra delays.

All hands will see the great necessity of promptness and dispatch; every minute of time is valuable as the Company are under heavy forfeit if the mail is behind time.

Conductors must note the hour and date of departure from Stations, the causes of delay, if any, and all particulars. They must also report the same fully to their respective Superintendents.

JOHN BUTTERFIELD, Pres't.

* The Station referred to on Gila River, is 12 miles west of Maricopa Wells.

Summary of 1858 Stagecoach Trips
by the Overland Mail Co.

The *Report of the Postmaster General* dated December 4, 1858, reports on page 718:

> *"At the last session of Congress I reported fully the steps that had been taken to carry into execution the act of Congress, approved 3rd March, 1857, authorizing the Postmaster General to contract for the conveyance of the enter letter mail between the Mississippi river and San Francisco.*
>
> *The contract was executed on the 15th September, 1857, and service commenced within the twelve months, namely, on 15th September, 1858, agreeably to the provisions of said act.*
>
> *The department is happy to announce its conclusive and triumphant success. Its departure and arrival were announced with unbounded demonstrations of joy and exultation. I submit a detailed report of Mr. Bailey, the agent of this department, not less instructive at the present time than it may be interesting and curious to those who, in after times, may be desirous to know by what energy, skill, and perseverance the vast wilderness was first penetrated by the mail stages of the United States, and the two great oceans united by the longest and most important land route ever established in any country,"*

Did the Overland Mail Run on Schedule?

Three months after the above report, the *Report of the Postmaster General* dated March 3, 1859, lists the following arrival and departure dates for 1858 on pages 11 and 12 of the report.

All of these 1858 trips would have been by stagecoaches and stage wagons since the steamboats *Jennie Whipple* and Charm did not make any attempts to carry the Overland until 1859.

A table showing the time in carrying the great overland mail between St. Louis and Memphis and San Francisco, route No. 12578, from September 16, 1858, to December 31, 1858

Date of departure from Memphis*	Date of arrival at San Francisco	Number of days in making trip.
September 16, 1858	October 10, 1858	24
September 20, 1858	October 15, 1858	25
September 23, 1858	October 17, 1858	24
September 27, 1858	October 23, 1858	26
September 30, 1858	October 23, 1858	26
October 4, 1858	October 30, 1858	26
October 7, 1858	November 1, 1848	25
October 11, 1858	November 5, 1848	25
October 14, 1858	November 7, 1848	24
October 18, 1858	November 12, 1848	25
October 21, 1858	November 15, 1848	25
October 25, 1858	November 19, 1848	25
October 28, 1858	November 22, 1848	25
November 1, 1858	November 27, 1858	26
November 4, 1858	November 29, 1858	25
November 8, 1858	December 2, 1858	24
November 11, 1858	December 6, 1858	25
November 15, 1858	December 11, 1858	26
November 18, 1858	December 16, 1858	28
November 22, 1858	December 18, 1858	26
November 25, 1858	December 20, 1858	25
November 29, 1858	December 25, 1858	26
December 2, 1858	December 29, 1858	27
December 6, 1858	January 3, 1859	28

[*The report also list identical departure and arrival dates for the stage leaving St. Louis except for the Dec. 2 & 6th departures from St. Louis which arrived in 23 days.]

Date of departure from San Francisco	Date of arrival at Memphis	Number of days in making trip.
September 16, 1858	October 13, 1858	27
September 20, 1858	October 18, 1858	28
September 24, 1858	October 21, 1858	27
September 27, 1858	October 28, 1858	31
October 1, 1858	October 29, 1858	28
October 4, 1858	November 1, 1858	28
October 8, 1858	November 7, 1848	30
October 11, 1858	November 9, 1848	29
October 15, 1858	November 12, 1848	28
October 18, 1858	November 18, 1848	31
October 22, 1858	January 6, 1848 returned back to San Francisco by mistake	
October 25, 1858	November 23, 1848	29
October 29, 1858	November 25, 1848	27
November 1, 1858	December 1, 1858	30
November 5, 1858	December 5, 1858	30
November 8, 1858	December 6, 1858	28
November 12, 1858	December 11, 1858	29
November 15, 1858	December 11, 1858	26

November 19, 1858	December 17, 1858	28
November 22, 1858	December 28, 1858	36
November 26, 1858	December 28, 1858	32
November 29, 1858	December 28, 1858	29
December 3, 1858	January 3, 1859	31
December 6, 1858	January 6, 1859	31

[The report also included a chart of arrivals at St. Louis. Typically the stage arrived at St. Louis 3 or 4 days less than the arrival of the stage at Memphis.]

Where Chidester's Stages Always on Time?

Although the above schedule of the 1858 trips from Memphis to San Francisco are impressive, on closer inspection it will be noted that the *"25 days or less"* cross country schedule was only met 30% of the time (14 out of 47 trips).

We do not have arrival details when Chidester carried the Overland Mail across Arkansas. However, we do have the comment of a special agent of the Postmaster General, George Bailey who was a passenger on the first Butterfield stage out of San Francisco. In his detailed five page report recorded on pages 739-744 of the December 4, 1858 *Report of the Postmaster General*, he writes:

> *...the Memphis branch ...the contractors on this route ...have been behind time on all their trips from Memphis to Fort Smith...*

One reason for the delays may be because it was not uncommon for the Military Road across Arkansas to be impassable due to snow, ice, severe weather, and flooded roads.

Another reason for the Chidester stages being "behind time" may be because the Chidester, Reeside & Brimmer company had another mail contract (#7831) that covered the same Memphis to Fort Smith route three times and week.

The mail will hereafter leave for Van Buren and Fort Smith in post coaches on Monday, Wednesday and Friday mornings, and go through in 54 hours, without detention.

Source: Weekly Arkansas Gazette, Little Rock, Arkansas, April 7, 1860, Sat., Page 2

Mr. Walton, agent of the Overland Mail Company, report-d to the *Des Arc Citizen* on December 4, 1858: *"He finds that wing to other contracts of the sub-contractors, the mail is laid over bout 48 hours at Fort Smith, and about 24 at Des Arc. At present his cannot be remedied..."* Based on Mr. Walton's comments, it ppears that Chidester often delayed the Overland mail so he ould carry both route #7831 and Overland Mail route #12578 nailbags on the same stagecoaches.

Therefore when the Postmaster General reported on de-ays of Route #7831, he may indirectly have been recording elays of Chidester to meet his sub-contract with Butterfield.

The following "failed to arrive" and "failed to arrive on me" were reported for route #7831.

Terminal	Dates	Place	Nature	Fine
		1858		
Des Arc to Fort Smith	Dec, 7 times	Des Arc	Failed to arrive on time	70.00
		1859		
Des Arc to Fort Smith	Jan-Feb, 5 times	Des Arc	failed to arrive on time	50.00
Des Arc to Fort Smith	Jan-Feb, 6 times	Des Arc	Failed to arrive	240.36*
Des Arc to Fort Smith	March 11	Ft. Smith	Failed to arrive	40.06*
Des Arc to Fort Smith	March 16	Fort Smith	Inferior service	10.00
Des Arc to Fort Smith	Dec. 22	Des Arc	Total failure	---
		1860		
Madison to Fort Smith	Jan 2, Feb 2	Fort Smith	Failed to arrive	80.12*
Madison to Fort Smith	Jan 5, 12, 23, 25	Fort Smith	Failed to depart	160.24*
			*these amounts were 'deductions' not fines	

How Does This Compare to Butterfield's Record?

John Butterfield not only had a contract to carry Overland Mail from St. Louis/Memphis to San Francisco, he also had n overlapping contract to carry local mail from Fayetteville o Fort Smith. This second contract, #7909, paid $3,250 per ear. Apparently Butterfield carried route #7909 mail in the ame stages he carried the Overland Mail (route #12578).

Butterfield never failed to deliver this second route, how-ver the mail was delivered wet on one occasion.

Terminal	Dates	Place	Nature	Fine
t Smith to Fayetteville	Sept. 3, 1859	Fayetteville	Wet Mail	$5

On the Overland Mail route #12578, the Postmaster General mentions this route twice in his *"Fines and Deductions of Mail Contractor"* letter of January 9, 1861 to the 2nd session of the 36th Congress.

First, during the week ending July 30, 1859, it reports that route #12578 under contract with Alexander Holland paying $600,000 per year, to carry mail from St. Louis and Memphis to San Francisco, that on April 5, 1859 the mail failed to deliver to Memphis, resulting in a fee of $721.15.

Secondly, during the week ending January 28, 1860, that route #12578 under contract with "Alexander Holland and others," *"Postmaster at Fort Smith, September 10, 1859, certifies that the mail from San Francisco, with dates of October 22, 1858, was changed at his office Nov. 17, 1858; that frequently the labels were lost off, and, as there was no key at that time to the brass locks at his office, it was impossible to separate the pouches after they got mixed; therefore remit fine of $1,442.30."*

The above quote refers to locks. The Pony Express, that operated from April 3, 1860, to October 26, 1861 had the riders carry the mail in six pouches permanently attached to the saddle. Each of the mail pouches were locked at the beginning point in Missouri or California, and were not unlocked from that saddle until arriving at it's final destination across country. Does this quote from September 10, 1859 also reveal that Overland Mail bags also had brass locks attached?

Did the Train Carrying Overland Mail From Hopefield (Ark) to Memphis Run on Time?

The Memphis and Little Rock Railroad Company had the contract to carry the mail from Madison to Hopefield by train. At Hopefield the mail crossed the Mississippi River by ferry to Memphis. This route #7997, paid $3,000 per year.

The railroad was fined several times:

Terminal	Dates	Place	Nature	Fine
		1859		
Madison to Hopefield	Mar 5 to Apr 1	Memphis	Failed to arrive & depart	211.10*
Madison to Hopefield	Sept. 39	Memphis	Failed to deliver	$4.80*
Madison to Hopefield	Jan. 21 Feb 15	Memphis	Wet Mail	$4.00*
		1860		
Madison to Hopefield	Jan. 27	Memphis	Failed to arrive	$4.80*
Madison to Hopefield	Oct 17, 22, 28, Nov 24, 30		Failed to arrive	24.00*

During the week of March 31, 1860, it was reported: *"It appearing that the failures of October 17 and 22, and Nov. 30, were caused by railroad company receiving no mails at Madison on those dates, and consequently could not deliver mails at Memphis, therefore remit $14.40 of the deduction imposed."*

How Many Pieces of Mail Were Carried?

This same report of the Postmaster General also gives an estimate of the number of letters sent in 1858 from Memphis at 5,367 yielding $247.74 in postage, and letters sent from St. Louis numbered 60,800 yielding $2,723.27. The St. Louis postmaster estimated that of the 60,800 pieces of mail, 1,800 were sent free, 25,000 went all the way through with 10¢ postage *(10¢ was the rate for letters traveling over 3,0000 miles)*, and 25,000 were to destinations along the way with 3¢ postage *(3¢ was the rate for letters traveling less than 3,000 miles)*. About 22 packages were sent with each stage out of St. Louis. Also, the stages carried, for free, Memphis, St. Louis, and San Francisco newspapers to be exchanged with other newspapers along the route. This free postal service for newspapers was based on Congressional act of 1825 that allowed *"every printer of newspapers to send one paper to each and every other printer of newspapers within the United States free of postage..."*

The report did not include the number of letters or packages that originated at San Francisco. Also, the report did not include a passenger count from any of these three cities.

In the March 4, 1859 issue of the *Chicago Tribune*, on page 2, the paper reported on the Senate's discussion of the Post Office appropriation bill. The paper expressed its disapproval of an amendment by Mr. Rice of Minnesota to establish an additional transcontinental route – from St. Paul to Puget's Sound at an expense of $200,000 per year. The paper also expressed its disapproval of the cost to support the Overland Mail to California when it wrote:

> *"...Butterfield & Co. do carry an occasional passenger, and now and then a few letters – the latter at an expense of $35 to $60 each... the Postmaster-General and all his underlings are clamorous for an increase of postal*

rates; but so mean a thing as economy in a matter which swallows up three-quarters of a million per annum is not thought of. When will this humbugging come to an end?"

The Early History of Des Arc by Ted Worley states that in 1859, Missouri Congressman Francis Preston Blair offered an amendment to the Post Office appropriation bill *"authorizing the Butterfield Company to carry the mail by any route it chose. In support of his amendment, Blair charged that the reason for the Memphis-Fort Smith branch in the first place was the Postmaster General's interest in Arkansas lands. The face that the Missouri Congressman was also an ardent Republican Free Soiler seemed to Southerners to be connected with his interest in abolishing the Memphis branch."*

The following year the *Report of the Postmaster General* dated December 1, 1860, reports on page 436 that postage received on the Overland via El Paso route totaled $119,766.76 during the past year. If we assume each letter was at 10¢ postage, that would amount to 1,197,667 letters. If we also assume they were equally distributed among the 208 Overland Mail trips during the year, it would amount to 5,758 letters in each stagecoach that year. The postmaster general was concerned that the cost of the route at $600,000 per year, far exceeded the revenue of $119,766. He suggested that the $600,000 should come from the general budget of the U.S. treasury and not from his postal budget. On page 435 he wrote:

"In view of this extremely limited revenue, as compared with the outlay, and of the fact that these route were established and are maintained mainly for the advancement of certain national objects and not at all postal in their character, I respectfully but earnestly renew the recommendation contained in my last annual report, that they shall be at once put upon the public treasury."

The following year, the *Report of the Postmaster General* dated December 2, 1861, repeated this request on pages 576-577:

"I have in a previous part of this report alluded to the refusal at the treasury to pay the appropriation for

the overland mail service to California. It seems to me so evidently to have been the purpose of Congress to require the payment of the amount stipulated from the treasury, under the 9th and 11th sections of the act, that I again call the attention of Congress to the subject for further legislation as may be required. It certainly cannot be supposed that a contract of that magnitude could be required by postal interest alone. The general interest of the country required it, and the compensation should therefore be made by a general appropriation from the treasury, as this department presumes to have been the intention of the law."

During the first 24 weeks of operation, the Butterfield stages averaged carrying 689 letters on each trip. On December 1, 1860 the Butterfield stages averaged carrying 5,758 letters on each trip.

The volume of mail carried by Butterfield's Overland Mail Co. skyrocketed in January of 1860. For example, the Overland Mail stage arrived in San Francisco May 9, 1860 carrying 10,000 letters, and 15,000 in July. The reason for the increase is that in mid December of 1859, the Postmaster General did not renew the ocean steamer contracts. So, starting at that date, the default carrier for all transcontinental mail was Butterfield's Overland Mail Co. instead of the steamers on the ocean route to Panama Isthmus or around South America.

The overland mail, with St. Louis dates to April 16th, reached San Francisco on the 9th, bringing over 10,000 letters, the largest number ever received here at one time. The next subsequent mail is telegraphed and will arrive this evening.

Source: June 1, 1860 Memphis Weekly Bulletin, page 3

The Overland mail, with St. Louis dates to the 2d July, arrived yesterday, bringing 15,000 letters, which is the largest mail ever received overland.

Source: August 9, 1860 Memphis Daily Avalanche, page 3

Was Memphis as Excited About the Overland Mail as Fort Smith and San Francisco?

While Fort Smith and San Francisco held great celebrations when Butterfield's Overland Mail arrived, apparently Memphis did not. Fort Smith and San Francisco continue to celebrate and appreciate the Overland Mail's existence, but it appears that the citizens of Memphis barely took notice of this great transcontinental enterprise.

On April 6, 1860, the following letter was printed in the *Memphis Daily Appeal*:

> *"THE GREAT OVERLAND MAIL, For and From California – Memphis as one of the Points of Departure and Arrival.*
>
> *EDITORS APPEAL: Feeling a deep interest in this, one of the great enterprises of the age, I have thought it would perhaps tend to promote the growing interests of your important city to direct renewed attention, on the part of your real estate owners, bankers, merchants, hotel keepers, railroad stockholders and citizens, to the present and prospective advantages of this mode of travel and means of keeping up an active correspondence with our Pacific sister States and territory.*
>
> *The demonstration that a mail could be safely carried between St. Louis and Memphis, as points of departure and arrival, to and from San Francisco within twenty-five days, was, twelve month since, actually doubted; and experience has shown that even with the deviations from a more direct course, the trip is generally made in an average of twenty days and nights.*
>
> *From inquiry and clear observation, it is found there is a want of general information among your citizens of the existence of such a means of communication with our Pacific coast, whereas it comes home to every individual feeling any interest in the promoting, sustaining of legitimate avenues of intercommunication, to be thoroughly posted in relation to so great an undertaking as this overland mail for and from California. Strangers*

visiting your city, a center already from its position, find even the hotel proprietors, merchants and others, ignorant of the days, hours of departure, name of the local agent, where the office is located; and one would suppose that the stockholders of the Little Rock Railroad would feel sufficient interest to have a sign put up over the ferryboat landing at their crossing, to let the multitude passing know the fact of such a connection.

It would be a subject of interest to the chamber of commerce of your city to submit to en efficient committee the advantages at present and prospective to the city of Memphis, to encourage and sustain the great overland mail to and from California. The same body in the city of San Francisco have had their attention directed to a similar branch of the subject, and its president made a report giving statistics, etc., a short time since.

Why is it that upon arrival of a mail within twenty days, Tuesday afternoon last, no notice is made of such event? Is it of no importance to a city like Memphis? Are her real estate owners, merchants, hotel keepers, railroad stockholders, citizens, about to allow one of her arteries to be cut lose? It may not be generally known, that strong efforts are being made to discontinue this portion of so great a route.

Memphis has decided claims for less distance, better travel, hence to Fort Smith, than from St. Louis. The writer contents that it is just as practicable for the traveler to make the trip hence to San Francisco, as it was to do so by stage from Portland to this point twenty years since.

For general information, the office of the overland mail is for the present at the Commercial Hotel, Jefferson street, B. F. Candy local agent. Days of departure, Wednesday and Saturday, at 8 a.m. Ferry boat for Little Rock Railroad foot of Jefferson street.

An Old Californian.

The Port of Memphis

Casey Swank, Archival Assistant of the Tennessee State Library and Archives in Nashville ask@tsla.libanswers.com, reports that two Memphis newspapers reported on steamboat arrivals and departures during the 1858 to 1861 years of the Butterfield's Overland Mail Co. The *Memphis Daily Avalanche* (the *'River News'* column), and *Memphis Daily Appeal* (the *'Port of Memphis'* column) newspapers are the primary sources for most of the information on the next 150 pages of this book.

Little Rock's *Weekly Arkansas Gazette*, and *Arkansas True Democrat* newspapers from this time period are available on newspapers.com and chroniclingamerica.loc.gov respectively. Both of these newspapers listed the daily arrivals and departures from the port of Little Rock. The Gazette called the column, *"Steamboat Register."* The *True Democrat* called the column, *"Steamboat Register - Furnished by Merrick & Wassell."*

The *Des Arc Citizen* printed a weekly *"River News & c."* column, however it only listed the arrivals and departures of its steamboat line advertisers. The weekly *Des Arc Citizen* issues from November 13, 1858 to August 29, 1860 are available online at the Smithsonian Institution's site: www.chroniclingamerica.loc.gov

A second Des Arc newspaper, *The Constitutional Union* existed from Nov. 16, 1860 to March 29, 1861. This paper printed a weekly column entitled *"River Intelligence"* where they listed arrivals, departures, and any White River related news. These issues are available online at the Smithsonian Institution's site: www.chroniclingamerica.loc.gov

Unfortunately, only one or two issues have survived from any of the newspapers of Fort Smith, 1858-1861. The same sad news is also true of the old newspapers published at Napoleon, Clarendon, and Pine Bluff, Arkansas – so the record of steamboat arrivals and departures at those ports are not available.

It is known, however, that at Pine Bluff, steamboat landings occupied several different sites between Alabama and Tennessee streets. In 1867 one was at the foot of Tennessee

Street and was still in use in 1888. In 1870 a new steamboat landing was built at the north end of Court Square.

Mississippi River Levee from the Custom House
Memphis, Tennessee, circa 1900

QUICKEST AND CHEAPEST ROUTE

TO

Little Rock, Fort Smith, Northern Texas, New Mexico and California!

THE OVERLAND MAIL,

WILL leave MEMPHIS, via Memphis and Little Rock railroad, every WEDNESDAY and SATURDAY, at 7 A M, for the above points, making much shorter time than any other line.

AN EXPRESS MESSENGER

will accompany each Train, and all packages left at the office of Adams & Co.'s Express will be promptly forwarded.

Tickets can be procured at the office of the Company, Commercial Hotel.

J. B. ROBINSON,
Superintendent.

Source: May 29, 1860 Memphis Daily Appeal, page four

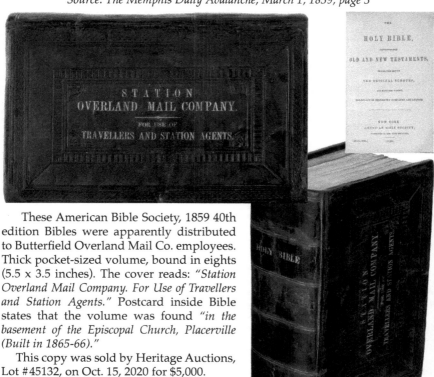

Regular United States Mail Passenger Packet

For Arkansas River.

The splendid passenger steamer

JENNIE WHIPPLE,

C. C. GRAY..... ....Master,

HAVING ENTERED REGULARLY in the Memphis and Arkansas River trade, will leave for Little Rock, Fort Smith, and all points on the Arkansas River every FRIDAY, commencing on Wednesday, 19th inst., at 5' o'clock, P. M. For freight or passage apply to HARMSTAD & HAYMAN, Agents.

17 Madison street

N. B—All orders for freight will be filled by this boat at Cincinnati prices. ja17d3m

Source: The Memphis Daily Avalanche, March 1, 1859, page 3

These American Bible Society, 1859 40th edition Bibles were apparently distributed to Butterfield Overland Mail Co. employees. Thick pocket-sized volume, bound in eights (5.5 x 3.5 inches). The cover reads: "*Station Overland Mail Company. For Use of Travellers and Station Agents.*" Postcard inside Bible states that the volume was found "*in the basement of the Episcopal Church, Placerville (Built in 1865-66).*"

This copy was sold by Heritage Auctions, Lot #45132, on Oct. 15, 2020 for $5,000.

The Bibles distributed to Pony Express employees contain the additional inscription: "*Presented by Russell, Majors & Waddell 1858.*"

CHAPTER TWO
Brief Summary of the *Jennie Whipple's* Trips

Below is a brief summary listing of the *Jennie Whipple's* arrivals and departures between the ports of Memphis / Napoleon / Pine Bluff / Little Rock and occasionally, Fort Smith.

When the date is listed as "Dec __" this indicates that no newspaper record was found of that arrival or departure's date, but it must have taken place since the next newspaper records the *Jennie Whipple's* arrival from that city.

1858

Dec 15	Butterfield & Co. purchased the *Jennie Whipple*		
Dec __	departed St. Louis	for	Memphis
Dec __	arrived Memphis	from	St. Louis
Dec __	departed Memphis	for	Little Rock
Dec 20	arrived Little Rock	from	St. Louis
Dec 22	departed Little Rock	for	Fort Smith
Dec __	arrived Fort Smith	from	Little Rock
Dec __	departed Fort Smith	to	Little Rock
Dec 28	arrived Little Rock	from	Fort Smith
Dec 29	departed Little Rock	for	Fort Smith

1859

Jan __	arrived Fort Smith	from	Little Rock
Jan __	departed Fort Smith	to	Little Rock
Jan 3	arrived Little Rock	from	Fort Smith
Jan 4	departed Little Rock	for	Fort Smith
Jan __	arrived Fort Smith	from	Little Rock
Jan __	departed Fort Smith	for	Little Rock

Jan 8/9	arrived	Little Rock	from	Fort Smith
Jan 11	departed	Little Rock	for	Memphis
Jan 14	arrived	Memphis	from	Arkansas[+]

[NOTE: [+]Frequently the Memphis paper listed the *Jennie Whipple* as arriving from or departing to the generic port of "Arkansas." The community of Arkansas Post was historically just called 'Arkansas,' however in this case the newspapers seem to be referring to the Arkansas River in general as a destination, not just Arkansas Post.]

Jan 20	departed	Memphis	for	Fort Smith[*]

[NOTE: [*]Frequently the Memphis paper listed the destination of the *Jennie Whipple* as Fort Smith, but in fact she did not go farther upstream than Little Rock.]

Jan 22/23	arrived	Little Rock	from	Memphis
Jan 22/24	departed	Little Rock	for	Memphis
Jan 27	arrived	Memphis	from	Arkansas[+]
Jan 28	departed	Memphis	for	Little Rock
Feb 5	arrived	Little Rock	from	Memphis
Feb 6	departed	Little Rock	for	Memphis
Feb __	arrived	Memphis	from	Little Rock
Feb 11	departed	Memphis	for	Fort Smith[++]
Feb __	arrived	Little Rock	from	Memphis

[NOTE: [++]Since this trip only lasted 3 or 4 days, it is physically impossible for the *Whipple* to have made a round trip to Fort Smith. Most likely she stopped at Little Rock.]

Feb __	departed	Little Rock	for	Memphis
Feb __	arrived	Memphis	from	Little Rock
Feb 14	departed	Memphis	for	Arkansas River[+]
Feb 17/18	arrived	Little Rock	from	Memphis
Feb 18	departed	Little Rock	for	Memphis
Feb __	arrived	Memphis	from	Little Rock
Feb 25	departed	Memphis	for	Fort Smith[*]
Feb 28	arrived	Little Rock	from	Memphis
Mar 1	departed	Little Rock	for	Memphis
Mar __	arrived	Memphis	from	Little Rock
Mar 2	departed	Memphis	for	Little Rock
Mar __	arrived	Little Rock	from	Memphis
Mar __	departed	Little Rock	for	Memphis
Mar __	arrived	Memphis	from	Little Rock
Mar 9	departed	Memphis	for	Arkansas River[+]
Mar 10	arrived	Little Rock	from	Memphis

Mar 11	departed	Little Rock	for	Memphis
Mar __	arrived	Memphis	from	Little Rock
Mar 18	departed	Memphis	for	Little Rock
Mar. 21	arrived	Little Rock	from	Memphis
Mar. 22	departed	Little Rock	for	Memphis
Mar __	arrived	Memphis	from	Little Rock
Mar 26	departed	Memphis	for	Little Rock
Mar 29	arrived	Little Rock	from	Memphis
Mar 29	departed	Little Rock	for	Memphis
Apr 2	arrived	Memphis	from	Little Rock
Apr 2/4	departed	Memphis	for	Little Rock
Apr 8	arrived	Little Rock	from	Memphis
Apr 9	departed	Little Rock	for	Fort Smith
Apr	arrived	Fort Smith	from	Little Rock
Apr __	departed	Fort Smith	for	Little Rock
Apr. 15	arrived	Little Rock	from	Fort Smith
Apr 15	departed	Little Rock	for	Memphis
Apr 18	arrived	Memphis	from	Little Rock
Apr 21	departed	Memphis	for	Fort Smith
Apr 24/25	arrived	Little Rock	from	Memphis
Apr 25/26	departed	Little Rock	for	Memphis
May __	arrived	Memphis	from	Little Rock
May 2	departed	Memphis	for	Fort Smith
May 5	arrived	Little Rock	from	Memphis
May 6	departed	Little Rock	for	Memphis
May 9	arrived	Memphis	from	Little Rock
May 12	departed	Memphis	for	Fort Smith
May 15	arrived	Little Rock	from	Memphis
May 15	departed	Little Rock	for	Memphis
May 17	arrived	Memphis	from	Little Rock

*"The **Jennie Whipple** came in from the Arkansas River yesterday (17th) before two o'clock P.M., having made the trip from Memphis to Little Rock and back inside of four and half days, the fastest trip on record."*

May 20	departed	Memphis	for	Little Rock

Date	Action	Place		To/From
May 22	arrived	Little Rock	from	Memphis
May 23	departed	Little Rock	for	Memphis
May 25	arrived	Memphis	from	Little Rock
May 28	departed	Memphis	for	Little Rock
May 30/31	arrived	Little Rock	from	Memphis
May 31	departed	Little Rock	for	Memphis
June 2	arrived	Memphis	from	Little Rock
June 4	departed	Memphis	for	Fort Smith
June 7	arrived	Little Rock	from	Memphis
June 7	departed	Little Rock	for	Memphis
June 9	arrived	Memphis	from	Little Rock
June 11	departed	Memphis	for	Arkansas River
June 13	arrived	Little Rock	from	Memphis
June 14	departed	Little Rock	for	Memphis
June 16	arrived	Memphis	from	Little Rock
June 18	departing	Memphis	for	Fort Smith
June 21	arrived	Little Rock	from	Memphis
June 20/21	departed	Little Rock	for	Memphis
June 23	arrived	Memphis	from	Little Rock
June 25	departed	Memphis	for	Little Rock
June 28	arrived	Little Rock	from	Memphis
June 28	departed	Little Rock	for	Memphis
June 31	arrived	Memphis	from	Little Rock
July 2	departed	Memphis	for	Arkansas River
July 4/5	arrived	Little Rock	from	Memphis
July 5	departed	Little Rock	for	Memphis
July 7	arrived	Memphis	from	Little Rock
July 9	departed	Memphis	for	Arkansas River
July 10/12	arrived	Little Rock	from	Memphis
July 11/12	departed	Little Rock	for	Memphis
July 15	arrived	Memphis	from	Little Rock
July 16	departed	Memphis	for	Arkansas River
July 20	arrived	Little Rock	from	Memphis
July 21	departed	Little Rock	for	Memphis

"We regret to learn that the Memphis and Little Roc

– 118 –

> packet, **Jennie Whipple**, is hard aground in the Arkansas River. She will, in all probability, get off and arrive in ample time to depart at her regular hour tomorrow for Little Rock."

July __	arrived	Memphis	from	Little Rock
July 23	departed	Memphis	for	Arkansas River

[Note: This trip was too short to reach Little Rock and return. Apparently she stopped in Napoleon or Pine Bluff and returned.]

July 25	arrived	Memphis	from	Arkansas River
July 27	departing	Memphis	for	Little Rock
July __	arrived	Little Rock	from	Memphis
Aug __	departed	Little Rock	for	Memphis
Aug 5	arrived	Memphis	from	Arkansas River

> "The **Jennie Whipple** will not return to the Arkansas River during the present season, but will take advantage of the low water and go to Cincinnati for repairs."

Aug 10	departed	Memphis	for	Cincinnati
Aug 13				

> "The mail route from this place [L. Rock] to Napoleon has been stocked with stages all the way through."

Sept 5	arrived	Memphis	from	Louisville

> "The **Jennie Whipple**... with her hull thoroughly overhauled and painted. She will enter the Arkansas River trade in a few days."

Sept 5	departed	Memphis	for	Arkansas River

> "We regret to learn that the **Jennie Whipple** met with an accident while ascending the Arkansas River a few days ago, about forty miles above Napoleon. She struck a snag, which knocked a hole in her bow, causing her to fill rapidly. Capt. Gray found it necessary to run her on a bar. She was afterward pumped out, and proceeded on her way to Little Rock."

Sept 10	arrived	Little Rock	from	Memphis
Sept __	departed	Little Rock	for	Memphis
Sept 15	arrived	Memphis	from	Arkansas River
Sept 17	departed	Memphis	for	Arkansas River
Sept 21	arrived	Little Rock	from	Memphis
Sept __	departed	Little Rock	for	Memphis
Sept 25	arrived	Memphis	from	Arkansas River
Sept 26	departed	Memphis	for	Little Rock

*"The Arkansas River continues quite low, and the **Jennie Whipple** was delayed on her upward trip."*

Oct __	arrived	Little Rock	from	Memphis
Oct __	departed	Little Rock	for	Memphis
Oct __	arrived	Memphis	from	Little Rock
Oct 5	departed	Memphis	for	Little Rock

[Note: Apparently the river was too low to go up the Arkansas so she returned to port.]

Oct 6	arrived	Memphis	from	Little Rock
Oct 8	departed	Memphis	for	Little Rock
Oct __	arrived	Little Rock	from	Memphis
Oct __	departed	Little Rock	for	Memphis
Oct __	arrived	Memphis	from	Little Rock
Oct 15	departed	Memphis	for	Little Rock

*"**Jennie Whipple** hard aground, just below Richland, having been in that condition twenty-four hours. Capt. Gray had reshipped his Little Rock freight at Pine Bluff, and attempted to return from that point."*

Oct __	arrived	Little Rock	from	Memphis
Oct __	departed	Little Rock	for	Memphis
Oct __	arrived	Memphis	from	Little Rock
Oct 26	departed	Memphis	for	Arkansas

*"JENNIE WHIPPLE SUNK - We learn from persons who came up on the Ingomar from Napoleon, that the **Jennie Whipple** struck a snag and sunk near White River cut-off, in the Arkansas River, Tuesday. the South Bend, which arrived yesterday, reported the **Whipple** aground in the same vicinity. We infer that she got off, and stuck a snag afterward and sank in the vicinity of the wreck of the Irene. She was bound down, and crowded with passengers and freight. Captain Gray thought he would be able to raise her. She was insured at Louisville, but we did not learn to what amount."*

Nov 11	arrived	Memphis	from	Arkansas

*"Mr, Rogers has succeeded admirably in his repairs to the **Jennie Whipple**. She is all afloat again, and doesn't look at all the worse for her late accident."*

Nov 15   *"Navigation has been almost suspended in the Arkansas River owing to the low water."*

Nov 26	departed	Memphis	for	Arkansas River

*"The fog and bad weather... detained... **Jennie Whipple** on Arkansas River."*

Nov 29				

"Above Little Rock... upper river too low to ascend beyond the foot of McLean's Bottom."

Dec __	arrived	Little Rock	from	Memphis
Dec __	departed	Little Rock	for	Memphis
Dec 4/5	arrived	Memphis	from	Arkansas River
Dec 8	departed	Memphis	for	Arkansas River
Dec __	arrived	Little Rock	from	Memphis
Dec __	departed	Little Rock	for	Memphis
Dec 18/19	arrived	Memphis	from	Arkansas River
Dec 20	departed	Memphis	for	Little Rock
Dec __	arrived	Little Rock	from	Memphis
Dec __	departed	Little Rock	for	Memphis
Dec 28	arrived	Memphis	from	Little Rock
Dec 30	departed	Memphis	for	Little Rock

1860

Jan 2	arrived	Little Rock	from	Memphis
Jan 2	departed	Little Rock	for	Memphis
Jan __	arrived	Memphis	from	Little Rock
Jan 10	departed	Memphis	for	Little Rock

*"The **Jennie Whipple** and South Bend were at Napoleon Thursday, having been detained by the fog."*

Jan 14	arrived	Little Rock	from	Memphis
Jan 14	departed	Little Rock	for	Memphis
Jan 17	arrived	Memphis	from	Little Rock
Jan 18/19	departed	Memphis	for	Arkansas River
Jan 21	arrived	Little Rock	from	Memphis
Jan 21	departed	Little Rock	for	Memphis
Jan __	arrived	Memphis	from	Arkansas River
Jan __	departed	Memphis	for	Arkansas River
Jan 23	arrived	Little Rock	from	Memphis
Jan __	departed	Little Rock	for	Memphis
Jan 24/25	arrived	Memphis	from	Arkansas River

Jan 25	departed Memphis	for	Little Rock

*"In the storm, Tuesday evening, the **Jennie Whipple**, bound up, was blown ashore in the vicinity of Commerce, and remained in that condition last evening, the water falling rapidly from her. She will be relieved, if at all, with great difficulty."*

Jan 28	arrived Little Rock	from	Memphis
Jan 28	departed Little Rock	for	Memphis

[NOTE: During a storm, the *Jennie Whipple* was blown out of the Mississippi River channel on January 31st at Commerce, forty miles south of Memphis. She remained aground until February 28th.]

Feb 4 -   *"The **Whipple** still remains on the bar near Commerce and was fully twenty feet from water yesterday."*

Feb. 11 –   *"**Jennie Whipple**, was blown so far out of the channel in the storm of the 31st ult., [of last month] about 40 miles below Memphis, that she now lies in a critical condition, high and dry, some distance from the water's edge."*

Feb 28   *"...it would require a rise of about three feet more to float the **Jennie Whipple** from her position in 'Gray's Inlet.'"*

Mar __	arrived Memphis	from Little Rock	

Mar 2   *"The tidy little **Jennie Whipple** was at the landing yesterday, receiving [passengers] for Arkansas River. She has been caulked, thoroughly overhauled and repainted since she got aground, and was never in better condition..."*

Mar 6	departed Memphis	for	Fort Smith
Mar __	arrived Little Rock	from	Memphis
Mar __	departed Little Rock	for	Memphis
Mar 11/12	arrived Memphis	from	Arkansas River
Mar 15	departed Memphis	for	Arkansas River
Mar 18	arrived Little Rock	from	Memphis
Mar 18	departed Little Rock	for	Memphis

Mar 23 –   *"The **Jennie Whipple** met the Bracelet at Pine Bluff, on Monday, and took her trip for Fort Smith and the Upper Arkansas."*

Mar 27 –   *"The **Jennie Whipple**, Undine and Lake City were, at the last intelligence, lying at Vane's Bar, above Little Rock. They could not get over the bar on account of the low water."*

April 6 –   *"The **Whipple** still above Little Rock, with a heavy cargo* *for Fort Smith, awaiting a rise in order to get up."*

April __	arrived	Little Rock	from	Memphis
April __	departed	Little Rock	for	Fort Smith
April __	arrived	Fort Smith	from	Little Rock

The following is a first person report, printed in the April 19, 1860 issue of the Memphis Daily Appeal (page two). This Overland Mail passenger mentions reaching Fort Smith by steamer, but it cannot be the *Jennie Whipple* since she was still stuck aground above Fort Smith.

"A LETTER FROM FORT SMITH – THE OVERLAND MAIL., FORT SMITH, ARK., APRIL 12, 1860. EDITORS APPEAL: Leaving your city [Memphis] *on the morning of Saturday, April 7, '60, to connect with the Little Rock Railroad at half past eight o'clock by skiff, the very punctual ferryboat leaving quarter before the hour (8 A.M.) (and at the north it is considered punctuality to keep the time fixed) to take overland stage at Madison, we reached this point* [Fort Smith], *(after a very pleasant trip, excepting one upset Monday night, but no one hurt) Tuesday at 8:30 A.M., giving about two days and nights respite for the balance of this interesting route to travelers. We had a good* **steamer** *Tuesday night here.* [Fort Smith]
If the citizens of Arkansas..."

[NOTE: In mid-March 1860, the *Jennie Whipple* set course for the upper Arkansas, above Fort Smith into Indian Territory. By March 27, the Arkansas River level was too low to get past Vane's Bar. By May 8th, the Arkansas River had risen enough for her to steam farther upstream past Little Rock and Fort Smith, only to end up stranded by low water in Indian Territory (Oklahoma). A year later, at last she was able to steam south out of Webber Falls, Oklahoma (30 mile south of Ft. Gibson) and arrive at the port of Little Rock on February 19, 1861.]

April 10 –	*The **Jennie Whipple**... still hard aground at Carson's Landing..."*
April 21 –	*"**Jennie Whipple**... still above"*
May 8 –	*"**Whipple** is somewhere up in the Indian Nation, and aground of course."*

1861

Feb 20 –	*"...boats have been stuck there a year, the **Jennie Whipple** being of them."*

– 123 –

Feb __	departed	Fort Smith	for	Little Rock
Feb __	arrived	Little Rock	from	Fort Smith

[NOTE: At some point during this week in February, the Arkansas River level rose enough for her to steam downstream past Fort Smith to Little Rock. At Little Rock, she was held by the U.S. Marshal for payment of past due debts.]

Feb. 26 –   *"**Jennie Whipple** has been calaboosed in Little Rock... by some of her creditors."*

Feb 6	departed	Little Rock	for	Memphis
Mar 4	arrived	Memphis	from	Little Rock

Mar 5	departed	Memphis	for	Little Rock
Mar 8	arrived	Little Rock	from	Memphis
Mar 9	departed	Little Rock	for	Fort Smith
Apr 6	arrived	Fort Smith	from	Memphis

[NOTE: This April 6th arrival at Fort Smith appears to be the last Overland Mail Co. trip across Arkansas. The last Overland mailbag left St. Louis on March 18, 1861 and arrived in Fort Smith about two days later, and in San Francisco April 13, 1861. Therefore this April 6th mailbag would have missed the last stage.]

Apr __	departed	Fort Smith	for	Memphis
April 11	arrived	Memphis	from	Fort Smith

April 11	departed	Memphis	for	St. Louis

April 12 –   *"The Memphis Bulletin says the steamer **Jennie Whipple** has quit the Arkansas River trade, very unexpectedly, leaving a number of bills unsettled. The **Whipple** was laid up in the Arkansas River for nearly twelve months, went to Memphis a few weeks since and loaded for Fort Smith, has returned, and gone no one knows where."*

April 20 –   *"**Jennie Whipple** sold to Mr. Adams for the Dubuque trade..."*

May 6 -   *"**Whipple** confiscated by U.S. Marshal for debts.."*

June 1 –   *"**Jennie Whipple** sold for $1,760 to Captain David White... for Davenport to Keokuk route."*

Late 1800's maps of the Arkansas, White and Mississippi Rivers indicate the location of many of the landings and location references used in the newspaper reports of steamboats being aground, sunk, or holding in place until the river level rises.

For river maps, refer to the appendices at the end of this book.

CHAPTER THREE
Detailed Record of the
Jennie Whipple's Arkansas River Trips

This chapter contains a more detailed listing of arrivals and departures of the *Jennie Whipple* on the Arkansas River between Memphis and Fort Smith. Arkansas River water levels, and a few of the major accidents by other steamers on the Arkansas are also recorded below as well.

In the following 1858 quotes from the Memphis and Arkansas newspapers, there are numerous mentions of the low water in the Arkansas and well as the Mississippi River. It was this low water in the fall of 1858 that kept John Butterfield from proceeding with his original plan to only use steamboats to carry mail and passengers on the Memphis and Fort Smith leg of the Overland Mail Co. route.

The low water in the fall of 1858 required John Butterfield to only use the stagecoaches of John T. Chidester, Reeside & Co. until the Arkansas River water levels improved.

When the Arkansas River water rose in January, 1859, John Butterfield's steamboat, *Jennie Whipple* was able to be put into service. The *Memphis Daily Avalanche*, on January 17, 1859 made note of the event:

> THE *JENNIE WHIPPLE* FOR ARKANSAS RIVER –
>   *The fine steamer Jennie Whipple, Captain C. C. Gray, has arrived here and will run hereafter as a regular packet between Memphis and Little Rock and all other points on the Arkansas River. She will leave Memphis*

*on Wednesday next at five o'clock, and every Wednesday thereafter during the season. The **Jennie Whipple** is in fine condition, is admirably adapted to the trade, and is well officered, Captain Gray being just the man for the position. We are therefore pleased to welcome him and his boat to the trade. Messrs. Harmstad & Hayman, No. 17 Madison Street are the agents.*

However, the Memphis papers of 1859 - 1861, recorded below, reveal that on a multitude of weeks low water or accidents continued to keep the **Jennie Whipple** out of service. When the **Jennie Whipple** was out of service, the Overland Mail Co. passengers and mail bags were carried by the stagecoaches of John T. Chidester, Reeside & Co. between Memphis and Fort Smith.

For an entire month, January 31 to February 28, 1860 the **Jennie Whipple** was hard aground about forty miles south of Memphis. She had been blown out of the Mississippi River channel by a storm on January 31st.

About two weeks after getting back into service, in mid-March, 1860, the **Jennie Whipple** set course for the upper Arkansas, above Fort Smith into Indian Territory. By March 27, the Arkansas River level was too low to get past Vane's Bar. By May 8th, the Arkansas River had risen enough for her to steam farther upstream past Little Rock and Fort Smith, only to end up hard aground in Indian Territory (Oklahoma). A year later, at last she was able to steam south out of Webber Falls, Oklahoma and arrive at the port of Little Rock on February 19, 1861.

During these thirteen months between January 31, 1860 and February 19, 1861, Overland Mail Co. passengers and mail travelled exclusively without the steamboat. Butterfield's Overland Mail left Memphis on a ferry to Hopefield, Arkansas. There it was transferred to a train for a 24 mile trip to Madison, Arkansas. At Madison it was transferred to a John T. Chidester stage wagon or stagecoach for the journey across Arkansas to Fort Smith.

1858

Monday, September 18, 1858 Memphis Daily Avalanche
"The Little Rock Democrat of the 8th says that the [Arkansas] river has risen about an inch, and has attained what may be understood as a 'low water mark.' No steamer has left here [Little Rock] since last week's report, except the Lone Star, a small craft built at this place by our enterprising fellow-citizen, Thomas Barrett."

Saturday, September 25, 1858 Memphis Daily Appeal
"The [Mississippi] river continued falling slowly yesterday."

Tuesday, September 28, 1858 Memphis Daily Appeal
"The [Mississippi] river continued declining..."

Friday, October 1, 1858, Memphis Daily Appeal
"The Ohio River is getting into very bad condition, as much so that navigation at present is almost impossible, even for the smallest boats."

Tuesday, October 5, 1858 Memphis Daily Appeal
"The Ohio River has gone nearly dry. The Illinois River is falling... with a scant five feet in the channel. The Upper Mississippi is becoming very low. The Missouri River is falling and becoming very bad."

Thursday, October 8, 1858 Memphis Daily Appeal
"In the morning we were visited by the first front of the season."

Wednesday, October 13, 1858 Memphis Daily Appeal
"...the Ohio continues so low that the boats running on that river continually get aground, making their time of landing uncertain."

Thursday, October 14, 1858 Memphis Daily Appeal
"Low and yet lower falls the [Mississippi] river, presenting a wide contrast to the mighty flood that rolled on in overwhelming grandeur."

Friday, October 15, 1858 Memphis Daily Appeal
"We are now.. reduced to low water with all its losses, delays, accidents and vexations. The bluff is covered with cotton, which the holders are anxious to ship, boats are laid up in idleness at different parts of the river, and little improvement in this state of things is to be expected until the Mississippi once more shows a respectable channel."

Sunday, October 17, 1858 Memphis Daily Appeal
"The [Mississippi] river still continues to fall. It was declining yesterday at an accelerated rate, and pilots are having a difficult task in navigation to perform.

The Little Rock Gazette of October 2, reports: Near low water mark and on a stand. The light steamer... Rough and Ready sunk, on her downward trip [to Napoleon]*... At low water, and no prospect of a rise."*

Wednesday, October 20, 1858 Memphis Daily Appeal
"The [Mississippi] river continues to fall steadily at this point, and is now at almost extreme low water mark."

Sunday, October 24, 1858 Memphis Daily Appeal
"The [Mississippi] river is still falling, and accounts from the upper rivers continue gloomy enough... The latest arrivals from above report a very bad river, and daily getting worse, with 6 feet from St. Louis to Cairo, 6 ½ at Island 18, and about the same at Plum Point. the officers of the Cora Anderson report several boats aground between this [Memphis] *and Cairo."*

Wednesday, November 3, 1858 Memphis Daily Appeal
"The [Mississippi] river was slowly rising yesterday... rain is looked for... give us hope of increased shipment facilities."

Saturday, November 6, 1858 Memphis Daily Appeal
"The Little Rock Gazette, of October 30th, says: The [Arkansas] *river, which up to Thursday evening has risen about fifteen inches, rose nine inches on Thursday night, and, at this writing (Friday noon) is still rising. It may, therefore, be now set down, that there are from three to three and a half feet water in the channel; and there is a prospect for at least some more water. We hope that the season of regular navigation may soon open."*

Sunday, November 7, 1858 Memphis Daily Appeal
"The [Mississippi] river, we rejoice to say, is still rising briskly. It rose a foot in the last twenty-four hours."

Friday, November 12, 1858 Memphis Daily Appeal
"The Napoleon Planter of November 6, says: A nine feet rise is reported in the Arkansas River. This is quite a fortunate circumstance, not only to the steamboatmen but to the planters on the river, as they are enabled to ship their cotton as fast as they may

see proper."

"The Little Rock Gazette of November 6, reports: The river has risen about fourteen feet, and is still rising. The Quapaw came to the landing Saturday night last, and left on Tuesday for New Orleans. The Little Rock left for New Orleans on Monday. The Arkansas arrived on Monday evening, the Lightfoot on Thursday, and the Irene on Thursday night. Navigation has fairly opened and the opening looks propitious."

Tuesday, November 16, 1858 Memphis Daily Appeal

"The Brownsville (Ark.) Echo, of November 10th says: The Arkansas River is in fine boating order, and was still rising on the 4th inst. The Little Rock merchants will have better facilities for getting their goods this fall than they have had for several years, as we learn they often have to haul them from Des Arc, through by the way of Brownsville, a distance of sixty miles."

Friday, November 19, 1858 Memphis Daily Appeal

"The Pine Bluff (Ark.) Independent, of November 5 reports: Our [Arkansas] river has risen six or eight feet, and is therefore now in fine boating stage. The boats are passing so frequently that we cannot keep the run of them."

Thursday, December 9, 1858 Memphis Daily Appeal

"The [Mississippi] river continues to rise, and is now over three feet higher than on Saturday last."

Thursday, December 16, 1858 The Louisville Daily Courier

*"The steamer **Jenny Whipple**, a very excellent light-draught stern wheel boat, was yesterday sold to Messrs. Butterfield & Co., for the sum of $8,000. She is intended to run as a packet between Little Rock and Fort Smith, in the Arkansas River, for the accommodation of the Overland Mail."*

Tuesday, December 21, 1858 Vicksburg Daily Whig

*"Butterfield & Co. have purchased the steamer **Jennie Whipple**, to run as a packet between Little Rock and Fort Smith, in the Arkansas River, for the accommodation of the Overland Mail."*

Saturday, December 25, 1858 Weekly Arkansas Gazette

ARRIVALS *Dec. 20 – **Jennie Whipple** at Little Rock from St. Louis*
DEPARTURES *Dec. 20 – **Jennie Whipple** from Little Rock to Ft Smith*
The New Orleans newspaper, *The Times-Picayune*, on Feb-

ruary 7, 1860 reports:

> *"In 1858, there was not a single steamboat running from Memphis up the Arkansas; now there is the Red Wing, S. H. Tucker, Lady Walton, South Bend, **Jennie Whipple** and Favorite - in all, six - all doing a heavy business. In 1856, there was not a bale of cotton shipped out of the Arkansas River to Memphis; now the amount is near 5,000 bales; and in 1858, $1,000 would cover the amount of groceries, liquor, lime, flour, etc. purchased in Memphis for the planters on the Arkansas; now there is $200,000 - quite a considerable increase."*

The introduction of the steamboat *Jennie Whipple* on the Arkansas River was part of this growing river traffic. The record of her arrivals and departures from the port of Memphis are reproduced below.

1859

Saturday, January 1, 1859 Weekly Arkansas Gazette
*Arrivals – Dec. 28 **Jennie Whipple** at Little Rock from Fort Smith*
*Departures – Dec. 29 **Jennie Whipple** from Little Rock to Fort Smith*

Saturday, January 1, 1859 Memphis Daily Appeal
"The Little Rock Gazette of Dec. 25 says: "Mississippi River bank full, and rising slowly - fears are entertained of an overflow." The same paper states that there is sufficient water in the Arkansas for the largest boats to Fort Smith."

Tuesday, January 4, 1859 Memphis Daily Appeal
"The river is now at a very high stage, but.. commenced falling."

Thursday, January 5, 1859 Arkansas True Democrat
Note: This paper printed a lengthy letter from John Butterfield where he encourages Arkansas to improve the Military Road. Butterfield ends his letter with the comment:
*"P. S. Since writing the above, I have purchased a boat the **Jennie Whipple**, with which I shall leave in the early part of the week to establish and start the route, and hope, yet to satisfy the people that, if they will lend their aid to improve the roads, tha they will reap the benefits that they desire. J. B."*
*Arrivals – Dec. 28 **Jennie Whipple** at Little Rock from Fort Smith*
*Departures – Dec. 29 **Jennie Whipple** Little Rock for Fort Smith*

Wednesday, January 5, 1859 Memphis Daily Appeal

"The Little Rock True Democrat, of the 29th December says: 'Eight feet water in the channel and falling slowly, though the prospects are for a considerable rise. The weather is warm at this time (Tuesday). An unusual number of boats are in the river, as regular packets at this time, showing an increase of business. There are now two lines running to Cincinnati, and several fine boats are regular traders to New Orleans, besides several regular packets from Napoleon to this place and Fort Smith. Emigrants and travelers now, need fear no detention, as all can be accommodated.'"

Thursday, January 6, 1859 Memphis Daily Appeal

"The river continued falling rapidly yesterday."

Friday, January 7, 1859 Memphis Daily Appeal

"The river... still falling with considerable rapidity."

Saturday, January 8, 1859 Weekly Arkansas Gazette

ARRIVALS JAN. 3 – ***Jennie Whipple*** *at Little Rock from Fort Smith*
DEPARTURES JAN. 4 – ***Jennie Whipple*** *from Little Rock to Fort Smith*

Saturday, January 8, , 1859 Memphis Daily Appeal

"...the weather was cold, and the mud frozen."

Tuesday, January 11, 1859 Memphis Daily Appeal

"St. Louis... the weather was dreadfully cold yesterday. It was emphatically a winter day... the ground was thickly covered with snow, and all day a sharp, cutting wind blew in the face of everybody that ventured out. There was ice floating in the river."

Wednesday, January 12, 1859 Arkansas True Democrat

ARRIVALS – *Jan. 9* ***Jennie Whipple***, *from Fort Smith*

Wednesday, January 12, 1859 Memphis Daily Appeal

"The river continues to fall..."

Thursday, January 13, 1859 Memphis Daily Appeal

"Business at the landing was not very brisk."

Friday, January 14, 1859 Memphis Daily Appeal

"The river continues to fall. The weather was rainy yesterday, and the wharf and streets are in a bad condition with mud."

Saturday, January 15, 1859 Weekly Arkansas Gazette

ARRIVALS JAN. 9 – ***Jennie Whipple*** *at Little Rock from Fort Smith*

Saturday, January 15, 1859 Weekly Arkansas Gazette

ARRIVALS JAN. 11 – *Jennie Whipple from Little Rock to Memphis*

Saturday, January 15, 1859 Memphis Daily Avalanche

"The ice at St. Louis was thin and soft, and not heavy enough to embarrass navigation."

"The little Jennie Whipple, all the way from the Arkansas River, was in port last evening."

Sunday, January 16, 1859 Memphis Daily Appeal

"The river was still falling yesterday."

Monday, January 17, 1859 Memphis Daily Avalanche

"The Mississippi is now entirely clear of ice at St. Louis...

THE JENNIE WHIPPLE FOR ARKANSAS RIVER - *The fine steamer Jennie Whipple, Capt. C. C. Gray, has arrived here and will run hereafter as a regular packet between Memphis and Little Rock and all other points on the Arkansas River. She will leave Memphis on Wednesday next at five o'clock, and every Wednesday hereafter during the season. The Jennie Whipple is in fine condition, is admirably adapted to the trade, and is well officered, Capt. Gray being just the man for the position. We are therefore pleased to welcome him and his boat to the trade. Masters Harmstad and Hayman, No. 17 Madison street, are the agents."*

Regular United States Mail Passenger Packet
For Arkansas River.
The splendid passenger steamer
JENNIE WHIPPLE,
C. C. GRAY...... ....Master,

HAVING ENTERED REGULARLY in the Memphis and Arkansas River trade, will leave for Little Rock, Fort Smith, and all points on the Arkansas River every FRIDAY, commencing on Wednesday, 19th inst., at 5 o'clock, P. M. For freight or passage apply to HARMSTAD & HAYMAN, Agents.
17 Madison street
N. B.—All orders for freight will be filled by this boat at Cincinnati prices.   ja17d3m

Butterfield's advertisement for passengers on his steamboat, *Jennie Whipple*
Source: The Memphis Daily Avalanche, Monday, January 17, 20, 22, 24, 25, 27 and February 1,3, 4,5,11, 17, 18, 19, 23, 26, 28 and March 1 1859

Tuesday, January 18, 1859 Memphis Daily Avalanche

"The river is still falling... weather clear... but very cold. Total shipments of cotton yesterday amounted to 3,359 bales..."

Wednesday, January 19, 1859 Memphis Daily Avalanche

"The citizens of the White River Valley in Arkansas, are preparing a petition to Congress, praying for the establishment of a river mail in connection with Memphis, Augusta, and Little Red River. The mail facilities in Arkansas are altogether inadequate to the wants of the people, and the services alluded to is greatly needed..."

"FOR ARKANSAS RIVER - The fine regular packet Jennie Whipple, Capt. C. C. Gray, will leave for Little Rock, Fort Smith, and all points on the Arkansas River, at five o'clock this afternoon. The Whipple has embarked in a trade which is a very important one to our business community, and they should see that Capt. Gray, who is a worthy man, is properly encouraged. Masters Harmstad and Hayman, No. 17 Madison Street, are the agents."

Thursday, January 20, 1859 Memphis Daily Avalanche

DEPARTURES YESTERDAY - *Jennie Whipple for Arkansas River.*

Friday, January 21, 1859 Memphis Daily Avalanche

"According to the statistics, the total value of the steamboats running on the Mississippi River and its tributaries, is over $60,000,000 and they number over fifteen hundred, with a tonnage three fold greater than the steamer tonnage of Great Britain, and more than that of all the nations of Europe and the rest of the world put together."

Saturday, January 22, 1859 Memphis Daily Avalanche

"The Arkansas River was rising slowly at Fort Smith on Saturday last, with three feet water in the channel. The weather at Fort Smith has been warm, cloudy, and rainy during the week, but was quite cold on the 15th."

Monday, January 24, 1859 Memphis Daily Avalanche

"The tributaries to the Upper Mississippi, so far as they are free of ice, are in good boating order."

Tuesday, January 25, 1859, The Memphis Daily Avalanche

"We now have three Arkansas River packets running in connection with this city - the Arkansas Traveler, Capt King; the Jennie Whipple, Captain Gray; and the Virginia Belle, Captain Gray.

*The trade and travel of that section with Memphis is amply suf-
ficient to support three packets, if properly concentrated, and we
hope they will all be properly encouraged."*

Wednesday, January 26, 1860 Arkansas True Democrat
ARRIVALS – *Jan. 23* ***Jennie Whipple*** *from Memphis*
DEPARTURES – *Jan. 24* ***Jennie Whipple*** *for Memphis*

Wednesday, January 26, 1859 Memphis Daily Avalanche
*"The **Jennie Whipple**, Captain Gray, is advertised for Arkansas River today, but, as she had not arrived last evening, we
presume her departure will be delayed."*

Thursday, January 27, 1859 Memphis Daily Avalanche
*"The first trip of the Virginia Belle in the Arkansas River trade
was a very profitable one. She went out yesterday with a good
freight and passenger list."*

Friday, January 28, 1859 The Memphis Daily Avalanche
*"FOR ARKANSAS RIVER - The fine steamer **Jennie Whipple** Capt.
Gray, will leave for all points below Little Rock, on the Ar-
kansas, at five o'clock this afternoon. Her accommodations are
most superb, and her officers are efficient and attentive, Messrs.
Harmstad & Hayman, No. 17 Madison Street are the agents. "*

Saturday, January 29, 1859 Weekly Arkansas Gazette
ARRIVALS JAN. 22 – ***Jennie Whipple*** *at Little Rock from Memphis*
DEPARTURES JAN. 22 – ***Jennie Whipple*** *from Little Rock for Memphis*

Saturday, January 29, 1859 Memphis Daily Avalanche
ARRIVALS YESTERDAY - ***Jennie Whipple***, *Arkansas River.*
*"According to the Fort Smith Herald, of the 22nd, the Arkansas
River was falling slowly, with about three feet water in the chan-
nel. The weather there was cool and pleasant. "*

Tuesday, February 1, 1859 Memphis Daily Avalanche
FOR ARKANSAS RIVER - *The fine steamer **Jennie Whipple**, Capt.
"C. C. Gray, having been detained, will leave most positively for
all points on the Arkansas River, this afternoon at the usual hour.
The **Whipple** has excellent accommodations and accomplished
officers. Messrs. Harmstad & Hayman and Capt. McDowell are
the agents."*

Wednesday, February 2, 1859 Memphis Daily Avalanche
DEPARTURES YESTERDAY - ***Jennie Whipple***, *Arkansas River*

Thursday, February 3, 1859 The Memphis Daily Avalanche

"The weather in this latitude for the past day or two has been hard on steamboatmen. There was a dark, misting rain on the river Tuesday night, and very high winds prevailed Wednesday..."

Friday, February 4, 1859 Memphis Daily Avalanche

"The river was falling pretty rapidly.. six inches... 24 hours."

Saturday, February 5, 1859 Memphis Daily Avalanche

"The river is still falling..."

Monday, February 7, 1859 The Memphis Daily Avalanche

"The Arkansas River was falling slowly on Thursday last, with three feet water in channel. The navigation of the Arkansas River is now tedious and at considerable risk."

"The steamer Little Rock met with an accident below Pine Bluff the other day, that nearly destroyed the boat. By mere accident she took fire in the hold; and had it not been for the greatest exertion of the captain, who was considerably burnt in the face, the whole would have been a total loss."

Tuesday, February 8, 1859 Memphis Daily Avalanche

"CHANGE OF OWNERS - The former proprietors of the Memphis and Hopefield ferryboat Nashoba, have sold the boat and ferry privileges for a term of years to Messrs. Richardson & Everett, who have improved the boat, and rendered the line in many respects more efficient than heretofore."

Wednesday, February 9, 1859 Arkansas True Democrat

ARRIVALS – Feb. 5 Jennie Whipple from Memphis
DEPARTURES – Feb. 6 Jennie Whipple for Memphis

Wednesday, February 9, 1859 Memphis Daily Avalanche

"The Virginia Belle arrived at Napoleon from Arkansas River on the 4th with a light trip. She was unable to get up to the 'Rock.' She reports but twenty inches water in the river."

Wednesday, February 9, 1859 Memphis Daily Appeal

"The river continues to fall gradually..."

"The neat boat Jennie Whipple is the regular packet for Little Rock and other ports on the Arkansas River today; she leaves at 6 o'clock in the evening. This boat connects with the Mary Cook for Fort Smith, and with the Overland Mail route for California.

The clever clerk, George Hynson, will not fail to make his passengers comfortable – it is a habit he has."

Thursday, February 10, 1859 Memphis Daily Avalanche

"FRIDAY PACKETS - The following regular packets will leave at the usual time on Friday... Jennie Whipple, for Little Rock."

Friday, February 11, 1859 Memphis Daily Avalanche

STEAMBOAT DEPARTURES TODAY – Jennie Whipple, Capt. Gray, Arkansas River.

"FOR ARKANSAS RIVER - The fine steamer Jennie Whipple, Captain C. C. Gray, will leave for Pine Bluff, Little Rock, Fort Smith, and way places at the usual hour this afternoon. Travelers will find the Jennie Whipple one of the most pleasant modes of conveyance on the Arkansas River. Messrs. Harmstad & Hayman are the agents."

Saturday, February 12, 1859 Memphis Daily Avalanche

"The river is still falling..."

Saturday, February 12, 1859

Note: On this date, Governor Conway signed an act of the legislature for the removal of all free Negroes and mulattoes over 21 years of age from Arkansas by the first day of January, 1860 or face sale into slavery for a period of one year. At the time, about 700 free black people lived in Arkansas, less than in any other slave state.

Saturday, February 12, 1859 Weekly Arkansas Gazette

ARRIVALS FEB 5 – Jennie Whipple at Little Rock from Memphis
DEPARTURES FEB 6 – Jennie Whipple from Little Rock for Memphis

Monday, February 14, 1859 Memphis Daily Avalanche

STEAMBOAT DEPARTURES TODAY – Jennie Whipple, Capt. Gray, Arkansas River.

"The Arkansas River, at Little Rock, has fallen to low water mark. The steamers Little Rock and Henry Fitzhugh are caught between Little Rock and Fort Smith, and are unable to get out The steamers Dardanelle, Arkansas, and Hickman are above the mouth, awaiting a rise. There was a rain at Little Rock on Tuesday last, with a prospect for a speedy rise."

"Dense fogs have prevailed in this latitude recently, and boat have lost considerable time by being forced to tie up."

*"FOR ARKANSAS RIVER - The fine low water steamer **Jennie Whipple**, Captain Gray, will leave as above, this afternoon, at the usual hour. She is a pleasant boat, with careful and attentive officers, Messrs. Harmstad & Hayman, corner of Front and Madison streets are the agents."*

Tuesday, February 15, 1859 Memphis Daily Avalanche
"The river... commenced rising... five or six inches."

Thursday, February 17, 1859 Memphis Daily Avalanche
"The Mississippi is still rising slowly at this point."

Friday, February 18, 1859 Memphis Daily Avalanche
"The ice, however, has become so soft and scarce that it offers little or no obstruction to navigation."

Saturday, February 19, 1859 Weekly Arkansas Gazette
ARRIVALS FEB 17 – **Jennie Whipple** *at Little Rock from Memphis*
DEPARTURES FEB 18 – **Jennie Whipple** *from Little Rock for Memphis*

Saturday, February 19, 1859 Memphis Daily Avalanche
"The river is rising slowly at this point."

Monday, February 21, 1859 Memphis Daily Avalanche
"The total shipments of cotton for the week... 7,149 bales."

Tuesday, February 22, 1859 Memphis Daily Avalanche
"Large sales of wild and as well as improved Arkansas lands have been made in the last few days to parties who intend to take up their residence at once in this growing and prosperous state... Should the same amount of emigration continue, it will be only a few years before Arkansas becomes the richest and most populous of our Southern States."

Wednesday, February 23, 1859 Arkansas True Democrat
ARRIVALS – *Feb. 18* **Jennie Whipple** *from Memphis*
DEPARTURES – *Feb. 18* **Jennie Whipple** *for Memphis*

Wednesday, February 23, 1859 Memphis Daily Avalanche
STEAMERS LEAVING THIS DAY - **Jennie Whipple**, *Capt. Gray, Arkansas River*
*"The fine steamer **Jennie Whipple**, Capt. Gray, is advertised for Little Rock today, but we presume she will remain over until tomorrow."*

Thursday, February 24, 1859 Memphis Daily Avalanche
STEAMERS LEAVING THIS DAY - **Jennie Whipple**, *Capt. Gray, Ar-*

kansas River.

"FOR LITTLE ROCK - *The excellent passenger packet* **Jennie Whipple**, *Captain Gray, will leave for all points on the Arkansas River at three o'clock this afternoon. The* **Jennie Whipple** *has become one of our permanent institutions, and she owes her popularity to Captain Gray's admirable management. Messrs. Harmstad & Hayman are the local agents."*

Friday, February 25, 1859 Memphis Daily Avalanche

STEAMERS LEAVING THIS DAY - *Jennie Whipple, Capt. Gray, Arkansas River.*

"*This is the season of fogs, and the heavy vapors have hung lazily over the Mississippi in this latitude during the past forty-eight hours, operating as a prohibition almost to navigation... fog-bound... boats were delayed both in arriving and departing."*

"FOR ARKANSAS RIVER - *The fine and staunch* **Jennie Whipple**, *Capt. C. C. Gray, will leave for Pine Bluff, Little Rock and Fort Smith, at five o'clock this afternoon. The* **Whipple** *is most admirably adapted to the trade, and Capt. Gray is admirably adapted to the command of such a craft. Messrs. Harstad & Hayman are the agents."*

"THE IRENE BROKE IN TWO - *We learn from from a gentleman who came by the overland route from Little Rock yesterday, that the steamer Irene, one of Captain Adams' line of mail-boats from Little Rock to the mouth of the Arkansas River, had run upon a bar and broken in two. We have no particulars of the accident."*

Saturday, February 26, 1859 The Memphis Daily Avalanche

"*The river was rising..."*

Monday, February 28, 1859 The Memphis Daily Avalanche

"*The river is still rising... water has broken over the levees a short distance above this city* [Memphis] *, and has spread out over the bottom between the Mississippi and the St. Francis Rivers. There will be no diminution, but a constant accumulation of water in the Mississippi Valley for some time to come... levels below the this city* [Memphis] *have been broken, and the flood is pouring out into the lowlands. The rise at this time is a great calamity, as the levees that have been completed are so new as to be useless to resist the tide, while those that are but partly built* *will, in many cases, be utterly destroyed."*

> Regular United States Mail Passenger Packet
> # For Arkansas River.
> The splendid passenger steamer
> # JENNIE WHIPPLE,
> C. C. GRAY . . . . Master,
>
> HAVING ENTERED REGULARLY in the Memphis and Arkansas River trade, will leave for Little Rock, Fort Smith, and all points on the Arkansas River every FRIDAY, commencing on Wednesday, 19th inst., at 5 o'clock, P. M. For freight or passage apply to HARMSTAD & HAYMAN, Agents.
> 17 Madison street
> N. B —All orders for freight will be filled by this boat at Cincinnati prices. ja17d3m

Butterfield's advertisement for passengers on the *Jennie Whipple*
Source: The Memphis Daily Avalanche, February 28, 1859

Tuesday, March 1, 1859
"The Mississippi is still rising slowly... four inches... 48 hours."
Wednesday, March 2, 1859 Arkansas True Democrat
ARRIVALS – *Feb. 28 **Jennie Whipple** from Memphis*
DEPARTURES – *Mar. 1 **Jennie Whipple** for Memphis*
Wednesday, March 2, 1859 Memphis Daily Appeal
*"The **Jennie Whipple** - a neat boat, well adapted to the trade, being light and capable of running at all stages of water - in the regular packet for Little Rock and Arkansas River ports today, leaving at six o'clock this evening; the gentlemanly and accommodating clerk, George Hynson, will leave no effort untried to make his passengers comfortable. "*
Thursday, March 3, 1859 Memphis Daily Appeal
"The river came to a stand... 20 inches below high-water mark."
Friday, March 4, 1859 Memphis Daily Appeal
"The water is now very high, and drift continues to descend..."
Saturday, March 5, 1859 Weekly Arkansas Gazette
ARRIVALS FEB 28 – ***Jennie Whipple** at Little Rock from Memphis*
DEPARTURES MAR 1 – ***Jennie Whipple** from Little Rock for Memphis*
Saturday, March 5, 1859 Memphis Daily Appeal
"The Little Rock Gazette of February 26th reports: 'The river, which has been very high for the past week, has commenced falling. The weather has been unusually warm. Vegetation is com-

mencing, and the peach trees are in bloom. We fear cold weather, between this and the first of April may seriously injure the fruit, or entirely destroy it.'"

Sunday, March 6, 1859 Memphis Daily Appeal

"We learn from Captain Bugher, of the Resolute, that the Arkansas River is low. There were only thirty inches at Fort Smith on Saturday last."

Tuesday, March 8, 1859 Memphis Daily Appeal

"The river... ten inches below high water mark."

Wednesday, March 9 1859 Memphis Daily Appeal

*"The **Jennie Whipple** was advertised for the Arkansas River yesterday. She is a light, neat, trim boat, and her clerk, George Hynson, is one of the cleverest fellows afloat. On such a boat, and with such an officer, an agreeable trip is certain. The boat is announced to leave at 6 o'clock this evening."*

Thursday, March 10, 1859 Memphis Daily Appeal

"Cairo is still safe from the flood, but there is a large accumulation of water inside the levees, caused by frequent rains..."

***Jennie Whipple* Advertisement**
Source: Memphis Daily Appeal, January 16 until March 11, 1859

Friday, March 11, 1859 Memphis Daily Appeal

"...the river... fallen a half inch... lacked 8½ inches of June rise."

Saturday, March 12, 1859 Weekly Arkansas Gazette
ARRIVALS MAR 10 – *Jennie Whipple* at Little Rock from Memphis
DEPARTURES MAR 11 – *Jennie Whipple* from Little Rock for Memphis
Saturday, March 12, 1859 Memphis Daily Appeal
"The river... 6 ½ inches below high water mark."
Sunday, March 13, 1859 Memphis Daily Appeal
"The river... 7 ½ inches below high water mark."
Monday, March 14, 1859 The Memphis Daily Avalanche
"Total shipments of cotton... this week... 5,343 bales"

For Arkansas River.

THE splendid fleet passenger steamer JENNIE WHIPPLE, C. C. Gray, Master, having entered regularly in the Memphis and Arkansas River trade, will leave for Little Rock, Fort Smith, and all points on the Arkansas River every **FRIDAY**, commencing on Wednesday, 19th inst, at 5 o'clock P. M. For freight or passage apply to   HARMSTAD & HAYMAN, Agents, 17 Madison street.

N. B.—All orders for freight will be filled by this boat at Cincinnati prices.   ja17 d3m

Butterfield's advertisement for passengers on his steamboat, the *Jennie Whipple*
Source: *The Memphis Daily Avalanche*, March 14, 19, 23, 24, 25, 1859
April 20, 21, 22, 23, 24, 25, 26, 27, 28, 1859
May 2, 3, 5, 6, 7, 9, 10, 12, 13, 16, 17, 18, 19, 1859

Tuesday, March 15, 1859 The Memphis Daily Avalanche
"Business on the levee was brisk."
Wednesday, March 16, 1859 Arkansas True Democrat
ARRIVALS – Mar. 10 *Jennie Whipple* from Memphis
Wednesday, March 16, 1859 Memphis Daily Appeal
*"The **Jennie Whipple** is advertised to leave today as the regular weekly Little Rock and Arkansas River packet. The boat is excellently adapted to the trade she runs in, and passengers will receive at the hands of Geo. Hynson, the clever and popular clerk, every necessary attention. "*
*"Geo. Hynson, clerk of the **Whipple**, informs us that the S. H. Tucker had broken her cylinder timber on the Arkansas River. She was obliged to turn back to Little Rock. The Lady Walton,*

on the Arkansas River, ran on a snag, a few days ago, knocking a very large hole in her hull. A bulkhead was built and the boat so far repaired as to be able to proceed."

Early Snag Boat, circa 1861
There was a specialty boat called a "snag boat" designed to lift and remove logs out of snags to open up the river and remove hazards.

"There is about six feet water in the [Arkansas River] channel, and stationary. There are prospects of a rise."
"BURNING OF THE STEAMER D. H. MORTON. The steamer D. H. Morton, was burned about sixty miles above Little Rock, on the Arkansas River, on Friday, the 11th. The Morton was a stern-wheeler, and belonged to the government. She was bound for Fort Smith at the time, and had about eight hundred bales of hay on freight, all of which, with the boat, was consumed. She was about three years old, and was valued at $6,000. Captain John T Washington was her commander. Captain W. came a passenger to this city yesterday by the steamer Lady Walton."

Thursday, March 17, 1859 The Memphis Daily Avalanche
STEAMERS LEAVING THIS DAY - ***Jennie Whipple***, *Captain Gray Little Rock.*

Friday, March 18, 1859 The Memphis Daily Avalanche
STEAMERS LEAVING THIS DAY - ***Jennie Whipple***, *Captain Gray Little Rock.*

Saturday, March 19, 1859 The Memphis Daily Avalanche

"There is plenty of water in the Arkansas River for boats to ascend to Fort Smith."

Source: Memphis Daily Appeal, March 20, 1859

Tuesday, March 22, 1859 The Memphis Daily Avalanche

"The weather yesterday was cloudy and unpleasant, with considerable... heavy rains... lightning and heavy thunder."

Wednesday, March 23, 1859 The Memphis Daily Avalanche

"The levee... limited in width as it is by the high water."

Wednesday, March 23, 1859 Arkansas True Democrat

*Arrivals – March 21 **Jennie Whipple** from Memphis*
*Departures – March 22 **Jennie Whipple** for Memphis*

Thursday, March 24, 1859 The Memphis Daily Avalanche

"The Lady Walton, from the Arkansas River, arrived at Louisville Sunday with a hole in her bottom."

Friday, March 25, 1859 The Memphis Daily Avalanche

*"For Little Rock - the fine steamer **Jennie Whipple**, Captain Gray, is announced for the Arkansas River after the arrival of the train this afternoon. Captain Gray has rendered the **Whipple** the very thing for the trade, and invariably takes the crowd. Remember the **Jennie Whipple** today. Messrs. Harmstad & Hayman are the agents."*

Saturday, March 26, 1859 Weekly Arkansas Gazette

*Arrivals March 21 – **Jennie Whipple** at Little Rock from Memphis*

DEPARTURES MAR 22 – *Jennie Whipple from Little Rock for Memphis*

Monday, March 28, 1859 The Memphis Daily Avalanche

"The new levee at Napoleon has not been completed, and Napoleon is in imminent danger of immediate inundation."

"BRONSON, THE ARTIST – This distinguished artist left this city, on the Jennie Whipple, Saturday for Little Rock, for the benefit of his health. It is his intention to return at an early date."

Wednesday, March 30, 1859 The Memphis Daily Avalanche

"The Arkansas River was falling from Little Rock down to Pine Bluff and that from Pine Bluff to the mouth the river was full of back water."

Thursday, March 31, 1859 The Memphis Daily Avalanche

"Total shipments of cotton yesterday embraced 3,254 bales..."

Friday, April 1, 1859 The Memphis Daily Avalanche

"The weather... very cold... with a killing frost."

Saturday, April 2, 1859 Weekly Arkansas Gazette

ARRIVALS MARCH 29 – *Jennie Whipple at Little Rock from Memphis*
DEPARTURES MAR 29 –*Jennie Whipple from Little Rock for Memphis*

Saturday, April 2, 1859 The Memphis Daily Avalanche

STEAMERS LEAVING THIS DAY - *Jennie Whipple*, Capt. Harmstad, for Little Rock.

"The popular steamer Jennie Whipple, Capt. Larry Harmstad, arrived from Little Rock yesterday. Included in her manifest were 200 bales of cotton for Napoleon, and a large consignment of hides for this city [Memphis].*"*

"FOR ARKANSAS RIVER - The popular steamer Jennie Whipple, Capt. Larry Harmstad, will leave for all points on the Arkansas River at 5 o'clock this afternoon. The Jennie seems to have usurped the greater part of the trade and travel hence to the "Rock" and she is admirably adapted to its performance. Mr. Geo. W. Hynson has charge of the office. Messrs. Harmstad and Hayman are the agents."

Monday, April 4, 1859 The Memphis Daily Avalanche

"The river... 7 ¼ inches below high water mark..."

Tuesday, April 5, 1859 The Memphis Daily Avalanche

"The fine little steamer Jennie Whipple, Capt. Larry Harmstad, left last evening for the Arkansas River with an excellent

trip, both of passengers and freight. Capt. Larry is an old steamboatman, and if he can't make a trip pleasant we don't know who can."

Tuesday, April 5, 1859 The Memphis Daily Appeal

*"Mr. James Gray, brother to Captain Charley, has taken Mr. George Hynson's place in the office of the **Jennie Whipple**, and is assisted by our popular young friend, Mr. James A. Parker."*

Regular U. S. Mail Passenger Packet.
MERCHANTS' AND PLANTERS' LINE,
JENNIE WHIPPLE,
C. C. GRAY, Master......JAMES A. GRAY, Clerk.

THIS splendid, swift running passenger steamer will run regularly between Little Rock and Memphis, leaving Little Rock weekly for Memphis.— Passengers ticketed through to Louisville, St. Louis or Cincinnati, by this boat.
For freight or passage, apply to
MERRICK & WASSELL, Agents,
April 6, 1859.   3m   Or on Board.

Source: Arkansas True Democrat, April 6, 1859, page 3

Wednesday, April 6, 1859 The Times Picayune (N. Orleans)

*"We learn from Mr. Hynson, of the **Jenny Whipple**, that when that boat left the Arkansas River on Wednesday, it was falling as far as the backwater above the mouth."*

Wednesday, April 6, 1859 Arkansas True Democrat

ARRIVALS – *March 29 **Jennie Whipple** from Memphis*
DEPARTURES – *March 29 **Jennie Whipple** for Memphis*
*"MR. EDITOR: ... One week ago, I left Memphis for Monticello, per steamer '**Jennie Whipple**,' and ascended the Arkansas River to this place [Pine Bluff], and made the residue of the way in a hack chartered especially for the trip. And here, let me remark by the way, that the **Jennie Whipple** is a beautiful little craft, with a gentlemanly captain and an obliging clerk, whose endeavors to render their passengers safe and satisfied, were unremitting. Speed, comfort, and safety seem to be their watch-words."*

Friday, April 8, 1859 The Memphis Daily Avalanche

"The river... just six inches below... high water mark of last year."

Saturday, April 9, 1859 Weekly Arkansas Gazette

ARRIVALS APRIL 8 – ***Jennie Whipple*** *at Little Rock from Memphis*

Saturday, April 9, 1859 The Memphis Daily Avalanche

"Ice in the upper Mississippi has broken up, which has had the affect of creating a rise in the river..."

"RESOLUTE AGROUND – From the officers of the Henry Fitzhugh we learn that the steamer Resolute, bound for Fort Smith, was hard aground in the Arkansas River about seventy-five miles above Little Rock, and as the river was falling fast, she would have to lighten herself considerable before she would get off."

"ARKANSAS RIVER – The latest accounts from the Arkansas River are to the effect that above Little Rock there were thirty inches water in the channel, and three and a half feet from Little Rock to the mouth."

"Steamboat business is represented as brisk on the Arkansas River. The Henry Fitzhugh, Capt. Windsor, arrived from Fort Smith yesterday with a large cargo consisting principally of hides, poultry, 12,000 lbs. bacon, pecans, beeswax and Indian ponies."

Monday, April 11, 1859 The Memphis Daily Avalanche

"...rain late last evening, which will have the effect of swelling the rivers and streams hereabout."

Tuesday, April 12, 1859 The Memphis Daily Avalanche

"The water is now within 8 ¼ inches of the highest point reached in the flood last year."

Wednesday, April 13, 1859 Arkansas True Democrat

ARRIVALS – *April 8* **Jennie Whipple** *from Memphis*

DEPARTURES – *April 9* **Jennie Whipple** *for Fort Smith*

*"RIVER, ETC. – The river has reached what may be termed low water mark, with little prospects of a rise. The mail steamers to Napoleon, make their regular trips in good time. From this point [Little Rock] to Fort Smith, navigation is suspended except to boats of very low draught. ...**Jennie Whipple**, however, may make the trip."*

*"Just received per steamer **Jennie Whipple**, 10 kegs best rifle*

powder; 2 cases best canister powder; 500 lbs. bar lead. Apply to A, J, Hutt, April 13, 1859."

Wednesday, April 13, 1859 The Memphis Daily Avalanche
"Business on the levee was not very active during the day."

Thursday, April 14, 1859 The Memphis Daily Avalanche
"The river... stationary for... days, commenced rising slowly..."

Friday, April 15, 1859 The Memphis Daily Avalanche
"The river here was rising... 1 ½ inch"

Saturday, April 16, 1859 Weekly Arkansas Gazette
DEPARTURES APRIL 9 – *Jennie Whipple* from Little Rock for Memphis

Saturday, April 16, 1859 The Memphis Daily Avalanche
"The weather... stiff, cool breeze prevailing last night."

Saturday, April 16, 1859 The Memphis Daily Appeal
*"At our last advice from Fort Smith, there was but eighteen inches water reported thence to Little Rock, and we would infer that the **Jennie** would rub the bottom all along with her heavy freight list. If anybody could take her through, however, Captain Larry is the man, and we expect to see the **Jennie** in port here with flying colors."*

Monday April 18, 1859 The Memphis Daily Avalanche
"...levee at Bedford's Plantation... Vicksburg... gave way"

Tuesday, April 19, 1859 The Memphis Daily Avalanche
"The river at this point declined three inches in 24 hours..."

Wednesday, April 20, 1859 Arkansas True Democrat
ARRIVALS – April 15 *Jennie Whipple* from Fort Smith
DEPARTURES – April 15 *Jennie Whipple* for Memphis

Wednesday, April 20, 1859 The Memphis Daily Avalanche
STEAMBOATS LEAVING TODAY - *Jennie Whipple*, Capt. Harmstad, for Little Rock.

*"Among other freight brought by the **Jennie Whipple** from Arkansas River, were 83 barrels of green apples, the product of Arkansas, 17 bales of cotton, and about 6,000 pounds of dry hides"* (page 3).

"SINKING OF THE STEAMER RESOLUTE - The packet Resolute struck a snag on Sunday morning last four miles below Van Buren on the Arkansas River, and sunk almost immediately in deep

water. The Resolute had no cargo of any consequence and the loss, therefore, to her owner, Capt. Dean of Cincinnati will not be great. The Arkansas Traveler was near by when the accident occurred and engaged immediately... The machinery and other valuables... were placed on the Traveler... No lives were lost."

*"The **Jennie Whipple**, commanded by the indefatigable (tireless) Larry Harmstad, arrived from Fort Smith late Monday night. While the **Whipple** was at the wharf at Fort Smith the river rose six feet in almost as many hours."*

For Little Rock and Fort Smith.

THE MERCHANTS' AND PLANT-ERS' LINE Light-Draught passenger packet JENNIE WHIPPLE, Larry Harmstad, Master, will leave as above THIS DAY, Wednesday, April 20 at five o'clock. For freight or passage apply on board, or to a20-1t HARMSTAD & HAYMAN.

Butterfield's advertisement for passengers on his steamboat, the *Jennie Whipple*
Source: The Memphis Daily Avalanche, April 20, 21, 1859

Thursday, April 21, 1859 The Memphis Daily Avalanche
*"Steamboats leaving today: **Jennie Whipple**, Capt. Harmstad, for Little Rock... the **Jennie Whipple** did not get off yesterday, but will leave positively today. A large party of gentlemen in this city intend paying a visit to the celebrated Hot Springs, and the **Whipple** is awaiting their movements..."*

*"FOR FORT SMITH - The **Jennie Whipple**, Capt. Larry Harmstad, will leave as above at five o'clock this evening."*

Friday, April 22, 1859 The Memphis Daily Avalanche
*"The **Jennie Whipple** left last evening for Arkansas River, having on board a fair trip... The river falling slowly at Napoleon yesterday. The Arkansas was falling all the way down and was quite low for the season."*

Saturday, April 23, 1859 Weekly Arkansas Gazette
ARRIVALS APRIL 15 – **Jennie Whipple** at Little Rock from Fort Smith
DEPARTURES APR 15 – **Jennie Whipple** from Little Rock for Fort Smith

Saturday, April 23, 1859 The Memphis Daily Avalanche
"IMPROVEMENT OF THE NAVIGATION OF WHITE RIVER - The Bates

ville Balance has the following in relation to a proposition made by a well known steamboatman, to improve the navigation of White River: We understand that a gentleman well known as a steamboatman in White River, made a proposition the other day, to make White River always navigable to Batesville, for the sum of $20,000, and to work on the "no cure no pay" principle. Being perfectly satisfied of the feasibility of the project, he is willing to agree that if he does not accomplish it he shall be paid nothing. He has been upon the river long enough to be able to form a correct idea of the difficulties to be overcome and the means of doing it, and we have no doubt but he is safe in his calculation that the navigation of the river to this point can be made perpetual with an expenditure of less than $20,000.

Monday, April 25, 1859 The Memphis Daily Avalanche
"Levee after levee continue to yield to the resistless power of the mighty flood waters which is being poured out upon the bottoms of the lower Mississippi... water is rushing through with great force and violence."

Tuesday, April 26, 1859 The Memphis Daily Avalanche
"The river is falling... one inch in twenty-four hours."

Wednesday, April 27, 1859 The Memphis Daily Avalanche
"The river at this point has come to a stand..."

Wednesday, April 27, 1859 Arkansas True Democrat
ARRIVALS – *April 24* **Jennie Whipple** *from Memphis*
DEPARTURES – *April 26* **Jennie Whipple** *for Memphis*

Thursday, April 28, 1959 The Memphis Daily Avalanche
"The Arkansas Traveler arrived at Cincinnati on Tuesday with the engines and machinery of the Arkansas and Resolute, which were recently sunk in the Arkansas River."

Friday, April 29, 1859 The Memphis Daily Avalanche
"The Arkansas is falling all the way down from Little Rock, and is now quite low."

Saturday, April 30, 1859 Weekly Arkansas Gazette
ARRIVALS APRIL 25 – **Jennie Whipple** *at Little Rock from Memphis*
DEPARTURES APR 25 – **Jennie Whipple** *from Little Rock for Memphis*

Monday, May 2, 1859 The Memphis Daily Avalanche
"STEAMBOATS LEAVING TODAY: **Jennie Whipple***, Capt. Harms-*

tad, for Fort Smith."

*"FOR THE ARKANSAS RIVER - The fine little passenger packet **Jennie Whipple**, Capt. Larry Harmstad, having been unavoidable detained, will leave for Pine Bluff, Little Rock, and all points on the Arkansas River at five o'clock this afternoon. There may be boats with better capacities than then **Jennie**, but none with better accommodations, or more attentive officers than Capt. Harmstad and Charley Gray."*

"A REQUEST TO STEAMBOATMEN - General Gideon J. Pillow, through a dispatch to the press of this city, earnestly requests that all steamboatmen will keep a constant lookout for the body of his son, who was lost by the explosion of the St. Nicholas, on Sunday night last. This request, coming from a distressed parent, we are sure, will be complied with by those to whom it is addressed."

*"The remains of Mr. Beckell, who died on board the steamer Chancellor a few days since, were yesterday removed from Morris Cemetery, where they had been deposited, and placed on board the **Jennie Whipple** for transportation to Fort Smith, the former place of residence of the deceased. His remains were followed to the boat by the Odd Fellows, of which he was a member."*

Tuesday, May 3, 1859 The Memphis Daily Avalanche
"The river level at this point is still stationary."

Wednesday, May 4, 1859 The Memphis Daily Avalanche
"The river here was rising yesterday... one inch in 24 hours."

Thursday, May 5, 1859 The Memphis Daily Avalanche
"The shipments of cotton yesterday comprised 505 bales..."

Saturday, May 7, 1859 Weekly Arkansas Gazette
*ARRIVALS MAY 5 – **Jennie Whipple** at Little Rock from Memphis*
*DEPARTURES MAY 5 – **Jennie Whipple** from Little Rock for Fort Smith*

Saturday, May 7, 1859 The Memphis Daily Avalanche
"The Lady Walton will run between Fort Smith and Little Rock until business ceases, when she will return to Cincinnati, where her machinery will be transferred to a new boat."

Monday, May 9, 1859 The Memphis Daily Avalanche
"Jennie Whipple arrived today from the Arkansas River."

Tuesday, May 10, 1859 The Memphis Daily Avalanche

*"From the officers of the **Jennie Whipple**, which arrived yesterday from the Arkansas River, we learn that the stream continues to fall steadily, there being only eighteen inches from Little Rock up, and three feet from that point down to the mouth."*

*"DEATH OF WALTER R. LEAK, ESQ., OF NORTH CAROLINA – The steamer **Jennie Whipple**, which arrived here yesterday from the Arkansas River, brought with her the remains of Walter R. Lean, the President of the Bank of Wadesborough, North Carolina, who died on Wednesday last, at the residence of Col. Francis A. Perry, in Poinsett County, Arkansas. Mr. Leak was a prominent and wealthy citizen of Wadesborough, Anson County, North Carolina, and the announcement of his death will be received with unusual regret, by a large community, to whom he was well known and by whom he was highly esteemed. Mr. Leak passed through this city about three weeks ago, on a visit to relatives and friends in Arkansas, stopping at the house of his relative Col. Perry, was taken sick and soon breathed his last. His remains, in charge of his nephew, Mr. L. P. Leak, were forwarded last evening over the Memphis and Charleston Railroad, to his home in North Carolina, there to be interred.*

For Arkansas River.

THE SPLENDID PASSENGER PACK-
et JENNIE WHIPPLE, Capt.
C. C. Gray, will leave for all points as
above on WEDNESDAY May 11th at 5 P.
M. Through tickets for the Hot Springs for slae on board
or by   LARRY HARMSRAD, Agent.
m10-2t

Butterfield's announcement of *Jennie Whipple's* May 11th planned departure.
Source: The Memphis Daily Avalanche, May 10, 1858

Wednesday, May 11, 1859 Arkansas True Democrat
ARRIVALS – *May 5 **Jennie Whipple** from Memphis*

Wednesday, May 11, 1859 The Memphis Daily Avalanche
STEAMBOATS LEAVING TODAY: ***Jennie Whipple**, Capt. Harmstad, for Fort Smith.*

Thursday, May 12, 1859 The Memphis Daily Avalanche
STEAMBOATS LEAVING TODAY: ***Jennie Whipple**, Capt. Gray, for*

Fort Smith.

"The [Mississippi] water now stands at the highest mark reached the present year, and is only five inches below the great flood of 1858."

*"FOR THE ARKANSAS RIVER - The **Jennie Whipple** did not get off last evening as announced, owing to the large amount of business offering, but will positively leave at six o'clock P.M. today for Little Rock and all points on the Arkansas River. Capt. C. C. Gray is her commander, and a better officer cannot be found. Passengers going up the Arkansas had better secure rooms at once on board the **Jennie**."*

Friday, May 13, 1859 The Memphis Daily Avalanche

*"The **Jennie Whipple** for the Arkansas River, went out at six o'clock last evening loaded down to the guards with freight, and having a cabin full of passengers."*

Saturday, May 14, 1859 The Memphis Daily Avalanche

"...seventeen miles below Natchez... another break in the levee... near the Esperance plantation of Dr. Frederick Stanton."

Monday, May 16, 1859 The Memphis Daily Avalanche

"Passengers report having seen a dead body floating in the river about forty miles below Memphis, on yesterday morning."

"The Fort Smith Times says the steamer Violet, coming to the first bend in the river above that place recently, got into a pocket, where she now remains surrounded by sand bars, waiting for a rise."

"FOR ARKANSAS RIVER - The Oakland, Capt. Fleming, is advertised to leave for Little Rock and Fort Smith this evening at five o'clock. The Oakland is a light draught boat and will go through."

NOTE: The author of this column had a sense of humor including the following: DIABOLICAL MURDER - *On the last trip up of one of our most popular packets, a most diabolical murder was committed on the person of A. Rooster - an individual well known in this community, having a large circle of relatives and friends in this city. The deed was committed about eleven o'clock on the morning of the 13th, and for atrocity and cold bloodedness is without parallel in the annals of crime. The* commission of the deed lies between the cook of the boat and his assistant - probably both - one holding the unfortunate individual while the other deliberately chopped off his head with an axe, and then threw the head into the river. The traces of blood upon the guards of the boat lead to an investigation and discovery of the criminal or criminals upon the part of the officers and passengers and on the arrival of the boat at Memphis the two were paid off. The police are in search of the guilty parties, and we trust such punishment as they deserve will be meted out to them. The friends of Mr. Rooster are making a loud noise over the matter, and they have the sympathy of all, while the foul murderers are execrated...

P. S. - Since writing the above we have imbibed deeply with Larry Harmstad [captain of the **Jennie Whipple**], and are under obligations to him."

Tuesday, May 17, 1859 The Memphis Daily Avalanche
"The Arkansas was reported as rising at Fort Smith..."

Wednesday, May 18, 1859 Arkansas True Democrat
*"We make our lowest bow to Messrs. Gray and Parker, the gentlemanly clerks of the steamer **Jennie Whipple**, for a bundle of late Memphis and New York papers."*

[NOTE: It was usual for mail packets to deliver and exchange newspapers up and down their routes between editors free of charge. This free postal service was based on Congressional act of 1825 that allowed *"every printer of newspapers to send one paper to each and every other printer of newspapers within the United States free of postage..."*]

Wednesday, May 18, 1859 Arkansas True Democrat
ARRIVALS – *May 15* **Jennie Whipple** *from Memphis*
DEPARTURES – *May 15* **Jennie Whipple** *for Memphis*

Wednesday, May 18, 1859 Des Arc Citizen, page 2
*"From the Memphis Appeal, 10th inst. MELANCHOLY DEATH – About two weeks since Walter R. Leake, Esq., the worthy President of the Bank of Waydesborough, N.C., embarked on the steamer **Jennie Whipple**, in the enjoyment of health, on a business visit to Terry's Landing, Arkansas. He sickened on the way and died, and his dead body was brought to this city [Memphis]*

yesterday by the same boat that bore him away a fortnight ago, when he was in the vigor of health and manhood."

Wednesday, May 18, 1959 The Memphis Daily Avalanche

*"The officers of the **Jennie Whipple**, which arrived yesterday at two o'clock, report the Arkansas River rapidly rising at Little Rock on Sunday. this doubtless must be the June rise, and from the color of the water - almost a blood red - is thought to come from the Canadian River."*

*"The **Jennie Whipple** came in from the Arkansas River yesterday before two o'clock P.M., having made the trip from Memphis to Little Rock and back inside of four and half days, the fastest trip on record. The **Jennie** is an established institution in the Memphis and Arkansas River trade, and well deserves the patronage which we are gratified to learn she is receiving from our merchants and planters along her route. She brought up this trip orders for groceries, etc., almost sufficient to load her on her return trip. The **Whipple** is advertised to leave on tomorrow evening at five o'clock. To her attentive officers, the Masters Gray and James A. Parker, we are indebted for memoranda and other information."*

*"MEMORANDA OF STEAMER **JENNIE WHIPPLE** - **Jennie Whipple** left Little Rock at Sunday, 15th, at two o'clock P.M. ...river rising at the rate of three inches per hour - rise supposed to come from the head waters of the river. **Whipple** will leave for Little Rock and all way points on Thursday the 19th after the arrival of the railroad trains."*

*"THE LITTLE ROCK MURDER – CONVICTION OF THE MURDERER – We learn from the officers of the steamer **Jennie Whipple**, which arrived yesterday, that the trial of Cosgrove, for the murder of young Lester, of Georgia was concluded at Little Rock on Saturday last, the prisoner being found guilty on murder in the first degree, and sentenced to be hung on the 10th... The remains of the murdered man were brought to this city by the steamer **Jennie Whipple**, in charge of his uncle, Maj. J. B. Lester, and Mr W. H. McClain. From here they will be taken to Georgia, by the Adams Express company, for burial."*

For Arkansas River.

THE SPLENDID PASSENGER PACK-
et JENNIE WHIPPLE, Capt.
C. C. Gray, will leave for all points as
above on THURSDAY May 19th at 5 P.
M. Through tickets for the Hot Springs for sale on the
boat, or by   LARRY HARMSTAD, Agent
my18-2t

Source: Memphis Daily Avalanche, May 19, 1859, page 3

Thursday, May 19, 1859 The Memphis Daily Avalanche

STEAMBOATS LEAVING TODAY - *Jennie Whipple*, *Capt. Gray, for Fort Smith.*

"FOR ARKANSAS RIVER - *The fleet little steamer Jennie Whipple, Capt. Gray, leaves this evening at six o'clock for Arkansas River. The Whipple is a crack boat, and travelers may rely upon a pleasant time, Larry Harmstad is agent.*"

Friday, May 20, 1859 The Memphis Daily Appeal

"FOR ARKANSAS RIVER – *The fastest and finest of all the light-draught boats in our knowledge, is the Jennie Whipple, Captain C. Gray. She will leave for Little Rock at the usual hour this afternoon. Passengers will find the two Jameses – Gray and Parker – in the office. Captain Harmstad is the agent.*"

Saturday, May 21, 1859 Weekly Arkansas Gazette

ARRIVALS MAY 15 – *Jennie Whipple at Little Rock from Memphis*
DEPARTURES MAY 15 – *Jennie Whipple from Little Rock for Memphis*

For Arkansas River.

MERCHANTS' AND PLANTERS' LINE

THE splendid fleet passenger steamer
JENNIE WHIPPLE. C. C.
Gray Master, having entered regularly
in the Memphis and Arkansas River trade
will leave for Little Rock, Fort Smith and all points on
the Arkansas River every FRIDAY, commencing on Wednesday 19th inst. at 5 o'clock P M. For freight or passage apply to   HARMSTAD & HAYMAN, Agents
                                        17 Madison street
   N. B.—All orders for freight will be filled by this boat
at Cincinnati prices.   Ja17 d3m

Source: Memphis Daily Avalanche, May 21, 1859, page 3

Saturday, May 21, 1859 The Memphis Daily Avalanche
"The river... receding rapidly... four inches"

Monday, May 23, 1859 The Memphis Daily Avalanche
"...the river fell about three inches..."

Tuesday, May 24, 1859 The Memphis Daily Avalanche
"The river... fell two and three inches in the 24 hours..."

Wednesday, May 25, 1859 Arkansas True Democrat
ARRIVALS – *May 22* **Jennie Whipple** *from Memphis*
DEPARTURES – *May 23* **Jennie Whipple** *for Memphis*

Wednesday, May 25, 1859 The Memphis Daily Avalanche
"The river at this point was falling very slowly..."

Thursday, May 26, 1859 The Memphis Daily Avalanche
*"The **Jennie Whipple** came in from the Arkansas River yesterday, having made one of the most profitable trips on record. She brought a large number of passengers, who publish below a most complimentary card to her officers. She is advertised to return to Little Rock this evening at six o'clock. We are indebted to her officers for special favor."*

*"LATE PAPERS – For late papers we are indebted to... Messrs. Gray and Parker, of the steamer **Jennie Whipple**."*

*"The officers of the **Jennie Whipple** report twenty feet of water in the channel of the Arkansas, and the river still rising at a rapid rate."*

*"COMPLIMENTARY CARD - The undersigned, passengers by the Steamer **Jennie Whipple**, take this method of tendering their most sincere and grateful acknowledgements to her commander - Capt. Charley Gray, J. A. Gray, J. E. Parker and A. Storm, clerks and also to her other officers, for their many kind and prompt attentions during the trip. They also must cheerfully commend the **Jennie Whipple** to the traveling public as one of the fastest and best conducted steamboats on the Arkansas River. May 20th, 1859. James B. Stone, Desha County, Arkansas; Dr. Byrd Smith, Virginia; Franklin Mapes, Desha County, Ark.; L. F. Graves, Red Fork, Ark.; S. Coats, Red Fork, Ark.; L. R. Moore, Red Fork, Ark.; S. F. Richards, Chester, Desha County, Ark.; John A. Richards, Chester, Desha County, Ark.; W. S. Mullen, Raymond, Hinds County, Miss.; T. O. Thornpure, Pine Bluff,*

Ark.; J. Justifer, Vicksburg, Miss.; and fifty others."

"ONE OF THE 'FANCY' IN LIMBO – Jim Coburn, the man who gave several sparring exhibitions in this city last spring, is now on trial at Napoleon, Arkansas, for the robbery of a gentleman on board the steamer Irene... was brought down from Pine Bluff to Napoleon, together with five other prisoners, on the Jennie Whipple."

Friday, May 27, 1859 The Memphis Daily Avalanche

"FOR ARKANSAS RIVER - The fleet and popular packet Jennie Whipple, Capt. Gray, is up for White River at five o'clock. The Jennie is well known as a favorite packet and her officers are well known as clever and attentive gentlemen." [NOTE: The paper's mention of White River is apparently a misprint].

Saturday, May 28, 1859 Weekly Arkansas Gazette

ARRIVALS MAY 22 – Jennie Whipple at Little Rock from Memphis
DEPARTURES MAY 23 – Jennie Whipple from Little Rock for Memphis

Saturday, May 28, 1859 The Memphis Daily Avalanche

STEAMBOATS LEAVING TODAY - Jennie Whipple, Capt. Gray, for Fort Smith.

"Whipple, which was announced to leave last evening... for Arkansas River, being induced to remain over by irresistible prospects of heavy additions to their freight and passenger lists. The Whipple goes out at six this evening for the wide Arkansas."

"FOR LITTLE ROCK - The fleet, neat and pretty Jennie Whipple, with 'veteran' Gray master, is up for the Arkansas River at five P.M. Her light draft insures a trip without detention."

Sunday, May 29, 1859

The book, *Negro Slavery in Arkansas* by Olivia Taylor (page 64) reports: *"On May 29, 1859* [Nathan Bedford] *Forrest placed Dick and Edmond, two negro boys whom Sheppard had purchased in person two days earlier, on board the steamboat Jennie Whipple, bound for Pine Bluff and points above. Late the next day, after a voyage down the Mississippi and up the Arkansas, Captain James A. Gray delivered the slaves to Sheppard's overseer in Pine Bluff, who paid these charges incurred in delivery: two days board at the Forrest slave jail at forty cents each per day, board and room from Memphis to Pine Bluff, $14."*

For Arkansas River.

MERCHANTS' AND PLANTERS' LINE.

THE SPLENDID PASSENGER PACK-
et **JENNIE WHIPPLE**, Capt
C. Gray will leave for all points as
above on SATURDAY May 28th at 5 P
f. Through tickets for the Hot Springs for sale at the
LARRY HARMSTAD Agent

my28-1t

Butterfield's advertisement for passengers on the *Jennie Whipple*
Source: *The Memphis Daily Avalanche, Monday, May 30, 1859*

Monday, May 30, 1859 The Memphis Daily Avalanche
"The river at this point fell... three inches"
Tuesday, May 31, 1859 The Memphis Daily Avalanche
"... Arkansas River, at last account, was falling fast."
Wednesday, June 1, 1859 Arkansas True Democrat
ARRIVALS – *May 30 **Jennie Whipple** from Memphis*
DEPARTURES – *May 31 **Jennie Whipple** for Memphis*
*"We are indebted to the gentlemanly officers of the **Jennie Whipple** for late papers."*
Wednesday, June 1, 1859 The Memphis Daily Avalanche
"The river falling more rapidly... 10 inches in 24 hours."
Friday, June 3, 1859 The Memphis Daily Avalanche
*"...the **Jennie Whipple** from Arkansas River, arrived yesterday and last night... having done a good business for the season..."*
*"The Arkansas River is reported by the **Jennie Whipple** as falling rapidly, but with a good stage of water for steamboats."*
*"Capt. C. C. Gray of the **Jennie Whipple**, we regret to say, was taken sick at Little Rock, previous to that boat's departure and remained there. The **Whipple** will leave on Saturday, at her usual hour, under direction of Capt. Storm."*
*"We are indebted to the officers of the ...**Jennie Whipple** for the usual favors."*
Saturday, June 4, 1859 Weekly Arkansas Gazette
ARRIVALS MAY 31 – ***Jennie Whipple** at Little Rock from Memphis*
DEPARTURES MAY 31 – ***Jennie Whipple** from Little Rock for Memphis*
Saturday, June 4, 1859 The Memphis Daily Avalanche

STEAMBOATS LEAVING TODAY - **Jennie Whipple**, *Capt. Storm, for Fort Smith.*

"For Arkansas River - The popular Arkansas packet **Jennie Whipple**, *Capt. A. D. Storm, in the absence of Capt. Gray, commanding, with Messrs. Gray and Parker in the office, is off at five o'clock this evening for Little Rock and all points on the Arkansas River.* **Jennie** *is a staunch, commodious and pleasant packet and her officers polite and attentive. She will take passengers and freight to the head of navigation in the quickest possible time. Her accommodations for travel are most excellent, and persons bound to the wilds of Arkansas should make haste to secure rooms, as she always goes out full. Larry Harmstad is the agent of the* **Whipple**."

Monday, June 6, 1859 The Memphis Daily Avalanche

"The river... receding at the rate of 1 foot in 24 hours..."

"The St. Francis No. 2... met... **Jennie Whipple** *at foot of Old Town Bend."*

Tuesday, June 7, 1859 The Memphis Daily Avalanche

"The river... falling at the rate of 1 foot in 24 hours"

Wednesday, June 8, 1859 Arkansas True Democrat

ARRIVALS – *June 7* **Jennie Whipple** *from Memphis*

"Memphis Packets – The steamer S. H. Tucker, will hereafter make weekly trips between Memphis and this point [Little Rock]. ... The **Jennie Whipple** *is also in the same trade. So that we now have two regular Memphis and Little Rock packets."*

"Flour! Flour! Just received per **Jennie Whipple**, *50 barrels of St. Louis extra flour; 50 barrels of Illinois extra flour; and for sale low by John Collins & Co., June 8, 1859."*

Wednesday, June 8, 1859 The Memphis Daily Avalanche

"The river continues to recede at the rate of 1 foot in 24 hours."

Thursday, June 9, 1859 The Memphis Daily Avalanche

"Boats yesterday were taking freight at the following figures: to St. Louis - pound freight, 25¢ per 100 lbs.; wheat 20¢ per sack. To New Orleans – cotton $1 per bale; freight 25¢ per 100 lbs."

Friday, June 10, 1859 The Memphis Daily Avalanche

"The **Jennie Whipple** *which arrived yesterday from Little Rock, reports the Arkansas River in good boating stage and rising*

slowly. We are indebted to Mr. James Parker, her clever clerk, for a memoranda. ...late papers and other favors."

Saturday, June 11, 1859 Weekly Arkansas Gazette

ARRIVALS JUNE 7 – **Jennie Whipple** *at Little Rock from Memphis*
DEPARTURES JUNE 7 – **Jennie Whipple** *from Little Rock for Memphis*

Saturday June 11, 1859 The Memphis Daily Avalanche

STEAMBOATS LEAVING TODAY - **Jennie Whipple**, *Capt. Storm, for Fort Smith.*

*"*FOR ARKANSAS RIVER *- The popular Arkansas River packet* **Jennie Whipple**, *Capt. Gray, commanding, with Messrs. Gray and Parker in the office, is off at five o'clock this evening for Little Rock and all points on the Arkansas River. The **Jennie** is a staunch, commodious and pleasant packet, and her officers polite and attentive. She will take passengers and freight to the head of navigation in the quickest possible time. Her accommodations for travelers are most excellent, and persons bound to the wilds of Arkansas should make haste to secure rooms, as she always goes out full. Larry Harmstad is the agent for the **Whipple**."*

Sunday, June 12, 1859 Daily Missouri Republican

A DAILY LINE OF MAIL STAGES,

From Pilot Knob, via Greenville, Missouri, to Pocahontas and Batesville, Arkansas, connecting at Pocahontas with a semi-weekly Steamboat Mail Line for Powhatan, Jacksonport, Napoleon, and all points on Black and White rivers. Connecting at Batesville with Hanger and Ayliff's Daily Mail Stage Line for Little Rock, which intersects the Mail Stage Line from Des Arc to Fort Smith, at a point fifty miles South of Batesville; also, intersecting with the semi-weekly Overland Mail Route from Memphis via Fort Smith to San Francisco, at a point fifteen miles North of Little Rock. At Little Rock, stages leave daily for Hot Springs and Camden, Arkansas, and for Clarksville, San Antonio, and other prominent points in Texas, thus forming an entire

John T. Chidester Advertisement for his Stage Line
Source: Sunday, June 12, 1859 Daily Missouri Republican, page 4

Monday, June 13, 1859 The Memphis Daily Avalanche

The fall of the river... eight inches in 24 hours.

Tuesday, June 14, 1859 The Memphis Daily Avalanche

"The river still continues to recede... fully eight inches..."

Wednesday, June 15, 1859 Arkansas True Democrat

ARRIVALS – *June 7 **Jennie Whipple** from Memphis*

ARRIVALS – *June 13 **Jennie Whipple** from Memphis*

DEPARTURES – *June 7 **Jennie Whipple** for Memphis*

*"The steamers S. H. Tucker and **Jennie Whipple** kindly furnished us with late papers."*

*"From the Pine Bluff Independent we learn... 'The last trip of that star little boat, **Jennie Whipple**, is the quickest on record, from Memphis to this place [Pine Bluff]. The **Jennie** is a nice boat. Captain A. D. Storm commending and J. A. Gray in the office is a sufficient recommendation. Thanks for late favors.'"*

Wednesday, June 15, 1859 The Memphis Daily Avalanche

"The river continues to decline at the same rate..."

Thursday, June 16, 1859 The Memphis Daily Avalanche

"The river... continues to decline... 24 hours... six inches."

Friday, June 17, 1859 The Memphis Daily Avalanche

*"The **Jennie Whipple** arrived from Little Rock yesterday with a good freight. We are indebted to her clever clerk, Parker, for favors."*

*"EARLY COTTON – We yesterday received from Mr. N. B. Marshall, through the politeness of Mr. James Parker, the clever clerk of the steamer **Jennie Whipple**, a stalk of cotton from the plantation of Dr. Peyton Graves, near Red Fork, Arkansas, containing forty-five squares and one bloom. The bloom opened on the 12th inst., and is the first of this season in the latitude of its growth. Great credit is due to Dr. G.'s excellent manager, 'Dutch Frank,' for his success in forwarding to this city the first cotton bloom yet received. Mr. Marshall, in forwarding the cotton stalk writes: 'The crops in this vicinity are finer than they have ever been at this season. We had a splendid rain on the 13th.'"*

"SINKING OF THE GRAPESHOT - The steamer Grapeshot... sunk a few days ago in the Arkansas River when fifteen miles below Van Buren. She was owned by Capt. Ed. Carter, and is the third boat he has lost in the last ten months. She was heavily loaded, just off the docks and was in excellent running order. The boat and cargo are a total loss..."

*"MEMORANDA OF STEAMER **JENNIE WHIPPLE** - Steamer **Jennie***

Whipple left Little Rock, Tuesday 14th at 10:30 A.M. Left steamer Medora in port for Fort Smith, and S. H Tucker for Napoleon. Met steamer Ona Parr fifty miles below, bound for Fort Smith. Steamer Medora reports Cincinnati steamer Grapeshot sunk in twelve feet water thirty miles below Van Buren - boat and cargo a total loss; one life lost - said to be a clerk of another boat; could not learn the name. Arrived at Napoleon 12 P.M. Wednesday. Steamer Red Wing in port for Arkansas River, and Sam Hale for White River. Met Kate Frisbee at Island 73; passed Scotland at 69; met Simonda at 70; passed Emma Bett at Cow Island; Imperial passed us twelve miles below Memphis. Arkansas and Mississippi Rivers falling fast, but a rise reported in the upper Arkansas. JIM PARKER, Clerk."

Butterfields advertisement for passengers on his steamboat, the *Jennie Whipple*
Source: The Memphis Daily Avalanche, June 18, 1859

Saturday, June 18, 1859 Weekly Arkansas Gazette

*Arrivals June 16 – **Jennie Whipple** from Memphis*
*DEPARTURES JUNE 14 – **Jennie Whipple** from Little Rock for Memphis*

Saturday, June 18, 1859 The Memphis Daily Avalanche

*STEAMBOATS LEAVING TODAY - **Jennie Whipple**, Capt. Gray, for Fort Smith.*

> *JENNIE WHIPPLE FOR ARKANSAS RIVER - The very punctual and always popular packet **Jennie Whipple**, Capt. Charley Gray Commanding, with Messrs. James Parker, James Gray and A. D. Stone in the office, will leave at five o'clock this evening for*

*Little Rock and all points on the Arkansas River. The **Jennie** is a staunch, commodious and pleasant packet, and her officers polite and attentive. She will take passengers and freight to the head of navigation in the quickest possible time. Her accommodations for travelers are most excellent, and persons bound to the wilds of Arkansas should make haste to secure rooms, as she always goes out full. Messrs. Thomas H. Williams & Co. are agents for the **Whipple**.*

Monday, June 20, 1859 The Memphis Daily Avalanche
"The river... still receding but more slowly than it has..."

Monday, June 20, 1859 Memphis Daily Appeal
"Boatmen have abandoned all hope of an immediate rise in the Arkansas River. ...there had been a rise of two or three inches at Little Rock, and that the water had then commenced receding again."

Tuesday, June 21, 1859 The Memphis Daily Avalanche
"The river... continues to recede but at a greatly reduced rate..."

Wednesday, June 22, 1859 Arkansas True Democrat
DEPARTURES – *June 14 **Jennie Whipple** for Memphis*
ARRIVALS – *June 20 **Jennie Whipple** from Memphis*
DEPARTURES – *June 21 **Jennie Whipple** for Memphis*

Collins & Co. ad for Flour Delivered by the *Jennie Whipple*
Source: June 22, 1859, Arkansas True Democrat

Saturday, June 25, 1859 Weekly Arkansas Gazette
ARRIVALS JUNE 21 – ***Jennie Whipple** at Little Rock from Memphis*

Wednesday, June 22, 1859 The Memphis Daily Avalanche
"The Arkansas River is still in good boating stage for the class of steamers running upon it, the receding of the river cutting out the bars."

"The authorities of the town of Napoleon (Ark) have had the

levee in front of that place cut in several places, and the result is that the seep water has nearly disappeared, and in most localities the streets and ground are becoming dry."

Thursday, June 23, 1859 The Memphis Daily Avalanche

"The river yesterday was rising ...for two days seven inches."

Source: Memphis Daily Appeal, June 24, 1859

Friday, June 24, 1859 Memphis Daily Avalanche

*"The **Jennie Whipple** came up yesterday evening from Little Rock, with a splendid trip of passengers and considerable freight. She reports the Arkansas River rising very rapidly, it having come up altogether nearly eighteen feet at Little Rock."*

Friday, June 24, 1859 Memphis Daily Appeal

*"The **Jennie Whipple**, from Little Rock yesterday, brought a few bales of cotton and a consignment of cotton. We are indebted to Messrs. Gray and Storm for papers and other favors. It having been reported along the Arkansas River that the **Jennie Whipple** was running for 'glory' only, we are pleased to inform her friends along the route, that she 'still lives' and is yet able to stand the 'press.' She leaves for Little Rock and all way points Saturday afternoon, at 5 P.M. positively."*

Saturday, June 25, 1859 Weekly Arkansas Gazette

DEPARTURES JUNE 20 – ***Jennie Whipple*** *from Little Rock for Memphis*

Saturday, June 25, 1859 Memphis Daily Appeal

STEAMBOATS LEAVING TODAY: *For Arkansas River, **Jennie Whipple**, Capt. Gray*

"The river was rising every more rapidly than on Thursday having swollen fully 10 inches during the twenty-four hours

*ending at 5 o'clock last evening. There was considerable drift running during the day, and a heavy raft lodged against the **Jennie Whipple**."*

*"The **Jennie Whipple** took on board yesterday, for Little Rock, ten coaches for Messrs. Chidester, Rapley & Co., for the California Overland Mail Service. They were all the way from Concord, New Hamshire."*

*"FOR ARKANSAS RIVER - Faithful to the hour, the **Jennie Whipple**, Capt. C. C. Gray, will leave for all points on the Arkansas River at 5 o'clock this afternoon. She is one of the old merchant's and planters' line, and while she is ever for the profit of the owner, the conveniences of passenger and shippers is never forgotten. There are no pleasanter traveling companions than Messrs. Gray, Storm and Parker."*

Saturday, June 25, 1859 Memphis Daily Avalanche

*STEAMBOATS LEAVING TODAY - **Jennie Whipple**, Capt. Gray, Fort Smith.*

*[Repeating the June 18th description:] "JENNIE WHIPPLE FOR ARKANSAS RIVER - The very punctual and always popular packet **Jennie Whipple**, Capt. Charley Gray Commanding, with Messrs. James Parker, James Gray and A. D. Stone in the office, will leave at five o'clock this evening for Little Rock and all points on the Arkansas River. The **Jennie** is a staunch, commodious and pleasant packet, and her officers polite and attentive. She will take passengers and freight to the head of navigation in the quickest possible time. Her accommodations for travelers are most excellent, and persons bound to the wilds of Arkansas should make haste to secure rooms, as she always goes out full. Messrs. Thomas H. Williams & Co. and Priest & Rowen are agents for the **Whipple**."*

Sunday, June 26, 1859 Memphis Daily Appeal

*"All the regular packets which departed yesterday had excellent trips including the... **Jennie Whipple** for the Arkansas."*

Tuesday, June 28, 1859 Memphis Daily Avalanche

"The shipments of cotton yesterday amounted to only 35 bales..."

Tuesday, June 28, 1859 Memphis Daily Appeal

"The Lady Walton arrived from the Arkansas River yesterday

morning. Mr. Bidwell, the accommodating clerk, reports the Arkansas River in excellent boating stage, but falling."

Wednesday, June 29, 1859 Arkansas True Democrat
No arrivals or departures of *Jennie Whipple* listed.

Wednesday, June 29, 1859 Memphis Daily Appeal
"The weather yesterday was very hot, the thermometer ranging at ninety-six degrees in the shade at noon."

Thursday, June 30, 1859 Memphis Daily Appeal
"Shipments of cotton yesterday embraced 158 bales..."

Friday, July 1, 1859 Memphis Daily Appeal
ARRIVALS YESTERDAY - *Jennie Whipple from Arkansas River*
"The Jennie Whipple arrived from the Arkansas River last evening. We are indebted to Messrs. Gray and Storm for favors."

Saturday, July 2, 1859 Weekly Arkansas Gazette
ARRIVALS JUNE 28 – *Jennie Whipple at Little Rock from Memphis*
DEPARTURES JUNE 28 – *Jennie Whipple from Little Rock for Memphis*

Saturday, July 2, 1859 Memphis Daily Appeal
*Steamboats Leaving Today - For Arkansas River, **Jennie Whipple**, Capt. Gray.*

*"The weather has become so oppressively hot that the laborers have deserted the landing, and it is with the greatest difficulty that deck hands and laborers can be procured to perform needful service either at the landing or on the boats. The deck hands of the **Jennie Whipple** deserted her yesterday, and a portion of the hands on the steamer Return also threw up for the cause above stated."*

*"We learn from the officers of the **Jennie Whipple** that the Arkansas River is falling from Fort Smith to Little Rock, and stationary from the 'Rock' to the mouth."*

*"FOR ARKANSAS RIVER - The clipper packet **Jennie Whipple** Capt. Gray, will depart at 5 o'clock this afternoon for the Arkansas River, and will take freight and passengers for all points on the Arkansas River from Napoleon to Little Rock. Capt. Gray with his boat, has diverted a heavy trade from the Arkansas River country to this port, and deserves the encouragement of all our business men. She was the pioneer in the trade, and we are gratified that the enterprise has proved successful. Traveler*

will find Messrs. Gray, Parker and Storm, efficient officers and pleasant travelling companions."

Sunday, July 3, 1859 Memphis Daily Appeal

DEPARTURES YESTERDAY - ***Jennie Whipple*** *for Arkansas River.*

"Business was somewhat brisk at the landing yesterday, as there were no less than five regular packet departures, including... the ***Jennie Whipple****, for Arkansas River..."*

Wednesday, July 6, 1859 Arkansas True Democrat

ARRIVALS – *June 28* ***Jennie Whipple*** *from Memphis*

DEPARTURES – *June 28* ***Jennie Whipple*** *for Fort Smith*

ARRIVALS – *July 4* ***Jennie Whipple*** *from Memphis*

DEPARTURES – *July 5* ***Jennie Whipple*** *for Memphis*

Wednesday, July 6, 1859 Memphis Daily Appeal

"We present in our commercial column this morning the annual report of our efficient Wharfmaster, Mr. Tobias Wolf."

"There was about twelve feet water in the Arkansas River at Little Rock on the 30th ult. [of last month], and river falling slowly. The True Democrat says that at this time there are three regular lines of steamers from that point to Memphis, Napoleon and Fort Smith. The mail boats to Napoleon are a tri-weekly line, to Memphis a semi-weekly line, and to Fort Smith the same."

Thursday, July 7, 1859 Memphis Daily Appeal

"Within the 24 hours... river had fallen nine inches..."

Friday, July 8, 1859 Memphis Daily Appeal

ARRIVALS YESTERDAY - ***Jennie Whipple****, Arkansas River*

"The steamer ***Jennie Whipple*** *arrived from Little Rock last evening, with a large number of passengers. We are indebted to Messrs. Gray and Parker for favors.*

MANIFEST OF THE JENNIE WHIPPLE - *The steamer* ***Jennie Whipple*** *left Little Rock on Wednesday, July 5th, 11 ½ A.M., left the steamer Medora in port for Fort Smith, Virginia Belle undergoing repairs, and Lady Walton putting in new machinery, preparatory to entering permanently the "Merchants and Planters Line" from Memphis to Little Rock. Met steamer Red Wing above Pine Bluff, arrived at Napoleon Wednesday at 6 o'clock P.M., steamers Daniel Boone for Memphis, Kate Frisbee for Vicksburg, Irene for Arkansas River, and San Hale for*

*White River, in port. Steamers Sancen and Little Rock laid up for the season. The Arkansas River is falling fast all the way to the mouth. The **Jennie Whipple** will leave at the usual hour on Saturday afternoon for Arkansas River.*

THE LOUISVILLE JOURNAL *says that a passenger on the Moses McLellan... informs that paper that there was a family of negroes on board from near Shawneetown, Ill., in route to Michigan to settle, consisting of a great grandfather, one hundred and five years old, a son eighty years old, a daughter seventy-five years old, and numerous children and grand children, and great grand children. The old man has been a member of a church for fifty years, his son has been a preacher for forty years, and the brother of the old man was a servant to General Washington. He is familiar with all the incidents of the Revolutionary War. He is worth several thousand dollars. His object in removing to the northeast is to buy land for, and settle down, the younger members of the family."*

Saturday, July 9, 1859 Weekly Arkansas Gazette

ARRIVALS JULY 5 – **Jennie Whipple** *at Little Rock from Memphis*
DEPARTURES JULY 5 – **Jennie Whipple** *from Little Rock for Memphis*

Saturday, July 9, 1859 Memphis Daily Appeal

STEAMBOATS LEAVING TODAY - *For Arkansas River,* **Jennie Whipple**, *Captain Gray.*

*"*FOR ARKANSAS RIVER *- The pioneer of the 'Merchants and Planters' Line,' the popular packet **Jennie Whipple**, will leave at 4 o'clock this afternoon for all points on the Arkansas River hence to Little Rock, connecting with the regular packet for Fort Smith. The **Whipple** affords an admirable opportunity for through travelers to avail themselves of a quick and pleasant passage to the 'Rock.' Her accommodations are good, and her officers unsurpassed. Messrs. Gray and Parker at the clerks."*

Sunday, July 10, 1859 Memphis Daily Appeal

DEPARTURES YESTERDAY - **Jenny Whipple**, *Arkansas River*
"The regular departures yesterday embraced the... **Jennie Whipple**, *for the Arkansas River.. They all had good trips. Capt. Charles Gray, of the **Jennie Whipple**, was a passenger by the Southerner yesterday in route for Chicago. The **Whipple** is*

under the command of Capt. J. W. Sears, for the present."

Tuesday, July 12, 1859 Memphis Daily Appeal

"The river has fallen one foot... during 48 hours..."

Wednesday, July 13, 1859 Memphis Daily Appeal

"The Arkansas River is still receding, with about five feet of water in the channel."

"The navigation of the Arkansas River is closed to the larger class of steamers for the season. Every facility will be afforded to the traveling community by the regular packets. The Quapaw and Little Rock have been laid up at Napoleon."

Wednesday, July 13, 1859 Arkansas True Democrat

ARRIVALS – *July 10* **Jennie Whipple** *from Memphis*

DEPARTURES – *July 11* **Jennie Whipple** *for Memphis*

Thursday July 14, 1859 Memphis Daily Appeal

"WONDERS OF THE MISSISSIPPI - ... immense additions are made to the quantity of water in the channel, by large streams from both the eastern and western sides of the Mississippi. The question naturally arises, what becomes of this vast added volume of water? It certainly never reaches New Orleans, and as certainly does not evaporate, and of course it is not confined to the channel of the river, for it would rise far above the entire region south of us. If a well is sunk anywhere in Arkansas River bottom, water is found as soon as the water level of the Mississippi is reached. When the Mississippi goes down, the water sinks accordingly in the well. The owner of a saw mill, some twenty miles from the Mississippi, in Arkansas, dug a well to supply the boilers of his engine, during the late flood. When the water receded, his well went down till his hose would no longer reach the water, and finally his well was dry. He dug a ditch to an adjacent lake to let the water into his well; the lake was drained and the well was dry again – having literally drank ten acres of water in less than a week. The inference is, that the whole valley of the Mississippi, from its banks to its highlands on either side, rests on a porous substratum, which absorbs the redundant waters, and thus prevents that degree of accumulation which would long since have swept New Orleans into the Gulf but for this provision of nature."

Thursday, July 14, 1859, Memphis Daily Avalanche

"The river at this point declined seven inches in the twenty-four hours... all the upper streams are reported quite low and falling."

Friday, July 15, 1859 Memphis Daily Appeal

"The water is gradually receding from the sunken Grapeshot, in the Arkansas River, and an effort will soon be made to recover her freight."

Saturday, July 16, 1859 Weekly Arkansas Gazette

ARRIVALS JULY 12 –**Jennie Whipple** at Little Rock from Memphis

DEPARTURES JULY 12 –**Jennie Whipple** from Little Rock for Memphis

Saturday, July 16, 1859 Memphis Daily Appeal

Arrivals Yesterday – **Jennie Whipple**, L. Rock

STEAMBOATS LEAVING TODAY – For Little Rock, **Jennie Whipple**, Capt. Sears.

"The officers of the steamer **Jennie Whipple***, which arrived yesterday, report four feet water in the Arkansas River, and the river falling."*

"The refreshment saloon of the **Jennie Whipple** *is now under the supervision of Dick Weatherton, a gentleman who is familiar with the taste of Arkansas travelers, and who has furnished the bar with the very best refreshments the market affords. The traveling public can rely upon our young friend Weatherton's taste."*

"FOR THE ARKANSAS RIVER – Travelers for all points on the Arkansas River, and especially those for the Hot Springs, should avail themselves of the fine steamer **Jennie Whipple***, Capt. J. W. Sears, which will leave positively at 4 P. M. She is officered by such choice spirits as Capt. Storm and the two James's – the Messrs. Gray and Parker."*

Sunday, July 17, 1859 Memphis Daily Appeal

DEPARTURES YESTERDAY - **Jennie Whipple**, Arkansas River

"All the regular packets that went out last evening were well freighted either with passengers or freight. This remark includes... the **Jennie Whipple** *for Arkansas River..."*

Tuesday, July 19, 1859 Memphis Daily Appeal

"The decline of the river at this point has fallen off, the water

having receded but four inches during the twenty-four hours..."

Wednesday, July 20, 1859 Arkansas True Democrat
No arrivals or departures of *Jennie Whipple* listed.

Wednesday, July 20, 1859 Memphis Daily Appeal
"The Mississippi at this point was about stationary yesterday, it did not change one half an inch in twenty-four hours. We have no arrivals to report."

Thursday, July 21, 1859 Memphis Daily Appeal
"So intense is the heat that work on the river cannot be performed but with difficulty and some danger... river receded four inches."

Friday, July 22, 1859 Memphis Daily Appeal
"The river declined four inches at this point [Memphis]."
*"We regret to learn that the Memphis and Little Rock packet, **Jennie Whipple**, is hard aground in the Arkansas River. She will, in all probability, get off and arrive in ample time to depart at her regular hour tomorrow for Little Rock."*

Saturday, July 23, 1859 Weekly Arkansas Gazette
*ARRIVALS JULY 20 – **Jennie Whipple** at Little Rock from Memphis*
*DEPARTURES JULY 21 – **Jennie Whipple** from Little Rock for Memphis*

Saturday, July 23, 1859 Memphis Daily Appeal
*STEAMBOATS LEAVING TODAY – For Arkansas River, **Jennie Whipple**, Capt. Sears*
"On many of the White River [Arkansas] plantations, owing to the great heat of the sun, and the opportunities to labor afforded by the moonlight, the order of work has been reversed, and the hands are permitted to perform field labor during the night-time, while they rest in the shade during the day."
*"FOR ARKANSAS RIVER – The fine, light draught steamer **Jennie Whipple**, Capt. Sears, is the regular Merchants and Planter's packet for Little Rock today, and will leave at the usual hour this afternoon. Having splendid passenger accommodations, she makes all her connections with perfect regularity. Messrs. Gray and Parker, gentlemen of accommodation and experience, are the clerks. Every thing about the **Whipple** is complete, including the saloon, under the direction of Dick Weatherton."*

Sunday, July 24, 1859 Memphis Daily Appeal

"The decline in the river continues steady in a rate of about 4 inches in 24 hours."

*"Two of three of our regular packets did not arrive, owing to the low water. Of this number were... the **Jennie Whipple**, from Little Rock."*

*"The **Jennie Whipple**, which was aground in the Arkansas River, had got off, arrived at Little Rock, and returned to the lower Arkansas. She was therefore due here last night. Capt. Charlie Gray is in the city, awaiting her arrival."*

*"A correspondent of Little Rock, writing under the date of the 20th July, informs us that the Arkansas River has nearly dried up, there being only eighteen inches water between Little Rock and Fort Smith. The **Jennie Whipple** had not arrived at Little Rock in the evening of the 19th, and was then fifteen hours behind time. This statement is in accordance with the report that the **Whipple** had got aground. The Arkansas Traveler had arrived within five miles of Little Rock and laid up from want of water. The mail boat Red Wing had not arrived at Little Rock from Napoleon on time, and it was feared that she was aground. The Violet, from Fort Smith, had not arrived at Little Rock, and the Medora had left her aground at Galley Rock on Sunday last. The charter of the steamer Medora, in the trade between Fort Smith and Little Rock, expired last week, and the Medora has been engaged to take the place of the Irene in the mail line between Napoleon and Little Rock – the Irene having gone to Cincinnati for repairs."*

Tuesday, July 26, 1859 Memphis Daily Appeal

*ARRIVALS SINCE SATURDAY – **Jennie Whipple**, Arkansas River ... the river at this point [Memphis] had fallen six inches...*

*"The **Jennie Whipple** arrived from Little Rock yesterday several days behind time. She found about twenty-four inches water in the Arkansas River, and several boats aground, heretofore reported. There was a heavy and protracted rain at Little Rock on Thursday last, and there is a prospect of a rise. The **Whipple** will leave for Little Rock tomorrow afternoon."*

"Ninety-five bales of cotton were received by the river at this port yesterday - all from Arkansas – including fifty bales by the

Jennie Whipple...*"*

*"Capt. John McDowell was a passenger to this city by the **Jennie Whipple** from Little Rock, and departed by the Philadelphia for St. Louis last evening. The object of his visit in St. Louis is to secure a light draught boat to take the place of the Medora in the Fort Smith and Little Rock trade."*

Wednesday, July 27, 1859 Arkansas True Democrat

ARRIVALS – *July 20 **Jennie Whipple** from Memphis*

DEPARTURES – *July 21 **Jennie Whipple** for Memphis*

*"New Flour. 50 sacks of extra new flour; 50 bbls. of extra new flour just received; per steamer **Jennie Whipple** and for sale by John Collins & Co. June 22, 1859."*

Wednesday, July 27, 1859 Memphis Daily Appeal

STEAMBOATS LEAVING TODAY – *For Little Rock, **Jennie Whipple**, Capt. Gray.*

"The heavy rains in this latitude Tuesday morning somewhat checked the decline in the river yesterday..."

*"FOR LITTLE ROCK – The popular steamer **Jennie Whipple**, Captain Gray, is the regular packet for all points on the Arkansas River today, and will leave at 4 o'clock this afternoon. She is of very light draught, and affords the best passenger accommodations. Messrs. Gray and Parker, the clerks, are attentive and efficient officers."*

Thursday, July 28, 1859 Memphis Daily Appeal

DEPARTURES YESTERDAY – ***Jennie Whipple**, Little Rock*

Friday, July 29, 1859 Memphis Daily Appeal

"The river has commenced declining again... fallen 2 inches..."

Saturday, July 30, 1859 Memphis Daily Appeal

... the river declined two and a half inches...

"SINKING OF THE STEAMER RETURN - the sinking of the steamer Return, at Devall's Bluff, in the Arkansas River, Wednesday morning. She stuck a snag, which entered the bow on the larboard [port] side, causing her to fill with water in an extraordinary short time. No lives were lost, but the boat will prove an entire loss. The cargo, consisting mainly of cattle, grain and cotton, for this city, it was thought would be saved. The Return was the regular Memphis and White River packet, and done

good service, and was nearly used up, although in good running condition. She was under command of Capt. Pete Flemming, but was owned by Capt. J. Riley Jones, of the Gen. Pike. She was uninsured."

Sunday, July 31, 1859 Memphis Daily Appeal

"The river at this point is falling 2 inches in twenty-four hours..."

Tuesday, August 2, 1859 Memphis Daily Appeal

"The river has been at a stand at this point since Saturday."

Wednesday, August 3, 1859 Memphis Daily Appeal

"...the river rose one inch and a half at this point."

Thursday, August 4, 1859 Memphis Daily Appeal

"There was a fall of one inch and a half inches in the river..."

Friday, August 5, 1859 Memphis Daily Appeal

"...the river declined two inches..."

"Our young friend Billy Page... has been quite ill in this city for sometime, left for the Hot Springs in Arkansas yesterday with the hope of restoring his health."

"James Noyes, engineer of the steamer Favorite... was caught by the pitman shaft, while the engine was in motion, and his body literally crushed. The call of the pilot, some minutes afterward, not being answered, a person was sent back to the engine and his body was found so mangled as to be hardly recognized. He resided at St. Paul, and leaves a wife and two children."

Saturday, August 6, 1859 Memphis Daily Appeal

*ARRIVALS YESTERDAY – **Jennie Whipple**, Arkansas River*

*"The steamer **Jennie Whipple** arrived from the Arkansas River last evening with a fair trip, including a large number of passengers. Her officers report but sixteen inches water to Little Rock. The **Whipple** went within twenty miles of Little Rock, and found it impossible to get higher."*

*"The **Jennie Whipple** will not return to the Arkansas River during the present season, but will take advantage of the low water and go to Cincinnati for repairs. In all probability she will take the place of the Kate May, on Wednesday next."*

[Apparently the paper's editor feared the **Jennie Whipple** might sink like the Kate May did near Cincinnati.]

"We regret to announce the sinking of Capt. A.H. Bugher's new steamer Kate May, below Cincinnati on Thursday night. She was entirely new, having been built in Cincinnati for the Cincinnati and Arkansas River trade, at a cost of $20,000."

*"LYNCH LAW IN NAPOLEON – We learn from the officers of the steamer **Jennie Whipple**, from Napoleon last evening, that a party of twenty-five citizens took John Lewis from his room at the hotel in that place, Wednesday night, put him to death and threw his body in the river. He had been warned to leave the place within a given time, with which order he failed to comply. Lewis was a river gambler, and it was believed that he was connected with the murder of Dr. Harding, at Napoleon, a few days ago. Lewis' partner barely escaped with his life, and came to this city on the **Jennie Whipple** last evening."*

Sunday, August 7, 1859 Memphis Daily Appeal

*"The officers of the **Jennie Whipple** report that they saw two dead bodies floating in the water during the last trip. One body was seen sixty miles below the city, and the other at Cora's Bar, in the Arkansas River. the later was evidently that of a deck hand, and the skull was fractured."*

Tuesday, August 9, 1859 Memphis Daily Appeal

*"Captain Gray, of the **Jennie Whipple**, announces his determination to leave this port for Cincinnati tomorrow afternoon. She draws but sixteen inches water, and will go through like a top. The **Whipple** will take two or three hundred bales of cotton, if sent down in time."*

Wednesday, August 10, 1859 Arkansas True Democrat

No arrivals or departures of any steamboats listed.

Wednesday, August 10, 1859 Memphis Daily Appeal

*"FOR LOUISVILLE AND CINCINNATI – The popular steamer **Jennie Whipple**, Capt. Gray, will leave as above at four o'clock this afternoon, As she draws but sixteen inches water, she will suffer no detention from low water. No boat of her class has better accommodations, and no boat of any class has better officers, from Capt. Charlie to the keeper of the saloon, Dick Weatherton. Messrs. Gray and Parker are the clerks, and Capt. Worman will be at the wheel."*

Thursday, August 11, 1859 Memphis Daily Appeal

Departed Yesterday - ***Jennie Whipple***, *for Cincinnati*

*"The river has risen one inch at this point since our last report. There were but two regular packet departures yesterday, including... the steamer **Jennie Whipple**, for Cincinnati."*

*"The **Jennie Whipple** departed for Cincinnati yesterday for repairs. She had a large number of passengers and as much freight as was desirable, including sixty bales cotton."*

*"The contemplated repairs to the **Jennie Whipple** will be completed within three weeks, and Captain Gray confidently expects to return in time to commence the trade hence to the Arkansas River between the 10th and 15th of September."*

"Statistical — It appears that more disasters have occurred on our Western waters, during the past six months, than any former period of the same length. The statistics are given as follows: Boats snagged, 22; boats exploded, 4; boats burned, 26; lost by collision, 13; lost by Rock Island Bridge, 1; lost by running against bank, 2; lost in storm, 1; Total number of boats lost, 74. Flatboats lost, 36. Lives lost, 327. Value of boats and cargoes, $1,770,520."

Friday, August 12, 1859 Memphis Daily Appeal

"Business was quite dull at the landing yesterday."

*"The **Jennie Whipple** had about 60 bales cotton yesterday for Cincinnati, which she took at $1.25 per bale. Cotton was offered to her freely at $1.00 per bale, but Capt. Gray very sensibly concluded that the price wouldn't pay."*

Saturday, August 13, 1859 Memphis Daily Appeal

"The river commenced declining... fell one inch during the day."

Saturday, August 13, 1859 Weekly Arkansas Gazette

"The River — low water — The mail route from this place [Little Rock] to Napoleon has been stocked with stages all the way through."

Sunday, August 14, 1859 Memphis Daily Appeal

"The river... declined nearly two inches in the 24 hours..."

Tuesday, August 16, 1859 Memphis Daily Appeal

"The river has declined 5 inches since our last report..."

Wednesday, August 17, 1859 Memphis Daily Appeal

"During the 24 hours... the river declined 3 inches..."
"There is eight feet of water in the channel of the Mississippi from St. Louis to Cairo, and from four to five feet in the river from Louisville to Cairo."

THE SEA SERPENT—THE MONSTER CAUGHT. The Yarmouth (Mass.) *Register* says that the far-famed sea serpent has lately visited that port, and was chased up a narrow creek and caught. He turned out to be a horse mackerel, measuring over eight feet in length and weighing three hundred and sixteen pounds. The *Register* says:

It is the opinion of experienced fishermen that this is the fish which has given rise to the belief in a sea serpent. When it is running at its ordinary speed in search of prey it moves along just under the surface of the water, producing a wave which rises up in a series of corrogations for about one hundred feet in a straight line, before it falls off into the ordinary spreading wave produced by a body moving through the water. This appearance in moderate weather so closely resembles that of a huge serpent moving over the surface of the water that it is difficult, even for those accustomed to the appearance, to realize that it is nothing but a wave, and it is not strange that, when seen for the first time, it should strike the beholder with terror.

Source: Memphis Daily Appeal, August 16, 1859

Thursday, August 18, 1859 Memphis Daily Appeal
"The river is still falling rapidly... declined about four inches..."
Friday, August 19, 1859 Memphis Daily Appeal
"There was a decline of three inches in the river..."

*"The **Jennie Whipple** has arrived at Louisville. It was Capt. Gray's intention to go in the canal dock at Louisville for repairs, after reshipping his Cincinnati freight and passengers. After repairing, the **Whipple** will go to Cincinnati for a cargo for the Arkansas River."*

Saturday, August 20, 1859 Memphis Daily Appeal
ARRIVALS YESTERDAY - *Conway and Medora, Arkansas River*

Sunday, August 21, 1859 Memphis Daily Appeal
"The river declined 3 inches at this point..."

Tuesday, August 23, 1859 Memphis Daily Appeal
"...during 48 hours... the river declined 5 inches at this point..."

Wednesday, August 24, 1859 Memphis Daily Appeal
"DEPARTURES YESTERDAY - Conway for the Arkansas River"
*"Captain Worman, having taken the **Jennie Whipple** to Louisville, has returned to the city [Memphis]."*

Thursday, August 25, 1859 Memphis Daily Appeal
"There was no apparent variation in the river at this point..."

Friday, August 26, 1859 Memphis Daily Appeal
"There was a very slight decline in the river at this point..."

Saturday, August 27, 1859 Memphis Daily Appeal
"There was a very slight decline in the river..."

Sunday, August 28, 1859 Memphis Daily Appeal
"The river fell about 3 inches at this point..."
*"The **Jennie Whipple**, Capt. Gray's Arkansas River and Memphis packet, was brought from the dock at Louisville, Wednesday, with her hull thoroughly overhauled and painted. She will enter the Arkansas River trade in a few days."*
"The Mississippi River from Cairo to New Orleans is rapidly approximating to low water mark, and has the appearance of having been planted in saw logs, as a formidable looking snag or sawyer rears its lofty head at almost every turn."

[Note: A "sawyer' is a type of snag. It consist of a group of trees that have fallen into the river. The roots have embedded themselves into the silt of the bottom. Subject to the pressure of the current, the tops of the trees appear above and disappear under the river water at intervals mimicking the motion of a saw at a saw mill. Thus it is called "sawyer."]

Tuesday, August 30, 1859 Memphis Daily Appeal
"The river declined 3 inches at this point..."

Wednesday, August 31, 1859 Memphis Daily Appeal
"The river at this point declined two or three inches..."

Thursday, September 1, 1859 Memphis Daily Appeal
*"The steamer **Jennie Whipple**, having been thoroughly repaired and refitted, left Louisville Tuesday for this port. She will in all probability depart for the Arkansas River on Saturday next. Orders left with Mr. Wm. G. Priest or Capt. O'Neal, the agents, will be attended to promptly."*

Friday, September 2, 1859 Memphis Daily Appeal
"The river declined about one inch at this point yesterday."

Saturday, September 3, 1859
"The river declined an inch... There were no arrivals or departures of transient steamers yesterday."

Sunday, September 4, 1859 Memphis Daily Appeal
"The river has ceased falling at this point, and rose one inch..."

Tuesday, September 6, 1859 Memphis Daily Appeal
ARRIVALS SINCE SATURDAY - ***Jennie Whipple*** *from Louisville*
DEPARTURES SINCE SATURDAY – ***Jennie Whipple**, for Arkansas River*
"The river... commenced rising Sunday... had risen 10 inches...
*"The **Jennie Whipple** arrived from Louisville yesterday, fully repaired and elegantly refitted. She left Louisville with 275 tons of freight and a large number of passengers. The **Whipple** departed for Arkansas River last evening. If there is not sufficient water to warrant an immediate resumption of her old trade, she will return to the Ohio River for another trip. When the **Whipple** lay here, we regret to say, Capt. Gray was confined to his state room through sickness."*

Wednesday, September 7, 1859 Arkansas True Democrat
No arrivals or departures of any steamboats listed.

Wednesday, September 7, 1859 Memphis Daily Appeal
"The river swelled one inch..".

Thursday, September 8, 1859 Memphis Daily Appeal
No mention of Arkansas arrivals or departures.

Friday, September 9, 1859 Memphis Daily Appeal

"There has been no change in the river at this point..."

Saturday, September 10, 1859 Memphis Daily Appeal

*"The **Jennie Whipple** will be due from the Arkansas River to-morrow. In all probability she will make another trip to Louisville."*

Sunday, September 11, 1859 Memphis Daily Appeal

"The river fell three inches..."

Tuesday, September 13, 1859 Memphis Daily Appeal

"The river has fallen about 6 inches during the 48 hours... All the principal western rivers are very low."

"Messrs. Chidester, Rapley & Co., of the mail service are negotiating for the purchase of the Indian, a little side-wheel steamer at present in the mouth of Wolf River. Their object is to make a short connection with her between their mail coaches in the Arkansas River country."

*"The **Jennie Whipple** is due from Little Rock. As that stream is yet quite low, we presume the **Jennie** will return to Louisville for a trip."*

Wednesday, September 14, 1859 Arkansas True Democrat

*"The river is still falling, with about three and a half feet in the channel from this point [Little Rock] to Napoleon. The navigation from here to Fort Smith is about closed. The steamers Red Wing and **Jennie Whipple**, both arrived last week in a slightly damaged condition, and enters protested. We learn that the goods on the latter boat [**Jennie Whipple**] are very much depreciated in value, owing to the water rising over a portion of them before the damage could be repaired."*

Wednesday, September 14, 1859 Memphis Daily Appeal

"The little steamer Kershena, Capt. Dorr, all the way from Lake Winnebago, left this point yesterday for White River, having been chartered by Messrs. Chidester, Ripley & Co. to run in that river in connection with their mail coaches."

Thursday, September 15, 1859 Memphis Daily Appeal

*"We regret to learn that the **Jennie Whipple** met with an accident while ascending the Arkansas River a few days ago, about forty miles above Napoleon. She struck a snag, which knocked a hole in her bow, causing her to fill rapidly. Capt. Gray found i*

necessary to run her on a bar. She was afterward pumped out, and proceeded on her way to Little Rock."

"The Arkansas River commenced rising at Little Rock Saturday, but in now falling again. There is every prospect, however, that there will be enough water for navigable purposes for some time."

Friday, September 16, 1859 Memphis Daily Appeal

ARRIVALS YESTERDAY – *Jennie Whipple*, Arkansas River

"The **Jennie Whipple** met a rise in the Arkansas River as she went up, but the river was declining again when she came out, with about 3 feet water in the channel. Business is unusually brisk in the Arkansas River country."

"There were no boats aground in the Arkansas River when the **Whipple** came out, but the Irene and South Bend had left Napoleon for Little Rock, and it was thought there would not be sufficient water to enable them to return. The **Whipple** was forced to come out through the White River cut-off."

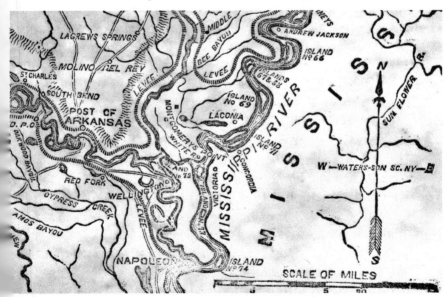

Map showing the White River cut off.
Steamers may avoid Napoleon altogether, by taking the short cut connection between the Mississippi, the White River and the Arkansas River.

"We have already given particulars of the accident to the **Jennie Whipple**. She struck a submerged snag, about forty miles above Napoleon, breaking a knuckle plank and causing her to leak somewhat. She was immediately run on the bank, a false bulkhead was built, and the boat proceeded on her way. The freight in the hold was damaged but slightly, and the **Whipple** arrived here yesterday, with eight bales cotton and some other freight. She brought about 600 bales cotton to Napoleon, and there reshipped it for New Orleans. The **Whipple** recommenced receiving again yesterday for Arkansas River, and will be fully repaired today. She will therefore leave for Little Rock tomorrow – her regular day. She has fine accommodations and accommodating officers, being under command of Capt. Charles C. Gray, with Messers. James Gray and Parker in the office."

Saturday, September 17, 1859 Weekly Arkansas Gazette
"The **Jennie Whipple** came in from Memphis on Saturday last."

Saturday, September 17, 1859 Memphis Daily Appeal
"FOR LITTLE ROCK – The favorite packet **Jennie Whipple**, Capt. Gray, will leave for all points on the Arkansas River at 4 o'clock this afternoon. She is of the old "Merchant's and Planter's Line," and is opposed to nothing but monopoly. We commend the **Jennie** and her officers to the traveling public. Messrs. Gray and Parker are the clerks, and the saloon is under the control of Dick Weatherton, an experienced caterer."

Sunday, September 18, 1859 Memphis Daily Appeal
DEPARTURES YESTERDAY – **Jennie Whipple**, Arkansas River
"...the **Jennie Whipple**, for Arkansas River, was to have left last evening. The **Whipple** had a good trip."

Tuesday, September 20, 1859 Memphis Daily Appeal
"Capt. C. C. Gray, of the **Jennie Whipple**, is in the city, having remained over here during a trip of his boat."
"Freight for the Arkansas and White Rivers are plentiful at Louisville, and are being obtained at good prices."

Wednesday, September 21, 1859 Memphis Daily Appeal
"The river is declining... at the rate of one inch in 24 hours."

Thursday, September 22, 1859 Memphis Daily Appeal
"The **Jennie Whipple** will be due from the Arkansas River today."

Friday, September 23, 1859 Memphis Daily Appeal
"The river continues to decline at this point."

Saturday, September 24, 1859 Weekly Arkansas Gazette
"Jennie Whipple arrived from Memphis on Wed. morning."

Saturday, September 24, 1859 Memphis Daily Appeal
*"The **Jennie Whipple**, Capt. Gray, is due from the Arkansas River, with a very heavy freight, and will in all probability depart for Little Rock at the usual hour this afternoon."*

Sunday, September 25, 1859 Memphis Daily Appeal
*"The **Jennie Whipple** arrived from the Arkansas River about 9 o'clock last evening, bringing a large number of passengers and a vast amount of freight. She brought about 650 bales cotton out of the river, 500 of which she reshipped for New Orleans at Napoleon, bringing 150 bales for Memphis. Dick Weatherton reports the Arkansas River quite low, but says business is excellent."*

*"The **Whipple** will leave for Little Rock at 4 o'clock tomorrow afternoon. She has splendid accommodations and officers unsurpassed for courtesy and efficiency. She will be under command of Capt. Charlie Gray, with the two Messrs. Gray and Parker in the office. Capt. O'Neal, No. 6, Howard's Row, is the agent."*

Tuesday, September 27, 1859 Memphis Daily Appeal
"The river has swollen fully one foot... since Saturday..."

*"Since our last report our local packets have been busy. ... **Jennie Whipple**, for Arkansas, departed, all with paying trips each way.*

*"Capt. C. C. Gray was quite ill again yesterday, and unable to take command of the **Jennie Whipple**. Capt. Sears will therefore make another trip for Capt. Gray."*

Wednesday, September 28, 1859 Memphis Daily Appeal
"The river rose about three inches at this point..."

Thursday, September 29, 1859 Memphis Daily Appeal
"...the river at this point had risen 5 inches, and was still rising.
"The Arkansas River is falling slowly, with 32 inches water in the channel at Little Rock, on Monday. The Gazette and Democrat say that freights appear to be plenty, and some little cotton is already being sent forward, and if too many free-soil boats

don't come on the river, the prospects for this coming season, are certainly looming and bright. The Leon passed Little Rock Monday for Fort Smith."

Friday, September 30, 1859 Memphis Daily Appeal

"The river at this point rose fully one foot during 24 hours..."

Saturday, October 1, 1859 Memphis Daily Appeal

"The river was rising... swollen fully ten inches..."

"In the attempt to transfer a lot of Arkansas cattle from the ferry boat Mound City Belle to the Belfast, twelve head fell overboard into the river, but were all rescued."

Sunday, October 2, 1859 Memphis Daily Appeal

"...the river at this point rose five inches."

"The shipments of cotton during the month of September embraced 8,424 bales of which 3,724 were taken for the Ohio River, 2,942 for New Orleans, and 1,832 for St. Louis."

Miller informs us that the little Charm was sold at Louisville, on Thursday, to parties from White River, for $2,000, which she cost her owners. She was taken to Jeffersonville to undergo repairs."

[John T. Chidester, Rapley & Co. bought the Charm.]

Butterfield advertisement seeking passengers for the steamboat *Jennie Whipple*
Source: Memphis Daily Appeal, October 4, 1859

Tuesday, October 4, 1859 Memphis Daily Appeal

"By the report of Wharfmaster Wolfe we learn that the number of steamboat arrivals at this port during the month of Sep

tember aggregated 158, from which wharfage to the amount of $1,790.65 was collected. The number of flatboat arrivals during the same period was six, and the wharfage from the same $120. total wharfage receipts of the month $1,910.65.

"The little *Charm*, recently sold at Louisville to Chidester, Rapely & Co., mail contractors in Arkansas, for the mail service in White River, took from Louisville Saturday, her departure. Mr. Chidester, one of the owners is on board."

Wednesday, October 5, 1859 Memphis Daily Appeal

"The Arkansas River continues quite low, and the *Jennie Whipple* was delayed on her upward trip. Capt. Gray received a letter from her yesterday, dated Little Rock. The *Whipple* will bring 700 bales cotton out of the river. She was due here last night."

"FOR LITTLE ROCK – The fine little Arkansas River packet *Jennie Whipple*, Capt. C. C. Gray, will leave for Little Rock at the usual hour this afternoon. She compasses the Independent Merchants' and Planters' Line, and is all that shippers and the traveling public would desire, having excellent accommodations and attentive officers. Messrs. Gray and Parker are the clerks."

Thursday, October 6, 1859 Memphis Daily Appeal

"Laborers of all kinds are in great demand in Mobile. Deck hands on the Alabama River are getting from $60 to $70 per month."

Friday, October 7, 1859 Memphis Daily Appeal

ARRIVALS YESTERDAY - *Jennie Whipple* from Arkansas River.

"The body of a drowned man was found floating in the river at the foot of Beal Street yesterday."

"The *Jennie Whipple* arrived about 9 o'clock last evening, and brought about 500 bales cotton out of Arkansas River, 75 of which were for this port."

"FOR ARKANSAS RIVER – The fine light draught packet *Jennie Whipple*, Capt. C. C. Gray, will leave for Little Rock at 4 o'clock this afternoon. She is the old favorite in the line, Capt. Gray having made the trade himself. Passengers will find their old friend Mr. James Gray, in the office and our young friend Mr. James A. Parker among the freight."

Saturday, October 8, 1859 Memphis Daily Appeal

ARRIVALS YESTERDAY - Charm from Louisville
DEPARTURES YESTERDAY - Charm for White River

"The Charme (sic.), Messrs. Chidester, Rapley & Co's beautiful little new steamer for the mail service between Des Arc and Clarendon, passed down yesterday, Captain Chidester in command." [NOTE: The Charm was owned by Butterfield's sub-contractor, John. T. Chidester.]

*"FOR ARKANSAS RIVER - The fine little steamer **Jennie Whipple**, Capt. C. C. Gray, is the regular packet as above at 4 o'clock this afternoon. As a low-water packet she is not excelled; while her accommodations are superb, her officers are pleasant companions and skilled in their duties, Messrs. Gray and Parker being the clerks."*

Sunday, October 9, 1859 Memphis Daily Appeal

*DEPARTURES YESTERDAY – **Jennie Whipple** for Arkansas River.*

Tuesday, October 11, 1859 Memphis Daily Appeal

"The river is still falling pretty fast... 10 inches... in 48 hours."

Wednesday, October 12, 1859 Memphis Daily Appeal

"The river is still falling... declined about 2 inches... 24 hours."

Thursday, October 13, 1859 Memphis Daily Appeal

"The river is falling at this point... declined about 3 inches..."

Friday, October 14, 1859 Memphis Daily Appeal

*"Mr. James A Parker, of the **Jennie Whipple**... in the city yesterday."*

Saturday, October 15, 1859 Memphis Daily Appeal

"The new steamer Charm got aground ten miles below Duval's Bluff, in White River, a few days ago, and broke her rudder in the effort to get off."

*"FOR LITTLE ROCK - The favorite packet **Jennie Whipple**, Captain C. C. Gray, will leave for Little Rock as the usual hour this afternoon. She is superior in these waters, and her officers are attentive and experienced."*

Sunday, October 16, 1859 Memphis Daily Appeal

*"Owing to an unusually heavy freight business, the **Jennie Whipple** did not arrive yesterday."*

Tuesday, October 18, 1859 Memphis Daily Appeal

"The Arkansas River is quite low and falling."

*"The officers of the Red Wing, from the Arkansas River yesterday, report the **Jennie Whipple** hard aground, just below Richland, having been in that condition twenty-four hours. Capt. Gray had reshipped his Little Rock freight at Pine Bluff, and attempted to return from that point."*

Wednesday, October 19, 1859 Memphis Daily Appeal

*"The **Jennie Whipple** had not arrived from Arkansas River last evening."*

"...the Kate Frisbee arrived in a crippled condition, having picked up a snag twelve miles below the city [Memphis], *by which her larboard* [port side] *wheel house was torn away, the wheel considerably damaged, and her cooking apparatus literally thrown overboard. She went to the upper landing yesterday for repairs.* [The Kate Frisbee is know to have carried Butterfield passengers occasionally from Des Arc to Memphis.]

Thursday, October 20, 1859 Memphis Daily Appeal

"The river is falling slowly... declined about three inches..."

Friday, October 21, 1859 Memphis Daily Appeal

"The river is still falling slowly at this point."

Saturday, October 22, 1859 Memphis Daily Appeal

*"The **Jennie Whipple** had not arrived at a late hour last evening and she will not, in all probability, leave for Arkansas River today. We infer that she is still aground in the Arkansas."*

Sunday, October 23, 1859 Memphis Daily Appeal

"... bales of cotton shipped... during the week... 12,196"

Tuesday, October 25, 1859 Memphis Daily Appeal

ARRIVALS SINCE SATURDAY - *Jennie Whipple, from Arkansas River.*

"Arkansas River is also falling, with about two feet six inches water in the shallowest places – less than has been known to the oldest inhabitant."

*"Of the regular packets, the **Jennie Whipple**, from Arkansas River... arrived since our last report. The **Whipple** had been aground several days below Richland, but got off by unloading her cotton... The **Whipple** notwithstanding the exceedingly low water, brought 80 bales cotton from Arkansas River, and 166 bales to this port."*

*"For Arkansas - The fine little steamer **Jennie Whipple**, Capt.*

C. C. Gray, the lightest boat of her capacity afloat, will leave for Little Rock at 5 o'clock this afternoon. A lady passenger of taste and experience, who was a passenger from this city by the **Whipple** *for Pine Bluff, writing from that point, says: 'the best passenger packet that ever visited the Rock. Her staterooms,' she says, 'are not only well furnished, but clean and even the plates and knives and forks, at the table are clean, in addition to which Capt. Gray is so nice that, if he were not already married, if he passes the next leap year in single-blessedness, it would be at the risk of his character for gallantry.' For her gratification, we assure our fair correspondent that, if Capt. Gray is married, there are single gentlemen in the clerk's office of the* **Whipple** *whose sacrifices for the comfort of passengers would lead them almost into matrimony. Messrs. Gray and Parker are the clerks."*

Wednesday, October 26, 1859 Memphis Daily Appeal

DEPARTURES TODAY - ***Jennie Whipple*** *for Little Rock*

"There has been heavy rains in the vicinity of Fort Smith, with a rise of 16 inches in the Arkansas River above Little Rock. The swell in the upper portion of the river, however, had no effect below Little Rock."

Thursday, October 27, 1859 Memphis Daily Appeal

"The river continues to decline at [Memphis]... the heavier boats, with fair cargoes experience great difficulty even below [Memphis] on account of the low water."

"The Arkansas River was about at a stand at Pine Bluff on Monday last."

Friday, October 28, 1859 Memphis Daily Appeal

"...number of bales of cotton shipped from this port yesterday was about 3,700"

Saturday, October 29, 1859 Memphis Daily Appeal

"FOR ARKANSAS RIVER - Capt. Gray's popular little packet ***Jennie Whipple***, *should she arrive, will leave for Little Rock at the usual hour this afternoon."*

Sunday, October 30, 1859 Memphis Daily Appeal

"Number of bales shipped during the week: 15,244"

Tuesday, November 1, 1859 Memphis Daily Appeal

"The Arkansas River is very low... stream still falling."

Wednesday, November 2, 1859 Memphis Daily Appeal
"The river... declined about two inches" [Memphis]

Thursday, November 3, 1859 Memphis Daily Appeal
"There has been no change in the Arkansas River since our last report, with 3 inches water to Pine Bluff and 30 inches at the Rock. The low water is becoming a serious obstruction even to Mississippi River boats..."

Friday, November 4, 1859 Memphis Daily Appeal
"...steamboat... Lady Walton departed for Little Rock..."

Saturday, November 5, 1859 Memphis Daily Appeal
"The Arkansas River is still falling with thirty inches Little Rock and twenty inches to Pine Bluff."
ARRIVALS YESTERDAY - THE South Bend from Arkansas River
"JENNIE WHIPPLE SUNK - We learn from persons who came up on the Ingomar from Napoleon, that the **Jennie Whipple** *struck a snag and sunk near White River cut-off, in the Arkansas River, Tuesday. the South Bend, which arrived yesterday, reported the* **Whipple** *aground in the same vicinity. We infer that she got off, and stuck a snag afterward and sank in the vicinity of the wreck of the Irene. She was bound down, and crowded with passengers and freight. Captain Gray thought he would be able to raise her. She was insured at Louisville, but we did not learn to what amount."*

Sunday, November 6, 1859 Memphis Daily Appeal
"The South Bend... will leave for Little Rock Tuesday afternoon."

Tuesday, November 8, 1859 Memphis Daily Appeal
"The river having declined almost to the standard of extreme low water mark, is still falling at... [Memphis]"

Wednesday, November 9, 1859 Memphis Daily Appeal
"The river was about stationary... clear and placid..."

Wednesday, November 9, 1959 Des Arc Citizen
"The steamer **Jennie Whipple** *struck a snag and sunk near White River cut-off, in the Arkansas River, on the 1st inst."*

Thursday, November 10, 1859 Memphis Daily Appeal
"The total shipment of cotton yesterday... 3,300 bales"

Friday, November 11, 1859 Memphis Daily Appeal
"We were gratified to hear the report yesterday, that the steamer

Jennie Whipple had been raised, and that she was on her way to this port [Memphis], with a prospect that she would arrive last night."

Saturday, November 12, 1859 Memphis Daily Appeal

ARRIVALS YESTERDAY - *Jennie Whipple* from Arkansas River.

"The *Jennie Whipple*, recently sunk in the Arkansas River, arrived yesterday morning. She had been badly snagged and badly sunk, and Captain Gray has displayed almost superhuman energy in reclaiming her after she was thought to be irrevocably lost. At the time the accident occurred her cargo was composed of cotton, all of which was recovered. The **Whipple** will be repaired here, and she will be ready to resume her place in the Arkansas River trade on Tuesday next."

Sunday, November 13, 1859 Memphis Daily Appeal

ARRIVALS YESTERDAY – *Jennie Whipple* from Arkansas River.

Tuesday, November 15, 1859 Memphis Daily Appeal

"Navigation has been almost suspended in the Arkansas River, owning to the low water, and the weather was very dry at Little Rock on the 10th..."

"Shipments of cotton during the week... 16,412 bales"

"Captain Gray is progressing rapidly with the repairs necessary to put the *Jennie Whipple* fairly afloat again, and she will be out in a day or two."

Wednesday, November 16, 1859 Memphis Daily Appeal

"The river continues at about a stand..."

Thursday, November 17, 1859 Memphis Daily Appeal

"Captain Gray is progressing with the repairs to the *Jennie Whipple* with his usual energy, and she will be receiving again in a day or two for Little Rock."

Friday, November 18, 1859 Memphis Daily Appeal

"Mr, Rogers has succeeded admirably in his repairs to the *Jennie Whipple*. She is all afloat again, and doesn't look at all the worse for her late accident. She will be ready to leave for the Arkansas River on Tuesday next. Capt. McDowell, in company with Mr. Jas. Gray, the clerk of the **Whipple**, has gone to Napoleon to attend to the shipment of the cotton lost overboard from the *Jennie Whipple* by the late accident. The damaged cargo *will be sent to New Orleans."*

Saturday, November 19, 1859 Memphis Daily Appeal

"There is now but thirty inches water in the Arkansas River. None of the boats now attempt to go above Pine Bluff, and they find navigation to that point, even, very difficult and hazardous."

Sunday, November 20, 1859 Memphis Daily Appeal

"Total shipment of cotton from [Memphis] during the week... embraced 21,904 bales."

Tuesday, November 22, 1859 Memphis Daily Appeal

*"The **Jennie Whipple**, having been repaired, will make a trip to Cairo, as the low water in Arkansas has almost effectively barred navigation in that stream. She will depart for Cairo on Thursday."*

"FOR ARKANSAS RIVER - The fine regular packet Lady Walton, W. B. Nowland captain, will leave for all points on the Arkansas River at 4 o'clock this afternoon. As the water is very low in the Arkansas at present, and as the Lady is of very light draught, those who do not wish to meet with detention should register on her."

Wednesday, November 23, 1859 Memphis Daily Appeal

"The steamer S. H. Tucker... will leave for Little Rock..."

Thursday, November 24, 1859 Memphis Daily Appeal

"We learn from the officers of the S. H. Tucker that there has been a rise in the Arkansas River, and that there is now three feet at Pine Bluff, and thirty inches water at Little Rock, with a prospect of plenty of water for the purposes of navigation."

*"The S. H. Tucker brought up from Napoleon, 143 bales cotton that had been sunk on the **Jennie Whipple** in the Arkansas River. The shipment was in a slightly damaged condition."*

*"FOR THE ARKANSAS RIVER - All her repairs having been completed, the fine little steamer **Jennie Whipple**, Captain Gray, will leave for all points on the Arkansas River at 5 o'clock Saturday. She will be under command of the "old veteran,' Captain Charley, and Captain A. D. Storm in her office. Everybody will be delighted with the announcement that the **Whipple** is coming out so soon."*

Saturday, November 26, 1859 Weekly Arkansas Gazette

"The Julia Roane, Captain Danley, attempted to go to Fort Smith, but found the upper river too low to ascend beyond the foot of McLean's Bottom."

Saturday, November 26, 1859 Memphis Daily Appeal

"The river was rising.. swollen about 2 feet..."

*"The Undine and Lake City will go into the Memphis and Arkansas River trade at an early day, forming, in connection with the **Jennie Whipple**, an independent tri-weekly line, to be called the "Merchant's and Planter's Line." One of the boats will leave this port on each Tuesday, another on Thursday, and a third on Saturday."*

*"Mr. Homer W. Baren has been engaged to superintend the stewart's department on the **Jennie Whipple**. Mr. B. is one of the most popular and successful caterers on the western waters."*

*"FOR THE ARKANSAS RIVER – The elegant packet, **Jennie Whipple**, Captain C. C. Gray, having been substantially repaired, will leave for all points on the Arkansas River, at 4 o'clock this afternoon. She has been refurnished and refitted during the low water season, and is now more complete than ever. Capt. Storm has been engaged to take charge of the office, and our young friend Parker may still be found aboard."*

Sunday, November 27, 1859 Memphis Daily Appeal

DEPARTURES YESTERDAY – **Jennie Whipple** for Arkansas River.

"A letter from Little Rock to Capt. Pritchard, dated the 23d last, says that the Arkansas River is still rising at that point, with 6 feet in the channel, and a prospect of 12 feet waters."

"...cotton... shipments during the [week] 22,352 bales..."

*"The regular packet departures yesterday... **Jennie Whipple** had fair trip..."*

Tuesday, November 29, 1859 Memphis Daily Appeal

"The Red Wing arrived from the Arkansas River at a late hour last evenings, bringing 100 bales of cotton. The Red Wing picked up a snag in the Arkansas River as she came out, which tore away her after bulk-head and guards, and did some other slight damage. She will repair here, in order to effect which, she will be detained until Thursday."

Wednesday, November 30, 1859 Memphis Daily Appeal
"The river is still rising... eighteen inches in 24 hours..."

Thursday, December 1, 1859 Memphis Daily Appeal
"The shipment of cotton... for the month... 81,885 bales"

Friday, December 2, 1859 The Louisville Daily Courier
*"There is a new line to be formed for the Memphis and Arkansas River trade, to consist of the **Jennie Whipple**, Captain Gray, the Lake City, Captain blake, and the Northerner, Captain Alford. The Undine is also talked of for the same trade."*

Friday, December 2, 1859 Memphis Daily Appeal
"There was not much general activity at the landing."

Saturday, December 3, 1859 Memphis Daily Appeal
*"The fog and bad weather have detained many... packets. **Jennie Whipple** from Arkansas River... due yesterday, had not arrived at a late hour last night."*

*"The elegant steamer **Jennie Whipple**, Capt. Gray, is the regular packet for Little Rock and all ports on the Arkansas River, at the usual hour this afternoon. She has excellent accommodations and popular officers. Messrs. Storm and Parker are the clerks."*

Sunday, December 4, 1859 Memphis Daily Appeal
"NEW RULES FOR STEAMBOAT PILOTS – From and after the first day of January, 1860, it shall be unlawful to navigate passenger steamers in the night time, on rivers flowing into the Gulf of Mexico and their tributaries, unless such steamer is provided with a red light in front, and attached to the larboard [port side] chimney, from six to ten feet below its top, and a green light attached the same way to the starboard chimney."

Tuesday, December 6, 1859 Memphis Daily Appeal
*"ARRIVALS SINCE SATURDAY - **Jennie Whipple** from Arkansas River."*

"The river commenced rising... 15 inches."

"The Arkansas River is now in excellent navigable condition, with at least eighteen feet water in the channel."

*"...the **Jennie Whipple**... had fair trip both of passengers and freight."*

*"FOR ARKANSAS RIVER – The elegant steamer, **Jennie Whipple**, Captain C. C. Gray, will leave for all points on the Arkansas River at 4 o'clock this afternoon. She is of the independent Mer-*

chant's and Planter's line, and has the very best accommodations for passengers, with careful, attentive officers, Capt. Storm and our young friend Parker being the clerks."

Wednesday, December 7, 1859 Memphis Daily Appeal

"... the river rose 12 inches... heavy fall of snow and sleet..."

"There were 2,127 bales of cotton shipped from [Memphis]"

"The majority of the regular packets announced to depart yesterday were detained by the bad weather... includes... the *Jennie Whipple*, for Arkansas River..."

"FOR ARKANSAS RIVER – The popular steamer *Jennie Whipple*, Captain C. C. Gray, having been detained, will leave most positively for all points on the Arkansas River, at 4 o'clock this afternoon. Travelers will find her one of the most desirable packets in the trade. Captain A. D. Storm and Mr. James A. Parker are the clerks."

Thursday, December 8, 1859 Memphis Daily Appeal

"Owing to the exceedingly inclement weather yesterday it was utterly impossible to get freights down to the river, and several boats posted to leave were forced to remain over, among which were the *Jennie Whipple*, for Arkansas River..."

"FOR ARKANSAS RIVER – Captain C. C. Gray informs us that his fine steamer *Jennie Whipple* will leave for Little Rock mot positively at 4 o'clock this afternoon. She is fleet and substantial and has superb passenger accommodations. Messrs. Parker and Green are the clerks."

Friday, December 9, 1859 Memphis Daily Appeal

"DEPARTURES YESTERDAY – *Jennie Whipple* for Arkansas River."

"The *Jennie Whipple* has a big passenger and freight list, and awaited the arrival of the 9 o'clock train last evening."

"The recent bad weather has thrown the Memphis and St. Louis packets out of time... and we may not expect much regularity in the boats of the line until the weather "settles." The people may rely upon one thing, however, that the company will always have a packet here on the regular day of departure."

Saturday, December 10, 1859 Memphis Daily Appeal

"The river was rising more rapidly... 8 inches in 24 hours..."

Sunday, December 11, 1859 Memphis Daily Appeal

"The river was rising more rapidly... one foot... in 24 hours..."

Tuesday, December 13, 1859 Memphis Daily Appeal

"The river was rising rapidly... 1 foot 6 inches... in 24 hours..."

Wednesday, December 14, 1859 Memphis Daily Appeal

"The river has risen about 12 inches..."

"The showboat Banjo remained over yesterday, and there was an entertainment given on board last evening."

Thursday, December 15, 1859 Memphis Daily Appeal

"The river was rising even more rapidly... eighteen inches..."

"The steamer Lady Walton, of the Arkansas River mail line, was aground above Little Rock at last accounts.

Friday, December 16, 1859 Memphis Daily Appeal

"The river was still rising rapidly... almost one inch per hour."

"The Arkansas River is falling again, with 8 feet water in the channel to Pine Bluff and six feet up to Little Rock."

Saturday, December 17, 1859 Memphis Daily Appeal

"The river was rising... 6 inches in twenty-four hours."

Sunday, December 18, 1859 Memphis Daily Appeal

"The shipment of cotton during the week.. 15,725 bales..."

Tuesday, December 20, 1859 Memphis Daily Appeal

*"ARRIVALS SINCE SATURDAY - **Jennie Whipple** from Arkansas River."*

*"The regular packets had a large number of passengers and good lists of freight... the **Jennie Whipple** 60 bales... "*

"The Arkansas River is falling, with 4 feet 6 inches water at Little Rock on Friday last."

"The Lady Walton, the regular Little Rock and Memphis packet, is reported badly aground at Trustee Island, a short distance below Van Buren. There is not truth, however, in the report that she had broken in two."

*"FOR THE ARKANSAS RIVER – The fine steamer **Jennie Whipple**, Captain C. C. Gray, will leave for Little Rock at four o'clock this afternoon. She has unsurpassed accommodations and careful, attentive officers, including Messrs. Green and Parker, of the clerk's office."*

Wednesday, December 21, 1859 Arkansas True Democrat

*"There is a new line to be formed for the Memphis and Arkansas River trade. It will consist of the **Jennie Whipple**, Captain*

*Gray; the Lake City, Captain H. Blake; and the Northerner, Captain P. A. Alford. The **Whipple** will leave this evening, and the Lake City on Wednesday. Each boat will make weekly trips, forming a tri-weekly line. We are glad to note the fact as an indication of the increase of trade between our city [Memphis] and one of the most fertile regions in the south. Messrs. B. E. Dill & Co., will be the agents of the line. – Avalanche."*

Wednesday, December 21, 1859 Memphis Daily Appeal

*"DEPARTURES YESTERDAY – **Jennie Whipple** for Arkansas River."*
"Now that the Arkansas River is navigable... mail steamers will make their trips between this port and Arkansas River with unbroken regularity... This arrangement will be appreciated by our traveling and shipping public, who have long felt the necessity of a sure connection with the people of the valley of the Arkansas River."

Thursday, December 22, 1859 Memphis Daily Appeal

"The river is falling more rapidly... declined almost one foot..."
"All the southern streams are in good boating condition, including... the Arkansas..."
"The steamer Lady Walton which as hard aground in Arkansas River, has been relieved from her last perilous position, and is now on her way to this city."

Friday, December 23, 1859 Memphis Daily Appeal

"The river is still falling rapidly... eighteen inches in 24 hours."
"The Lady Walton, which had been aground in the Arkansas River, as we have before remarked, had got off, and proceeded down to Napoleon. She was to return to the Rock, however, to take her regular day."

Saturday, December 24, 1859 Memphis Daily Appeal

"The river... falling... about 6 or 10 inches during the 24 hours..."

Sunday, December 25, 1859 Memphis Daily Appeal

"The river declined about six inches..."

Wednesday, December 28, 1859 Memphis Daily Appeal

"Since Saturday the river has declined about one foot..."
*"**Jennie Whipple**, from Arkansas River... due yesterday, but... not arrived at a late hour last night."*

Thursday, December 29, 1859 Memphis Daily Appeal

"ARRIVALS YESTERDAY – **Jennie Whipple** *from Arkansas River."*
"The fog in this latitude has amounted to almost a prohibition to navigation."
"Mr. James Gray, of the **Jennie Whipple**, *are in the city."*
"There was a rumor in circulation yesterday to the effect that the **Jennie Whipple** *has been burned in the Arkansas River. It was altogether unfounded, however, as the officers of the H. R. W. Hill saw her at Napoleon Tuesday, and she arrived here last evening."*

Friday, December 30, 1859 Memphis Daily Appeal

"From all accounts there is to be considerable competition on the Arkansas River trade. Including Captain Adams' mail line and the **Jennie Whipple**, *there are already five packets hence to Little Rock. Added to these, the Lake City and Undine are making arrangements to enter the list, and it is reported that the Favorite will run hereafter in the same trade, making a fleet of eight boats in a trade, that, one year ago, did not afford encouragement enough to pay a single craft. Our business men do not remember, perhaps, that Capt. Charles C. Gray, of the* **Jennie Whipple**, *was the pioneer in the trade, and that the little* **Jennie** *was the entering wedge opened up the immense traffic between this city and the valley of the Arkansas. Such is the case, however, and Capt. Gray now looks with confidence to our business men to sustain him in an enterprise that has been far more profitable to them than to him."*

"FOR ARKANSAS RIVER – The popular steamer **Jennie Whipple**, *Captain C. C. Gray, will leave for Pine Bluff, Little Rock, and all points on the Arkansas River at 4 o'clock this afternoon. the* **Whipple** *is the pioneer in the trade, and merits all the popularity she enjoys. She has excellent accommodations and popular officers, among whom are Messrs. Parker and Green, the clerks."*

Saturday, December 31, 1859 Memphis Daily Appeal

DEPARTURES YESTERDAY - **Jennie Whipple** *for Little Rock.*
"The Arkansas River has declined fully a foot, leaving but four feet to Little Rock. There have been heavy rains at the vicinity of Fort Smith recently, and there will be ___ immediately."

1860

Wednesday, January 4, 1860 The Memphis Daily Appeal
"The White, Little Red, Arkansas and all the southern streams are in fine navigable condition."

Sunday, January 8, 1860 The Memphis Daily Appeal
*"FOR ARKANSAS RIVER – The elegant steamer **Jennie Whipple**, Capt. C. C. Gray will leave for Pine Bluff, Little Rock, etc. at 4 o'clock tomorrow. She … is deservedly popular with passengers and skippers. Messers. Gray and Patterson are the clerks."*

Tuesday, January 10, 1860 The Memphis Daily Appeal
"The Arkansas River is about at a stand, with fully 4 feet to Little Rock, and about 3 feet to Fort Smith."

*"FOR THE ARKANSAS RIVER – The fine little steamer **Jennie Whipple**, Captain C. C. Gray, having been detained will leave most positively for Little Rock at 10 o'clock this morning. She is the independent boat, and has excellent accommodations and popular officers. Messrs. Green and Patterson are the clerks, both of whom are attentive and experienced."*

Wednesday, January 11, 1860 Arkansas True Democrat
*ARRIVALS – Jan. 2 **Jennie Whipple**, Capt. Gray, from Memphis*
*DEPARTURES – Jan. 2 **Jennie Whipple** for Memphis*

Wednesday, January 11, 1860 The Memphis Daily Appeal
"The Arkansas River is falling slowly, with scant four feet to Little Rock, with a prospect of an immediate rise, however, as there had been heavy rains at Fort Smith. There have been no boats aground recently between Fort Smith and Little Rock.
*"The departures yesterday embraced the South Bend and **Jennie Whipple** for the Arkansas River…"*
*DEPARTURES YESTERDAY – **Jennie Whipple** for Little Rock*

Thursday, January 12, 1860 The Memphis Daily Appeal
"The river is falling at this point, having declined fully 10 inches."

Saturday, January 14, 1860 The Memphis Daily Appeal
"Arkansas River is rising at Little Rock, but when the Lady Walton left, was falling at points below."
*"The **Jennie Whipple** and South Bend were at Napoleon Thursday, having been detained by the fog."*

Sunday, January 15, 1860 The Memphis Daily Appeal
"The receipts of cotton during the week... 2,218 bales..."

Tuesday, January 17, 1860 The Memphis Daily Appeal
"The river has risen 3 feet since Saturday..."
"Arkansas... rising rapidly, with fully 7 feet in the Arkansas to Little Rock."

Wednesday, January 18, 1860 Arkansas True Democrat
ARRIVALS – *Jan. 14* **Jennie Whipple**, *Capt. Gray, from Memphis*
DEPARTURES – *Jan. 14* **Jennie Whipple** *for Memphis*

Wednesday, January 18, 1860 The Memphis Daily Appeal
ARRIVALS YESTERDAY – **Jennie Whipple** *from Arkansas River*
"BOATS LEAVING TODAY FOR ARKANSAS RIVER - The fine steamer **Jennie Whipple***, Captain C. C. Gray, will leave for all points on the Arkansas River at 4 o'clock this afternoon. She is of the ... excellent accommodations and attentive officers. Messrs. Green and Patterson are the clerks."*

Thursday, January 19, 1860 The Memphis Daily Appeal
"The shipment of cotton yesterday embraced 3,587 bales..."
"The **Jennie Whipple** *was detained last evening, but will leave positively today for the Arkansas River."*

Friday, January 20, 1860 The Memphis Daily Appeal
"The river rose about two feet... during 24 hours... the river has been full of heavy drift during the past two or three days."

Saturday, January 21, 1860 The Memphis Daily Appeal
"The river is still rising rapidly... about three feet..."
"The Arkansas River is falling at Little Rock, but is stationary below that point, with fully eighteen feet of water to Little Rock."

Sunday, January 22, 1860 The Memphis Daily Appeal
"No boats arrived from the Arkansas, but the Skylark departed yesterday for Fort Smith and the S. H. Tucker departed yesterday for the Arkansas River."

Tuesday, January 24, 1860 The Memphis Daily Appeal
"...the Arkansas River... falling, with plenty of water, however, for navigation to Fort Smith."

Wednesday, January 25, 1860 Arkansas True Democrat
ARRIVALS – *Jan. 21* **Jennie Whipple**, *Capt. Parker, from Memphis*

DEPARTURES – *Jan. 21* ***Jennie Whipple*** *for Memphis*

Wednesday, January 25, 1860 The Memphis Daily Appeal

"The Arkansas is falling rapidly."

"ARRIVED YESTERDAY - ***Jennie Whipple****, from the Arkansas River"*

"BOATS LEAVING TODAY FOR ARKANSAS RIVER – The popular packet ***Jennie Whipple****, Captain C. C. Gray, will leave for Pine Bluff, Little Rock and all points on the Arkansas River at 4 o'clock this afternoon. She has the very best accommodations and efficient officers, including Messrs. Green and Patterson, the clerks."*

Thursday, January 26, 1860 The Memphis Daily Appeal

"The ***Jennie Whipple*** *departed yesterday..."*

"The ***Whipple*** *received considerable freight from the Interchange, from Louisville, for the Arkansas River. Both the Simmons and the* ***Whipple*** *delayed their departure until after the arrival of the nine o'clock train."*

Friday, January 27, 1860 The Memphis Daily Appeal

"The Arkansas River is falling, with 8 feet to Little Rock and 4 feet 6 inches thence to Fort Smith."

Saturday, January 28, 1860 The Memphis Daily Appeal

"The river fell... about 4 inches during the 24 hours..."

Sunday, January 29, 1860 The Memphis Daily Appeal

"The river fell at least six inches..."

Tuesday, January 31, 1860 The Memphis Daily Appeal

"The Arkansas is also falling, with some very shoal places above Little Rock."

"We learn from the officers of the H. Fitzhugh that the Skylark and Arkansas Traveler are both hard aground at Sycamore Shoals in the Arkansas River."

Wednesday, February 1, 1860 Arkansas True Democrat

ARRIVALS – *Jan. 28* ***Jennie Whipple****, Capt. Gray, from Memphis*

DEPARTURES – *Jan. 28* ***Jennie Whipple*** *for Memphis*

Wednesday, February 1, 1860 The Memphis Daily Appeal

"The river declined about 2 feet during 24 hours... snow and sleet, with the ground covered last evening to the depth of two or three inches."

"The ***Jennie Whipple*** *and Lady Walton were due from Arkan*

sas River last evening, but had not arrived as of late last night."

Thursday, February 2, 1860 The Memphis Daily Appeal

"The Arkansas River is falling rapidly, with, however about five feet to Little Rock."

"Captain Riley did not find enough water to float his craft above the "Rock" and wisely determined to reship his Fort Smith freight and return."

"...the Cincinnati and Arkansas River packet Hickman struck a snag and sprang a leak in the Arkansas River, a short distance below Little Rock."

*"In the storm, Tuesday evening, the **Jennie Whipple**, bound up, was blown ashore in the vicinity of Commerce, and remained in that condition last evening, the water falling rapidly from her. She will be relieved, if at all, with great difficulty."*

Friday, February 3, 1860 The Memphis Daily Appeal

*"The **Jennie Whipple** is still high and dry on a bar in the vicinity of Commerce. Her owner, Captain C. C. Gray, went down to her last evening on board the Lady Walton, to see what can be done toward getting her off. "*

Saturday, February 4, 1860 The Memphis Daily Appeal

*"The **Whipple** still remains on the bar near Commerce and was fully twenty feet from water yesterday. She is well located, however, and in little or no danger of being broken, run into my passing steamers, as they cannot get near her. An officer of the boat was in the city [Memphis] yesterday, and procured the necessary materials for caulking her. She will at once be rendered perfectly tight, and will then await the coming of a second flood."*

Sunday, February 5, 1860 The Memphis Daily Appeal

"The Arkansas River was falling Sunday at Little Rock, with thirty inches in the channel to Fort Smith. A heavy rain fell, however, in the latitude of Fort Smith, and one Tuesday the river had risen three feet at Little Rock."

Tuesday, February 7, 1860 The Memphis Daily Appeal

"The river... declined a full two feet since Saturday."

*"Captain C. C. Gray, of the **Jennie Whipple**, left this city for Louisville last evening to charter a boat to take the place of the*

*Jennie in the Arkansas River trade. It is said he is in quest of the Silver Star. The **Jennie** is now about three quarters of a mile in the country - fully that distance from the river."*

Wednesday, February 8, 1860 The Memphis Daily Appeal
"There was twelve feet water in the channel of the Arkansas River to Little Rock."

Thursday, February 9, 1860 The Memphis Daily Appeal
"The shipments yesterday aggregated 2,363 bales..."

Friday, February 10, 1860 The Memphis Daily Appeal
"The Arkansas River was stationary at Little Rock Tuesday, but falling above that point, with plenty of water for all navigable purposes."

Saturday, February 11, 1860 Weekly Arkansas Gazette
*"We regret to learn that the independent Memphis packet **Jennie Whipple**, was blown so far out of the channel in the storm of the 31st ult.* [of last month], *about 40 miles below Memphis, that she now lies in a critical condition, high and dry, some distance from the water's edge."*

Saturday, February 11, 1860 The Memphis Daily Appeal
"The river rose six inches... during the 24 hours..."

Sunday, February 12, 1860 The Memphis Daily Appeal
"The Arkansas River was stationary on Thursday, with seven feet of water to Little Rock, and five feet thence to Fort Smith."
"The little steamer Mugangno struck a snag and sunk in four feet of water, Sunday last, a short distance from Fort Gibson, in the Arkansas River. She was a regular packet between Van Buren and Fort Gibson, and had a cargo of dry goods and other merchandise."

Tuesday, February 14, 1860 The Memphis Daily Appeal
"The river is still rising... in a rate of one foot in 48 hours."

Wednesday, February 15, 1860 The Memphis Daily Appeal
"The river rose one foot... during the 24 hours..."

Thursday, February 16, 1860 The Memphis Daily Appeal
"The river rose about 5 inches... during the 24 hours..."

Friday, February 17, 1860 The Memphis Daily Appeal
"The Arkansas River is falling from Fort Smith to the mout with plenty of water, however, for boating purposes."

Saturday, February 18, 1860 The Memphis Daily Appeal

"The river commenced rising again... swelled about 9 inches..."
*"Captain C. C. Gray, of the **Jennie Whipple**, was in Louisville Thursday, in search of a boat to take the place of the **Whipple** The Silver Star is for sale, but cannot be chartered."*

Sunday, February 19, 1860 The Memphis Daily Appeal

"The river rose about 4 inches... 24 hours..."

Tuesday, February 21, 1860 The Memphis Daily Appeal

"The shipments yesterday embraced about 4,000 bales..."

Wednesday, February 22, 1860 The Memphis Daily Appeal

"The river rose 6 inches... in 24 hours..."

Thursday, February 23, 1860 The Memphis Daily Appeal

"The Arkansas River has been higher at Fort Smith, during the past week, than at any former period during the season, but is now falling, with twelve feet water at Little Rock.
*"If the river should continue to rise a day or two at the present rate, there will be sufficient water to float the **Jennie Whipple** from her ugly position in the vicinity of Commerce."*

Friday, February 24, 1860 The Memphis Daily Appeal

"The [Mississippi] river was rising more rapidly... having swollen fully 1 foot."
"The Arkansas River is falling all the way from Fort Smith to the mouth, but is in good boating condition."

Saturday, February 25, 1860 The Memphis Daily Appeal

"The river is still rising... 1 foot in twenty four hours."

Sunday, February 26, 1860 The Memphis Daily Appeal

"The river at this point rose 6 inches during the 24 hours..."

Tuesday, February 28, 1860 The Memphis Daily Appeal

"The river is still rising at this point, ...almost 15 inch in 48 hr"
"The Arkansas River is also full and rising."
*"Dating from last evening it would require a rise of about three feet more to float the **Jennie Whipple** from her position in "Gray's Inlet." From present appearances, however, she will get off in a day or two. Captain C. C. Gray of the **Whipple** was a passenger by the Goody Friends, which left Cincinnati Friday for this port."*

Wednesday, March 1, 1860 The Memphis Daily Appeal

The river having risen fully 6 inches in the 24 hours...
The report of the Wharfmaster Wolfe... month of February

> *Steamboats arrived - 227*
> *Flatboats arrived - 16*
> *Wharfage receipts from steamers - $2,892.50*
> *Wharfage receipts from flatboats - $493.00*
> *Cotton bales shipped to New Orleans - 35,083*
> *Cotton bales shipped to Ohio River - 13,532*
> *Cotton bales shipped to St. Louis - 21*

When the Gladiator passed up yesterday, the **Jennie Whipple** *had steam, and she doubtless got off last evening. Captain Gray, of the* **Whipple**, *will arrive here today by the Goody Friends."*

"The **Jennie Whipple** *arrived last night in fine condition for another campaign in the Arkansas River. The Goody Friends arrived about 9 o'clock last evening, among her passengers was Captain Gray, of the* **Jennie Whipple**.*"*

ARRIVALS YESTERDAY - **Jennie Whipple**, *Captain Gray*

Friday, March 2, 1860 The Courier-Journal (Louisville)

"The Memphis Appeal of Wednesday says: The **Jennie Whipple**, *it is thought, will float off today or tomorrow from her late position in the vicinity of Commerce, and will leave for Arkansas River at an early day next week."*

Thursday, March 2, 1860 The Memphis Daily Appeal

"The Arkansas River was still falling all the way down when the Red Wing, which arrived yesterday, came out... brought 55 bales of cotton for our merchants."

"The tidy little **Jennie Whipple** *was at the landing yesterday, receiving for Arkansas River. She has been caulked, thoroughly overhauled and repainted since she got aground, and was never in better condition for a summer campaign. She will leave for all points on the Arkansas at the usual hour tomorrow."*

Friday, March 3, 1860 The Memphis Daily Appeal

*"*BOATS LEAVING TODAY FOR THE ARKANSAS RIVER *− The fine steamer* **Jennie Whipple**, *Captain C. C. Gray; will resume her old trade today, in the Arkansas River trade, leaving for all points hence to Fort Smith at 4 o'clock this afternoon. She will be remembered by planters and shippers and travelers gener-*

ally as the old "accommodation line," and has never yet forfeited their confidence or her claims to their patronage."

Saturday, March 4, 1860 The Memphis Daily Appeal

"Notwithstanding the adverse weather, the local packets were all fortunate as to freight, and had fair passenger lists."

Tuesday, March 6, 1860 The Memphis Daily Appeal

*"STEAMERS LEAVING TODAY – **Jennie Whipple**, Captain Gray, for the Arkansas River."*

*"The last arrivals from the Arkansas River report that stream rising again, with plenty of water for all purposes to Fort Smith. BOATS LEAVING TODAY FOR THE ARKANSAS RIVER – The **Jennie Whipple** will leave for Fort Smith at 4 o'clock this afternoon She has unsurpassed accommodations and careful, attentive officers."*

Wednesday, March 7, 1860 The Memphis Daily Appeal

"The Arkansas River is falling all the way down from Fort Smith.

*Departing yesterday... of the regular packets... **Jennie Whipple** for the Arkansas River."*

*DEPARTURES YESTERDAY – **Jennie Whipple** for Arkansas River*

Thursday, March 8, 1860 The Memphis Daily Appeal

ARRIVALS YESTERDAY – Lady Walton from Arkansas River
DEPARTURES TODAY – J. H. Tucker & Lake City for Arkansas River

Friday, March 9, 1860 The Memphis Daily Appeal

DEPARTURES TODAY – Kate May for Arkansas River

Saturday, March 10, 1860 The Memphis Daily Appeal

Departures Today - Kate May for Arkansas and Indian Territory
Lady Walton for Arkansas River

*"We have already given particulars of the robbery on the **Jennie Whipple** Wednesday night. Steamboat men and passengers should be on their guard."*

Sunday, March 11, 1860 The Memphis Daily Appeal

ARRIVED TODAY – Red Wing from the Arkansas River
DEPARTURES YESTERDAY – Lady Walton for the Arkansas River
"The Hickman burned on the Arkansas River."

Tuesday, March 13, 1860 The Memphis Daily Appeal

*ARRIVALS SINCE SATURDAY – **Jennie Whipple** from Arkansas River*

DEPARTURES SINCE SATURDAY – *Skylark for Arkansas River*
STEAMERS LEAVING TODAY – **Jennie Whipple** *for Arkansas River*
Red Wing for Arkansas River
"The **Whipple** *brought 11 bales of cotton."*

Wednesday, March 14, 1860 Arkansas True Democrat
ARRIVALS – *March 8* **Jennie Whipple** *from Memphis*
DEPARTURES – *March 9* **Jennie Whipple** *for Memphis*

Wednesday, March 14, 1860 The Memphis Daily Appeal
ARRIVALS YESTERDAY – *South Bend from Arkansas River*
DEPARTURES YESTERDAY - *Red Wing for Arkansas River*
STEAMERS LEAVING TODAY – **Jennie Whipple** *for Arkansas River*
"The Arkansas River is also falling, with 5 feet water in Little Rock and 30 inches thence to Fort Smith."
"There will be several new boats built for the Memphis trade during the approaching season. For example... Captain Gray... will build one..."
*"*BOATS LEAVING TODAY FOR THE ARKANSAS RIVER *– The neat and popular* **Jennie Whipple***, Captain C. C. Gray, having been unavoidably detained, will leave for all points on the Arkansas River at 5 o'clock this afternoon. She is of the merchants' and planters' line, the pioneer in the trade, and she and her officers never fail to give satisfaction either to passengers and shippers."*

Thursday, March 15, 1860 The Memphis Daily Appeal
STEAMERS LEAVING TODAY – **Jennie Whipple** *for Arkansas River*
South Bend for Arkansas River
*"*BOATS LEAVING TODAY FOR ARKANSAS RIVER *– The* **Jennie Whipple***, Captain C. C. Gray, was detained again yesterday, but will leave for all points on the Arkansas River at 4 o'clock this afternoon. She has long been in the trade, and well known to passengers and shippers."*

Friday, March 16, 1860 The Memphis Daily Appeal
"The Arkansas River is falling very rapidly, and there was but __ feet to Little Rock on Tuesday, and about two feet to Fort Smith."
ARRIVED – *S. H. Tucker from Arkansas... 1,507 bags cotton seed*
DEPARTED – **Jennie Whipple***, South Bend, and Bracelet for the Arkansas River*

"Owing to the rapid decline in the Arkansas River the Skylark was unable to get up with her full cargo."

"The steamers Parallel and Little Rock were both above the 'Rock' when the S. H. Tucker left, and there was but a poor prospect that either would get down until another rise should intervene."

Saturday, March 17, 1860 The Memphis Daily Appeal
STEAMERS LEAVING TODAY – *S. H. Tucker for Arkansas River*

Sunday, March 18, 1860 The Memphis Daily Appeal
DEPARTURES YESTERDAY – *S. H. Tucker for Arkansas River*

Tuesday, March 20, 1860 The Memphis Daily Appeal
ARRIVED SINCE SATURDAY – *Lady Walton from Arkansas River*
DEPARTURES SINCE SATURDAY – *H. Fitzhugh for Arkansas River*
STEAMERS LEAVING TODAY – *Lady Walton for Arkansas River*

"The Arkansas River is falling, with ½ feet to Little Rock and 22 inches to Fort Smith."

"The Lady Walton, which arrived yesterday from the Arkansas River met the Skylark, Lake City and Red Wing at Pine Bluff, and the Bracelet at the White River cut-off. The Skylark would proceed no father up the river than Little Rock, at which point she would reship her Fort Smith freight by the Lake City, that best going through."

Wednesday, March 21, 1860 The Memphis Daily Appeal
ARRIVED YESTERDAY – *Red Wing from the Arkansas River*
DEPARTED YESTERDAY – *Lady Walton for the Arkansas River*

"The Arkansas River is still falling, with about four feet to the Rock and eighteen inches to Fort Smith."

Thursday, March 22, 1860 The Memphis Daily Appeal
STEAMERS LEAVING TODAY – *Red Wing for the Arkansas River*

Friday, March 23, 1860 The Memphis Daily Appeal
ARRIVALS YESTERDAY – *South Bend, Bracelet and Skylark from the Arkansas River*
DEPARTING TODAY – *Red Wing for the Arkansas River*

"The Arkansas River is also falling, and the officers of the South Bend, which arrived yesterday, report three feet six inches to Little Rock, and but fourteen inches to Fort Smith."

"The Skylark and Bracelet arrived from the Arkansas River

*Wednesday night, having re-shipped her Little Rock freight at Pine Bluff by the **Jennie Whipple**, which boat turned back from that point."*

"...the steamer Hickman [after burning on the Arkansas, had her] *...machinery removed to Little Rock. The safe has not been found* [containing gold], *and has evidently fallen overboard and become embedded in the sands of the Arkansas."*

Friday, March 23, 1860 Memphis Weekly Bulletin

*"The **Jennie Whipple** met the Bracelet at Pine Bluff, on Monday, and took her trip for Fort Smith and the Upper Arkansas."*

Saturday, March 24, 1860 Arkansas True Democrat

ARRIVALS – *March 18 **Jennie Whipple** from Memphis*

DEPARTURES – *March 18 **Jennie Whipple** for Memphis*

Saturday, March 24, 1860 The Memphis Daily Appeal

LEAVING TODAY – *South Bend for the Arkansas River*

Sunday, March 25, 1860 The Memphis Daily Appeal

DEPARTURES YESTERDAY – *South Bend and Hyland for Arkansas River*

"Receipts of cotton during the week... 5,155 bales..."

Tuesday, March 27, 1860 The Memphis Daily Appeal

ARRIVED YESTERDAY – *S. H. Tucker from the Arkansas River*

LEAVING TODAY – *S. H. Tucker for the Arkansas River*

"The officers of the Kate May report only 2 ½ feet water up to Little Rock in the Arkansas River, and but 10 inches above that point."

*"The **Jennie Whipple**, Undine and Lake City were, at the last intelligence, lying at Vane's Bar, above Little Rock. They could not get over the bar on account of the low water."*

"The Arkansas Traveler... ran on a sawyer on Thursday night at Marshall's cut-off, on the Arkansas River, a few miles below Pine Bluff. [see note at Aug. 28, 1859 for definition of sawyer.]*Her entire bottom was torn off, and she went down with five feet of water over her main deck. She had a cargo of sugar, molasses, salt, and dry goods from New Orleans. A passenger, named William Parsley, was so alarmed by the accident that he jumped into the river and was drowned. He was from Dardanelles, Arkansas. The boat careened so much that her chimneys and cabin fell overboard. She was owned by Captain John Timmons and*

Captain Albert thomas, her commander. She was worth $7,000, and had on board 200 lbs. of sugar, 800 sacks of salt, which will prove a total loss The remainder of the freight will be saved in a damaged condition."

Wednesday, March 28, 1860 The Memphis Daily Appeal
DEPARTED YESTERDAY – *S. H. Tucker for the Arkansas River*

Thursday, March 29, 1860 The Memphis Daily Appeal
"The Arkansas River has two feet four inches to Little Rock and falling."
ARRIVALS – *The Lady Walton from the Arkansas River with a large lot of hides, and 18 bales of cotton.*

Friday, March 30, 1860 The Memphis Daily Appeal
ARRIVALS YESTERDAY – *E. M. Ryland from Arkansas River*
DEPARTURES YESTERDAY – *The Lady Walton left for Arkansas River with a first rate load of freight and a large number of passengers.*

Saturday, March 31, 1860 Arkansas True Democrat
No *Jennie Whipple* arrivals or departures for March 20-30

Tuesday, April 3, 1860 The Memphis Daily Appeal
"The river [Mississippi] *has fallen a foot... "*

Wednesday, April 4, 1860 The Memphis Daily Appeal
"The officers of the Skylark report Arkansas River still falling, with only two feet water to Little Rock, and navigation above that point entirely suspended."

Thursday, April 5, 1860 The Memphis Daily Appeal
"The river is still falling slowly - two inches..."

Friday, April 6, 1860 The Memphis Daily Appeal
"DEPARTURES FOR LITTLE ROCK AND FORT SMITH – The excellent passenger and freight steamer Conewago, Captain E. Eugene Bowers commander, will leave for the above and intermediate points this evening at three o'clock..."
"The Great Overland Mail, for and from California – Memphis... the office of the overland mail is for the present at the Commercial Hotel, Jefferson Street, B. F. Candy local agent. Days of departure, Wednesday and Saturday, at 8 a.m. Ferry boat for Little Rock railroad foot of Jefferson street." (page 2)

Saturday, April 7, 1860 The Memphis Daily Appeal

"We have nothing further from the Arkansas River."

*"Captain A. D. Storm, clerk of the **Jennie Whipple**, also arrived yesterday. He reports the **Whipple** still above Little Rock, with a heavy cargo for Fort Smith, awaiting a rise in order to get up."*

Sunday, April 8, 1860 The Memphis Daily Appeal

"The Arkansas, as we learn from the officers of the Lady Walton, is still falling slowly, with only twenty-eight inches water to Little Rock, and fifteen inches thence to Fort Smith."

"Departures – Red Wing for the Arkansas River"

*"Arrivals Yesterday – The Lady Walton came in from the Arkansas with a goodly number of people and eight bales of cotton and a lot of poultry on freight. From a memoranda furnished by her attentive officers, we learn that the Henry Fitzhugh is at Paine's Landing, twelve miles below Pine Bluff, and the Little Rock and Pine Bluff at Carson's, six miles above the landing, unable to proceed on account of low water. The **Jennie Whipple** and Undine are still at Vaun's Bar, forty miles above Little Rock, heavily laden, and unable to get up or down the river. On Wednesday last, the Lake City, South Bend, and Delta were at Little Rock, awaiting the adjournment of the Democratic Convention. The Lady Walton will return to the Arkansas on Tuesday next – her regular day.*

Tuesday, April 10, 1860 The Memphis Daily Appeal

Steamers Leaving This Day – Lady Walton for Arkansas River

"The Arkansas River continues to decline, with thirty inches to Pine Bluff, and two feet to Little Rock."

Arrivals Since Saturday – South Bend from Arkansas River

*"The **Jennie Whipple**, Julia Roane, and Undine are still hard aground at Carson's Landing, and the Henry Fitzhug at Haine's. The S. H. Tucker descended the river to Napoleon, and returned again to Little Rock with the mails The Lady Waldon and South Bend are at this port..."*

Wednesday, April 11, 1860 The Memphis Daily Appeal

Departures Yesterday – Lady Walton for the Arkansas River

"Captain Chidester, the great southern mail contractor, left for Vicksburg by the steamer Kentucky yesterday. He has sold the

– 210 –

steamer Charm, and she is now in upper White River."

Thursday, April 12, 1860 The Memphis Daily Appeal
DEPARTURES YESTERDAY – *Bracelet for the Arkansas River*
STEAMERS LEAVING THIS DAY – *South Bend for the Arkansas River*

Friday, April 13, 1860 The Memphis Daily Appeal
"DEPARTURES YESTERDAY – South Bend for the Arkansas River... one of the heaviest trips of freight of the season, and actually refused freight before her departure."

Saturday, April 14, 1860 Arkansas True Democrat
No arrivals or departures listed for the *Jennie Whipple.*

Saturday, April 14, 1860 The Memphis Daily Appeal
ARRIVALS YESTERDAY – *Lake City from the Arkansas River*
DEPARTURES YESTERDAY – *Skylark for the Arkansas River*
BOATS LEAVING TODAY – *Red Wing for Arkansas River*
"The Arkansas River is declining, with twenty-six inches in Little Rock."

Sunday, April 15, 1860 The Memphis Daily Appeal
Attempting to reach Little Rock... The Conewago, Captain E. Eugene Bowers, proceeded as far as Napoleon, and found that, owning to the low water, it was impracticable to proceed up the [Arkansas] river... so returning to Memphis.

Tuesday, April 17, 1860 The Memphis Daily Appeal
Arrivals Yesterday – Red Wing from the Arkansas River ...with 9 bales of cotton
STEAMERS LEAVING THIS DAY – *Red Wing for Arkansas River*
"The Arkansas River continues to recede slowly, and the officers of the Red Wing, the last arrival, report twenty-four inches to Pine Bluff and twenty inches to Little Rock."
"The safe of the steamer Hickman, which was lost in the late fire which consumed that boat in the Arkansas River, has been found... [empty. The suspects] ...are now in Little Rock spending the money profusely..."
"The pilots of the upper Mississippi River are on a strike for an increase of pay. They received, last season $250 per month for running a boat, and now demand $600..."

Wednesday, April 18, 1860 The Memphis Daily Appeal
"At last accounts there was but 20 inches water in the Arkansas

River to Pine Bluff, and 26 inches to Little Rock."
DEPARTED YESTERDAY – *Red Wing and J. H. Dune for Arkansas River*

Thursday, April 19, 1860 The Memphis Daily Appeal

Arrivals Yesterday – NEW *South Bend from the Arkansas River*
STEAMERS LEAVING TODAY – *New South Bend for Arkansas River*
"The pilots of the South Bend, which arrived from the Arkansas River yesterday, found 30 inches water to Pine Bluff, the channel having washed out in many places."

Friday, April 20, 1860 The Memphis Daily Appeal

Departures Yesterday – South Bend for Arkansas River

Saturday, April 21, 1860 The Memphis Daily Appeal

"The last arrival from the Arkansas River reports but 18 inches water to Little Rock."

Sunday, April 22, 1860 The Memphis Daily Appeal

"The S. H. Tucker was due from the Arkansas River yesterday, but had not arrived as a late hour last night."

Tuesday, April 24, 1860 The Memphis Daily Appeal

STEAMERS LEAVING TODAY – *Red Wing for Arkansas River*
"Since the Red Wing, which arrived yesterday, left Pine Bluff, there had been a rise of four inches in the Arkansas River at that point. Recent rains, we are pleased to learn, have been general, especially throughout Arkansas, and the streams of that State will at once become navigable again, especially the Arkansas River, which is doubtless open all this to Fort Smith."

Wednesday, April 25, 1860 The Memphis Daily Appeal

DEPARTURES YESTERDAY – *Red Wing for Arkansas River*
"The Lady Walton arrived from Pine Bluff yesterday, and reported that there had been a rise of two feet at Little Rock previous to her departure. The Arkansas is therefore open for the largest class of boats that navigate that stream... Of course the Walton brought out a light freight, as the lower Arkansas had not risen any when she left Pine Bluff."
*"The present rise in the Arkansas will release all the boats that have been detained at various points in that stream by low water. This consummation will be a relief to Captain Charlie Gray, o, the **Jennie Whipple**, whose lamentations are loudly expressed in a letter from "Poker Point" to Capt. Dill, his agent in thi*

city."

Thursday, April 26, 1860 The Memphis Daily Appeal

STEAMERS LEAVING THIS DAY — *Lady Walton for Arkansas River*
"We have nothing later from the Arkansas streams, but they are no doubt all rising, and in good navigable condition."

Friday, April 27, 1860 The Memphis Daily Appeal

"The officers of the South Bend, which boat came in from the Arkansas River yesterday, report the river open to Fort Smith."
ARRIVED YESTERDAY - *South Bend from the Arkansas River*
DEPARTURES YESTERDAY - *Lady Walton for the Arkansas River*
Cedar Rapids for the Arkansas River

Saturday, April 28, 1860 Daily Missouri Republican

STAGE CONNECTIONS.
The Missouri Stage Company is now running in close connection with the cars of this Company.
A TRI-WEEKLY line of Mail Stages from Pilot Knob, via Greenfield, Mo., to Pocahontas and Batesville, Ark., connecting at Pocahontas with a semi-weekly steamboat mail line for Powhatan, Jacksonport, Napoleon, and all points on Black and White Rivers. Connecting at Batesville with Hanger & Ayliff's Daily Mail Stage Line for Little Rock, which intersects the Mail Stage line from Des Arc to Fort Smith, at a point fifty miles south of Batesville; also, intersecting with the semi-weekly Overland Mail route from Memphis via Fort Smith to San Francisco, at a point fifteen miles north of Little Rock. At Little Rock, stages leave daily for Hot Springs and Camden, Arkansas, and for Clarksville, San Antonio, and other prominent points in Texas, thus forming an entire new line to the Southwest.
d27   JAMES A. FELPS, Superintendent.

Saturday, April 28, 1860 Daily Missouri Republican, page 5

Saturday, April 28, 1860 Arkansas True Democrat

No arrivals or departures listed for the *Jennie Whipple*.

Saturday, April 28, 1860 The Memphis Daily Appeal

DEPARTURES YESTERDAY — *Skylark for the Arkansas River*
STEAMBOATS LEAVING THIS DAY - *South Bend for Arkansas River*
"The Bracelet has quit the Arkansas trade for Louisville..."

Sunday, April 29, 1860 The Memphis Daily Appeal

DEPARTED YESTERDAY — *South Bend for Arkansas River*
"When the H. Tucker left Little Rock Wednesday, the Arkansas River had risen twelve feet."
"Shipments of cotton by river during the week.. 4,364 bales."
"We learn from Mr. Frank Pearce, that the S. H. Tucker left Napoleon Sunday, the 22 inst., for Little Rock; met Julia Ralne

*15 miles below the Rock, the Julia having been laid up at Piney; returning left Little Rock Wednesday, 25 inst., at which time the **Jennie Whipple** and Undine were hourly expected from Fort Smith for Memphis. The H. Fitzhugh, Pine Bluff and Little Rock, which had been laid up a short distance below Pine Bluff during the low water, had left Little Rock for Fort Smith. Met the Parallel, Conewago, and S. H. Slone Wednesday night. Arrived at Napoleon Friday morning, at which time the Quapaw and Cedar Rapids left for Fort Smith. The Tucker had been absent from Memphis five weeks, but in the meantime, has been doing yeoman service in the Arkansas River. She brought to this port [Memphis] yesterday 10 bales cotton and 1,180 bags cotton seed."*

"The S. H. Tucker will leave this port for Arkansas River Tuesday evening."

Wednesday, May 2, 1860 The Memphis Daily Appeal

ARRIVALS YESTERDAY – *Red Wing from the Arkansas River... including a large number of passengers and 2,000 sacks cotton seed.*

DEPARTURES YESTERDAY – *S. H. Tucker for the Arkansas River*

"We learn from Captain Morris, of the Red Wing, from Arkansas River, yesterday, that the stream was falling rapidly when the Red Wing came out – about as rapidly as it rose."

"The Quapaw, of the Arkansas River, is on her way to this port [Memphis]. Captain Thomas Bruce, who reached this city last evening, will be her future commander."

Thursday, May 3, 1860 The Memphis Daily Appeal

STEAMERS LEAVING THIS DAY – *Red Wing for Arkansas River*

"The Arkansas River is falling rapidly."

"The Conewago, Captain Bowers, will arrive from the Arkansas River today."

Saturday, May 5, 1860 Arkansas True Democrat

No arrivals or departures listed for the **Jennie Whipple**.

Saturday, May 5, 1860 The Memphis Daily Appeal

"The river [Mississippi] fell 18 inches at this point yesterday.

Sunday, May 6, 1860 The Memphis Daily Appeal

"...cotton shipments of the week... 4,088 bales."

"The Quapaw and Conewago, from the Arkansas River for Cincinnati were due yesterday, but had not arrived at a late hour last evening."

Tuesday, May 8, 1860 The Memphis Daily Appeal

ARRIVALS SINCE SATURDAY – *Skylark, South Bend, and Conewago from the Arkansas River*

STEAMERS LEAVING THIS DAY – *South Bend for the Ark river*

"The Conewago, which arrived yesterday from the Arkansas River, found two feet water from Fort Smith to Little Rock and three feet out from the Rock, and the river falling."

*"The steamboat business in the Arkansas River is in status quo again. The J. H. Dune is laying up below Van Buren, and the Parallel is in the same condition at Sitworth's. The Bela Creole, bound up, is hard aground twelve miles below Little Rock. The Quapaw was at Darnanelles on Wednesday, reshipping her up-river cargo by the W. E. Miller. The **Jennie Whipple** is somewhere up in the Indian Nation, and aground of course. The Lady Walton has been laid up at Little Rock. We are informed that Captain Watt___ interest in the Walton is offered for sale."*

"The Undine has arrived at Cincinnati, from the Arkansas River, after an absence of two months."

Wednesday, May 9, 1860 The Memphis Daily Appeal

ARRIVALS YESTERDAY – *S. H. Tucker and Quapaw from Arkansas*

DEPARTURES YESTERDAY – *South Bend for the Arkansas River*

"The S. H. Tucker will be the regular packet for the Arkansas River at 5 o'clock tomorrow afternoon."

"The Lady Walton is for sale at Little Rock."

Thursday, May 10, 1860 The Memphis Daily Appeal

STEAMERS LEAVING THIS DAY – *S. H. Tucker for Arkansas River*

"Our latest advices from the Arkansas River represent that stream is still declining, with no prospect of an immediate rise."

Friday, May 11, 1860 The Memphis Daily Appeal

DEPARTURES YESTERDAY – *S. H. Tucker for the Arkansas River... with a fine trip, with a full passenger list.*

Saturday, May 12, 1860 Arkansas True Democrat

No arrivals or departures listed for the **Jennie Whipple**.

Saturday, May 12, 1860 The Memphis Daily Appeal

*"*ARRIVALS YESTERDAY *– Red Wing from the Arkansas River...*

brought 1,508 sacks of cotton seed and 14 bales of cotton for this city. She was crowded with passengers each way during the trip."

"STEAMERS LEAVING THIS DAY – Red Wing for the Arkansas River"

"The Arkansas continues to decline, with scant three feet in the channel to Little Rock."

*"The navigation of the Arkansas River is becoming embarrassing and hazardous again. The Red Wing, which arrived yesterday. reported less than three feet water in the channel to Little Rock, and the Julia Roane laid up three miles below Swan Lake, unable to get up. the Belle Creole was in the same condition a short distance below Pine Bluff and the Muskogee was relieving her of her freight. The **Jennie Whipple** is still high and dry above Fort Smith."*

Sunday, May 13, 1860 The Memphis Daily Appeal
"Cotton by river during the week... shipment... 3,357 bales."

Tuesday, May 15, 1860 The Memphis Daily Appeal
"Either the Medora or South Bend will take the place of the Lady Walton today, and will leave for Little Rock..."

Tuesday, May 16, 1860 The Memphis Daily Appeal
ARRIVALS YESTERDAY – Arago from the Arkansas River
DEPARTURES YESTERDAY – Sky Lark for the Arkansas River
"Cincinnati... where a new Arkansas River packet shall be completed."

Wednesday, May 17, 1860 The Memphis Daily Appeal
DEPARTURES YESTERDAY – Undine for the Arkansas River
ARRIVALS – South Bend from the Arkansas River
STEAMERS LEAVING THIS DAY – South Bend for Arkansas River
"The Arkansas River continues to decline, with about 30 inches in the channel at present to Little Rock."

Thursday, May 18, 1860 The Memphis Daily Appeal
ARRIVALS YESTERDAY – S. H. Tucker from the Arkansas River
DEPARTURES YESTERDAY – South Bend for the Arkansas River
"The Arkansas River continued to decline, with about four feet water in the channel to Little Rock at the last account."
"A deck hand, from Van Buren, was lost overboard from the steamer, Delta, on a recent trip to Fort Smith."

Friday, May 19, 1860 The Memphis Daily Appeal
ARRIVALS YESTERDAY – Skylark from the Arkansas River

STEAMERS LEAVING THIS DAY – *S. H. Tucker for Arkansas River*

Saturday, May 20, 1860 The Memphis Daily Appeal

DEPARTURES – *Samuel H. Tucker for Arkansas River*

"Cotton.. shipments during the week... 3,162 bales..."

"A dense fog prevailed in this latitude Friday night, which embarrassed the movement of steamers."

Tuesday, May 22, 1860 The Memphis Daily Appeal

ARRIVALS SINCE SATURDAY – *Red Wing from the Arkansas River*

STEAMERS LEAVING TODAY – *Red Wing for Arkansas River*

"Private advices from Little Rock answers us that there has been a slight swell in the Arkansas as that point, and that the river was still rising, having risen in all about six inches."

"In view of the low water in the Arkansas River, the Arapo and Skylark have withdrawn from the trade, and will run until the opening of navigation between St. Louis and Vicksburg."

Wednesday, May 23, 1860 The Memphis Daily Appeal

DEPARTURES – *H. Fitzhugh & Red Wing for the Arkansas River*

Friday, May 25, 1860 The Memphis Daily Appeal

ARRIVALS – *South Bend from the Arkansas River*

"The Science arrived from the Arkansas River yesterday..."

DEPARTURES – *South Bend for the Arkansas River*

"Captain Houston's new Arkansas River packet will leave Louisville on Monday. She has been named the Frontier City."

Tuesday, May 29, 1860 The Memphis Daily Appeal

ARRIVALS - *S. H. Tucker from the Arkansas River*

"There has been a swell of about 10 inches in the Arkansas River at Fort Smith, which amounted to 5 inches at Little Rock, but that stream is falling again, with about 22 inches to Little Rock."

"As the S. H. Tucker, Captain Henry W. Stark, was backing out from Rob Roy landing, in the Arkansas River, Wednesday night, her stern swung round against a snag, which knocked a whole in her. She commenced filling rapidly, when the leak was observed and she was run upon a bar, when it was discovered that she had made three feet six inches water. A bulkhead was built at once, the leak stopped, and the water pumped from her hold, when she proceeded on her way after a detention of but a few hours and no other damages to the boat and no injury to cargo. In consequence

the Tucker will be detained here until Thursday, making the necessary repairs. About $250 will pay for the repairs."

"The Red Wing is a complete wreck. The S. H. Tucker finished the wrecking process, and took her engine, machinery, cabin, fixtures, etc. down to Napoleon, the Meadors having taken her Arkansas River freight. A small quantity of the freight is in the hold, including about $500 worth of white lead and a lot of flour and hay, were abandoned with the wreck, which was sold by Captain Adams to a planter near-by. Captain Morris, the commander, and some of the crew came up yesterday to this city on the S. H. Tucker. The sand had washed from the bow and stern of the Red Wing, and she had broken amidships."

"We hear from Captain Storm of the S. H. Tucker, that the steamers Little Rock, H. Fitzhugh and Pine Bluff are at Napoleon awaiting a rise and the Undine at Smith's Cut-off, the Providence at Dr. Waddell's, and the Julia Roane at Swan Lake, all detained by low water. the Leon and ___ are "crashing it" in the latitude of Fort Smith. The **Jennie Whipple** is in the mountain region."

Wednesday, May 30, 1860 The Memphis Daily Appeal

"Cincinnati... two new Arkansas River packets building there – one for Captain Pritchard and the other for Captain John D. Adams – will be ready by the middle of July."

Thursday, May 31, 1860 The Memphis Daily Appeal

STEAMERS LEAVING TODAY – S. H. Tucker for Arkansas River

Saturday, June 2, 1860 The Memphis Daily Appeal

"It may not be generally known that the most desirable route at present to Little Rock and Hot Springs is up the White River, and thence overland by stage. By this route there is but seventy-two miles staging, a saving of fifty miles over the old route. Passengers for either of these points would do well to take the Quarrier today for Aberdeen, the point of embarkation."

Sunday, June 3, 1860 The Memphis Daily Appeal

"Shipments during May... 16,253 bales..."

"Shipments during the week... 3,649 bales..."

"The Alarm, a very light boat for the upper Arkansas passed down Friday night."

"The South Bend will arrive from the Arkansas River today."

Tuesday, June 5, 1860 The Memphis Daily Appeal

STEAMERS LEAVING THIS DAY – *Lake City for the Arkansas River*
"There is no improvement in the Arkansas River, the last boats out reporting 22 inches to Little Rock."
"The South Bend has not arrived from the Arkansas River, having returned up the Arkansas River from Napoleon."

Wednesday, June 6, 1860 The Memphis Daily Appeal

*"*DEPARTURES YESTERDAY *– The Lake City left for the Arkansas River with more freight than she can take up the river."*

Thursday, June 7, 1860 The Memphis Daily Appeal

"The new Arkansas River packet Frontier City is on her way down from Pittsburg."

Friday, June 8, 1860 The Memphis Daily Appeal

"The river was declining slowly at this point yesterday."

Saturday, June 9, 1860 The Memphis Daily Appeal

BOATS LEAVING TODAY FOR THE ARKANSAS *– Rose Douglas*
"Captain Woodburn, of the Undine, is building a light draught packet for the Upper Arkansas River trade, He will name her Tahlequah..."

Sunday, June 10, 1860 The Memphis Daily Appeal

ARRIVALS YESTERDAY *– South Bend from the Arkansas River*
DEPARTURES YESTERDAY *– Frontier City, South Bend and Quapaw for the Arkansas River*
"Boatmen will be gratified to learn that there has been a material rise in the Arkansas River - say seven feet at Little Rock."

Tuesday, June 12, 1860 The Memphis Daily Appeal

ARRIVALS SINCE SATURDAY *– S. H. Tucker from the Arkansas*
"The rumor in reference to the rise of seven feet in the Arkansas River was premature. There had been heavy rains in the interior, but they had not affected the river. The S. H. Tucker, which arrived yesterday, did not encounter a swell, and will remain here until Captain Henry W. Smith hears of a rise."
"We copy the following paragraph from the Little Rock Gazette of the 9th inst.: The river continues at a very low stage, with twenty inches scant water in the channel from this point to Pine Bluff."

Wednesday, June 13, 1860 Memphis Daily Avalanche
DEPARTURES YESTERDAY – Rose Douglas for the Arkansas River

Thursday, June 14, 1860 Memphis Daily Avalanche
STEAMERS LEAVING TODAY – S. H. Tucker for the Arkansas River
"A gentleman who arrived from Little Rock overland yesterday, brings the intelligence of a rise in the Arkansas River of nine inches, with the prospect of plenty of water."
"Captain John D. Adams' new Arkansas River U.S. mail packet Sevier, will be launched at Cincinnati today."

Friday, June 15, 1860 Memphis Daily Avalanche
ARRIVALS YESTERDAY – Banjo from the Arkansas River
DEPARTURES YESTERDAY – S. H. Tucker for the Arkansas River
"Business will commence at once in the Arkansas River in right good earnest, as there is now no doubt of a considerable rise in that stream. This will be a cheering announcement to the owners of low water steamers."

Saturday, June 16, 1860 Memphis Daily Avalanche
ARRIVALS YESTERDAY – South Bend from the Arkansas River
STEAMERS LEAVING TODAY – South Bend for the Arkansas River
The reported rise in the Arkansas River was premature. The South Bend arrived from that stream yesterday, but heard nothing of a swell, although there there had been considerable rains along the shore."

Sunday, June 17, 1860 Memphis Daily Avalanche
DEPARTURES YESTERDAY – South Bend for the Arkansas River
"There has been a slight rise in the Arkansas River at last, as we learned overland from Little Rock, at which point the river had swollen ten inches."

Tuesday, June 19, 1860 Memphis Daily Avalanche
"The Arkansas.. rising, the rise in the Arkansas at Little Rock having amounted to nine inches Friday, with more water coming."

Wednesday, June 20, 1860 Memphis Daily Avalanche
STEAMERS LEAVING THIS DAY – Frontier City for Arkansas River
"Boatmen have abandoned all hope of an immediate rise in the Arkansas River. The Frontier City arrived from that stream yesterday, and her officers report that there had been a rise of two

or three inches at Little Rock, and that the water had then commenced receding again."

"The tidy little Frontier City... was brought here to be transferred to her new owners, but the contracting party failed to come to terms, and the transfer was not made."

Thursday, June 21, 1860 Memphis Daily Avalanche
"The little Frontier City departed for the Arkansas River with few passengers and little freight."

Friday, June 22, 1860 Memphis Daily Avalanche
"There has been a rise of at least two feet in the Arkansas River, as we learn by letter from Little Rock, with the prospect of plenty of water."

Saturday, June 23, 1860 Memphis Daily Avalanche
ARRIVALS YESTERDAY – Lady Walton from the Arkansas River after being absent some time.

STEAMERS LEAVING TODAY – Lady Walton for the Arkansas River
"Arkansas River is reported falling again at Little Rock, the rise having amounted to only fourteen inches in all."

"The S. H. Tucker, having reshipped her Little Rock freight at Pine Bluff, was due here last evening."

Sunday, June 24, 1860 Memphis Daily Avalanche
DEPARTURES YESTERDAY – The Lady Walton for Arkansas River

Tuesday June 26, 1860 Memphis Daily Avalanche
ARRIVALS SINCE SATURDAY – Tucker & South Bend from Ark.
STEAMERS LEAVING THIS DAY – South Bend for Arkansas River
"The Arkansas River is falling slowly, with less than three feet to Little Rock. The Freestone, with a locomotive aboard, was trying to work over the bar at Trichiett's, and the H. Fitzhugh was aground at Swan Lake. The Cedar Rapids, having broken a shaft below Pine Bluff, was towed up to the Bluff by the Lake City. The broken shaft was taken up for St. Louis yesterday by the New Falls City. The Frontier City, Pine Bluff and Leon were at Napoleon Friday, and the Frontier City left for Little Rock that evening. The officers of the South Bend report that they met the Julia Roane at Triplett's, Little Rock as Yell's, the Rose Douglas and Charm at Kimbrough's Lake City at New Gascony, and the J. J. Cadot at Notrets Place." [The Charm was owned by the

Chidester, Redside & Co. - Butterfield's sub-contractor.]
"The Tucker made a successful and worthwhile trip up the Arkansas, having gone through to the Rock on the rise with her freight. She returned to the Bluff for a cargo of corn for Little Rock, [edge of paper torn and missing] *safely, mere rubbing. Captain __ will perhaps lay up the Tucker a short time to __ visit to Louisville in the meantime."*

Saturday, June 30, 1860 Weekly Arkansas Gazette
[Although the *Jennie Whipple* was hard aground upstream in Indian Territory for 14 months, the Overland Mail continued by stagecoach as advertised below.]

Weekly Arkansas Gazette (Little Rock, Arkansas) ·June 30, 1860, Sat · Page 3

Saturday, July 7, 1860 Memphis Daily Avalanche
[Arkansas is mentioned but this issue is heavily stained and a large edge is missing on the left side.]

Sunday, July 8-10, 1860 Memphis Daily Avalanche
[No Arkansas River report, arrivals or departures.]

Wednesday, July 11, 1860 Memphis Daily Avalanche

"The Louisville Courier says the Arkansas River packet, S. H. Tucker, is now in the canal dock undergoing thorough repairs, and we lean from Captain H. W. Smith that she will be out Monday evening all right, ready for a trip to Memphis."

Thursday, July 12, 1860 Memphis Daily Avalanche
[No Arkansas River report, arrivals or departures.]

Friday, July 13, 1860 Memphis Daily Avalanche
ARRIVED YESTERDAY – *South Bend from Pine Bluff*
"The Arkansas is very low and declining, with nineteen inches water to Little Rock, and twenty seven inches to Pine Bluff."
"The South Bend went only as high up the Arkansas as Pine bluff the last trip, and reports NO water to Little Rock."

Saturday, July 14, 1860 Memphis Daily Avalanche
STEAMERS LEAVING THIS DAY – *South Bend for Arkansas River*

Sunday, July 15, 1860 Memphis Daily Avalanche
DEPARTED – *South Bend for the Arkansas River*
"The Arkansas was very low at last accounts – so low that the Indian ponies were fording it."
"The steamer Leon, on her way to Fort Smith, when about twenty miles above Little Rock, on Friday morning, the 29th June, about 5 o'clock, struck a snag, was run on a bar and sunk in about 3 feet water. She was principally loaded for Fort Smith. The Leon returned to Little Rock for repairs."

Tuesday, July 17, 1860 Memphis Daily Avalanche
ARRIVALS YESTERDAY – *Rose Douglas from the Arkansas River*
"There is about fourteen inches water in the Arkansas to Little Rock, the Rose Douglas having abandoned the river in despair of a rise. We are greatly in need of rain in this latitude."
"The Rose Douglas and S. H. Tucker have both abandoned the Arkansas River trade, the Rose having embarked in the trade hence to White River, and the Tucker going regularly into the Louisville trade..."

Wednesday, July 18, 1860 Memphis Daily Avalanche
[No Arkansas River report, arrivals or departures.]

Thursday, July 19, 1860 Memphis Daily Avalanche
"ARRIVED YESTERDAY – South Bend from the Arkansas River brought a number of passengers but no freight. Owning to the

low water, she, too, has abandoned the Arkansas River trade, and will leave for Cincinnati today. The South Bend went but thirty-five miles up the Arkansas River... to which point she found but 30 inches water..."

"The Arkansas is still declining, and the officers of the South Bend, which arrived yesterday, report but 20 inches in the channel to Pine Bluff."

Friday July 20, 1860 Memphis Daily Avalanche

"There has been no rise in the Arkansas River, and at last accounts there was but 20 inches to Pine Bluff."

Saturday July 21, 1860 Memphis Daily Avalanche

[No Arkansas River report, arrivals or departures.]

Sunday July 22, 1860 Memphis Daily Avalanche

Arrived Yesterday – Frontier City from the Arkansas River

"There has been no improvement in the Arkansas River, and we now report 15 inches in the channel to Pine Bluff."

Tuesday, July 24-25, 1860 Memphis Daily Avalanche

[No Arkansas River report, arrivals or departures.]

Thursday, July 26, 1860 Memphis Daily Avalanche

"The Arkansas River is very low, and for boats drawing more than 15 inches is unnavigable above Pine Bluff."

Friday, July 27, 1860 Memphis Daily Avalanche

"In regard to the condition of Arkansas River, we have received nothing later than that published yesterday. We would advise our steamboat friends not to move their boats in that direction, as the river is beyond all doubt unnavigable for boats drawing over twelve or fifteen inches."

Saturday, July 28, 1860 Memphis Daily Avalanche

"Boats of all draughts have withdrawn from the Arkansas River trade."

Sunday, July 29, 1860 Memphis Daily Avalanche

"Arkansas, White, Little Red and St. Francis rivers are all very low, and falling."

Wednesday August 1, 1860 Memphis Daily Avalanche

"Business at the levee was rather dull."

Thursday, August 2, 1860 Memphis Daily Avalanche

"Total receipts of cotton... past month 3,148..."

Friday, August 3, 1860 Memphis Daily Avalanche

"The weather yesterday was hot and sultry... 92^0 in the shade."

Saturday, August 4, 1860 Memphis Daily Avalanche

"The Arkansas is falling and from all appearances will soon "dry up." ...99^0 in the shade..."

Monday, August 6, 1860 Memphis Daily Avalanche

"THE ENGINEERS' ASSOCIATION - The Convention agreed yesterday upon a standard of salaries, classifying steamers into first, second and third rate basis. The standard of salaries agreed upon was as follows: for first class steamers - first engineer $175 per month; second engineers, $125. Second class boats – first engineers, $150; second engineers, $100. Third class boats – first engineers, $125; second engineer, $90."

Tuesday, August 7, 1860 Memphis Daily Avalanche

"The Mississippi... falling... 3 inches... ridiculously hot days..."

Wednesday, August 8, 1860 Memphis Daily Avalanche

"The weather yesterday was intensely hot, and business dull..."

Thursday, August 9, 1860 Memphis Daily Avalanche

"The number of boats at the wharf yesterday was few..."

Friday, August 10, 1860 Memphis Daily Avalanche

"The river decline continues... business rather dull on the Levee."

Saturday, August 11, 1860 Memphis Daily Avalanche

"The river... was about stationary..."

Monday, August 13, 1860 Memphis Daily Avalanche

"...the established rates of freight governing all steamboats New Orleans to Memphis:

Buggies	*5.00*
Carriages to dealers	*8.00*
Railroad Iron, per ton	*5.00*
Lumber per 1,000 feet	*9.00*
Dry goods, hardware, rope per 100 lbs.	*.25¢*
Pianos, each	*5.00*
Horses, Mules, Cattle, each	*5.00*

Tuesday, August 14, 1860 Memphis Daily Avalanche

"Of the up rivers... falling, some of them being lower than ever known before."

Wednesday, August 15, 1860 Memphis Daily Avalanche
[Its been weeks since any steamer departed for the Arkansas River.]

Saturday, August 18, 1860 Memphis Daily Avalanche
[This is the first steamer departed for the Arkansas in weeks.]
"For Arkansas River – The little low-water steamer, W. Henry, will start for Little Rock and Fort Smith, on the Arkansas River, this afternoon, at five o'clock. She will go through safely."

Monday, August 20, 1860 Memphis Daily Avalanche
"The steamer Choctaw... struck a rock, stove a large hole in her hull and sank in a short time... lying in a very ugly position - her bow and stern out of water... valued at $35,000..."

Tuesday, August 21, 1860 Memphis Daily Avalanche
No arrivals or departures for Arkansas River.

Wednesday, August 22, 1860 Memphis Daily Avalanche
"The Henry Fitzhugh, which has been all summer waiting for a rise in the Arkansas... the stream is lower than it has been for years, with "nary" prospect for a rise till next fall."
"The S. H. Tucker paid off her crew yesterday and will lay up here to wait for better times."

Friday, August 24, 1860 Memphis Daily Avalanche
"Captain Andy Byers arrived in the city yesterday from the steamer Quapaw, which has been laid up in the Arkansas during the summer. Up to the time he left, no rise had taken place but he received a dispatch by way of St. Louis last evening to the effect that it had rained for 36 hours at Fort Smith, and that the river was rising rapidly. A gentleman who came Overland from Van Buren, confirms the report, and says that the river had swollen one foot at that point. We have frequently reported a rise in the Arkansas upon what we considered good authority and been mistaken, but there seems to be no doubt of the truth of the present intelligence. At least, on the strength of it, the S. H. Tucker yesterday commenced taking on board the Arkansas River freight, which she has had stored here several months."

Saturday, August 25, 1860 Memphis Daily Avalanche
"We have no further news from the Arkansas, but the report

the rise coming down is very generally believed."

*"We have direct intelligence from Captain Charley Gray, the ill-fated commander of the **Jennie Whipple**. The report that he had supplanted Old Blueskin, the thief of the Busthead Indians, is not entirely without foundation. Charley has become Second Counsellor of the tribe, and rejoices in the cognomen of the Howling Panther - a distinguished appellation among the untutored sops of the forest. He has become reconciled to his fate and don't care a button whether the Arkansas rises or not."*

"Capt. Byers informs us that the planters along the Arkansas are beginning to get their cotton ready for market, and large quantities are stored along the banks awaiting shipment. There is a lot of 1,300 bales (old) at Williams; landing."

Monday, August 27, 1860 The Memphis Daily Avalanche

"The reported rise in the Arkansas needs positive confirmation, yet very little doubt of its truth is entertained by those most interested."

*"In our last compositor made us state that old Blueskin, of the Busthead Indians was the head thief of the nation, and that Capt. Charley Gray [of the **Jennie Whipple**] , it was reported, would supplant him. The assertion was a libel on old Blueskin's fair fame - he is the honored chief of his tribe."*

Tuesday, August 28, 1860 The Memphis Daily Avalanche

"The reported rise in the Arkansas lacks confirmation, yet we do not doubt the truth of the news."

Wednesday, August 29, 1860 The Memphis Daily Avalanche

"Those interested in the Arkansas River are again doomed to a disappointment. We saw a gentleman from Little Rock yesterday, who states that after rising about a foot, the river became stationary, and no doubt ere this it is declining. This will be a sad disappointment to those Cincinnati merchants who have their goods lying along the river, and who cannot get their money till they are delivered."

Thursday, August 30, 1860 The Memphis Daily Avalanche

"The river here declined three inches in 24 hours..."

Saturday, September 1, 1860 The Memphis Daily Avalanche

"There was a report in the city yesterday, that there had been an eight foot rise in Arkansas."

Sunday, September 2, 1860 The Memphis Daily Avalanche

"Arkansas River has at last risen. Our report yesterday of a rise of eight feet in that stream is verified by dispatch received yesterday. Never since the Arkansas has been navigated by steamboats has it remained as low for so long time as during the present."

"The Frontier City, as taken advantage of the recent rise in the Arkansas, and left for that stream last evening."

Wednesday, Sept. 5, 1860 The Memphis Daily Avalanche

"The Arkansas is reported to be rising rapidly at Van Buren — three feet in twenty-four hours."

Thursday, September 6, 1860 The Memphis Daily Avalanche

"A thunder storm was raging over in Arkansas in the afternoon, but the kindly drops were all poured into the swamps."

Friday, September 7-11, 1860 The Memphis Daily Avalanche

No Arkansas River report, arrivals or departures.

Wednesday, Sept. 12, 1860 The Memphis Daily Avalanche

No Arkansas River report, arrivals or departures.

"At last accounts there had been no rise in the Arkansas River."

Thursday, Sept. 13, 1860 The Memphis Daily Avalanche

No Arkansas River report, arrivals or departures.

"At Little Rock the Arkansas was rising slowly, with barely sixteen inches water in the channel. A rise of three feet is reported at Van Buren."

"The Judge Fletcher, a new boat for the New Orleans and Arkansas River trade, recently built at the cost of $23,000, may be looked for at our landing [Memphis] *in a few days, on her way to the Arkansas River."*

"The Belle Creole, now up the Arkansas River, was sold the other day for $4,520 to be delivered at Cincinnati."

Friday, September 14, 1860 The Memphis Daily Avalanche

DEPARTURES — *South Bend for the Arkansas River*

"The recent rise up the Arkansas River has created a stir among steamboatmen who affect those waters."

Saturday, Sept. 15-20 1860 The Memphis Daily Avalanche

No Arkansas River report, arrivals or departures.

Friday, September 21, 1860 The Memphis Daily Avalanche

No Arkansas River report, arrivals or departures.

"Captain Perry's new Arkansas packet is nearly completed."

Saturday, Sept. 22, 1860 The Memphis Daily Avalanche
No Arkansas River report, arrivals or departures.

Sunday, September 23, 1860 The Memphis Daily Avalanche
"By telegraph from Arkansas we learn the same old news, no water in the Arkansas. The stream is very low, and no prospects of a rise."

Tuesday, September 25, 1860 The Memphis Daily Avalanche
No Arkansas River report, arrivals or departures.

Wednesday, Sept. 26, 1860 The Memphis Daily Avalanche
No Arkansas River report, arrivals or departures.
*"Mr. James Parker, formerly of the **Jennie Whipple**, has accepted a clerkship on the Masonic Gem."*

Friday, Sept. 27 - Oct. 5, 1860 The Memphis Daily Avalanche
No Arkansas River report, arrivals or departures.

Saturday, October 6, 1860 The Memphis Daily Avalanche
No Arkansas River report, arrivals or departures.
"Telegraphic accounts from Fort Smith report, 'no rise, nor prospect.'"

Sunday, October 7-12, 1860 The Memphis Daily Avalanche
No Arkansas River report, arrivals or departures.

Friday, October 13, 1860 The Memphis Daily Avalanche
No Arkansas River report, arrivals or departures.]
"The A. H. Sevier, Captain Windsor, stuck a rock on her last trip up a little above Chiro, and sunk immediately. She left this point on Wednesday, for Cincinnati, well loaded with freight and passengers, a large portion of her cargo consisting of cotton. She was a new boat, and was built expressly for the Arkansas River, by Captain Adams of the Arkansas line, but has made several trips between this point [Memphis] and Cincinnati while waiting for a rise in the Arkansas. We understand that there are about three feet water in her hold, and presume she will be easily raised."

Tuesday, October 16-19, 1860 The Memphis Daily Avalanche
No Arkansas River report, arrivals or departures.

Saturday, October 20, 1860 The Memphis Daily Avalanche
No Arkansas River arrivals or departures.

"White and Arkansas Rivers continue at about the same stage – very low."

Sunday, Oct. 21 - Nov. 2, 1860 The Memphis Daily Avalanche
No Arkansas River report, arrivals or departures.

Tuesday, November 6, 1860 The Memphis Daily Avalanche
No Arkansas River report, arrivals or departures.

"The John Simonds came in from New Orleans... with... 1,280 bars of railroad iron for the Memphis and Little Rock railroad which she landed yesterday at the point on the Arkansas side just above this city... "

Wednesday, Nov. 7-9, 1860 The Memphis Daily Avalanche
No Arkansas River report, arrivals or departures.

Saturday, November 10, 1860 The Memphis Daily Avalanche
*"Captain Charley Gray and Dick Raymond will start today for the hunting grounds of the Busthead Indians. They fancy that a rise has taken place on the Arkansas, and are en route to bring out the famous **Jennie Whipple**. Our adventurers will please bear our kind regards to old Blueskin. The Howling Panther has a belt of wampum for the old fellow's squaw."*

Sunday, November 11, 1860 The Memphis Daily Avalanche
No Arkansas River report, arrivals or departures.

"Referring to the long awaited rise in the Mississippi: The little creek that has been running by us for some six months past, has all at once become a big river, broad and deep."

Friday, Nov. 23, 1860 The Constitutional Union (Des Arc)
"We learn from our Memphis exchanges that the Chester Ashley left that place last week, bound up the Arkansas. This is the first trip of the season, the unusual lowness of the Arkansas having rendered navigation impracticable."

NOTE: In the Butterfield advertisement below no mention is made of transportation by steamboat. The Arkansas River has been so low, for so long, there is no prospect of a rise in the near future.

Butterfield's advertisement for passengers for the Overland Mail Co. stagecoach.
Source: Memphis Daily Appeal, November 11, 1860, page 3

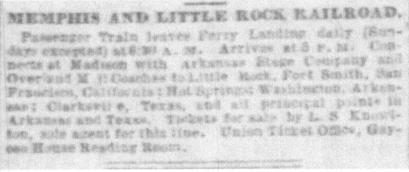

Butterfield's advertisement for passengers for the Overland Mail Co. stagecoach.
Source: Memphis Daily Appeal, November 15, 1860, page 4

Friday, Dec. 7, 1860 The Constitutional Union (Des Arc)

"We learn from the Little Rock Gazette of the 1st inst., that the Arkansas at that point had risen since Thursday morning about seven inches, and, at the time of writing (Friday morning) still swelling, with 30 inches in the channel. Old river men were looking for a rise of at least two feet from heavy rains which fell in the earlier part of the week."

1861

Tuesday, January 1, 1861 Daily Missouri Republican

*"Jennie Whipple – On or before the 1st of this month, the **Jennie Whipple**, bound up Arkansas River, ran aground out of the channel, and the water failing rapidly, left her high and dry out on the bank. When last heard from, she was reported broken in two and gone to pieces."* [This rumor of **Jennie Whipple** being "broken in two" proved to be false.]

Saturday, January 5, 1861 Arkansas True Democrat, page 2

*"The **Jennie Whipple** yet tarries among the Cherokees."*

Tuesday January 8, 1861 The Courier-Journal (Louisville)

*"The Little Rock True Democrat says that the fleet of boats which left for Fort Smith on the 20th and 22nd remain tied up above Norristown. The Belle Creole is at Bentley's bar hard and fast. Freestone at Five Islands, Lake City and Little Rock at Shoal Creek. The parallel yet remains in her summer quarters at McLeans's bottoms. The **Jennie Whipple** yet tarries among the Cherokees."* [Oklahoma Indian Territory]

Thursday, February 14, 1861 Memphis Daily Avalanche

"We saw a dispatch from Little Rock yesterday to Captain Carter of the 35th Parallel, which states that there had been a rise of two feet at Fort Smith, and heavy rains and prevailed in that section. This will be sufficient water to enable all the boats in the Arkansas to get out."

"The sternwheel steamers Quapaw and Sam Kirkman were sunk in Arkansas River last week."

"Captain Carter, of the 35th Parallel, that has been in the Arkansas River for the past eight months, unable to get either up or down, is at present in the city [Memphis]. *His report of the position of some of the craft "up that ar way," is as follows: Leon*

at Moore's; Undine, at mouth of Mulberry; Lake City and 35th Parallel, at Roseville; H Fitzhugh, at Norristown; Sam Kirkman, stuck at Swallow's; Key West, at Swallow's aground at the same place; and half a mile from water; and the Quapaw, badly sunk at Barraques's Bar, 50 miles below Little Rock."

Friday, February 15, 1861 Memphis Daily Avalanche
"A dispatch received from Fort Smith yesterday states that there has been three feet of rise in the Arkansas River at that point. There must be seven or eight feet water in the channel to Little Rock."

Wednesday, February 20, 1861 Memphis Daily Argus
*"Arkansas River is "looming" up rapidly. It rose nine feet at Fort Smith Saturday. This will enable all the boats which are not sunk in that stream to come out. Some of the boats have been stuck there a year, the **Jennie Whipple** being of them."*

Thursday, February 21, 1861 Arkansas true Democrat, page 2
*FEB. 19 ARRIVALS – **Jennie Whipple** from Webber Falls*

Monday, February 25, 1861 Memphis Daily Argus
*"Captain Charley Gray informs us that the **Jennie Whipple** will be here this evening. She has a load already, engaged to return to Fort Smith tomorrow."*

Tuesday, February 26, 1861 Memphis Daily Argus
*"The **Jennie Whipple** has been calaboosed in Little Rock, so we hear."*

Tuesday, February 26, 1861 The Memphis Daily Avalanche
*"We are sorry to learn that the **Jennie Whipple** has been calaboosed at Little Rock by some of her creditors. Captain Charley Gray has had ill luck – he and his boat [the **Jennie Whipple**] having been idle for about a year owing to circumstances that human foresight could not well guard against, and now that business has opened in earnest, he is deprived of the only means of 'paying out.' His hopeful father -in-law, Old Blueskin, cannot help him, and the Howling Panther only laments that he is not quartered again in the 'bosom of his family.'"*

Friday, March 1, 1861 Memphis Daily Argus
*"The **Jennie Whipple** left Little Rock for this port yesterday."*

Saturday, March 2, 1861 Louisville Daily Courier
*"The Memphis papers report the **Jennie Whipple** attached at*

Little Rock, and that the sheriff will sell one-half of the *Admiral* on Saturday, 9th of March, levied upon as the property of Captain A. Baird."

Monday, March 4, 1861 The Memphis Daily Avalanche

"The ***Jennie Whipple*** *is expected here daily from Little Rock, she having been released from the minions of the law.*"

Tuesday, March 5, 1861 The Memphis Daily Avalanche

"The ***Jennie Whipple*** *– the long lost* ***Jennie****, the heroine of Poker Point, the home of the Howling panther, the son-in-law of Old Blueskin, the Chief of the Busthead Indians – after a year's absence, returned to our wharf yesterday. She looks as bright and beautiful as ever. She has secured a load of Government hay, and will leave this evening for Fort Smith. Captain Charley Gray still stands on the fiery deck, and the redoubtable Sir Hayman may be found in the office.*"

Tuesday, March 5, 1861 Memphis Daily Argus

"The ***Jennie Whipple*** *made her appearance at our wharf last evening. Captain Gray has a full load and will depart at five p.m. today for Fort Smith.*"

Wednesday, March 6, 1861 the Memphis Daily Avalanche

"The ***Jennie Whipple*** *cleared for Fort Smith yesterday with 800 bales Government hay and a large trip in other respects.*"

Wednesday, March 6, 1861 Vicksburg Whig

"The Memphis Enquirer of the 26th says: The ***Jennie Whipple*** *having been detained about ten months in the Arkansas on the bars, is now on her way to Memphis.*"

Thursday, March 14, 1861 The Daily True Democrat

ARRIVALS - *March 8* ***Jennie Whipple*** *from Memphis*

DEPARTURES - *March 9* ***Jennie Whipple*** *for Fort Smith*

Friday, March 15, 1861 The Constitutional Union (Des Arc)

"WASHINGTON, MARCH 13. *– A contract has been signed for a daily mail to California, over the Central Route, and a tri-weekly by the Pony Express. Time of the former, sixteen days, and the latter, eight days.*"

Saturday, April 6, 1861 Thirty-Fifth Parallel (Ft Smith)

"*...arrived* [at Fort Smith] *...the* ***Jennie Whipple****... on the 4th each boat brought large lots of freight for our merchants.*"

March 1861
The End of Butterfield's Overland Mail

A proposal in the U. S. Senate to end Butterfield's Overland Mail southern ox bow route was considered in Congress in April of 1860. That substitute bill did not pass, according to the April 21, 1860 issue of the *Memphis Daily Appeal*:

"THE OVERLAND MAIL ROUTE THROUGH LITTLE ROCK – BILL BEFORE CONGRESS TO CHANGE IT.

Our latest advices from Washington indicate that the Senate bill for the establishment of the overland communication, between the Atlantic and Pacific States, which was reported as a substitute for the House Bill, which invites proposals for carrying the entire mail, will be passed.

The Butterfield Overland Mail contract, however, which passes through Little Rock according to the opinion of the attorney general, cannot be got rid of; but it is understood that Mr. Butterfield, who is now at Washington, is disposed to cancel the contract under certain arrangements with the Government.

The new bill provides for two routes, north and south – the latter to go by way of New Orleans and Texas, discontinuing the present one from Memphis, through Little Rock to Fort Smith. The northern route to go by way of Salt Lake.

This presents a suggestion to our citizens, whether they will be content to lay still and even without an expression on the part of our real estate owners, merchants and hotel keepers, railroad stockholders, and business men of every class, to the present and prospective advantage of the present route. Ought not our citizens generally in public meeting convened, and our city council as a municipal body, to forward at once a memorial to Congress protesting against any change in the Pacific mail arrangement, that takes us from our present advantages, of being on average only twenty days from San Francisco. – LITTLE ROCK TRUE DEMOCRAT

While the April 1860 substitute bill failed in the U. S. Senate, the following year a resolution to end the southern route passed. In the March 1, 1861 issue of Des Arc's *The Constitutional Union* reported that in Washington on February 20th, U. S. Congressman Hemphill offered the following resolution:

> "WHEREAS, *several States have withdrawn from the Union, and the lays of the United States are no longer enforced, therefore* RESOLVED, *that the Postmaster General be directed to discontinue the postal service in said Stages, and make arrangements with the governments of the same for inter-postal communication therein.*"

On March 12, 1861 the Postmaster General ordered the Overland Mail route to be discontinued (*Report of the Postmaster General*, 35th Congress, 2nd Session, Doc. No. 48). The transcontinental mail service was transferred to the Union-held Central Overland Trail, avoiding the southern states because of the impending start of Civil War. *The Report of the Postmaster General*, December 2, 1861 on page 560, reports:

> "*By the 9th section of an act of Congress approved March 2, 1861, entitled 'An act making appropriations for the service of the Post Office Department during the fiscal year ending June 30, 1862,' authority is given to the Postmaster General to discontinue the mail service on the southern overland route, (known as the 'Butterfield' route) between St. Louis and Memphis and San Francisco, and to provide for the conveyance, by the same parties, of a six-times-a-week mail by the 'central route;' that is, 'from some point on the Missouri River, connecting with the east, to Placerville, California.' In pursuance of this act, and the acceptance of its terms by the mail company, an order was mode on the 12th of March, 1861, to modify the present contract, so as to discontinue service on the southern route, and to provide for the transportation of the entire letter mail six times a week on the central route...*"

In the Friday, March 15, 1861 issue of Des Arc's *The Consti tutional Union* it reports that the mail to California, instead c being carried on the southern 'ox bow' route through Arkansas, would now be carried on the Central Route that avoided the southern Confederate states: *"WASHINGTON, MARCH 13. – A contract has been signed for a daily mail to California, over the Central Route, and a tri-weekly by the Pony Express. Time of the former, sixteen days, and the latter, eight days."*

The last eastbound mail successfully carried on the southern route departed San Francisco on March 27 and arrived at St. Louis on May 1, 1861. According to the April 5, 1861 issue of the *Sacramento Daily Union,* (*"Letter from St. Louis, From our Special Correspondent, St. Louis, March 19, 1861"*) the last westbound Overland mailbag left St. Louis on March 18, 1861. According to the April 14, 1861 issue of the *Daily Alta Californian,* this last westbound mailbag arrived in San Francisco on April 13, 1861.

The April 6, 1861 arrival at Fort Smith may have been *Jennie Whipple's* last mail and passenger run for Butterfield's Overland Mail Co. However, after being hard aground upstream on the Arkansas River in Indian Territory for almost a year, the *Jennie Whipple's* trip between Memphis and Fort Smith on April 6th may have just been for passengers and freight - so the *Whipple's* last time to actually carry an Overland mailbag may have been way back in March of 1860 before she was stuck upstream in Indian Territory.

Apparently John Butterfield's ownership and relationship with the steamboat *Jennie Whipple* ended sometime before April of 1861 after being stuck for a year upstream in Indian Territory due to low water on the Arkansas River.

The April 25, 1861 issue of the *Arkansas True Democrat* reported that on April 16th the *Jennie Whipple* was seen passing Memphis on her way to the Arkansas River with United States government arms and ammunitions of war. Her name s rubbed out.

On April 20, 1861 the Davenport, Iowa paper *Quad-City imes,* reported that the *Jennie Whipple* with Captain Gray vas about to fall into the regular trade service between Davinport, Iowa and St. Louis.

On June 8, 1861 it was reported that the *Jennie Whipple* was sold by the Marshal at St. Louis on Saturday for $1,760 to Mr. Adams, for the Dubuque trade.

April 1861
Activity of the *Jennie Whipple*
After Butterfield's Ownership

Thursday, April 11, 1861 Arkansas True Democrat

*ARRIVALS – April 7 **Jennie Whipple** from Fort Smith*

*DEPARTURES – APRIL 7 **Jennie Whipple** for parts unknown*

Friday, April 12, 1861 The Memphis Daily Avalanche

*ARRIVALS YESTERDAY – **Jennie Whipple** from Arkansas River*

*DEPARTURES YESTERDAY – **Jennie Whipple** for St. Louis*

Friday, April 12, 1861 The Courier-Journal (Louisville)

*"The Memphis Bulletin says the steamer **Jennie Whipple** has quit the Arkansas River trade, very unexpectedly, leaving a number of bills unsettled. The **Whipple** was laid up in the Arkansas River for nearly twelve months, went to Memphis a few weeks since and loaded for Fort Smith, has returned, and gone no one knows where."*

Wednesday, April 17, 1861 The Memphis Daily Avalanche

"THE TROOPS ON THE LOOKOUT FOR A STEAMBOAT – The recent news of the attack and capitulation of Fort Sumter – the proclamation of Old Abe, and the stirring news generally, has created such an excitement here as we have never before witnessed. The streets are thronged during the day by anxious citizens, and at night the tread of armed men preparing for war reverberate through the city. As we write, no less than three companies are being drilled within hearing of our office, while half a dozen others are confined to their armories engaged in the same business. Memphis will furnish at least five hundred men at a moment' notice. The union men of a month since are now the hottest of the hot in their denunciation of Lincoln, and a favorable opportunity is alone wanting to permit them to testify unmistakably their devotion to Southern rights...."

*"Later in the day, information was received that the steamer **Jennie Whipple**, with 6,000 stand of arms, was on her way down the river to supply a United States fort in Arkansas. Three*

companies of the 154th regiment were ordered out, and if the *Jennie* had come along, the muskets said to be on board her would have been appropriated, very properly, to our use. Up to a late hour last night she had not arrived, but a steady watch is being kept up for her. We want arms, and must have them."

Thursday April 18, 1861 Memphis Weekly Bulletin

"The Jennie Whipple was yesterday reported, by the Robert Campbell, as laid up at Bloody Island, opposite St. Louis..."

Saturday, April 20, 1861 Quad-City Times (Davenport, Iowa)

ARRIVED - *Jennie Whipple*, Capt. Gray, from St. Louis
DEPARTED – *Jennie Whipple*, Capt. Gray, to Lyons
"The Jennie Whipple, Captain Gray, is about to fall into the trade between this point [Davenport, Iowa] and St. Louis. The Jennie is a very light draught, and can make regular trips during low water. She leaves for St. Louis today. Grant Watson, agent."

Thursday, April 25, 1861 Arkansas True Democrat

"TELEGRAPHIC – Des Arc, April 16. TO GOV. RECTOR: It is reported here by the officers of the Golden State, just from Memphis, that the Jennie Whipple passed Memphis on her way to the Arkansas River with United States government arms and ammunitions of war. Her name is rubbed out."

Saturday, April 27, 1861 Quad-City Times (Davenport, Iowa)

ARRIVED - *Jennie Whipple*, Capt. Gray, from St. Louis
"The Jennie Whipple will depart for St. Louis this morning."

Monday, May 6, 1861 Daily Missouri Republican (St. Louis)

United States of America
Eastern District of Missouri
United States Marshal's Office, May 3, 1861
Proclamation in Admiralty –
I hereby give notice that, by virtue of a warrant of arrest and monition, issued out of the office of the Clerk of the United States District Court, in and for the Eastern District of Missouri, and to me directed, in the following cause, to wit: Isaac C. Sitton, libellant, against the steamboat Jennie Whipple, her engines, machinery, tackle, apparel and furniture, in a cause for marine wages, for a demand of one hundred and fifty six 50/100

*dollars, I did, on the 3rd day of May, A.D. 1861, at the port of St. Louis, in said, Eastern District of Missouri, arrest and take in my possession, for safe custody, and do now detain, the said steamboat **Jennie Whipple**, her engines, machinery, tackle, apparel and furniture. And I hereby also give public notice, that the time assigned for the return of said warrant is the 1st MONDAY to wit, the 3rd day, of the month of June, 1861, and I hereby admonish and summon all persons claiming any interest in the said steamboat **Jennie Whipple**, her engines, & c., or knowing or having anything to say, why the same should not be condemned and sold to answer the demand of said libellant, that they be and appear before the said District Court for the Eastern District of Missouri, at a special return term thereof, to be begun and holden at said District Court Room, in the United States Custom House, in said District, on the last named day, to wit: the 3rd day of June, 1861, when and where said case will be heard, then and there to interpose their claims, and answer said libel, and make their allegations in that behalf.*

D. A. Rawlings,
United States Marshal in and for said Eastern District

May 22, 1861 Daily Missouri Republican (St. Louis)

United States of America
Eastern District of Missouri
United States Marshal's Sale

*In the District Court of said United States, in an for said district. In the case number 864, of Isaac C. Setton, libellant, against the steamboat **Jennie Whipple**, her engines, machinery, tackle, apparel and furniture; whereas, by virtue of a writ and order of venditioni exponas, issued from the office of the Clerk of the United States District Court for the Eastern District of Missouri, dated (20th) twentieth day of May, A.D. 1861, I am directed, as Marshal of the United States, for the Eastern District of Missouri, to expose for sale the sail steamboat **Jennie Whipple**, with her engines, machinery, tackle, apparel and furniture, on ten days public notice of the time, place and terms of sale given by advertisement in three newspapers published in the city of St. Louis, Mo., and also by hand bills to be posted in* *six different places in said city of St. Louis, in said Eastern District.*

*Now, therefore, in obedience to said order of the District Court for the Eastern District of Missouri, dated as aforesaid, I hereby give public notice that I will, on SATURDAY, THE FIRST DAY OF JUNE, 1861, between the hours of nine o'clock in the forenoon and five o'clock in the aforenoon of said day, at public sale, and by public auction, sell to the highest bidder, the steamboat **Jennie Whipple**, with her engines, machinery, tackle, apparel and furniture, on the following terms...*

The sale will therefore take place on Saturday, the first day of June, 1861, at or near the foot of Plum Street.

D. A. Rawlings, U.S. Marshal, Eastern District of Missouri St. Louis, Mo., May 21st, 1861

Sunday, June 2, 1861 Daily Missouri Republican (St. Louis)
*"The **Jennie Whipple** was yesterday sold by the U.S. Marshal at this port. She brought $1,760 and was purchased, we learned, for Captain White."*

Wednesday, June 5, 1861, Daily Missouri Republican
*"Isaac C. Sitton, & c., vs. steamboat **Jennie Whipple** & c.; warrant of arrest in case No. 864 returned and filed. Proclamations made and defaults entered."*

Saturday, June 8, 1861 The Memphis Daily Avalanche
*"The Shreveport and **Jennie Whipple** were sold by the Marshal at St. Louis on Saturday; the former at $3,750, and the latter for $1,760. The first was bought in for Captain Northern, no doubt, and the buyer of the latter was for the Mesrs. Adams, for the Dubuqne trade."*

Monday, July 15, 1861 Daily Missouri Republican (St. Louis)
*"The **Jennie Whipple** has come to the wharf foot of Walnut Street. For what purpose we are not aware."*

Tuesday, July 16, 1861 Daily Missouri Republican (St. Louis)
*"The steamer J. Mussleman has come to the landing and taken her place beside the **Jennie Whipple**, at the foot of Walnut Street. Both are light draught boats, and are waiting for low water in some of the upper rivers."*

Wednesday, July 17, 1861 Quad-City Times (Davenport)

"Jennie Whipple — We understand that the Jennie Whipple is about to fall into the trade between this point [Davenport] and Keokuk, running on alternate days with the Kate Cassel. Both of these boats are very light draught, and probably will make regular trips during the low water season."

Thursday, July 18, 1861 Daily Courier-Journal (Louisville)

"The Jennie Whipple is at the St. Louis wharf repairing, and is expected to go North in a few days."

Tuesday, July 23, 1861 Daily Missouri Republican (St. Louis)

"The steamer Jennie Whipple, Captain David White, is receiving for St. Paul and way points on the Upper Mississippi, and will have this evening, at 4 o'clock. The Jennie Whipple has been purchased by Captain White for an Upper Mississippi packet."

Wednesday, July 24, 1861 Daily Missouri Republican

"THE STEAMER JENNIE WHIPPLE — Any thing like a steamboat enterprise, in these days, is a novelty, and we have one to record. Captain David White and Ben Campbell lately purchased the light draught steamer Jennie Whipple, and have docked her, painted her, and thoroughly fitted her up for business. This sort of business, in these times, is enough to excite general curiosity, and so it has, among steamboatmen. The boat was purchased by the before mentioned gentlemen, and put in order for a regular mail packet, to run between Rock Island and Keokuk. She is admirably adapted for this purpose — being of very light draught, and having a roomy and comfortable cabin, well furnished for the accommodation of passengers. — The Jennie Whipple will be able to run in all sorts of water, from a heavy dew to a flood... a fast steamboat of her power and capacity. We wish the new owners all the success which their enterprise deserves..."

Thursday, August 8, 1861 Muscatine Evening Journal (Iowa

"Mr. Bell informs us that the 7th Regiment, Col. Lauman, embarked for St. Louis, Tuesday morning on the steamer Jennie Whipple and two barges."

Friday, August 9, 1861 Daily Missouri Republican (St. Louis

"The steamer Jennie Whipple arrived from Burlington yesterday with the seventh Iowa Regiment on board of the boat an

barges. They numbered about one thousand men."

Friday, August 9, 1861 The St. Louis Democrat

*"The 7th Regiment of Iowa Volunteers arrived at the Arsenal at 2 o'clock yesterday morning on the steamer **Jennie Whipple**, Captain White, from Burlington, Iowa. The troops remained on board till sunrise, and then disembarked, and took quarters on the western slope of the Arsenal grounds..."*

Friday, August 16, 1861 Muscatine Weekly Journal (Iowa)

*"Arrival of the Seventh Iowa Regiment — Three More Iowa Regiments Expected.— The Seventh Regiment of Iowa Volunteers arrived at the Arsenal at two o'clock yesterday morning, on the steamer **Jennie Whipple**, Captain White, from Burlington, Iowa. The troops remained on board till sunrise, and then disembarked, and took quarters on the western slope of the Arsenal grounds..."*

Davenport, Keokuk & St. Louis.

THE LIGHT DRAUGHT PACKET

JENNIE WHIPPLE,

DAVID WHITE,.....................Master,
JOHN LOWRIE,.....................Clerk,

WILL MAKE REGULAR TRI WEEKLY trips between Davenport and Montrose, leaving this point

Tuesdays, Thursdays and Saturdays,

making direct connections with the Keokuk Packets for St. Louis. Passengers will arrive in St. Louis in 36 hours.

For further particulars enquire of
ag24-dtf]   F. W. WATSON, Agent.

Source: Quad City Times, Davenport, Aug. 26-27, 1861

Wed., August 28, 1861 Muscatine Evening Journal (Iowa)

"500 Troops from Camp McClellan - Yesterday afternoon,

the steamer **Jennie Whipple** arrived from Davenport with 500 troops which has been ordered suddenly, from Camp McClellan to reinforce Col. Moore, who is threatened by the secessionists of North Eastern Missouri...."

Friday, August 30, 1861 Muscatine Weekly Journal (Iowa)

*"Capt. Mahanna, of Co. B, Iowa City, arrived on the **Jennie Whipple**, last night with about twenty of his men. The remainder were expected on the Fred Lorenz in time to take the train this morning for their homes. This company suffered next to company C in the battle. One was killed and twenty nine wounded, three of whom have since died. Fourteen of the wounded are now with the company. The remainder were left at Springfield."*

Saturday, Aug. 31, 1861 Muscatine Evening Journal

*"Troops Returning.— The **Jennie Whipple** passed up last night with the 500 troops taken from Davenport to Keokuk by here on Tuesday last. It appears to us the extreme of folly to take these men back to Davenport. Keokuk is the point of danger in our State, and is the place where the main body of our troops should rendezvous..."*

Monday, Sept. 2, 1861 The Morning Democrat (Davenport)

*"River News.— ...**Jennie Whipple**... bringing five hundred troops she took down last week. She brought a barge with her, on which were a portion of the soldiers, to Burlington, but there she took them on board the boat, of course, crowding it, filling the state rooms and cabins."*

Friday, Sept. 13, 1861 Muscatine Evening Journal (Iowa)

*"Maj. Leffingwell, of the First Cavalry, was a passenger on the **Jennie Whipple** yesterday afternoon. He was on his return to Burlington from Davenport, where he had been on business with Gov. Kirkwood."*

Saturday, Sept. 14, 1861 The Rock Island Argus (Illinois)

*"Gone to Burlington.— Captain Ankeny's company of cavalry from Clinton County, which has been encamped here since last Saturday, left here yesterday on the **Jennie Whipple** for Burlington, where they go to join Col. Warren's regiment, which with this addition, will be completed. — Dav. Gaz. 13th."*

Friday, September 20, 1861 Muscatine Weekly Journal (Iowa

"*Departure of our Volunteers* – *Companies A and B of the 11th Iowa Regiment, from this city, departed on the steamer* **Jennie Whipple**, *Wednesday noon, for the rendezvous at Davenport. Forming at their respective halls, the two companies marched up Second Street as far as the Eichelberger House then they countermarched and returning repaired to the boat, [**Jennie Whipple**] at the wharf. As they passed through the crowded thoroughfares, the enthusiasm was intense. The streets were crowded with the friends of the boys, who, as they marched along, would press the hands of the patriotic volunteers and bid them God speed and the cause they were engaged to defend. At the boat the scene was truly impressive. Fathers, mothers, sisters, and sweethearts crowded around the little band to bid adieu to their sons, brothers, and lovers, some of them perhaps for the last time. As the boat [**Jennie Whipple**] was ready to move, Harry O'Conner came forward on the hurricane deck and made a few remarks to the immense assemblage... Men and boys tossed their hats into the air, and shouted with all their might; women waved their bonnets and handkerchiefs, and the rousing cheers testified how dearly the cause of the Union was loved in our city. The bells sounded, the wheels moved and two hundred more of Muscatine's best sons left their homes to battle for their country.*"

Wednesday, Sept. 25, 1861, Chicago Tribune

"*The 8th Iowa Regiment, Lieut. Col. Geddes, left Davenport yesterday morning for St. Louis in the steamer* **Jennie Whipple**, *with two barges in tow, for St. Louis.*"

Wednesday, Sept. 25, 1861, Quad City Times (Davenport)

"*... At about nine o'clock the entire Regiment had embarked upon the steamer* **Jennie Whipple** *and were on their way to St. Louis. The Regiment was without arms, and in many instances without comfortable clothing. We trust that both will be supplied in abundance upon arrival at their destination... We cannot say that we were at all proud of their appearance... to send them away thus ragged, is a blot upon our State – a shame to the government.*"

Wed., Sept. 25, 1861, The Morning Democrat (Davenport)

*"Preparations were made for starting the regiment early in the morning on the steamer **Jennie Whipple**. Quartermaster Price drew rations for two regiment three days, and all the volunteers leaving our camp were supplied with blankets...*

*Early in the morning the 8th regiment marched from Camp to the wharf, where the **Jennie Whipple** was lying. By means of two large barges, the steamer was enabled to take the whole regiment, although it crowded the transport to capacity of the vessels to their utmost extent. At 9 o'clock they left our wharf, where a large crowd of citizens had assembled, and soldiers and citizens cheered enthusiastically. The regiment was in command of Major Ferguson, as the Lt. Colonel is absent..."*

Sat., Sept. 28, 1861, The Morning Democrat (Davenport)

*"THE EIGHTH REGIMENT.— This regiment, temporarily under the command of Major Ferguson of Marion County, arrived here yesterday noon, on the **Jennie Whipple**, on their way from Davenport to St. Louis. It being impossible to accommodate so many on the boat, they were delayed here some time, while the men prepared their dinner on the wharf. Their culinary operations attracted a large crowd to the landing, to the most of whom this wholesale way of cooking for nine or ten hundred men was quite a novelty. No sooner had the boat touched the landing, than the cooks sprang out, and, starting their fires, brought forth their provisions, consisting of beef, bread, coffee, beans, & c. They proceeded to their work quietly and without confusion, each appearing to know exactly what to do, and in an exceedingly short time the huge pile of raw material was converted into a very palatable, if not a tempting dinner, which the boys appeared to enjoy highly.*

The men composing this regiment are all young and athletic. We predict that we shall hear a good account of the Eighth in Missouri before the war is closed. — Muscadine Journal."

Wed., October 2, 1861 Daily Missouri Republican (St. Louis

*"The steamer **Jennie Whipple**, Captain White, left [Burlington] today for St. Louis with 600 men and horses of Col. Warren's Cavalry Regiment."*

Thursday, Oct. 10, 1861 The Iowa Transcript (Toledo, Iowa)

*"The Iowa 8th left on the steamer **Jennie Whipple** some hours, before us, but we passed them the first evening and arrived at St. Louis in advance... the inhabitants on both sides of the river particularly the ladies showed their good feelings towards us by waving flags, handkerchiefs, hats, bonnets and aprons, which the boys reciprocated by many a rousing cheer..."*

Advertisement for the *Jennie Whipple,* which was no longer owned by John Butterfield. *Quad-City Times, Davenport, Iowa,* Aug. 31, Sept. 3-4, 6-7, 10-13, 18-21, 23-26, 28, 30, Oct. 1-2, 4, 7-10, 12, 14-18, 19-25, 26, 28-31, Nov. 2, 4, 9, 11-16, 18-19, 21-22, 1861

Saturday, Oct. 19, 1861 Muscatine Evening Journal (Iowa)

*"About thirty of them, including the Captain and two Lieutenants, were taken to Davenport on the **Jennie Whipple**, last Thursday..."*

Thursday, Oct. 24, 1861 Muscatine Evening Journal (Iowa)

*"The **Jennie Whipple** went up yesterday evening with another full company from Charaiton, Lucas County. This company is also destined for the 13th regiment and is under the command of Captain Baker, a tried and experienced officer."*

Friday, Oct. 25, 1861 Muscatine Weekly Journal (Iowa)

*"For the Fifteenth,– Captain Kettler's company from Lyons passed down on the **Jennie Whipple** Saturday afternoon, bound for Keokuk, where they design entering the 15th regiment now organizing at that place."*

Tuesday, Oct. 29, 1861 Quad City Times (Davenport, Iowa)

*"Excursion – A deputation from Muscatine arrives here today by the **Jennie Whipple** to visit the soldiers. They bring along an elegant dinner for the boys from that county, we are told. They will have a good time, undoubtedly."*

Wednesday, Oct. 30, 1861 Quad City Times (Davenport)

*"The **Jennie Whipple**, Captain White and Clerk Lowrie, will depart for Montrose this morning at 10 o'clock. Her passenger accommodations are of the first order, and everything pertaining to the comfort and safety of the traveller is connected with this packet. Of Captain White, it would be superfluous to say anything, as his attentive services as a S. B. C. have won him the respect and confidence of all. Try the **Jennie**."*

Friday, November 1, 1861 Muscatine Weekly Journal (Iowa)

*"A company from Des Moines County, under Captain Leonard, passed up to Davenport on the **Jennie Whipple**, Tuesday morning, for Camp McClellan, en route for Fort Randall."*

Monday, Nov. 18, 1861 The Morning Democrat (Davenport)

*"Departure of the 11th Regiment.– About 10 o'clock on Saturday, the 11th regiment, Col. Hare, came down from Camp McClellan to embark on the **Jennie Whipple** for Benton Barracks, near St. Louis. As the boat was not ready to start, the men stacked arms, and lounged around on the levee, near the positions assigned their several companies. The boat did not get off until about 1 o'clock. The means of transportation were the same as used on similar occasions. The **Jennie** had in tow one covered barge and an open flatboat. The accommodations were wholl*

inadequate to the number of men, considering the severity of the weather, and they they were yet unprovided with overcoats. As there were other steamboats to be had, there was no excuse for crowding the men into such close and uncomfortable quarters. We regard it as but poor economy at best, as the number of the sick list will attest hereafter."

Wednesday, Nov. 20, 1861 Quad City Times (Davenport)

*"Row in the 11th Regiment.— From Captain David, of the steamer Pomeroy, which arrived yesterday, we learn that the soldiers got tired of their close quarters on board of the **Jennie Whipple** and when they arrived at Keokuk a number of them flatly refused to go any further under such arrangements. Three companies bolted entirely and went aboard the Messenger, which was going down. It is said there was no small amount of swearing done about being shipped off in the way they left here. Sailing down the river in a flat boat at this time of year, without overcoats, may be a pleasant way of traveling, but we don't so consider it, and we should judge that the boys of the 11th, who tried it, failed to discover anything rational about such management."*

Friday, Nov. 22, 1861 Muscatine Weekly Journal (Iowa)

*"Our Army Correspondence – On Board the **Jennie Whipple**, St. Louis, Nov. 19.– Dear Journal: – Saturday morning at 4 o'clock the reveille was beat and the men were ordered to get breakfast, pack up, and be ready to march to the landing by 8 o'clock. Active preparations commenced immediately, and by the hour appointed the 11th bid adieu to Camp McClellan, and passed on our way to 'Dixie Land.'*

*Our first twenty-four hours on the boat [**Jennie Whipple**] was anything but pleasant, and the next day and night was not half as comfortable as it should have been if the government agent had not wanted to be saving at our expense and his profit.*

We were stowed in the boat and barges so close that the men could not lay down and straighten themselves, and still worse than all, the horses were put inside (when the men should have had all the room) and kept there until Sunday.

When we got to Keokuk (Sunday) the captain took on some hay and scattered over the floor of the boat and barges, which added very much to the comfort of those who tried to sleep. We laid at Keokuk long enough to cook dinner and attend church.

... We landed at St. Louis this evening about 5 o'clock, and the regiment immediately disembarked and went out to the Barracks. A heavy shower of rain was falling as they marched up through the city, yet the boys were jolly and went along singing the 'Happy Land of Cannan.' The boys will not be discouraged, but will be happy.

Henry Madden and myself will stay on the boat tonight [**Jennie Whipple**] to guard our company's baggage until it can be taken to camp.

One of the new gun boats went around the landing this evening. They are small, built with screw propellers and all the machinery is in the bottom, so as to be out of the way of shot, and is cased with rail-road iron. They run fast and are easily managed, and I think they will prove to be quite efficient 'teasers' among the rebels.

It is after ten and I must retire for the night. In a few days, when I have looked around I will write again and give our friends what particulars I can."

Thursday, Nov. 28, 1861 Muscatine Evening Journal (Iowa)

"THE FOURTEENTH — Three companies D, F, and I, of the 14th Regiment passed down on the **Jennie Whipple** last evening about 8 o'clock. Col. Shaw in command. The remainder of the regiment will leave Camp McClellan this morning for St. Louis by rail. This is right. Three companies can be comfortably accommodated on board the **Jennie**, but a regiment could not be transported to St. Louis by the river at this season of the year without a great deal of suffering among the men."

Thursday, Dec. 5, 1861 The Weekly times (Dubuque, Iowa)

"FOURTEENTH REGIMENT.— Three companies of this regiment left yesterday on the steamer **Jennie Whipple** for St. Louis... The regiment marched into the city about two o'clock in the afternoon, and after a little delay on the levee they went aboard the **Jennie**, and soon got underway. — Davenport Gazette, 28th inst."

Thursday, Dec. 12, 1861 The Memphis Daily Avalanche

*"The St. Louis Republican, of Saturday last says: ... The **Jennie Whipple** arrived from the Upper Mississippi without freight. She started up the Mississippi some days ago, and found the ice too heavy to proceed. The therefore stored her freight and returned."*

Wednesday, Dec. 25, 1861 The Memphis Daily Avalanche

*"The United States government has a line of packets running between this point and Cairo. The boats are the **Jennie Whipple** and D. A. January."*

Summer 1861

In the late summer of 1861, the **Jennie Whipple** began to be used frequently for the transportation of Union troops. The *Memphis Daily Avalanche* reports on December 25th that the *"United States government has a line of packet running between this point and Cairo. The boats are the **Jennie Whipple**, and..."*

However, before and after this date, the **Jennie Whipple** continued to advertise for passengers and freight. The Union government requisitioned into service the **Jennie Whipple** as the newspaper implies. However, General Grant permitted the **Jennie Whipple** to also continue its normal route.

William J. Peterson, in his book, *Steamboating on the Upper Mississippi*, writes:

*"Upper Mississippi steamboats did heroic work during the Civil War. Many of the boats were requisitioned into service by the government In this group were such well known steamboats as the Kate Cassel, the **Jennie Whipple**, and the Ad Hine. In this way transportation was often crippled – at least temporarily. There was general rejoicing when General Grant permitted the **Jennie Whipple** to continue plying between Fort Madison and Rock Island."*

1862

Wednesday, January 22, 1862 The Memphis Daily Avalanche

*"The St. Louis News, of the 9th, reports: ...A letter from the officers of the **Jennie Whipple** at Quincy, dated 6th, says that navigation is suspended for the present, both on account of the low water and ice."*

Monday, March 24, 1862 Tri-Weekly Missouri Democrat (St. L)

*"The **Jennie Whipple**, having come off the rocks, is now at the upper end of the wharf, where her repairs and improvements will be completed, after which there will be no prettier, as there are few faster boats than the **Jennie**."*

Monday, March 31, 1982 Daily Missouri Democrat (St. L.)

*"The **Jennie Whipple** has been carefully attended to. She is all right. She is neat, comfortable and attractive. She is unusually attractive. The **Jennie Whipple** will leave, we understand, tomorrow evening for all points to Debuque in command of Charles Morrison. Captain Morrison is one of the most popular commanders every on the upper rivers. Remember the **Jennie Whipple**."*

Tues, April 1, 1982 The Daily Missouri Democrat (St. Louis)

*"FOR DUBUQUE – Captain Charles Morrison, as we before stated, has assumed command of the rapid and elegant steamer **Jennie Whipple**. The **Jennie** has been greatly improved, is now loading, and will cast loose for the upper Mississippi this afternoon. The well known Captain Parkhurst officiates at the desk."*

Friday, May 2, 1862 Quad City Times (Davenport, Iowa)

*"FUNERAL OF JOHN S. CHRISTIAN.– The corpse of John S. Christian, who was wounded at Pittsburg, and died at Keokuk a few days since, came up yesterday morning on the **Jennie Whipple**..."*

Friday, May 2, 1862 The Morning Democrat (Davenport, IA)

*"RETURNED.– Lieut. Benton, of Co. B 8th regiment, arrived in town yesterday morning on the **Jennie Whipple**. Lieut. B. had been sick two weeks before the battle of Shiloh, and at that time was unable to leave his bed. During the first day's fight, the enemy got so near to where he was confined, that some of his men insisted on removing him, notwithstanding his earnest remonstrance. They took him to the landing, but were not permitted to take him on a steamboat, as he was not wounded, and he was left on the landing, where he lay from Sunday till Tuesday morning, without anything to eat, and exposed to the storms at night during the battle. He was wet through, and in that condition was taken back to the hospital, suffering from typhoid fever. H*

was subsequently brought to St. Louis and taken to a hospital, whence Mrs. Dougherty, a benevolent lady of that city, had him removed to a private house, where he was kindly cared for. Lieut. Benton's sister went to St. Louis and brought him to this city, whence he started for his home, in Blue Grass, yesterday. We hope for his early restoration to health under the genial skies of Iowa."

Saturday, May 3, 1862 Burlington Weekly Hawk-Eye (Iowa)

*"List of sick and wounded on board the steamer **Jennie Whipple** from the Hospitals at Keokuk and St. Louis:*

John Iback, Co. K, 5th Iowa	*George Sullers, Co. E, 5th Iowa*
N. H. Smith, Co. I, 5th Iowa	*H. C. Rouse, Co. C, 10th Iowa*
N. Tilliam, Co. C, 10th Iowa	*B. Dunbar, Co. C, 10th Iowa*
G. Guford, Co. C, 10th Iowa	*__ Cora, Co. A, 10th Iowa*
C. G. Bailey, Co A, 10th Iowa	*__ Clemers, Co. A, 5th Iowa*
Benton Ayres, Co. A, 5th Iowa	*C. J. Bales, Co. K, 5th Iowa*
C. L. Holcomb, Co. F, 10th Iowa	*S. Shockley, Co. B, 10th Iowa*
J. Ficer, Co. I, 10th Iowa	*__ Haller, Co. F, 5th Iowa*
__ Bassfield, Co. F, 2nd Iowa Cav.	*E. Estebrook, Co. F, 2nd Iowa Cav.*

Also Lieut. M. P. Benton, Co. F, 8th Iowa, wife in attendance
Capt. J. B. Hawley, Co. H. 45th Illinois, wife in attendance
Lieut. G. F. Vail, Co. K, 16th Wisconsin, brother in attendance;
also corpse of private Andrew Pye, 23d Missouri.

Monday, May 12, 1862 Muscatine Evening Journal (Iowa)

*"We learn that Ben Campbell has purchased the interest of Captain White in the **Jennie Whipple**."*

Thursday, May 15, 1862 Muscatine Evening Journal (Iowa)

*"A TRIP. – We wish it distinctly understood that we individually took a trip down the river last week, on a steamboat, and were never better pleased, nor had better accommodations or fared so well on any boat. It is needless to say that the above was owing to the fact that we went on the fine, fast running little packet **Jennie Whipple**, which is a decided favorite all along the river..."*

Friday, May 30, 1862 Muscatine Evening Journal (Iowa)

*"The mail packet **Jennie Whipple** arrived from above with a fair trip of freight and passengers. She received nine hundred sacks of grain at this place, besides a large number of passengers."*

[**NOTE:** The news clipping below mentions the use of a "yawl." A yawl, sometimes called a 'jolly boat,' is a small row boat used mainly to ferry personnel to and from the ship, or for other small scale activities.

Friday, May 30, 1862 Muscatine Weekly Journal (Iowa)

*"FELL OVERBOARD, Saturday evening last, four miles below Burlington, John McGraw, deck hand on board the steamer **Jennie Whipple**, and was drowned. The deceased was from Davenport, and leaves a wife and children. The yawl was sent out and everything done to save him, but he sunk in a few moments."*

Saturday, May 31, 1862 Muscatine Evening Journal (Iowa)

*"A FINE PAINTING.— Mr. George W. Girdon, the gentlemanly clerk of the steamer **Jennie Whipple** showed us yesterday one of the finest specimen of oil painting that we ever remember seeing. It is a scene in autumn, and represents a female seated near a decayed tree viewing the surrounding landscape. The painting was executed by Mr. Girdon, the design being entirely original, and reflects much credit on the skill and good taste of the artist."*

Thursday, June 5, 1862 The Morning Democrat (Davenport)

*"Report of Mr. L. C. Burwell – as a member of the Sanitary Committee... I render.. a report of my labors... After the patients had all been conveyed to the hospital, the officers commenced giving furloughs, and about thirty of our men having thus been released from the hospital, were put on board the steamer **Jennie Whipple** early next morning for up the river. By request I wen aboard and dressed all their wounds by the time the boat arrivec at Burlington...*

Friday, June 20, 1862 Muscatine Weekly Journal (Iowa)

*"A TRIP TO DAVENPORT. – We made one of a small party on th **Jennie Whipple** night before last, on an excursion to Davenport and Rock Island. To say that the trip was pleasant woul not express half enough – it was delightful. The night was beau*

tiful, and comfortably established on the hurricane deck, our little company whiled away the time in songs, music and story telling, until the increasing lights in the Eastern horizon, and the steeples and chimneys rising above the distant point, told us that morning and the twin cities were close at hand.

Landing first at Rock Island, we did the town, and then crossed over into Davenport. By this time the sun was shining fiercely, and together with the dusty streets of the bridge city, that luminary like to have 'did' us. Re-embarking about 11 o'clock, we started for home and reached our destination a few hours later after one of the most agreeable jaunts on record.

Our acknowledgments are due Captain Charley Morrison and Mr. Girdon, clerk for the **Jennie**, for courtesies, which we hope at some time to be able to return in full. The **Jennie** is one of the best little boats that plows on the Upper Mississippi, and her officers are thorough-bred and accomplished gentlemen. – Daily, 14th.

Wednesday, June 21, 1862 Muscatine Evening Journal (Iowa)

"THAT EXCURSION. – Our readers will please bear in mind that Captain Charley Morrison and Clerk George W. Girdon, also Pilots Bill Owens and Charles Wilds, and in fact all the crew of the decidedly popular mail and express steamer **Jennie Whipple** are going to considerable pains and expense, in order to give the 'gay and festive' youths of this city a 'turn' on their fine boat. It is hoped that all who have a curiosity to visit Nauvoo, the ancient Capitol of Mormonism, will be on hand. – It is not exactly determined yet about what time the excursion will take place, but will not be longer than two weeks. Captain Morrison has placed the fare extremely low, being only $2.50 per couple."

[NOTE: In late 1839, arriving Mormons bought the small town of Commerce, in Hancock County, Illinois. In April, 1840 it was renamed "Nauvoo" (a Hebrew word meaning 'beautiful place' or 'city beautiful') by Joseph Smith, the latter day prophet of the Latter Day Saint movement.]

Wed., June 25, 1862 The Morning Democrat (Davenport)

"GONE. – Lt. Col. Hall left yesterday on the **Jennie Whipple**, bound for the army. Col. H. is still weak, and one would think *hardly able to do military duty, but he preferred being at his post. Governor Kirkwood went down the river on the same boat."*

Wednesday, June 25, 1862 Muscatine Evening Journal (Iowa)

*"THAT EXCURSION. — It is proposed that the pleasure trip to Nauvoo on the **Jennie Whipple** be postponed till the next moon. This will be much more applicable, we think, to the larger portion of the participants. These excursions don't come every day, and we might as well have a big time while we are about it as a small one."*

Thursday, July 10, 1862 Muscatine Evening Journal (Iowa)

*"The fleet little steamer **Jennie Whipple**, with her popular commander, Captain Charley S. Morrison, came up a 'kiting' last evening, bound for Rock Island and Davenport. She returns this morning for Burlington and Fort Madison. Travelers will find her an A No. 1 boat to travel on."*

Saturday, July 12, 1862 Muscatine Evening Journal (Iowa)

*"The famous **Jennie Whipple** came at about her usual hour, and after delivering and receiving the mail, she 'skedaddled' for Rock Island."*

Friday, Aug. 15, 1862 Muscatine Evening Journal (Iowa)

*"PLEASURE EXCURSION. — A number of young gentlemen and ladies of our city had an excursion on the steamer **Jennie Whipple** yesterday. They had a decidedly gay time, enjoying themselves as all guest of Captian Morrison do. They return thanks to Mr Girdon for the amusement he furnished them, and will ever remember the steward for his kind attentions. They would recommend the **Jennie** to the traveling public as one of the best boat on the river."*

Wednesday, Oct. 15, 1862 Quad City Times (Davenport)

*"FOR THE IOWA RIVER. — A party of Nimrods — Messrs Joshu Burr, E. A. Tillebine, J. H. Sanders, O. S. McNeil, James Morrison and B. W. Burditt started off yesterday morning on th steamer **Jennie Whipple** for a duck hunt at the mouth of th Iowa river. They are amply provided with all that is necessar for having a 'big old time,' and it will be a mistake if they don' The party propose staying in that vicinity for about ten day and will, no doubt, slay a vast number of Teal and Mallard, b*

sides punishing a moderately fair quantity of whiskey."

U. S. MAIL AND EXPRESS
LINE OF BOATS.

The Steamers

JENNIE WHIPPLE,

C. S. MORRISSON,............Master

KATE CASSEL,

B. W. DAVIS,.................Master,

ARE N W MAKING DAILY TRIPS (SUNday's excepted) between Keokuk, Davenport and Rock Island, leaving both ends of the route at 7 o'clock A. M., connecting at Keokuk with the Keokuk and St. Louis Packet for St. Louis, and at Davenport with steamers Ad Hine and Bill Henderson for Galena and Dubuque.

☞ For Freight or Passage apply to
J. W. ROBINSON, Agent.
m17 tf

Source: Quad City Times, Davenport, Iowa,
May 26, June 7, 25, 27, 28, July 19, 26, August 8, 9, 12, 20, 23, 25, 26, 30, 1862

Friday, Nov. 14, 1862 The Morning Democrat (Davenport)
"Lieut. H. G. McNeil, of Co. C, Second Iowa Infantry, left of the Jennie Whipple yesterday, to rejoin his regiment at Rienzi, Miss. He took with him the new regimental flag for the Second Iowa."

Wednesday, Nov. 19, 1862 Muscatine Evening Journal (Iowa)
"Clothing for the 37th – Col. Kincaid came down from Davenport yesterday, on the steamer Jennie Whipple, and brought

with him several boxes containing drawers for the 37th regiment. The coats, pants, and shoes are expected to arrive today."

Monday, Nov. 24, 1862 Quad City Times (Davenport, Iowa)

"WRECKING. — The steamer **Jennie Whipple** has been engaged for several days past in raising up the machinery in the hull of the old steamer Gray Eagle, that went down at this point a year ago last spring. We believe everything of value has been removed or soon will be. The low stage of water is very favorable to the work."

*The steamer Grey Eagle, was salvaged by the **Jennie Whipple** Nov. 24, 1862*

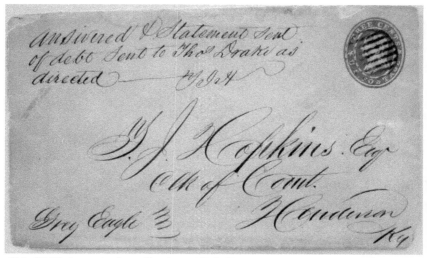

This 1860's letter in the collection of Bob Crossman, postage paid with an embossed star D U26, was written by Thomas Drake, and carried by the Sidewheel Grey Eagle, to Tignal J. Hopkins, who was Circuit Clerk of Henderson, Kentucky from 1860 to 1862.

Tuesday, Dec. 12, 1862 Quad City Times (Davenport, Iowa)
"REVIEW OF THE RIVER BUSINESS OF 1862. –... *Steamboating is one of the few professions to which the war times have proved advantageous...*

*The boats which have carried these mails were the Kate Cassel and **Jennie Whipple**... One hundred and two trips each comprised the mail career of the two... This they performed with almost unequaled punctuality... not a trip was lost, or even varying scarcely an hour from their appointed time of arrival. Much honor is due to the officers of these packets for the manner in which they acquitted the duties assigned them.*"

1863

Monday, Jan. 19, 1863 Daily Missouri Republican (St. Louis)
"*The Upper Mississippi is falling from Quincy down, and full of ice. The **Jennie Whipple** went up as far as Canton, turned back to Quincy, where she stored her freight, and arrived in this port Saturday morning.*"

Friday, Feb. 6, 1863 Daily Missouri Republican (St. Louis)
"*... and the **Jennie Whipple** up the Mississippi froze up.*"

Tue., March 3, 1863 Daily Missouri Republican (St. Louis)
"*The **Jennie Whipple**, having been thoroughly repaired, is now ready for business. She is receiving for Rock Island, and will leave tomorrow.*"

Tuesday, March 10, 1863 Quad City Times (Davenport, Iowa)
"*...the **Jennie Whipple** came up, having on board twenty wagons and one hundred and eight mules belonging to the government. They are intended for the Sixth Cavalry. The **Jennie** will run as a mail and passenger packet between here and Keokuk the coming season, commanded by Jim Campbell, a man of much steamboat experience. L. Parkhurst, of LeClaire, will preside in the office. Any boat under the supervision of these two gentlemen will never be found wanting of patronage where they are known.*"

Thursday, March 12, 1863 Muscatine Evening Journal (Iowa)
"*The **Jennie Whipple** experienced considerable difficulty in making a landing at the levee, on her trip down yesterday, owing to a high wind blowing from the west. She took down as passen-*

gers a number of soldiers belonging to different Iowa regiments, who have been at home on furlough and sick leave.

The **Jennie** has a new commander – Captain Worden. He is said to be an old steamboatman, and will add to the popularity already enjoyed by his boat."

Friday, March 13, 1863 Muscatine Weekly Journal (Iowa)

"A GREAT INVENTION. – *Captain Charlie Morrison, of Keokuk, (now in command of the ferryboat Davenport, which is attached to the 32d Iowa Infantry), well known in the entire length of the river as one of the most popular steamboat captains on the western waters, better known to our citizens as the courteous and affable commander of the* **Jennie Whipple** *last season, has just secured a patent for an invention for steering gunboats or other craft, which promises great results.*

It consists simply of a small engine, and additional wheel just forward of the stern of the boat. – This wheel is made to revolve at right angles to the stern or side wheels, and will throw the boat quickly around as if upon a pivot. – Suppose a ram is advancing upon a gunboat the pilot can shift the position of his boat so quickly as to avoid all danger whatever from collision. And in running over rapids, or around close abrupt bends in the river, it will prove of infinite advantage to any boat simply engaged in the carrying trade. Commander Porter has had this invention applied to his flag-boat, and Senator Grimes secured an appropriation to prove for its application to all vessels of war hereafter built for the Government.

Captain Morrison has placed himself upon a sure road to the possession of an ample fortune by this simple application of well known principles; and better yet, has rendered the Nation by its timely introduction, service of the very highest character By the international arrangements which now exist this paten is good for the next seventeen years in all of the leading European Governments. – We congratulate the lucky inventor, and we trust that his reward may be ample, for no man is more truly deserving.

Friday, March 27, 1863 Muscatine Evening Journal (Iowa)

"River Items. – *The Northern Line boats are making regula*

*trips, none of them having been taken for Government purposes. The packets **Jennie Whipple** and Kate Cassel, having been released, will hereafter run regularly between Keokuk and Davenport, carrying the mails."*

Friday, March 27, 1863 Muscatine Weekly Journal (Iowa)

"A WHOPPER. – Mahoony, the pioneer-trator of Iowa, is circulated an enormous lie throughout the East. He states that when he was arrested for treasonable practices, the United States Marshal chartered a steamboat all the way up from Burlington to Dubuque to arrest him.

*The truth of the matter is, that Mahony was taken down the river past this city on the regular packet **Jennie Whipple**, for which his fare was the same as is always charged passengers. Mahony must have an exalted opinion of his own importance, to suppose that the Government would charter a boat for his special accommodation."*

Tuesday, March 31, 1863 Quad City Times (Davenport, Iowa)

*"THE REAR. – A number of soldiers, who were left behind in a state of drunken obfuscation when the Brigade left on Sunday, were forwarded yesterday morning on the steamer **Jennie Whipple**. Some of them had peeled noses – the result of barking up the wrong tree, but they were all sober enough to travel."*

Thursday, April 2, 1863 The Iowa Transcript (Toledo, Iowa)

*"COMING IN. – About three hundred men of the 7th Iowa cavalry, arrived here yesterday, on board the steamboat **Jennie Whipple**, from Ottumwa, via Burlington. They took quarters at Camp Hendershot vacated last week by the Sixth Cavalry. This is the first installment. More will follow soon. The boys look well and hardy. – Dav. Gaz. March 26."*

Thursday, May 7, 1863 Muscatine Evening Journal (Iowa)

*"FOR VICKSBURG. – Captain Ben Beach left yesterday on the steamer **Jennie Whipple**, for his regiment (the Eleventh) bearing with him the best wishes of his numerous friends here, and many hopes for his safe return."*

Monday, June 15, 1863 The Rock Island Argus (Illinois)

*"STEAMBOAT RACE. – A nice little race between the **Jennie Whipple** and the Canada occurred coming up the river on Sunday.*

*When about opposite Buford's foundry the Canada shot ahead of the **Jennie** and seemed sure to make the landing first – but the **Jennie** rallied and in a few moments began to gain on her, and before reaching the landing was a full length ahead. The **Jennie** was loaded to the guards, and the Canada was light."*

Two Steamships, Eagle and Diana, race on the Mississippi River
Source: Lithographed and published by Currier & Ives, 1870

Monday, July 20, 1863 Muscatine Evening Journal (Iowa)
*"Departures – **Jennie Whipple**, Campbell, Ft. Madison for Rock Island. The mail and passenger packet **Jennie Whipple**, will be found at the levee today noon for Ft. Madison and way points Captain Campbel has charge of her, and Lemuel Parkhurst in the office.*

Tuesday, June 22, 1863 Quad City Times (Davenport, Iowa)
*"The **Jennie Whipple**, when opposite Rockingham on her up trip, Sunday morning, struck a rock which penetrated her hull and admitted water sufficiently to sink the boat. No great damage, however, will be incurred from this accident, we understand It is expected that the **Jennie** will be thoroughly repaired and in sailing order in the course of a few days. No lives were lost, and but little injury done to her cargo."*

Tuesday, June 23, 1863 Quad City Times (Davenport, Iowa
*'The **Jennie Whipple**, we are informed, has been raised, and gone to the Rock Island Boat Yard, where necessary repairs will be made."*

Thur., July 21, 23, 1863 Muscatine Evening Journal (Iowa)

"*Departures* — **Jennie Whipple**, Campbell, Rock Island for Fort Madison. The regular mail and passenger packet, **Jennie Whipple**, Captain Campbell, clerk Parkhurst, will be up tonight for Davenport."

U. S. MAIL AND EXPRESS.

SEASON ARRANGEMENT
—— OF THE ——
RAPIDS PACKET LINE.

KATE CASSEL,

B. W. DAVIS,.................Master,
B. F. WILLIAMS,.............Clerk,

JENNIE WHIPPLE,

JAMES CAMPBELL,.......... Master,
LEMUEL PARKHURST,........Clerk.

ONE OF THE ABOVE NAMED PACKETS will leave this point daily on the arrival of Eastern morning train, connecting at Muscatine with the cars for Iowa City and Washington ; at Burlington with the Burlington & Mi-souri River Railroad for Oskaloosa and Autumwa, and with the Chicago train ; at Fort Madison with the Keokuk & Mount Pleasant Railroad for Mount Pleasant and Keokuk, and at Keokuk with packets for St. Louis.

Passengers traveling on these boats will avoid all vexacious delays of passing the Rapids. Freight handled with care and dispatch.
mh17 tf

Advertisement of the *Jennie Whipple*,
Source: Quad-City Times, Davenport, Iowa
March 28, 31, April 9, 10, 17, 29, May 4, 6, 23, 25 June 30, July 23, 30 and Aug. 8, 1863

THE STEAMER

JENNIE WHIPPLE,

Capt. JAMES CAMPBELL,

Will leave every TUESDAY, THURSDAY and SAT-
URDAY morning on the arrival of the Cars from
Keokuk. These fine Passenger Steamers will arrive at
Burlington at 1 o'clock P. M., making connection with
the B. & M. R. R. for the West, and the C., B. & Q. R.
for the East, and arriving at Davenport at 5 A. M., for
trains leaving for Iowa City and Chicago.

For freight or passage apply at the company's office
at the Depot of the Keokuk and Fort Madison R. R.

GEO. W. GIRDON,

ap18-d'f   General Agent.

Source: The Daily Gate City (Keokuk, Iowa, Sept. 16, 1863, page 4

Saturday, Oct. 31, 1863 Quad City Times (Davenport, Iowa)
*"The mail and passenger packet **Jennie Whipple**, Captain Campbell, will depart for Keokuk and intermediate landings Monday morning. Lemuel Parkhurst in the office. E. A. Tilebein, agent."*
[NOTE: This same was repeated March 30, May 5, 12, 14, 16, June 2, 16, 18, July 7, 9, 14, 21, 23, 25, 28, 30, Aug. 1, 8, 11, 15, 18, 22, 27, Sept. 12, 15, 22, 26, Oct. 1, 6, 8, 10, 15, 20, 1863]

Thursday, Oct. 22, 1863 The Daily Gate City (Keokuk, Iowa)
*"The **Jennie Whipple** is the morning boat for Davenport and Rock Island and intermediate points. Leaves fort Madison on arrival of the cars, [train cars] and will make connection with trains at Burlington for Mt. Pleasant, Fairfield, Ottumwa, & c. also with trains East for Chicago."*

Thursday, Nov. 12, 1863 Muscatine (Iowa) Evening Journal
*"CLOSE OF NAVIGATION – This week will pretty much finish navigation for this season. The mail packets **Jennie Whipple** and Kate Cassel will withdraw, their contract for carrying the mail expiring on the 15th inst. –"*

1864

Friday, March 4, 1864 Quad City Times (Davenport, Iowa)

*"FOR ST. LOUIS. – The favorite passenger packet **Jennie Whipple**, Captain Campbell, Parkhurst Clerk, will leave this point for St. Louis and intermediate points next Monday morning. Passengers and shippers will bear this in mind. The **Jennie** will probably land here from Rock Island sometime today, and commence receiving. She has been put in excellent trim during the past winter, and is in complete condition for business. The public will be pleased to know that the same jovial and courteous officers that commanded her last, have been selected for that position this season. They are men of much experience, and in whom the people place the utmost confidence. E. A. Tilebein has been appointed agent for the **Jennie**, this season."*

Saturday March 5, 1864 The Rock Island Argus (Illinois)

*"FOR KEOKUK – The steamer **Jennie Whipple** was towed up from the Boat Yard to our levee this forenoon (Saturday) by the ferry boat Rock Island, and will leave for Keokuk on Monday."*

Tuesday, March 8, 1864 Muscatine Evening Journal (Iowa)

*"FIRST BOAT – The **Jennie Whipple**, Captain James Campbell, arrived yesterday from Rock Island, bound down the river. We understand that she will take her place at once as a regular packet between Montrose and Rock Island. Captain Parkhurst is again in the office of the **Jennie**. Success to her! The **Jennie** was also the first boat last year, having arrived at our wharf from below on the same day (March 7th).*

Monday, March 28, 1864 Muscatine Evening Journal (Iowa)

*"The **Jennie Whipple** was obliged to lay by at our levee until morning, on her way upward trip Friday night, owing to the dense fog. She did not continue on to Davenport, but turned around at this point in order to make up her lost time."*

Monday, April 18, 1864 Daily Davenport Democrat, page 1

*"Col. Wilson, in view of the riotous conduct of his men while coming up on the **Jennie Whipple** two days previous, made the following... speech... : 'Soldiers, since the commencement of your furloughs... lately you have been acting the devil. In coming upon the **Jennie Whipple** the other day, twenty-five of you*

got drunk and destroyed $700 worth of property... five have been arrested...'"

Friday, April 29, 1864 Muscatine Weekly Journal (Iowa)

"*Correl, the counterfeiter, who made the bold escape from our jail, last Wednesday evening, by cutting a hole through the wall, letting himself down with blankets and escaping in daylight, was nabbed by Marshal James, yesterday morning at the Island City Hotel, Rock Island, whilst in bed... He was brought down on the* **Jennie Whipple** *yesterday and lodged in his old quarters...*"

Monday, May 2, 1864 Muscatine Evening Journal (Iowa)

"*The* **Jennie Whipple** *broke some of her machinery at Burlington, and did arrive up until yesterday about noon. She made up her lost time handsomely, by increased speed in running. She will be down today.*"

Thursday, May 5, 1864 The Rock Island Argus (Illinois)

"*Yesterday while the* **Jennie Whipple** *was taking on some freight, by invitation we went on board and heard Prof. Chamberlain sing a patriotic song in a style hard to surpass. During the singing a lady in the cabin remarked that the singing was 'a great nuisance.' A gentleman on our right replied to her in the following laconic style: — "Madam, a patriotic song may seem a nuisance to you, but it is my opinion you are a nuisance to decent society.' She quietly subsided. May the Lord have Mercy on her, if she is worth saving. – Burnington Hawkeye, 29th ult.*

This is one side of the story. Captain Campbell, of the **Jennie***, furnishes us with the other. Prof. Chamberlin and severa[?] other gentlemen [?] having hoisted themselves outside of much essence of corn, took seats in the ladies' cabin and commenced singing in a boisterous manner. It happened that there was [?] lady aboard, the wife of Captain Robert H. Whitenack, of Cedar Rapids, commanding Company A of the 15th Iowa infan[?] try, which had just separated from her husband the day befor[?] at Keokuk, he to go to the field, and she to return to her lonel[?] home. She was very low in health and spirits – in fact had bee[?] confined to her state room nearly all day – too feeble to partake [?] any nourishment, but at the time had just come into the cabi[?]*

and she it was who remonstrated against such, a noise as was being created – a noise, as we are assured by the officers of the boat, that was more like a drunken brawl than like music; and she it was who was insulted in the language above given, by one Mr. Caffrey, who was then on his way to Davenport to obtain from General Baker a recruiting commission. Being a lady – weak and out of spirits (which is much more than can be said of the intoxicated 'local' of the Hawkeye), she modestly desisted from asserting her rights, or entering into any conversation with men bereft of feelings of politeness or decency – of course she 'quietly subsided' to the shame of the intruders, be is said.

It is very proper to sing patriotic songs, but no gentleman will intrude them into the presence of the sick – much less will they insult a sick lady who remonstrates against offensive noises. Such 'patriotism' is but the result of low breeding and whisky on the brain. It was this same crowd who plied some soldiers aboard the boat with whisky until they became uproarious, and then blamed the officers of the boat because they did not keep them quiet – Davenport Democrat & News.

Friday, May 13, 1864 Quad City Times (Davenport, Iowa)
" ARRIVED *– A squad of 57 men for the 100 days' service arrived this morning on the steamer* **Jennie Whipple***, at 4 ½ o'clock. Where they were from we know not, for up to this hour the officer in charge had not reported at headquarters. Where he had gone to, or what special service detained him that he omitted to observe the duty of reporting in due form, is unknown to the writer. The men went to Camp McClellan, and are there yet.*"

riday, May 13, 1864 Muscatine Evening Journal (Iowa)
"GOVERNOR STONE *went down the river on the* **Jennie Whipple** *yesterday morning. He reports that recruiting for the one hundred days' service is brisk in all parts of the state...*"

at., May 21, 1864 Burlington Weekly Hawk-Eye, page 7
"The Second Iowa Cavalry passed down last evening on the **Jennie Whipple***. They had a very fine band with them. "Captain Harper left for Keokuk with his Company yesterday evening, on the* **Jennie Whipple***. Hundreds of our citizens, including a large number of ladies, were at the landing, to give the*

Captain's brave boys a parting cheer. After the shaking of hands by mothers, fathers, sisters and sweethearts, the Second Iowa, who were on board the **Jennie Whipple***, gave the Company three rousing cheers, when they were marched on board, and amid cheers and the waving of handkerchiefs, and music by the band, the* **'Jennie'** *shoved from the shore with her living freight of brave hearts, beating strong and true for their country, and for whose rescue they have offered their services. Thus, again, had Des Moines county nobly responded to her country's call. May Heaven shield and protect those brave boys, is our prayer."*

Saturday, May 28, 1864 Muscatine Evening Journal (Iowa)

"ARREST OF THE NEGRO WHO ATTEMPTED AN OUTRAGE ON A WHITE GIRL – DISGRACEFUL PROCEEDINGS – AN EXCITED MOB TAKE HIM FROM THE OFFICES AND ALMOST KILL HIM – We briefly noticed in yesterday's issue the arrest of the negro who attempted an outrage on the daughter of Mr. Satterthwaite, in the outskirts of the city, last Sunday. He was overtaken near Burlington, on Wednesday evening, by Messrs. Soudder and Bell, of New Boston, and brought here on the **Jennie Whipple** *about 11 o'clock Thursday night, and lodged in jail...*

The crowd finally broke open the door and took the prisoner out upon the pavement, where Marshal James and Deputy Sheriff Connor again succeeded in getting him into their custody. They proceeded some distance towards the jail, followed by the crowd, when he was again seized and a rope placed over his head at each end of which excited men pulled, lustily, tightening the knot around his neck till the blood gushed from his mouth. He was then dragged, face downwards, across the street in front of the residence of W. H. Stewart, till his tormentors thought he was dead, when they suffered the officers to take charge of him. He soon after revived and was carried to jail.

We regret to record this lawless and barbarous proceeding. torture is brutal and inexcusable under any circumstances, and mob violence is always to be deplored. The negro gave his name as John English...

Monday, May 30, 1864 Muscatine Evening Journal (Iowa)

"EXCURSION TO DAVENPORT – An excursion to Davenport he

been arranged to come off the present week, probably tomorrow evening, on the **Jennie Whipple**, to visit Camp Roberts, where the 44th regiment is now in rendezvous. The party will be taken for half fare, and can return when convenient – either the next morning on the same packet, or the day following on the City of Keithsburg. Edibles will be taken along with which to set out a dinner to the boys. We will give further particulars when the time is definitely settled."

Saturday, July 2, 1864 Chicago Tribune

"Recapture of... Escaped Rebel Prisoners – June 30 – Ten rebel prisoners escaped... seven of them were retaken the same day. The other three made their escape... at Burlington ... their story did not seem at all probable... the Provost Marshall ... arrested and lodged in jail on suspicion of being escaped rebel prisoners... had them brought up on the **Jennie Whipple**, when they proved to be the very persons."

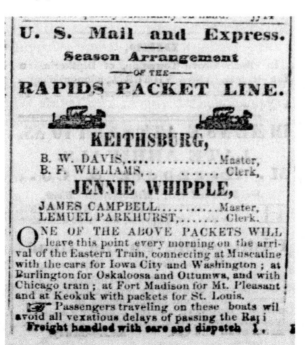

Source: Quad City Times, Davenport Iowa, July 21, 1864 page 2
reprinted in the same paper July 5, 6, 9, 21 June 7, 11, 13, 14, 21, 23, 29, 1864

Tuesday, July 5, 1864 Quad City Times (Davenport, Iowa)
*"A small excursion party embarked on the **Jennie Whipple** and went down the river as far as New Boston, and returned this morning on the Keithsburg... They had a band of music for the occasion."*

Monday, July 18, 1864 Muscatine Evening Journal (Iowa)
*"The Muscatine and the **Jennie Whipple** are the down boats this forenoon, and the Canada and the Keithsburg the up boats this evening."*

Saturday, July 23, 1864 Quad City Times (Davenport, Iowa)
*"RIVER ITEMS – The favorite mail and passenger packet **Jennie Whipple**, Captain Campbell, will depart for Fort Madison and way points Monday morning at 7 o'clock. Lemuel Parkhurst in the office. E. A. Tilebein, agent."*
[NOTE: This same report was reprinted March 29, April 7, 9, 12, 26, 28, May 5, 7, 11, 21, 26, June 2, 4, 9, 16, 23, 25. 28, 30, July 9, 23, 1864

Tues. July 26, 1864 The Morning Democrat (Davenport)
*"RIVER ITEMS – We learn that the **Jennie Whipple** is to be cut down and altered into a tow boat."*

Tuesday, Aug. 16, 1864, Daily Davenport Democrat, page 1
*"The favorite mail and passenger packet **Jennie Whipple**, Captain Campbell, will depart for Fort Madison and way points tomorrow morning at 7 o'clock. Lemuel Parkhurst in the office. E. A. Tilebein, agent."*

Thursday, Aug. 17, 1864 Daily Davenport Democrat, page 1
*"... T. B. Rhodes, President of the Northern Line Packet Company, purchased the entire stock and interest of the Rapids Packet Company, and the transfer of property took place this morning. The Rapids Line consisted of the New Boston, City of Keithsburg and the **Jennie Whipple**. ...the **Jennie Whipple** is comparatively worthless... In the freighting capacity she might serve for a year or so longer."*

Thursday, Oct. 27, 1864 Muscatine Evening Journal (Iowa)
*MUSCATINE POST OFFICE – RIVER MAIL, via Burlington to Keokuk Per Steamers Keithsburg and **Jennie Whipple**. {Arrives 6 a.m Closes 10 a.m.} Daily"*

Tuesday, Nov. 22, 1864 Quad City Times (Davenport, Iowa)
*"NAVIGATION CLOSED. – The boats of the Northern Line have discharged their crews, and laid up for the winter. The Davenport, Pembina, Muscatine, Keithsburg and Petrel are at Fort Madison, and the **Jennie Whipple** and New Boston have laid up in the Rockingham Slough. Even should the river open up a while, the Company will not run the risk of bringing out the boats again, there being too much uncertainly as to how long they would be able to run. The season has not been one of great prosperity in the river business. The boats have had to contend with adverse circumstances all the way through –continued low water, scarcity of help, high price of fuel, and inadequate railroad faculties around the lower rapids. This last obstacle has kept the boats from carrying thousands of tons of freight that they might otherwise have handled, but which had to reach the market through other channels. We wish them more prosperous times next season.*

1865

Monday, May 15, 1865 Muscatine Evening Journal (Iowa)
*"JENNIE WHIPPLE SOLD. – The old sternwheeler, **Jennie Whipple** was sold in St. Louis recently for $5,250. She is to be transformed into a tow boat."*

Thur., June 8, 1865 Daily Missouri Republican (St. Louis)
*"ARRIVALS 7TH – Steamer **Jennie Whipple**, Burt, Hennepin;..."*
*"The steamer **Jennie Whipple**, arrived from Hampin, Illinois River, with a good cargo of produce. She will leave for LaSalle and way points this evening at 4 o'clock."*

Saturday, June 10, 1865 The Cincinnati Enquirer
*"The **Jennie Whipple** brought a very nice cargo down the Illinois to St. Louis. Her officers are managing her very energetically, and she promises to put forth good fruits. The **Jennie** will leave again tomorrow morning at ten o'clock for Illinois River."*

Tue., June 20, 1865 Daily Missouri Republican (St. Louis)
*"The **Jennie Whipple** arrived from La Salle, with a good trip, on Sunday evening. Manifest published yesterday. The **Jennie Whipple** left for La Salle last evening."*

Tue., June 27, 1865 Daily Missouri Republican (St. Louis)

DEPARTED – ***Jennie Whipple*** *for Illinois river*

Monday, July 10, 1865 St. Louis Globe Democrat (St. Louis)
ARRIVED – ***Jennie Whipple***

Monday, July 17, 1865 Daily Missouri Republican (St. Louis)
*We are indebted to... the **Jennie Whipple**... for copies of boats manifests.*

Saturday, September 9, 1865 Cairo Evening Times
ARRIVALS – ***Jennie Whipple***

Wednesday, September 13, 1865 The Memphis Argus
ARRIVED ***Whipple*** *from Cincinnati*

Friday, Sept. 15, 1865 Daily Missouri Republican (St. Louis)
*"Cairo Port List. Cairo, Sept. 14. The following is our port list for the past twenty four hours: ... **Jennie Whipple** for Helena."*

Sunday, Sept. 17, 1865 The Times Democrat (New Orleans)
*"The St. Louis Democrat of the 11th says: ... arrived on the 9th... The **Jennie Whipple** from St. Louis for New Orleans, arrived at Cairo the same day."*

Tuesday, Sept. 18, 1865 The Times-Picayune (New Orleans)
*"The steamer **Jennie Whipple**, Captain DeLasley, arrived from St. Louis with a full cargo."*

Tuesday, Sept. 19, 1865 The Courier Journal (Louisville, KY)
*"The officers of the War Eagle report a stern-wheeler aground at Island No 21. They think it was the **Jennie Whipple**."*

Wed., Sept. 20, 1865 The Times-Picayune (New Orleans)
*"...150 bbls. flour – Rosewood, 150 bbls. flour – Moonlight, damaged on board steamer **Jennie Whipple**, on her voyage from St. Louis to this port."*

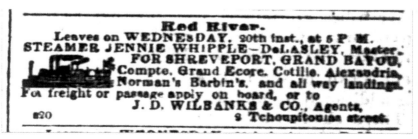

Source: The Times-Picayune, September 20, 1865, page 7

Thursday, Sept. 21, 1865 The Times-Picayune (N. Orleans)

"The arrivals were few, but we had a quite a number of departures, and most of them with tolerably good trips of freight and passengers... DEPARTURES. – *...* **Jennie Whipple**...*

Saturday, Sept. 23, 1865 The Times-Picayune (New Orleans)
"... 34 boxes soap, 18 boxes candles, damaged on board the steamer **Jennie Whipple***, on her voyage to this port."*

Saturday, Oct. 21, 1865 The Times-Picayune (New Orleans)
"The Red River packet Marshall... memoranda: ... **Jennie Whipple** *at Hickman's."*

"The Red River packet Navigator... memoranda: ... **Jennie Whipple** *at Alexandria, bound down;..."*

Tuesday, Oct. 24, 1865 The Times-Picayune (New Orleans)
"The Red River packet, **Jennie Whipple***, Captain De Lesley, arrived from Shreveport with 197 bales cotton, and will lay up for the present."*

Saturday, Nov. 11, 1865, The Times-Picayune (New Orleans)
*"*BOAT SOLD *– The steamer* **Jennie Whipple** *was sold at auction, yesterday, by the Sheriff. Messrs. Collen & Goodyn steamboat agents, were the purchasers."*

1866
The Way's Packet Directory, 1848-1994
by Fredrick Way Jr., states,
"The Jennie Whipple went off the lists in 1866."

1870
aturday, Nov. 19, 1870 Pittsburgh Weekly Gazette (Penn)
*"*CAPTAIN ANDY MILLER*, formerly of the* **Jennie Whipple***, and other steamers, and recently in the towing business for the St. Charles Bridge, has abandoned the river, and is proprietor of a saloon in St. Charles, Missouri, called the Arbor."*

1874
ugust 5, 1874 Cincinnati Daily Times
"...Captain David White's journey through life. ...a succession of years of disaster followed, and Mr. White was painting as

*a journeyman on the steamer **Jennie Whipple**, at St. Louis, in the beginning of the war of the rebellion. Friends came to his assistance and purchased for him one-third interest in the **Jennie Whipple**. In a very short time he was full owner of the steamboat, and before that year of the war ended he owned the Magenta and several other steamers, carrying for the Government and supplying the army South with ice and almost every article which no one else seemed willing to take hold of. After the war he organized the Mississippi Transportation Company with a full line of steamers plying between St. Louis and New Orleans..."*

"The April 11, 1865 Daily Davenport Democrat reported: SALE OF STEAMBOATS — *At Louisville, last week the steamers St. Nicholas and St. Charles were sold to the Ohio & Mississippi Transportation Co. for $77,500 each."*

1875
Wednesday, August 18, 1875 St. Louis Globe-Democrat

*"*DEATH OF AN OLD RIVER MAN *— The many friends of Mr. Clempson Stephens will be pained to hear of his death, which took place at his residence, No. 2903 Dickson Street, yesterday morning. Mr. Stephens was born in Carroll County, Md., in 1819 and came to St. Louis in 1845. Until shortly after the war he followed steamboating, and was half owner of the steamer **Jennie Whipple** when she was destroyed by fire. His affliction from inflammatory rheumatism caused him to abandon the river. He was a member of St. John's Methodist Episcopal Church, and also of Pride of the West lodge of Masons. He leaves a widow and two adopted children to mourn the demise of a kind husband and father. The funeral will take place at 3 o'clock this afternoon from the residence, to Bellefontaine Cemetery."*

[**NOTE:** The above obituary states that the **Jennie Whipple** was destroyed by fire, but does not mention the date or location of the fire. *Way's Packet Directory, 1848-1994* by Frederick Way, Jr. states that *"the **Jennie Whipple** went off the lists in 1866."* No clarity exist precisely on the location, date or method of the **Jennie Whipple's** demise.]

Thursday, August 19, 1875 St. Louis Globe-Democrat

"The funeral of Mr. Clempson Stephens was well attended yesterday. Rev. Drs. Lewis and Morris conducted religious exercises at the residence, and the regular Masonic services were observed at the grave."

1878

February 22, 1878 Cincinnati Commercial Tribune

*"In 1858 and 1860 the Arkansas packet **Jennie Whipple**, a fast one of her sort, and as good as she was speedy, used to run from the mouth of Arkansas to Memphis in 17 ½ hours. The distance was 30 miles more than now. Captain A. D. Storm, now of the Anchor Line, was Captain of the **Whipple** in those days."*

1888

Monday, March 24, 1884 St. Louis Globe Democrat

*"The widow of R. U. Deles-Dernier, No. 1710 North Grand Avenue, St. Louis, MO., offers a reward of $100 for the whereabouts of any of the crew, or soldiers, that were on board the steamer **Jennie Whipple** in October, 1865 when the boat was seized and pressed into the United States service by Col. McLaughlin, of the 47th Indian Infantry. Steamboatmen on this river knowing anything of the matter may help a widow by answering this card."*

Potts Station Welcoming Butterfield's Overland Mail Stagecoach
Built in 1858 by Kirkbride Potts, serving today as the Pope County Museum
Source: Pope County Museum, Potts Inn in Pottsville, Arkansas

The Landing at Van Buren, Arkansas
Source: History Makers of Arkansas, 1918, by John Hugh Reynolds

Earliest photo of Van Buren townscape along the Arkansas River, ca. 1860
Images of America: Van Buren, by Tom Wing

CHAPTER FOUR
Steamboats and the Arkansas River

In the 1800's steamboats significantly boosted the economic development of the communities and cities along the Arkansas River. Stretching 445 miles across Arkansas, the river was quickly recognized as the fastest way to travel. The steam powered boats played this role until the late 1800's when the development of the railroads gradually began to capture the bulk of the passenger and freight business. The growth of river traffic on the Mississippi River had a direct influence on Arkansas River's traffic.

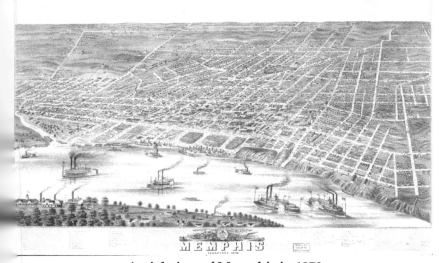

Aerial view of Memphis in 1870

Launched in 1811, the New Orleans was the first Mississippi River steamboat. Designed by Robert Fulton, her low-pressure Boulton and Watt steam engine was heavy and inefficient.

The New Orleans, 148' x 32', built 1811 at Pittsburg and sunk 1814 near Baton Rouge

Between 1813 and 1816, the Comet was the second Mississippi steamboat, followed by Vesuvius, Enterprise, Washington also entered the Mississippi River trade.

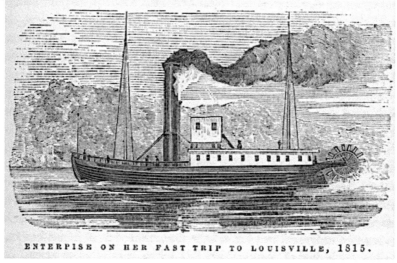

ENTERPISE ON HER FAST TRIP TO LOUISVILLE, 1815.

The Enterprise on her fast trip to Louisville, 1815
Source: Lloyd's Steamboat Directory, Cincinnati, O. : J. T. Lloyd & Co., 1856

By the end of the 1810's there were twenty steamboats on the Mississippi. By the 1830's there were more than 1,200 steaming the Mississippi. The steamboats carried crops cotton, rice, timber, tobacco and whiskey to market, and returned with stock for the shelves of mercantile stores up and down the length of the river.

Wood was the primary fuel initially, and was slowly replaced by coal.

The steamboats ranged in length from 40 to almost 300 feet, and from 10 to 80 feet in width. To allow them to navigate shallow waters, the draught was only 1 to 5 feet when fully loaded with freight and passengers. Due to river snags, collisions, boiler explosions and fire the average vessel only lasted about five years. It is estimated that 7,000 fatalities occurred between 1811 and 1853 due to steamboat boiler explosions on the Mississippi River and its tributaries.

On the Mississippi River at Mound City, Arkansas the worst steamboat disaster in history occurred in 1865 when the Sultana's four boilers exploded. She was only designed to hold 376 passengers, but on this occasion she was carrying 1,953 paroled Union prisoners-of-war, as well as another 177 guards, civilian passengers and crew for a grand total of 2,130 people. Of that number, an estimated 1,200 perished. The paroled prisoners came primarily from Ohio, Michigan, Indiana, Kentucky, and Tennessee.

Sultana on fire at Mound City near Helena, Arkansas
Source: Harper's Weekly

Some of the passenger vessels, to compete and attract more ticket sales, began to improve the cabin and common areas with velvet, gilt edging, plush chairs, and friendly staff. Honest gambling, pool tables, dancing, attentive cabin staff and amazing food were all apart of improving the experience of passengers aboard the steamboats.

In 1824 the Army Corps of Engineers was given the task of removing Arkansas and Mississippi River snags, sand bars, rapids and sawyers. As the years passed, the Corp was also tasked with deepening the river channel.

As improvements were made in engine and ship design, along with obstruction removals, and improved pilot skills - a trip upstream from New Orleans to the Ohio River was reduced from three weeks to only four days.

During the Civil War, steamboats like the *Jennie Whipple* played a major role in transporting troops and ammunition. Ironclad steamboats also played a significant role in the war.

USS Cairo
In June 1862, this City-class ironclad gunboat captured the Confederate garrison of Fort Pillow on the Mississippi, enabling Union forces to occupy Memphis.

In the University of Arkansas at Little Rock's on virtual e hibit, *"As Much as the Water: How Steamboats Shaped Arkansas* Leslie C. Stewart-Abernathy, Ph.D. writes:

"From the 1830's to the 1870's the steamboat was the most popular form of transport for people and their baggage from the Appalachians almost to the Rocky Mountains, and for shipping out everything from bags of corn and fresh produce to bales of cotton heading down river, and for bringing pianos to crates of dishes to fresh oysters going upstream. The steamboat allowed a person to go to the next town on the water or halfway across the country, usually in safety and comfort. Today it would be like if every small town had an airport with planes that could carry those people and cargo to destinations nearby and faraway.

Ozark Queen at Calico Rock, Arkansas on the White River

The big boats on the Mississippi, incredibly long and incredibly narrow, captured the glory with their towering white sides (pilot house at the top sitting on the "Texas" deck, then the "boiler" deck with its passenger cabins and the Grand Salon down the middle, all resting on the main deck with its elaborate machinery and steam boilers) elaborate jig sawn trim, enormously tall smokestacks, and huge paddle wheels whether on the sides of the hull or at the back end of the vessel. Smaller and smaller steamboats that drew as little as one foot of water also ran on the smaller and smaller streams, from the Cumberland River to the Tennessee River, to the Ohio River and on to the Mississippi, and from the Ouachita and Arkansas Rivers and the Black River to the White River to the Mississippi as well.

Landing at DeVall's Bluff, Arkansas on the White River, undated

The steamboat had to be invented, however, from adapting flat bottom wooden hulls, to developing engines powerful enough to push 300 foot boats loaded with over 1000 cotton bales, and perfecting steam boiler systems from which engineers could convince high-temperature steam to operate the hydraulic systems to push the paddle wheels that moved the vessels through the water. The 1820's was a decade of experimentation. The boats reached their near final form in the 1830's, but it was the 1840's if not the early 1850's before engineering skills, metalworking, and state and federal regulations came together to produce the best quality steamboats. They subsequently played a crucial role during the Civil War transporting troops and supplies, and some being turned into "tin clad" gunboats or built from the ground up as tough armored gunboats. Unfortunately, the Civil War also brought to maturity the railroads, and their advantages in areas not served by riverboats led them to dominate passenger and freight travel after the 1870's.

The steamboat as a form of transportation did have its disadvantages, not the least of which were regular seasons of the year (particularly summer and fall) in which there was not enough river water to float most boats. When there was enough water, there were the hazards of trees that fell into the water from collapsing banks due to rivers constantly chang-

ing their course. The trees would float or become fixed in the bottoms of the rivers, and when hit would easily pierce mortal holes in the wooden hulls. More significant perhaps was the combination of boilers fired by wood or coal and the lightly built wood structures in close proximity to those somewhat untrustworthy boilers. Fires, exploding boilers, sinkings, and other accidents ranging from human error to severe storms to failure of other equipment were often horrible and tragic events, but they were taken as hazards of normal travel worth the risk, much like later train wrecks and the daily car wrecks that kill people today.

The ultimate fragility of the relatively thin wooden hull was not overcome until the development of steel plates that can be used to make all metal hulls in the late 1900's. Metal hulls plus diesel engines plus propellers equal the big towboats of today that can push as many as 32 barges upstream on the Mississippi."

Reprinted here by permission of the author
Leslie C. Stewart-Abernathy, Ph.D. on Aug. 24, 2021
Source: *University of Arkansas at Little Rock's virtual exhibit, "As Much as the Water: How Steamboats Shaped Arkansas" by Leslie C. Stewart-Abernathy, Ph.D.*

Tom Dillard, in his *Arkansas Democrat Gazette's* article, *"Introducing Steamboats to Arkansas,"* April 12, 2020, writes:

"The arrival of the first steamboat in Arkansas in 1820 ushered in an era of commerce and travel for the newly created territory. Within a few years, it was possible to make a trip from Little Rock or Camden to New Orleans, conduct business, and return home in less than a week.

Cotton, deer hides, bear oil and countless other products of Arkansas forests and farms could be shipped to markets in a planned and timely manner. The steamboat soon became an integral part of the economy, and brought romance and drama to towns across the state.

Early settlers in Arkansas used flatboats and keelboats to traverse the rivers. As the name implies, flatboats had flat bottoms, which allowed more room for large cargoes, but made the craft less manageable.

The first recorded steamboat in Arkansas was probably the Comet, which docked at Arkansas Post about 10 p.m. March 31, 1820, having departed New Orleans eight days earlier. Despite the late hour, a crowd came out to see this revolutionary new contraption. This was 13 years after Robert Fulton's Clermont launched the commercial steamboat era in 1807. Suddenly, Arkansas was not so remote any more.

Little Rock received its first steamboat, the Eagle, in March, 1822.

The Eagle

The following month a steamboat reached Fort Smith with supplies for the military post that gave the fledgling town its name. Steamboats were threading their way up the Ouachita by 1830, while the Waverly reached Batesville on the upper White River in 1831. Just when the Black River received steamboat service is debated, but one reached Davidsonville in Randolph County at least by 1831.

Archaeologist and historian Leslie Stewart-Abernathy summed up the rapid growth and penetration of steamboats in the Encyclopedia of Arkansas: "By about 1875, steamboats had reached everywhere in the state, up the Little Red River, into the Fourche La Fave, up the St. Francis River and Bayou Bartholomew, and eventually up the Buffalo River as far as Rush."

Several steamboats were built in Arkansas prior to the Civil War. The first steamboat was constructed of bois d'arc wood on the Little River in Hempstead County about 1824. The bois d'arc tree, popularly known as the bodark or Osage orange, is intimately tied to many aspects of Arkansas natural and cultural history.

In late 1841, two partners at Lewisburg in Conway County built a steamboat and floated it down the Arkansas River to modern North Little Rock where it was fitted with boilers and engines. At the suggestion of the Arkansas Gazette, the new boat was named after recently inaugurated and wildly popular Gov. Archibald Yell. Wasting no time, Gov. Yell immediately set off for Cincinnati, a center of steamboat commerce.

The City of Lewisburg 1852
Source: This modern painting is displayed at the Morrilton Railroad Station Museum in downtown Morrilton (Lewisburg), Arkansas.

Several of the steamboats built in Arkansas were small and lightweight, with the goal of being able to travel during periods of low water. One was the Dime, built in Arkadelphia about 1830. Another was the Arkansas No. 6, which a female Protestant missionary on her way to Fayetteville to teach at a school for Indian girls described as "a perfect toy boat."

The Arkansas No. 6 had been called out of Van Buren to pick up the missionary and other travelers when their steamboat became stuck on a sandbar. The rescue boat had a "tiny stove with a thin tin stovepipe [and] scarcely gave out any heat, and as it was very, very cold, we suffered. There were no state-rooms, only thin, dark curtains to hide one bed from another."

Steamboat travel could be dangerous as well as uncomfortable. The rivers were home to hundreds of snags and sunken logs, which ripped the bottoms of steamboats with distressing regularity. Boilers exploded frequently due to neglect, clogging, and poor design.

BURNING OF THE CAROLINE.

On Sunday, March 5, 1854, the steamer *Caroline* caught fire as she traveled up the White River, with extensive loss of life. A boiler explosion on the lower Arkansas shortly after the Civil War took the lives of several members of the Ashley Band, a musical group made up of former slaves of Sen.

Chester Ashley of Little Rock.

By the time the Civil War ended in 1865, steamboats had been plying the state's waters for over 40 years. Towns like Little Rock, Clarendon, Jacksonport, and Camden had long prospered from the steamboat trade, but during the two decades following the end of the war, steamboat owners sought out markets up every navigable stream in the state, and some that stretched the definition of navigable.

Steamboats built after the Civil War were often more elaborately decorated and lighted as the austere simplicity of the antebellum era gave way to the generous ornamentation of the Victorian age. The larger boats could be four stories high with a main deck, a boiler deck, a Texas or hurricane deck, and atop that a pilot house.

The steamboat made it possible for goods from around the world to be shipped to interior Arkansas. A Camden merchant in 1851 advertised the arrival of three shipments containing 2,000 pounds of bacon, 1,000 pounds of cheese, 30 sacks of coffee, 15 kegs of lard, 50 barrels of molasses, and 60 barrels of flour. Salt was also a staple of the steamboat trade.

The same steamboats loaded up with local produce before leaving the landing. Practically every riverboat captain hauled large consignments of Arkansas cotton to markets down river. Lumber and other wood products were commonly exported. In 1881, more than 101,000 bales of barrel staves were shipped out of the Camden port.

Black Arkansans worked on steamboats long before the Civil War, often as slaves who were hired out to the boat captains. Some blacks were cooks and general helpers, but most worked as roustabouts, doing the heavy lifting when the boats were manually loaded or unloaded. Even after the Civil War, blacks continued the tradition of working as roustabouts.

John Quincy Wolf, who worked as a clerk aboard a steamer on the upper White River in the 1880's, remembered that about 15 blacks worked on a typical steamboat, including *"deck-hands, firemen, cooks, and cabin boys." He recalled the deckhands having spare time between ports, which they filled with playing Seven Up, a popular card game, or shooting craps after dark in the engine room.*

John Quincy Wolf Sr., 1864-1949
Buried at Oaklawn Cemetery, Batesville, Arkansas

In his memoirs, Wolf recalled the aromas of a steamboat--especially in the bars where "the preparation of egg-nog, mint juleps, rock and rye, cocktails, sour toddies, and other mixed and fancy drinks calling for the use of sugar, rock candy, lemons, whiskey, water (not very much), nutmegs, and other spices produced a sweet, pungent odor ... I like the smell of a steamboat."

The upper White, which winds its way from Newport in Jackson County through the Ozarks to the mouth of the James River in Stone County, Mo., was the last part of Arkansas to be served by railroads, so the steamboat trade persevered. Over this distance of 367 miles were nearly 100 steamboat landings.

The most famed riverboat captain of the upper White trade was Thomas Benton Stallings. Known as the Commodore of the White, he built the first and only steamboat in Boone County, launched in January 1881 at Dubuque north of Lead Hill. The Lady Boone was a light steamer with a length of 110 feet, capable of carrying only 400 bales of cotton, but that same lightness allowed it to travel over the threatening and unreliable upper White.

The same technology that made possible the steamboat also brought railroads, and before the century ended, the sounds of the train whistles almost completely replaced the familiar three-key whistles of the steamboats. By 1910 railroads had snaked their way into every area of the state, and the steamboats became floating relics.

Reprinted here by permission of the author, Tom Dillard on August 22, 2021
Tom Dillard is a historian and retired archivist living near Glen Rose in rural
Hot Spring County. Email him at Arktopia.td@gmail.com.
An earlier version of this column was published Sept. 7, 2008.

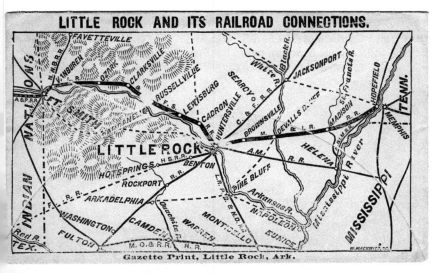

**Little Rock Railroad Connections
as displayed on the reverse of an envelope printed in 1869**

"City and Garrison of Fort Smith, Arkansas" and "United States Arsenal at Little Rock, Surrendered to the State Troops, February 1861"
Source: March 8, 1861 Harpers Weekly

Fort Smith, Arkansas, Recently Captured From the United States Secessionist
Source: Illustrated London News, May 20, 1861, page 499

CHAPTER FIVE
Butterfield's Use of Steamboats

The steamboats that traveled the Arkansas waterways were wooden-hulled, and their lives were short. Most of the losses were from boiler explosions, fire, striking a snag in the river, running hard aground, or stuck high and dry when water levels unexpectedly dropped. Despite these weaknesses, hundreds of steamboats traveled the rivers of Arkansas until the train tracks were built in the 1870's, and roadways were improved in the 1880's.

In September of 1858, John Butterfield was caught by surprise. The Arkansas River was too low for steamboats to make the trip from Fort Smith to Napoleon, and then on to Memphis carrying the Overland Mail. In haste, John Butterfield was forced to sub-contract with a successful Arkansas stage line run by John T. Chidester. Chidester already had a contract (Route #7831) with the United States Post Office to carry the mail on Monday, Wednesday and Friday from Fort Smith to Des Arc (90 miles west of the Mississippi and Memphis).

> Contract made with Brimmer, Chidester & Reeside, dated April 24, 1858, at $12,500 per annum.
>
> Leave Des Arc Monday, Wednesday, and Friday, at 6 a.m.; arrive at Fort Smith fourth days by 10 p.m.
>
> Leave Fort Smith Monday, Wednesday, and Friday, at 6 a.m.; arrive at Des Arc fourth days by 10 p.m.

In the sub-contract, Butterfield was asking Chidester to add two additional stagecoach trips weekly in each direction.

> Depart Memphis every Monday and Thursday at 8 a.m.; arrive at Fort Smith four days later, on Friday and Monday at 2:45 a.m.
>
> Depart Fort Smith every Sunday and Wednesday at 1 p.m.; arrive at Memphis four days later, on Thursday and Sunday.

In addition to stagecoaches, two steamboats were involved in carrying the Overland Mail between Fort Smith and Memphis. The steamboat Charm was used by sub-contractor John T. Chidester for six months. The steamboat *Jennie Whipple* was owned and used by John Butterfield for two years.

Apparently John T. Chidester was attempting to reduce the number of trips across Arkansas by combining them. Mr. Walton, agent of the Overland Mail Company, reported to the *Des Arc Citizen* on December 4, 1858: *"He finds that owing to other contracts of the sub-contractors, the mail is laid over about 48 hours at Fort Smith, and about 24 at Des Arc. At present this cannot be remedied..."*

The Charm

John Butterfield sub-contracted the Memphis to Fort Smith route to the stage line owned by John T. Chidester. Chidester lived in Camden, Arkansas where his home has been preserved and is available for tours. The McCullum-Chidester Museum maintains the home and property.

The September 14, 1859 issue of the *Memphis Daily Appeal* (page 3), reports: *"The little steamer Kershena, captain Door, all the way from Lake Winnegabo, left this point* [Memphis] *yesterday for the White River, having been chartered by Messrs. Chidester Ripley & Co. to run in that river in connection with their mail coaches."* There is no record of the Kershena ever arriving at the Des Arc port on the White River. Nor is the word *"Kershena"* found in any of the Memphis papers again.

Apparently the charter with the Kershena did not work out, because two weeks later, on September 29, 1859, John Chidester purchased a different steamboat, the Charm.

John T. Chidester purchased the steamboat the Charm to carry mail and passengers on the White River. He used the Charm to carry the Overland passengers from Des Arc, south on the White River to Clarendon instead of using his stage coaches. The *Des Arc Citizen* only records about fifteen trips by the Charm from Des Arc to Clarendon during the six months Chidester owned the Charm (October 1859 to April, 1860).

The exact number of times the official Overland Mail Co. passengers and mail were transported in this manner is not known.

NEW ARRANGEMENT !

FROM FORT SMITH TO MEMPHIS VIA. DES ARC IN THREE DAYS.
FROM DES ARC TO MEMPHIS IN 24 HOURS.

By Stage Steamboat and Railroad !

Having established a regular Semi-Weekly line of U. S. Mail Stages from Fort Smith to Des Arc—thence to Clarendon by Steamboat—thence to Madison by Stage—thence to Memphis by Railroad, the proprietors flatter themselves that they will receive a liberal patronage.

The U. S. Mail steamer CHARM, Capt. Hendrix, will leave Des Arc for Clarendon every Sunday and Thursday at 12 o'clock, M., and make regular connections through to Memphis, by Steamboat, Stage and Railroad, carrying passengers through in twenty-four hours. Extra coaches are in readiness to carry passengers from Clarendon to Madison, there connecting with the cars for Memphis.

Fare from Des Arc to Memphis, $8.
oct19-tf] CHIDESTER, RAPLEY & CO.

Source: Des Arc Citizen, October 19, 1859

In an advertisement in the *Des Arc Citizen*, dated October 9, 1859, John T. Chidester states:

> *"NEW ARRANGEMENT! From Fort Smith to Memphis... in three days... Having established a regular semi-weekly line of U.S. Mail Stages from Fort Smith to Des Arc – thence to Clarendon by Steamboat – thence to Madison by Stage – thence to Memphis by Railroad... through in twenty-four hours..."*

White River Steamboat Port and Ferry Site at DeVall's Bluff
Source: Photo by Bob Crossman November 11, 2021

The fare from Des Arc to Memphis was advertised to be $8. With 2.17% average inflation, $8 in 1859 is equivalent in purchasing power to about $263 in 2021, an increase of $255 over 162 years.

John T. Chidester purchased the Charm for $2,000 in Louisville, Kentucky. On October 2, 1859 the *Memphis Daily Appeal* reported:

> *"The little Charm was sold at Louisville, on Thursday, to parties from White River, for $2,000, which she cost her owners. She was taken to Jeffersonville to undergo repairs." Two days later, the paper reported: "The little Charm, recently sold at Louisville to Chidester, Rapely & Co., mail contractors in Arkansas, for the mail service in White River, took from Louisville Saturday, her departure. Mr. Chidester, one of the owners is on board."*

On Saturday, October 8, 1859 the *Memphis Daily Appeal* reported:

> *"The Charme (sic.), Messrs. Chidester, Rapley & Co.s' beautiful little new steamer for the mail service between*

– 294 –

Des Arc and Clarendon, passed down yesterday, Captain Chidester in command."

The Nov. 16, 1860 issue of Des Arc's *The Constitutional Union,* on page three, reported that the Fort Smith mails arrives at Des Arc on Mondays and Thursdays at 2 p.m., and departs for Fort Smith on Tuesdays and Saturdays at 10 p.m.

On October 12, 1859, the *Memphis Daily Appeal* reported the Charm's arrival and listed her length and engine size.

☞ The Charm, Messrs. Chidester, Rapley & Co.'s., new boat for the mail line between Des Arc and Clarendon, arrived here with the mail yesterday noon. She will hereafter leave Des Arc every Monday and Wednesday at 12 o'clock, M. The Charm is one of the prettiest little steamers afloat. Her length is 83 feet; depth of hold 3 feet; has two seven inch cylinders of 15 inches stroke; one twelve foot boiler and measures eighty-three tons.

Source: October 12, 1859, Des Arc Citizen. page 3

On Saturday, October 15, 1859 the *Memphis Daily Appeal* reported:

"The new steamer Charm got aground ten miles below DuVall's Bluff, in White River, a few days ago, and broke her rudder in the effort to get off."

The October 22, 1859 issue of the *Weekly Arkansas Gazette* reported that Chidester, Rapley & Company had purchased the steamboat Charm. They planned for the Charm to run daily between Clarendon and DeVall's Bluff - however, his actual route was between Clarendon and Des Arc.

Clarendon Button Factory
This barge holds a factory that made buttons out of shells harvested from the White River. On shore stands a large pile of shells. A steamboat is shown behind the barge.

☞ We are pleased to learn that Messrs. Chidester, Rapley & Co., have secured the service of Capt. Hendrix, to take charge of their mail boat "*Charm,*" which runs daily between Clarendon and Devall's Bluff. If the rest of their employees be as faithful and reliable, our Memphis mail matter will surely get through in time ; *provided* always it is furnished them by the agents of the Post Office department.

Chidester buys the Charm
Source: Weekly Arkansas Gazette, Little Rock, Arkansas, 22 Oct 1859, Sat

The Wednesday, April 11, 1860 issue of the *Memphis Daily Appeal*, reported: "*Captain Chidester, the great southern mail contractor, left for Vicksburg by the steamer Kentucky yesterday. He has sold the steamer Charm, and she is now in upper White River.*"

Ted Worley, in his book "*Early History of Des Arc and Its People,*" reports that the floating wharf at Clarendon was made of logs 50 feet long, and 4 feet in diameter. The wharf was anchored on the shore, and it rose and fell with the river water level. In constructing the wharf, saplings were laid over the ends of the logs, and anchored to the logs with wooden pins. Rough boards were then laid across the saplings to form a deck. Often, part of the decking was covered with a layer of dirt so that a fire for cooking or warmth could be built on the wharf.

At the site of the Clarendon port, the old Military Road crossed the White River. Jo Claire English, in her book, *Pages From the Past Revisited: Historical Notes on Clarendon, Monroe County and Early Arkansas*, written in 1991, includes a chapter on "Clarendon *Ferries*." She reports that Sylvanus Phillips operated the first ferry at this site starting in 1827. At that time, before Clarendon was founded, the site was called Mouth of Cache. To signal the ferry from the opposite bank, waiting passengers would signal the ferryman with the "gong." The gong consisted of a rusty plowshare hanging from a tree limb on a wire, and a bolt kept in the fork of the tree that was used to strike the plowshare. The ferry passed through a succession of owners, and at times there were two ferries in operation at Clarendon. The ferry owners and operators included: David Wilder 1839, George W. Ferebee, William Harrick 1844, William S. Grooms 1850, Samuel Martin 1851, Mayor B N. D Tannehill 1870, Governor Simon P. Hughes 1872-1874.

Clarendon's White River Steamboat Port and Ferry Site
Source: Photo by Bob Crossman November 11, 2021

Steamboat Chickasaw at Clarendon Port with a Load of Cotton for Market
(The location in this photo was identified by Clarendon Library staff.)
Built at cost of $65,000 by the Pittsburgh firm of James Rees & Sons, the Chickasaw
underwent its initial inspection on October 29, 1883. The wooden hull measured
185 feet in length by 38 feet in width, with a depth of 6.6 feet. Three boilers supplied steam to engines having 16-inch cylinders with a 7-foot stroke. With a light
draft of just 28 inches, the sternwheeler had a capacity of 1,650 cotton bales.
Source: Huddleston Steamboat Photograph Collection (UALR.PH.0070)

In *Steamboats and Ferries on the White River: A Heritage Re*
visited by Duane Huddleton, Sammie Chatrell Rose, and Pa:
Taylor Wood (1998, The University of Arkansas Press, pag
44) mention is made of the Charm:

> *"A new small steamer arrived in the Lower White*
> *River in 1859 to ply the mail and passenger line between*
> *Clarendon and Des Arc. Described as the prettiest little*
> *steamer afloat, the Charm was eighty-three feet long,*
> *has a three foot hold, two seven-inch cylinders of fifteen*
> *inch stroke, and displaced eighty-three tons. Owned by*
> *Chidester, Rapley & Company, the boat was under the*
> *command of Capt. H. B. Hendrix. By special arrange-*
> *ment utilizing the Charm, transportation service was of-*
> *fered from Fort Smith to Memphis, via Des Arc, in the*
> *amazingly short time of four days, or from Des Arc to*

Memphis in twenty-four hours. The trip involved traveling by stage, steamboat, and railroad. Passengers received one night's sleep on the steamer Charm, which connected with the stages to Des Arc, DeValls Bluff, and Clarendon. Fort Smith travelers could take the semi-weekly mail stage from Fort Smith to Des Arc, where they would ride aboard the steamboat Charm to Clarendon, then travel by stage to Madison and board a railroad car for the remaining trip to Memphis. The Charm left Des Arc every Sunday and Thursday."

Reporter Tom Dillard with the *Arkansas Gazette* writes in his article "*Chidester Stage Lines*" on December 20, 2015:

"...If rivers were sufficiently high to enable steamboat navigation, Butterfield-owned vessels were pressed into service. The **Jenny Whipple** plied the Arkansas between Little Rock and Fort Smith, while the Charm operated between Des Arc and Clarendon. The steamboats offered the advantages of a smooth ride, hot meals, and comfortable beds." [Butterfield owned the **Jennie Whipple**. Chidester owned the Charm.]

The April 11, 1860 issue of *The Memphis Daily Appeal* reported:

"*Captain Chidester, the great southern mail contractor, left for Vicksburg by the steamer Kentucky yesterday. He has sold the steamer Charm, and she is now in upper White River.*"

After only six months of ownership, Chidester sold the Charm and returned to only using stagecoaches or stage wagons on this portion of the Overland Mail route.

There are perhaps two reasons he sold the Charm. First, perhaps the short steamboat route did not significantly speed delivery of the Overland Mail. The distance between Des Arc and Clarendon is about 40 miles by land, or about 70 to 90 miles by water. Or Secondly, perhaps Chidester may not have been successful in attracting enough paying passengers or freight to make the route financially feasible.

DES ARC'S PORT and the JACKSON HOUSE

The Jackson House at Des Arc was a Home Station for the Butterfield Overland Mail. It served this function when the stagecoaches were used by Butterfield, but also when John T. Chidester used his steamboat, the Charm, to carry passengers and Overland Mail from Des Arc south to Clarendon on the White River.

The September 25 1858 issue of Little Rock's *Weekly Arkansas Gazette*, reprinted an article from the *Des Arc Citizen*. The article entitled, *"The Great Overland Mail,"* mentions that the trip from Memphis to Des Arc only took 14 hours. Therefore, when the Overland was on schedule, Butterfield's Overland Mail Co. stage from Memphis would arrive in Des Arc at 10 p.m. every Monday and Thursday evening on its westward journey.

The History of Des Arc by Thomas Eans, reports that the town of Des Arc takes its name from the bayou.

> *"Des Arc means 'the bow or curve' in French. A sharp bend in the White River at the mouth of Bayou Des Arc could have been the source for the name of the Bayou. The Bayou's mouth was uniquely in that curve... causing a whirlpool to be present at the mouth today and perhaps then. The Bayou was a landmark and a significant trapping area for the French."*

The spelling for this bayou that Des Arc takes it name from varies in early maps. The 1826 map of Missouri and the Territory of Arkansas, in the atlas by Anthony Finley labels the bayou: *"Bayou des Arc."* The 1836 map of Arkansas by David Hugh Burr labels the bayou: *"B. des Arques."* The 1838 map of Arkansas, by Thomas Gamaliel Bradford labels the bayou *"Bayou Desare."* The 1844 map of Arkansas, by Sidney Mors & Samuel Breese labels the bayou: *"Bayou des Arcs."* The 184 map of Arkansas, by Joseph Meyer & Carl Radefeld labels th bayou: *"Bayou d'Arques."* The 1847 map of Arkansas, by Samuel Augustus Mitchell labels the bayou: *"Bayou d'Arc."*

Old ferry crossing the White River at Des Arc.
Butterfield's Overland Mail crossed the White River by ferry at this point.
The dates of this particular ferry's operation at Des Arc are unknown.
Image courtesy of Lower White River State Park Museum of Des Arc

The History of Des Arc reports that a ferry was operating north of the mouth of Bayou Des Arc in 1844. On April 8, 1859 the *Des Arc Citizen* reported that W. W. Erwin had sold his ferry, and 400 acres of land connected to it, to Mr. Frith and Mr. Vaden of Des Arc.

On April 8, 1859 the *Des Arc Citizen* reported that the citizens of Des Arc began a petition to the county courts to establish a second ferry across the White River. About ten months later, in the January 25, 1860 issue of the *Des Arc Citizen*, the county court granted William H. Harvey a license to establish a second ferry at Des Arc from a site called Harvey's Fraction, to the opposite bank of the White River.

The Des Arc ferry at the White River was very popular. In fact, lines of wagons camped along the river waiting their turn to cross on the ferry. The November 02, 1859 issue of the *Des Arc Citizen* reported:

> "EMIGRATION – THE BEST ROUTE TO TEXAS IS DES ARC – *For several weeks past, long lines of wagons containing*

movers bound for Arkansas and Texas have crossed at the Des Arc ferry, and as we write, large numbers have camped on the opposite side of the river waiting their turn to be ferried over. Every one who has traveled the old Military Road and the route via Des Arc, give the last named route the preference for two reasons:

First, the route via Des Arc is the nearest to the ferriage and tolls less than the old route.

Second, the corn, fodder, meal, and every thing to sustain man or beast is cheaper on the Des Arc route, than that of the old Military Road.

This being the fact, to say nothing of the superiority of the roads, should movers and travelers to save time and annoyance by selecting the route by Des Arc."

The great demand for use of a ferry to cross the White River at this point may have been what prompted the construction of a new ferry at Des Arc named *"Tom Sugg"* owned by William Harvey. *The History of Des Arc* also reports that this new ferry had a steam powered wheel for propulsion and had a rope guideline across the river. The Friday, Nov. 16, 1860 issue of Des Arc's *The Constitutional Union*, page three, reports:

"A DES ARC ENTERPRISE. – While at the landing the other day, we noticed one of the finest models of a steamer that it has been our fortune to see for many a day. Upon inquire, we were gratified to learn that it was a 'home institution,' built to run as a ferry between Des Arc and the Surrounding Hill. She is christened the 'Tom Sugg,' and is under the command of our enterprising townsman, Captain Harvey, with H. T. Harrison as clerk. She was built in Cincinnati, by Mesrs. Johnson, Morton & Co., under the supervision of Captain Harvey, as a cost of $7,500. We understand it is as yet uncertain whether she will run as a ferry or packet, but in either case, she has our good wished for success."

Ten miles east of Des Arc and the White River ferry, there was another ferry. That ferry was at the Cache River. In the August 29, 1860 issue of the *Des Arc Citizen*, that ferry ran an advertisement:

> *"Best Route – Persons traveling eastward from Des Arc, will find it to their interest after travelling about ten miles, to take the left hand where the road forks and cross Cache River at the Upper Ferry, which is the oldest and best road, and ferry clear of causeway and mud. They can get ferried at half price and will get printed instructions to travel toward Memphis, which will save trouble and expense. Plenty corn and fodder. Attentive ferrymen always at hand.   George W. Mayberry, Proprietor"*

The above advertisement ran weekly in the Des Arc paper. Starting in October 3, 1860 two additional sentences were added:

> *"There is a Spring House, and a splendid spring of pure water, two hundred yards east of the river. There is a sign "Spring" near by it."*

The river port of Des Arc in Prairie County, located on the Lower White River, witnessed many steamboats travelling the White River. *The History of Des Arc* records that the *Des Arc Citizen* reported in 1858 that the Des Arc wharf had 370 arrivals by 27 different steamboats, and 8,000 bales of cotton were shipped from the wharf in 1859.

According to the December 4, 1858 issue of the *Des Arc Citizen*, the steamers Kate Frisbee and W. H. Langley charged cabin passengers $8 for passage between Memphis and Des Arc. The charge was less for passengers who rode on the open deck. The equivalent in value or purchasing power of $8 in 1850 is about $260 in 2021.

The History of Des Arc records that shipping cost were $1.25 per barrel of whisky, 50¢ for a sack of salt or barrel of flour; and that money or jewelry could be entrusted to the steamboat captain for ¼% of the value to protect it from robbery.

Many of the steamers passing through the Des Arc port were mail packets carrying mail up into central Arkansas.

Fortunately, the *Dec Arc Citizen* printed a weekly column called *"River News"* listing steamboat arrivals and departures. The issues of the Dec Arc Citizen between December 4, 1858 and September 26, 1860 have survived.

RIVER NEWS, &c.

☞ The U. S. mail packet Sam. Hale, Capt. C. W. Coles, passed up yesterday morning, bound for Jacksonport. Capt. W. Gibbes furnished us with late papers. The Hale will be down on Monday, bound for Napoleon.

☞ The U. S. Mail packet Fortune, Capt. Morg. Bateman, passed up Tuesday and returned Thursday morning. Henry E. Green, her clerk, has our thanks for late papers.

☞ The Return, Capt. Riley Jones, leaves Memphis this evening, and is due here Monday afternoon. She will pass down on her return trip to Memphis, on Tuesday night. Capt. Jim Booker furnished us with late papers last Tuesday morning.

☞ We learn from the Memphis papers that the price of cabin passage from Memphis to Des Arc, Ark., by either the Kate Frisbee or W. H. Langley, and the White river packets, has been fixed permanently at $8.

☞ Attention is directed to the advertisement of the steamer Grand Glaize. She will run from Jacksonport to Buffalo City.

Source: Des Arc Citizen, December 04, 1858 page 3

The steamboats gained favor with local newspapers b assisting them in exchanging papers with other cities. Th exchange of papers allowed the dissemination of news an provided stories for local papers to reprint for their subscri ers.

Other than a few passenger references in personal letter no Butterfield log books have been found from Arkansas' Bu terfield agents or from Chidester's stagecoach line to acc

rately report how many times Butterfield's Overland came up
the White River to Clarendon, DuVall's Bluff, or Des Arc.

JACKSON HOUSE,

AND STAGE OFFICE,

Des Arc, Arkansas.

M. M. ERWIN, Proprietor.

HAVING purchased this large and commodious public house, and erected additional buildings, the proprietor respectfully informs his friends, and the public generally, that he is prepared to accommodate all who may favor him with their patronage.

His Table

is supplied with the best the country affords, and the proprietor pledges himself to spare no pains or expense to promote the comfort of his guests.

The Rates of Charges are as follows:

Board and Lodging per month	$20 00
Board without Lodging per month	15 00
Board per day	1 50
Single meal—Dinner	50
Single meal—Breakfast or Supper	50
Supper, Lodging and Breakfast	1 00
Lodging	25

The stage office of CHIDESTER, REE-SIDE & Co.'s line of four-horse post-coaches, from Des Arc to Fort Smith, has been permanently located at the Jackson House.

oct2-tf

Source: Des Arc Citizen, November 13, 1858, page 4

However, we do know for certain that Butterfield Overland stages stopped at Des Arc's Butterfield Home Station at the Jackson House. In an advertisement on November 13, 1858 the Jackson House listed their room rates, which included a package of supper, lodging and breakfast for $1.

The Jackson House frequently printed a list of visitors who had checked in.

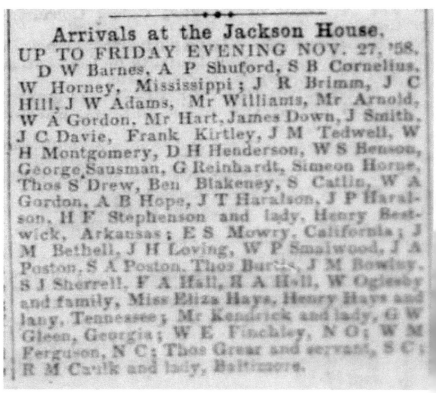

Arrivals at the Jackson House.
UP TO FRIDAY EVENING NOV. 27, '58.

D W Barnes, A P Shuford, S B Cornelius, W Horney, Mississippi; J R Brimm, J C Hill, J W Adams, Mr Williams, Mr Arnold, W A Gordon, Mr Hart, James Down, J Smith, J C Davie, Frank Kirtley, J M Tedwell, W H Montgomery, D H Henderson, W S Benson, George Sausman, G Reinhardt, Simeon Horne, Thos S Drew, Ben Blakeney, S Catlin, W A Gordon, A B Hope, J T Haralson, J P Haralson, H F Stephenson and lady, Henry Bestwick, Arkansas; E S Mowry, California; J M Bethell, J H Loving, W P Smalwood, J A Poston, S A Poston, Thos Burris, J M Bowley, S J Sherrell, F A Hall, R A Hall, W Oglesby and family, Miss Eliza Hays, Henry Hays and lady, Tennessee; Mr Kendrick and lady, G W Gleen, Georgia; W E Finchley, N O; W M Ferguson, N C; Thos Grear and servant, S C; R M Caulk and lady, Baltimore.

Source: Des Arc Citizen, November 27, 1858, page 3

About November 13, 1858, the Jackson House was put up for sale due to poor health of the owner M. M. Erwin. An advertisement with details of the sale began to run weekly in the *Des Arc Citizen*. The advertisement reveals that the Jackson House was:

> *...a brick building containing twelve rooms – connected therewith is a frame dining room, 45 feet long, 16*

feet wide. Also, connected is an office with a good Bar and a back room — each 18 feet square. There is also, another tenement disconnected from the main building, suitable for a barber shop — it is now occupied as a silver-smith shop. These is in all sixteen rooms. There is a good livery stable within 30 years of the premises... It is situated within 100 years of the steamboat landing, immediately on the main street. The U.S. Mail Stage Office is kept at this house."

Jackson House for Sale.

THE undersigned is desirous to sell the above House, which is situated in Des Arc. The house is a brick building containing twelve rooms—connected therewith is a frame dining room, 45 feet long, 16 feet wide. Also, connected is an office with a good Bar and a back room—each 18 feet square. There is, also, another tenement disconnected from the main building, suitable for a Barber Shop —it is now occupied as a Silver-smith Shop. There is in all sixteen rooms. There is a good Livery Stable within 30 yards of the premises.

I am not anxious to sell because the business will not pay, but on account of my health being bad, I cannot give my personal attention to the House. I venture the assertion that this tavern has cleared more money for the amount invested than any other business in the State. It is situated within 100 yards of the Steamboat Landing, immediately on the main street. The U. S. Mail Stage Office is kept at this House.

TERMS.—One-third cash ; balance in one and two years, with a lien on the property until the last payment is made.

☞ If not sold by the 1st day of January next, this property will be for rent or lease.

☞ For further information address me at Des Arc.   M. M. ERWIN.

nov. 13, 1858—t.1.j.

Source: Des Arc Citizen, Dec. 11, 1858

Based on the date an advertisement began in the *Des Arc Citizen*, the Jackson House was purchased about July 27, 1859 by J. F. and W. R. Welch. They renamed it Des Arc Hotel and Stage Office.

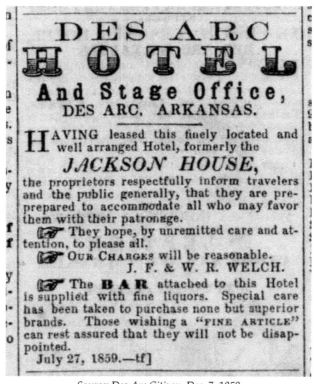

DES ARC
HOTEL
And Stage Office,
DES ARC, ARKANSAS.

HAVING leased this finely located and well arranged Hotel, formerly the **JACKSON HOUSE**, the proprietors respectfully inform travelers and the public generally, that they are pre-prepared to accommodate all who may favor them with their patronage.

☞ They hope, by unremitted care and attention, to please all.

☞ OUR CHARGES will be reasonable.

J. F. & W. R. WELCH.

☞ The **BAR** attached to this Hotel is supplied with fine liquors. Special care has been taken to purchase none but superior brands. Those wishing a "FINE ARTICLE" can rest assured that they will not be disappointed.

July 27, 1859.—tf]

Source: Des Arc Citizen, Dec. 7, 1859

The old Des Arc Hotel, on 4th and Main in Des Arc was demolished about 2011.
The Des Arc Library staff identify this as the original 1850's Jackson Hotel building.

The Louisville Daily Courier in the October 1, 1859 edition reported, *"The Charm, recently sold to Chidester, Rapley & Co., mail contractors in Arkansas, for the mail service on the White River, takes her departure this morning..."* John Chidester was aboard on that day as the Charm steamed for Arkansas.

The records are incomplete, but the Steamboat Registers published in the *Arkansas Gazette* do not record any departures for the Charm out of the port of Little Rock.

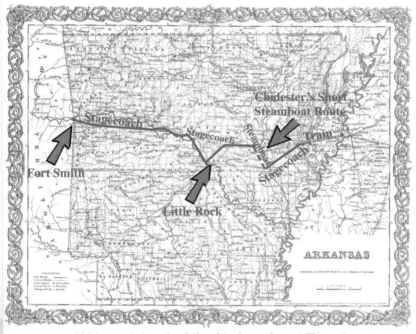

Chidester Advertised that his Steamboat "Charm"
would carry the Overland Mail and passengers from Des Arc to Clarendon.
The distance between Des Arc and Clarendon is about 40 miles by land,
or about 70 to 90 miles by water.

Arrivals and Departures of John T. Chidester's steamboat: the Charm at Des Arc

1859

turday, October 8, 1859 Memphis Daily Appeal
ARRIVALS YESTERDAY - Charm from Louisville

DEPARTURES YESTERDAY - *Charm for White River*
"The Charme (sic.), Messrs. Chidester, Rapley & Co.s' beautiful little new steamer for the mail service between Des Arc and Clarendon, passed down yesterday, Captain Chidester in command. "

October 12, 1859 Des Arc Citizen, page 3
"The Charm, Messrs. Chidester, Rapley & Co., new boat for the mail line between Des Ace and Clarendon, arrived here with the mail yesterday noon. She will hereafter leave Des Arc every Monday and Wednesday at 12 o'clock, p.m. The Charm is one of the prettiest little steamers afloat. Her length is 83 feet' depth of hold 3 feet; has two seven inch cylinders of 15 inches stroke; one twelve foot boiler and measures eighty-three tones."

Saturday, October 15, 1859 Memphis Daily Appeal
"The new steamer Charm got aground ten miles below DuVall's Bluff, in White River, a few days ago, and broke her rudder in the effort to get off."

October 19, 1859 Des Arc Citizen page 3
"The Des Arc and Clarendon U.S. Mail packet Charm, Captain H. B. Hendrix, will hereafter leave Des Arc for Clarendon every Sunday and Thursday, at noon."

October 26, 1859, Des Arc Citizen, page 3
"The Des Arc and Clarendon U.S.M. packet Charm, Captain H. B. Hendrix, arrived Sunday, and left on Monday. Captain Hendrix furnished us with Memphis papers of Saturday morning. Des Arc is now within one days travel of Memphis by this line. The Charm is due from Clarendon tomorrow noon, and will leave immediately on her return trip."

November 2, 1859, Des Arc Citizen, page 3
"The Des Arc and Clarendon U.S.M. packet Charm, Captain H. B. Hendrix, arrived Sunday, and left on Monday. Captain Hendrix furnished us with Memphis papers of Saturday morning. The Charm is due from Clarendon tomorrow noon, and will leave immediately on her return trip."

November 9, 1859 Des Arc Citizen, page 3
"The Des Arc and Clarendon U.S.M. packet Charm. Captain H. B. Hendrix, arrived Sunday, and left on Monday. Captain Hendrix furnished us with Memphis papers on Saturday morning. The Charm is due from Clarendon tomorrow noon, and will leave immediately on her return trip."

November 16, 1859 Des Arc Citizen page 3
"The Des Arc and Clarendon U.S.M. packet Charm, Captain H. B. Hendrix, arrived Sunday, and left on Monday. Captain Hendrix furnished us with Memphis papers on Saturday morning. The Charm is due from Clarendon tomorrow noon, and will leave immediately on her return trip."

November 30, 1859 Des Arc Citizen page 3
"The Des Arc and Clarendon U.S.M. packet Charm, Captain H. B. Hendrix, arrived Sunday, and left Monday. Captain Hendrix furnished us with Memphis papers of Thursday morning. The Charm is due from Clarendon tomorrow noon, and will leave immediately on her return trip."

December 7, 1859 Des Arc Citizen page 3
"The Des Arc and Clarendon U.S.M. packet Charm, Captain H. B. Hendrix, is due from Clarendon tomorrow noon, and will leave immediately on her return trip."

December 14, 1859 Des Arc Citizen page 3
"The Des Arc and Clarendon U.S.M. packet Charm, Captain H. B. Hendrix, is due from Clarendon tomorrow noon, and will leave immediately on her return trip."

December 21, 1859 Des Arc Citizen page 3
"The Des Arc and Clarendon U.S.M. packet Charm, Captain H. B. Hendrix, is due from Clarendon tomorrow noon, and will leave immediately on her return trip."

1860

January 4, 1860 Des Arc Citizen page 3
"The Des Arc and Clarendon U.S.M. packet Charm, Captain H. B. Hendrix, is due from Clarendon tomorrow noon, and will leave immediately on her return trip."

January 11, 1860 Des Arc Citizen page 3
"The Des Arc and Clarendon U.S.M. packet Charm, Captain H. B. Hendrix, arrived Sunday, and departed at noon on Monday. She is due again from Clarendon tomorrow noon, and will leave immediately on her return trip."

February 1, 1860 Des Arc Citizen, page 3
"The Des Arc and Clarendon U.S. Mail packet Charm, has broken her machinery, but will resume her trips as soon as the necessary repairs can be made."

March 14, 1860 Des Arc Citizen page 3
"The Charm, Captain Hendrix, arrived from Clarendon on Sunday evening, and left Monday noon."

March 21, 1860 Des Arc Citizen page 3
"The Charm, Captain Hendrix, arrived from Clarendon on Sunday evening, and left Monday noon."

Wednesday, April 11, 1860 The Memphis Daily Appeal
"Captain Chidester, the great southern mail contractor, left for Vicksburg by the steamer Kentucky yesterday. He has sold the steamer Charm, and she is now in upper White River."

Why did Chidester Re-Route the Overland?

John T. Chidester had a sub-contract to carry the Overland Mail and passengers by four horse stage from Fort Smith to Madison where it connected with the train to Memphis. From October 8, 1859 to April 11, 1860, instead once arriving in Des Arc, he used his steamboat Charm to carry the mail on the White River south to Clarendon, then by stage to Madison to connect with the train.

The reason for this re-routing may be because he had a separate contract with the Post Office to carry local mail from Clarendon to Madison (route #7846, paying $9,340 per year), and another contract to carry mail from Little Rock to Clarendon (route #7802, paying $7,150 per year).

Chidester was delinquent on these routes several times while he operated the Charm. The Report of the Postmaster General lists about a dozen failures to meet the contract during the time the Charm was in operation, October 8, 1859 to April 11, 1860:

Concerning route #7846 under contract to John T. Chidester, to carry mail between Madison and Clarendon, it was reported during the week ending April 28, 1860, that between January and March of 1860, that the mail failed to arrive at Camden 9 times, resulting in a fine of $134.73. During the week ending February 16, 1860 on this same route, under contract to Chidester, Rapley Hanger & Brimmer, it was reported that the *"failed to arrive"* at Clarendon on December 23, 24, 27, 27, resulting in a fine of $59.88. During the week of February 18, 1860 it was reported that the mail failed to arrive at Clarendon on Dec. 23, 24, 26 and 27, and therefore $59.88 was deducted also on October 28 at Madison, they *"failed to take the mail for Memphis,"* therefore $14.97 was deducted.

Concerning route # 7802 under contract to Chidester, Rapley, Hanger & Brimmer to carry mail between Little Rock and Clarendon, it was reported during the week ending Saturday April 28, 1860: *"It appearing that there were only fifty-four total failures, at $11.46, amounting to $518.8* *instead of $541.76, therefore remit $22.92."*

On this same route, it was also reported during the week ending April 28, 1860 that on March 10, the mail failed to arrive at Clarendon, resulting in a fine of $11.46.

Steamboats at Des Arc (Prairie County); 1860s.
Source: Courtesy of the Arkansas State Archives

White River Steamboat Port and Ferry Site at Des Arc
Source: Photo by Bob Crossman Oct. 29, 2021

The Return, Mary Cook & Kate Frisbee

There are several reports of occasions when Overland Mail Co. passengers or mail were carried by steamboats other than the *Jennie Whipple* or the Charm.

In the January 4, 1859 issue of the *San Francisco Daily Evening Bulletin*, a correspondent reported on his Overland Mail journey by boat from Des Arc to Memphis on the steamer The Return:

> *"On arriving in Des Arc, one of the passengers — that's myself — waited for a Memphis boat, while three of them took a passing steamer for New Orleans. The mail for Memphis was sent from Des Arc for Memphis on horseback over the country — being a distance of some 80 miles — while we were left to shift for ourselves in the way of getting to Memphis. The company paid our fare through. This was all right and according to agreement, but I am certain that the Department at Washington never contemplated that a delay of five days would take place owing to a want of means of conveyance — being two days at Fort Smith and three days at Des Arc... It is about 300 miles from Memphis to Des Arc by water, and about 80 or 90 by land... we left Des Arc ... The steamer Return ... It was near night when we entered the Mississippi River..."*

Occasionally Butterfield's passengers and mail were able to travel directly across Arkansas by steamboat on the Arkansas River. In the April 6, 1859 issue of Fayetteville's newspaper *The Arkansian*, there is an account a passenger "J. R. P." He successfully traveled by steamboat from Fort Smith to Memphis in March of 1859. The first leg of his journey from Fort Smith to Little Rock was on the steamboat Mary Cook. Initially the Mary Cook was to travel all the way to Memphis but arriving at Little Rock, the captain announced they were not going further. J. P. R writes, *"After staying at Van Buren four days we took passage on the steamboat Mary Cook for Napoleon. The accommodating Captain concluded that he would go no further than Little Rock..."*

J. R. P. then boarded the steamer *Jennie Whipple* to trav-

from Little Rock to Napoleon, Arkansas. J. R. P. writes, "... *Little Rock ...we remained one day and shipped on the Overland Mail steamer **Jennie Whipple** for Napoleon...*"

Arriving in Napoleon, Arkansas J. R. P. transferred to the mail packet steamboat Kate Frisbee to complete the last leg of this journey from Napoleon, Arkansas to Memphis. J. R. P. writes:

> "...*Napoleon, thence on the fine passenger mail packet, Kate Frisbee for Memphis. The Mississippi River at Napoleon was very high. It only lacked seven inches of being the high water mark of last spring. Memphis is beautifully situated, entirely above overflow and seems to be rapidly improving. Memphis will doubtless, ere many years, be one of the most important cities in the Southwest, on account of its situation, commerce and manufacturers, and being accessible from all parts of the United States by the Mississippi River and tributaries and numerous rail roads converging from every direction.*"

In the same month, referred to in the quote above, the steamboat Kate Frisbee ran an ad in the *Memphis Daily Avalanche* stating that she had a four year contract to carry the U.S. mail between Memphis and Napoleon, Arkansas and up the White River to Clarendon and Des Arc.

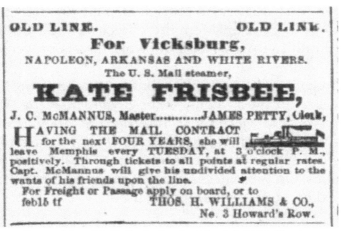

OLD LINE.   OLD LINE.

For Vicksburg,

NAPOLEON, ARKANSAS AND WHITE RIVERS.

The U. S. Mail steamer,

KATE FRISBEE,

J. C. McMANNUS, Master..........JAMES PETTY, Clerk,

HAVING THE MAIL CONTRACT for the next FOUR YEARS, she will leave Memphis every TUESDAY, at 3 o'clock P. M., positively. Through tickets to all points at regular rates. Capt. McMannus will give his undivided attention to the wants of his friends upon the line.

For Freight or Passage apply on board, or to
feb15 tf   THOS. H. WILLIAMS & CO.,
No. 3 Howard's Row.

Source: Memphis Daily Avalanche, March 1, 1859, Tuesday

Butterfield's steamboat *Jennie Whipple* traveling from Memphis to Fort Smith

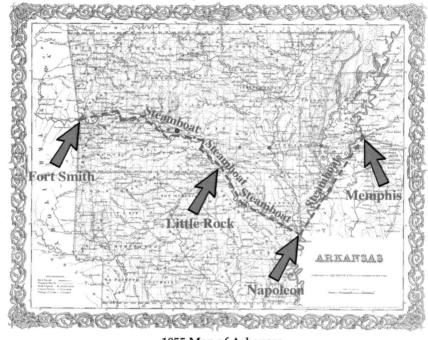

1855 Map of Arkansas
Published by J.H. Colton & Co., 112 Williams St., New York
The dotted lines show the approximate route
of the steamboat *Jennie Whipple.*

It was John Butterfield's original plan for the Overlan to travel by boat from Memphis direct through Little Roc to Fort Smith twice a week. Low water levels prevented th most of the time.

The records are incomplete, but we do have the *"Stean boat Register"* printed weekly in the *Arkansas Gazette, Memph Daily Appeal,* and *Memphis Daily Avalanche.* They record th the steamboat *Jennie Whipple* carried Overland mail and pa sengers the entire way from Memphis to Fort Smith on on 8 occasions. On those occasions the stage coaches, swing st tions, and home stations were not used.

This splendid, swift running passenger steamer will run regularly between Little Rock and Memphis, leaving Little Rock weekly for Memphis. Passengers ticketed through to Louisville, St, Louis or Cincinnati, by this boat.

Source: Weekly Arkansas Gazette, Little Rock, Arkansas
This ad ran frequently, starting on Saturday, April 2, 1859.

John Butterfield purchased the *Jennie Whipple* in St. Louis and it arrived in Little Rock on December 20. 1858.

1858

Dec	departed	St. Louis	for	Memphis
Dec __	departed	Memphis	for	Little Rock
Dec 20	arrived	Little Rock	from	St. Louis
Dec 22	departed	Little Rock	for	Fort Smith
Dec __	arrived	Fort Smith	from	Little Rock

1859

Jan __	departed	Fort Smith	for	Little Rock
Jan 8/9	arrived	Little Rock	from	Fort Smith
Jan 11	departed	Little Rock	for	Memphis
Jan 14	arrived	Memphis	from	Arkansas[+]

Apr 4	departed	Memphis	for	Little Rock
Apr 8	arrived	Little Rock	from	Memphis
Apr 9	departed	Little Rock	for	Fort Smith
Apr	arrived	Fort Smith	from	Little Rock
Apr __	departed	Fort Smith	for	Little Rock
Apr. 15	arrived	Little Rock	from	Fort Smith
Apr 15	departed	Little Rock	for	Memphis
Apr 18, 1859	arrived	Memphis	from	Little Rock
Mar 15, 1860	departed	Memphis	for	Arkansas River
April __	arrived	Little Rock	from	Memphis
April __	departed	Little Rock	for	Fort Smith
April __, 1860	arrived	Fort Smith	from	Little Rock
Feb __, 1861	departed	Fort Smith	for	Little Rock
Feb __	arrived	Little Rock	from	Fort Smith
Feb 6	departed	Little Rock	for	Memphis
Mar 4	arrived	Memphis	from	Little Rock
Mar 5	departed	Memphis	for	Little Rock
Mar 8	arrived	Little Rock	from	Memphis
Mar 9	departed	Little Rock	for	Fort Smith
Apr 6	arrived	Fort Smith	from	Memphis
Apr __	departed	Fort Smith	for	Memphis
Apr __	arrived	Little Rock	from	Memphis
Apr __	departed	Little Rock	for	Fort Smith
April 11	arrived	Memphis	from	Fort Smith

The *Jennie Whipple* was not the only steamboat connecting Fort Smith and Little Rock.

The December 25, 1858 *Weekly Arkansas Gazette*, ran an advertisement originally dated Dec. 15, 1858 promoting the steamboat S. H. Tucker and her commander, Reese Pritchard, connecting Fort Smith, Little Rock, and Napoleon.

> ## S. H. TUCKER,
> ### REESE PRITCHARD, COMMANDER,
> To connect at Little Rock, for Van Buren and Fort Smith, leaving Little Rock every Tuesday morning at 10 o'clock, and leaving Fort Smith on every Thursday evening at 2 o'clock, and Van Buren same evening. Passengers or freight ticketed through from Napoleon to Fort Smith, and from Fort Smith to Napoleon, at REGULAR RATES, and without detention.
>
> All business entrusted to this line will meet with prompt attention.
>
> JNO. D. ADAMS,
> *Dec.* 15, 1858.   *Contractor.*

Source: Weekly Arkansas Gazette, December 25, 1858, Saturday, page 3

In the October 22, 1859 issue of the *Weekly Arkansas Gazette*, an advertisement ran for the steamboat The Lady Walton, Captain Wm. B. Nowland, connecting Fort Smith and Little Rock.

> ## LADY WALTON,
> ### CAPT. WM B. NOWLAND,
> To connect at Little Rock, for Van Buren and Fort Smith, leaving Little Rock every Tuesday morning at 10 o'clock, and leaving Fort Smith on every Thursday evening at 2 o'clock, and Van Buren same evening. Passengers or freight ticketed through from Napoleon to Fort Smith, and from Fort Smith to Napoleon, at REGULAR RATES, and without detention.
>
> All business entrusted to this line will meet with prompt attention.
>
> JOHN D. ADAMS,
> *Dec.* 15, 1858.   *Contractor.*

Source: Weekly Arkansas Gazette, October 22, 1859, Saturday

It is possible that the Overland Mail occasionally used the H. Tucker or the Lady Walton eastward out of Fort Smith but the full record of the Overland's steamboat use does not exist.

The steamboat *Jennie Whipple* travelling from Memphis through Napoleon to Little Rock

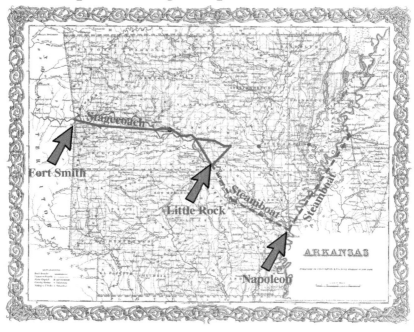

The solid and dotted lines show the approximate route
of Butterfield's Overland Mail.

The records are incomplete, but the records we have from the *"Steamboat Register"* printed weekly in the *Arkansas Gazette*, *Memphis Daily Appeal* and *Memphis Daily Avalanche* indicate that the steamboat ***Jennie Whipple*** carried the Overland mail and passengers direct from Memphis to Little Rock on 73 occasions.

On those occasions it bypassed all the swing and home stations between Memphis and Little Rock. However on the 73 occasions listed below, it appears that the stage coaches were still needed to carry the mail and passengers from Little Rock to Fort Smith.

In 1855, The *Traveller's and Tourist's Guide Through the United States of America*, by Wellington Williams reports on page 140:

"Passengers may go between Little Rock and Memphis by steamboat as follows: down the Arkansas River to its mouth, about 300 miles, thence up the Mississippi River to Memphis, 177 miles. Total, 477 miles."

1859

Jan 20, 1859	departed	Memphis	for	Fort Smith*

*Frequently the Memphis paper listed the destination of the *Jennie Whipple* as Fort Smith, but in fact she did not go farther upstream than Little Rock.

Jan 22/23	arrived	Little Rock	from	Memphis
Jan 22/24	departed	Little Rock	for	Memphis
Jan 27	arrived	Memphis	from	Arkansas+
Jan 28	departed	Memphis	for	Little Rock
Feb 5	arrived	Little Rock	from	Memphis
Feb 6	departed	Little Rock	for	Memphis
Feb __	arrived	Memphis	from	Little Rock
Feb 11	departed	Memphis	for	Fort Smith
Feb __	arrived	Little Rock	from	Memphis
Feb __	departed	Little Rock	for	Memphis
Feb __	arrived	Memphis	from	Little Rock
Feb 14	departed	Memphis	for	Arkansas River+

+Frequently the Memphis paper listed the destination of the *Jennie Whipple* with the generic 'Arkansas River.'

Feb 17/18	arrived	Little Rock	from	Memphis
Feb 18	departed	Little Rock	for	Memphis
Feb __	arrived	Memphis	from	Little Rock
Feb 25	departed	Memphis	for	Fort Smith*
Feb 28	arrived	Little Rock	from	Memphis
Mar 1	departed	Little Rock	for	Memphis
Mar __	arrived	Memphis	from	Little Rock
Mar 2	departed	Memphis	for	Little Rock
Mar __	arrived	Little Rock	from	Memphis
Mar __	departed	Little Rock	for	Memphis
Mar __	arrived	Memphis	from	Little Rock
Mar 9	departed	Memphis	for	Arkansas River+
Mar 10	arrived	Little Rock	from	Memphis
Mar 11	departed	Little Rock	for	Memphis
Mar __	arrived	Memphis	from	Little Rock

Mar 18	departed	Memphis	for	Little Rock
Mar. 21	arrived	Little Rock	from	Memphis
Mar. 22	departed	Little Rock	for	Memphis
Mar __	arrived	Memphis	from	Little Rock
Mar 26	departed	Memphis	for	Little Rock
Mar 29	arrived	Little Rock	from	Memphis
Mar 29	departed	Little Rock	for	Memphis
Apr 2	arrived	Memphis	from	Little Rock
Apr 2	departed	Memphis	for	Little Rock
Apr __	arrived	Little Rock	from	Memphis
Apr __	departed	Little Rock	for	Memphis
Apr __	arrived	Memphis	from	Little Rock
Apr 21	departed	Memphis	for	Fort Smith
Apr 24/25	arrived	Little Rock	from	Memphis
Apr 25/26	departed	Little Rock	for	Memphis
May __	arrived	Memphis	from	Little Rock
May 2	departed	Memphis	for	Fort Smith
May 5	arrived	Little Rock	from	Memphis
May 6	departed	Little Rock	for	Memphis
May 9	arrived	Memphis	from	Little Rock
May 12	departed	Memphis	for	Fort Smith
May 15	arrived	Little Rock	from	Memphis
May 15	departed	Little Rock	for	Memphis
May 17	arrived	Memphis	from	Little Rock
May 20	departed	Memphis	for	Little Rock
May 22	arrived	Little Rock	from	Memphis
May 23	departed	Little Rock	for	Memphis
May 25	arrived	Memphis	from	Little Rock
May 28	departed	Memphis	for	Little Rock
May 30/31	arrived	Little Rock	from	Memphis
May 31	departed	Little Rock	for	Memphis
June 2	arrived	Memphis	from	Little Rock
June 4	departed	Memphis	for	Fort Smith
June 7	arrived	Little Rock	from	Memphis
June 7	departed	Little Rock	for	Memphis
June 9	arrived	Memphis	from	Little Rock
June 11	departed	Memphis	for	Arkansas River
June 13	arrived	Little Rock	from	Memphis
June 14	departed	Little Rock	for	Memphis

June 16	arrived	Memphis	from	Little Rock
June 18	departing	Memphis	for	Fort Smith
June 20/21	arrived	Little Rock	from	Memphis
June 21	departed	Little Rock	for	Memphis
June 23	arrived	Memphis	from	Little Rock
June 25	departed	Memphis	for	Little Rock
June 28	arrived	Little Rock	from	Memphis
June 28	departed	Little Rock	for	Memphis
June 31	arrived	Memphis	from	Little Rock
July 2	departed	Memphis	for	Arkansas River
July 4/5	arrived	Little Rock	from	Memphis
July 5	departed	Little Rock	for	Memphis
July 7	arrived	Memphis	from	Little Rock
July 9	departed	Memphis	for	Arkansas River
July 10/12	arrived	Little Rock	from	Memphis
July 11/12	departed	Little Rock	for	Memphis
July 15	arrived	Memphis	from	Little Rock
July 16	departed	Memphis	for	Arkansas River
July 20	arrived	Little Rock	from	Memphis
July 21	departed	Little Rock	for	Memphis

*"We regret to learn that the Memphis and Little Rock packet, **Jennie Whipple**, is hard aground in the Arkansas River. She will, in all probability, get off and arrive in ample time to depart at her regular hour tomorrow for Little Rock."*

July 26	arrived	Memphis	from	Little Rock

*"The steamboat **Jennie Whipple** came in at an early hour yesterday morning, with a good trip, and reports the water in the Arkansas River as being in a very scant condition. The bars are all visible and navigation is much impeded. Captain Gray informs us that the **Jeannie Whipple** will make one more trip to Little Rock, after which, if the water does not rise, she will be removed to the Cincinnati and Memphis trade, in which she will run until the Fall business commences.*

The Mississippi at this point recedes at the rate of three inches per day, the fall since our last report, of Sunday morning, having been exactly six inches. The waters are falling with rapidity, and the tributaries below are getting so very low as to impede navigation to a great extent.

*The **Jennie Whipple** was detained during some hours in the Arkansas River, on her trip to this place, on the above accounts...."*

July 27	departing	Memphis	for	Little Rock
July __	arrived	Little Rock	from	Memphis
Aug __	departed	Little Rock	for	Memphis
Aug 5	arrived	Memphis	from	Arkansas River
Sept 5	departed	Memphis	for	Arkansas River
Sept 10	arrived	Little Rock	from	Memphis
Sept __	departed	Little Rock	for	Memphis
Sept 15	arrived	Memphis	from	Arkansas River
Sept 17	departed	Memphis	for	Arkansas River
Sept 21	arrived	Little Rock	from	Memphis
Sept __	departed	Little Rock	for	Memphis
Sept 25	arrived	Memphis	from	Arkansas River
Sept 26	departed	Memphis	for	Little Rock

The Arkansas River continues quite low, and the *Jennie Whipple* was delayed on her upward trip

Oct __	arrived	Little Rock	from	Memphis
Oct __	departed	Little Rock	for	Memphis
Oct __	arrived	Memphis	from	Little Rock
Oct 8	departed	Memphis	for	Little Rock
Oct __	arrived	Little Rock	from	Memphis
Oct __	departed	Little Rock	for	Memphis
Oct __	arrived	Memphis	from	Little Rock
Oct 15	departed	Memphis	for	Little Rock
Oct __	arrived	Little Rock	from	Memphis
Oct __	departed	Little Rock	for	Memphis
Oct __	arrived	Memphis	from	Little Rock
Nov 26	departed	Memphis	for	Arkansas River
Dec __	arrived	Little Rock	from	Memphis
Dec __	departed	Little Rock	for	Memphis
Dec 4/5	arrived	Memphis	from	Arkansas River
Dec 8	departed	Memphis	for	Arkansas River
Dec __	arrived	Little Rock	from	Memphis
Dec __	departed	Little Rock	for	Memphis
Dec 18/19	arrived	Memphis	from	Arkansas River
Dec 20	departed	Memphis	for	Little Rock
Dec __	arrived	Little Rock	from	Memphis
Dec __	departed	Little Rock	for	Memphis
Dec 28	arrived	Memphis	from	Little Rock
Dec 30	departed	Memphis	for	Little Rock

1860

Jan 2	arrived	Little Rock	from	Memphis
Jan 2	departed	Little Rock	for	Memphis
Jan __	arrived	Memphis	from	Little Rock
Jan 10	departed	Memphis	for	Little Rock

*"The **Jennie Whipple** and South Bend were at Napoleon Thursday, having been detained by the fog."*

Jan 14	arrived	Little Rock	from	Memphis
Jan 14	departed	Little Rock	for	Memphis
Jan 17	arrived	Memphis	from	Little Rock
Jan 18/19	departed	Memphis	for	Little Rock
Jan 21	arrived	Little Rock	from	Memphis
Jan 21	departed	Little Rock	for	Memphis
Jan __	arrived	Memphis	from	Little Rock
Jan __	departed	Memphis	for	Arkansas River
Jan 23	arrived	Little Rock	from	Memphis
Jan 24	departed	Little Rock	for	Memphis
Jan 24	arrived	Memphis	from	Arkansas River
Jan 25	departed	Memphis	for	Little Rock
Jan 28	arrived	Little Rock	from	Memphis
Jan 28	departed	Little Rock	for	Memphis
Jan __	arrived	Memphis	from	Little Rock
Mar 6	departed	Memphis	for	Fort Smith
Mar __	arrived	Little Rock	from	Memphis
Mar __	departed	Little Rock	for	Memphis
Mar 11/12	arrived	Memphis	from	Arkansas River
Mar 15	departed	Memphis	for	Arkansas River
Mar 18	arrived	Little Rock	from	Memphis
Mar 18	departed	Little Rock	for	Memphis

There are also passenger references to this leg of the Overland Mail being carried on other steamboats such as: The Rearn, H. Langley, and Kate Frisbee, but the complete record of which steamboats the Butterfield utilized has not been found.

The steamboat *Jennie Whipple* traveling from Little Rock direct to Fort Smith

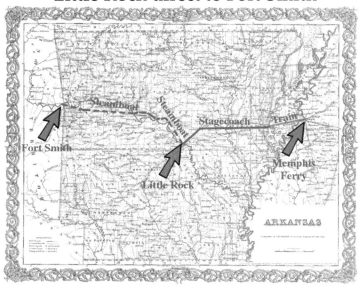

Dotted lines added to show the steamboat's Fort Smith - Little Rock route.

The *Jennie Whipple* carried the Overland mail and passengers from Little Rock to Fort Smith, instead of using stage coaches on 4 occasions in the winter of 1858/1859. No additional Little Rock to Fort Smith round trips are recorded other than the 8 times when the full round trip was from Fort Smith to Memphis and return.

1858

Dec __	departed	Fort Smith	to	Little Rock
Dec 28	arrived	Little Rock	from	Fort Smith
Dec 29, 1858	departed	Little Rock	for	Fort Smith
Jan __, 1859	arrived	Fort Smith	from	Little Rock

1859

Jan __	departed	Fort Smith	to	Little Rock
Jan 3	arrived	Little Rock	from	Fort Smith
Jan 4	departed	Little Rock	for	Fort Smith
Jan __	arrived	Fort Smith	from	Little Rock

Butterfield's Overland Mail by Steamboat from Memphis to Napoleon to Clarendon or Des Arc

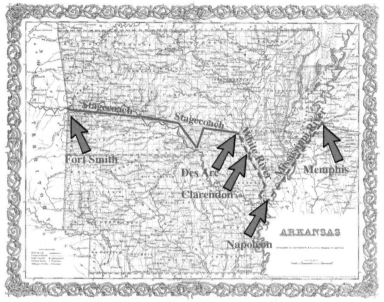

**Dotted lines added to show the steamboat route from
Memphis to Napoleon to Clarendon to Des Arc.**
The rest of the trip to Fort Smith would have been by stage.

When water levels were too low on the Arkansas River to reach Little Rock's port, yet water levels on the White River were still favorable, Butterfield's Overland Mail Co. took advantage of steamboats out of Memphis for the first leg of the journey to Fort Smith.

Leaving Memphis the steamboat would take the Mississippi River south, then at Napoleon turn north on the White River to the port at Clarendon or Des Arc.

No port registers or records have been found listing which steamboats carried Butterfield's Overland Mail Co. passengers and mail from Memphis to Napoleon and on to Clarendon, other than one or two passengers reference to their personal trip.

Butterfield's Overland Mail by Steamboat from Memphis through Napoleon to Pine Bluff

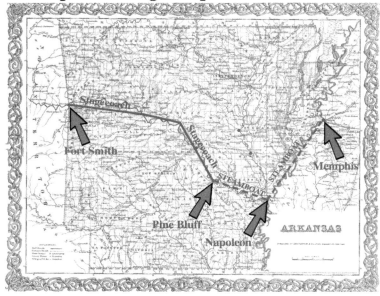

Dotted lines added to show the steamboat route from Memphis through Napoleon to Pine Bluff.
The rest of the trip to Fort Smith would have been by stage.

The Pine Bluff papers for this time period have not survived so port arrivals and departures are not available. However, it appears that every time the *Jennie Whipple* passed Pine Bluff on the way to Little Rock she would stop at the Pine Bluff port. This is based on numerous mentions in the Memphis papers, such as:

> "*For Arkansas River - The fine and staunch Jennie Whipple, Capt. C. C. Gray, will leave for Pine Bluff, Little Rock and Fort Smith, at five o'clock this afternoon.*"

There were occasions when the Arkansas River water levels were too low to continue on to Little Rock. On one occasion October 15, 1859 the *Jennie Whipple* ran aground, unloaded her freight at Pine Bluff, and returned to port at Memphis.

| Oct. 15, 1859 | departed | Memphis | for | Little Rock |
| Oct. 18 | arrived | Pine Bluff | from | Memphis |

"The **Jennie Whipple** was hard aground, just below Richland, having been in that condition twenty-four hours. Capt. Gray had reshipped his Little Rock freight at Pine Bluff, and attempted to return from that point."

| Oct __ | departed | Pine Bluff | for Memphis |
| Oct. 24/25 | arrived | Memphis | from Pine Bluff |

"The **Jennie Whipple** arrived with 80 bales of cotton from the Arkansas River.."

To arrive at Pine Bluff, the **Jennie Whipple** would leave Memphis taking the Mississippi River south, then at Napoleon turn north on the Arkansas River to the port at Pine Bluff. There was also a White River cut off several miles upstream on the Mississippi that led directly to the Arkansas River and bypassed the port of Napoleon altogether.

NAPOLEON

The town of Napoleon in Desha County, at the confluence of the Arkansas and Mississippi Rivers, served as a river port for steamboats carrying the Overland Mail between Memphis and Fort Smith to Clarendon to Des Arc. About a dozen years after the Overland, the town was deserted when the banks of the Mississippi overflowed and much of the Napoleon town and river port was destroyed.

Engraving of Napoleon, Arkansas

Mark Twain, Samuel Langhorne Clemens (1835 to 1910)

Samuel Clemens was known by the pen name Mark Twain. Photograph taken in his old age. The town of Napoleon was the subject of a chapter in Mark Twain's Life on the Mississippi, in which he tells a story of learning from a deathbed confession that $10,000 was hidden behind a brick in a building in Napoleon. When Twain tried to retrieve it, he discovered the entire town had been washed away. Twain reports that the early explorers De Soto, Marquette and Joliet, and La Salle visited *"the site of the future town of Napoleon, Arkansas"* in their pioneering journeys.

Do we have details on the steamboats construction?

Most of the steamboats were new because on average, the vessels only lasted about five years due to the wooden hulls being breached, poor maintenance, fires, general wear and tear, and the common boiler explosion. By the 1850's the average Mississippi River steamboat was about 250 feet long with a 40 foot beam and could carry 350 passengers as well as some 700 tons of freight. A steamboat this size could cost $50,000 to $75,000, but this amount could often be made back in one good season.

Duane Huddleston, in *Steamboats and Ferries on the White River* (page 15) describes the basic shape of the steamboats:

"A steamboat's design, however, was not for beauty but for practicality. The shallow nature of many rivers required vessels with a wide shallow hull or bottom. Decks stacked on top of one another provided needed space for both passengers and cargo, since there was little room in the hull of the boat for either. The position of the pilothouse afforded the pilot an excellent view of the waters ahead, and two smokestacks were used rather than one because a single stack in front of the pilothouse would have obstructed the pilot's view. The smokestacks were quite tall in order to increase their draft and enable the boilers to operate more efficiently. Gangplanks were necessary at most landings since few towns and none of the plantations and farms had docking facilities. While many of the steamboats displayed ornate trimmings, the fundamental design of the craft was very functional and related to the specific problems of river travel."

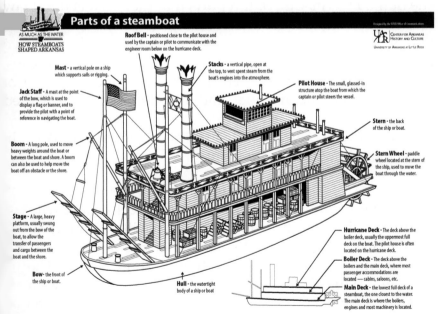

Duane Huddleston goes on to describe the basic propulsion of the steamboats:

"There were two basic types of steamboats, the stern-

wheeler and the side-wheeler. As the name imply, their difference came from the placement of the paddle wheel. The sternwheelers could operate in shallower water... Sidewheelers, however, were easier to maneuver and were faster."

Steamboats constructed for tributaries of the Mississippi River were typically narrower and shorter than those built for the mighty Mississippi River. The smaller size allowed the boats to navigate tight bends in the smaller rivers, and to have a shallower drought that allowed them to operate in shallow water.

The White River flows faster than the Arkansas River, resulting in fewer sand dunes and a deeper channel. Therefore, it was not uncommon for the White River to remain navigable during droughts, when such conditions shut down steamboat traffic on the Arkansas River.

In the *"River News"* column in the July 18, 1860 (page 3) issue of the *Des Arc Citizen* it reports that there is a Federal law known as *"The Protection for Passengers."* That law requires that any steamboat carrying passengers without having two life-boats, a certain number of water buckets and fire axes, shall forfeit and pay for each trip the sum of $500. Half of the fine went to the informer, and the other half to the United States.

Way's Packet Directory, 1848-1994 by Frederick Way, Jr gives the following information:

The *Jennie Whipple*

The *Jennie Whipple* was a sternwheel packet with a wood hull, built in 1857 at Brownsville, Pennsylvania. She was 138 tons, 135 feet long, and 30 feet wide. The engines were 15 ½'s 3 ½ ft, with three boilers. The *Jennie Whipple* was built for the Chippewa River with Capt. Charles C. Gray, but soon went to the Arkansas River from 1858 to 1859 with Capt. A. D. Storm running to Memphis. In August 1864, she loaded the 7th Infantry Volunteers at Burlington and took them to St.

Louis. The *Jennie Whipple* went off the lists in 1866.

The Charm

The Charm was a wood hulled sternwheel packet, built in 1860 at Cincinnati, Ohio. She was 223 tons. On Nov. 7, 1861 she was at the Battle of Belmont, ferrying Confederate troops, wounded, and bodies of the slain. On May 17, 1863 Confederates burned the boat to prevent her capture after the Battle of Big Black. The wreck of the Charm was found by skin divers in August 1962 and many souvenirs were brought up.

There were three other steamboats mentioned by passengers as carrying them, along with the Overland Mail over part of all of the route from Fort Smith to Memphis: The Return, The Mary Cook, and The Kate Frisbee. No records exist to report how frequent these three steamboats carried the Overland Mail Co. passengers or mail.

The Return

The Return was a sternwheel packet with a wood hull, built in 1852 at California, Pennsylvania. She was 219 tons, 152 feet long, 28 feet wide, and 5 ½ feet from bottom timbers to the main deck floor timbers in the body of the hull about midships. Last owner and master was Capt. J. R. Jones. The Return was lost at DeValls Bluff, Arkansas on July 27, 1859.

The Mary Cook

The Mary Cook was a sternwheel packet with a wood hull, built in 1857 at California, Pennsylvania. Transported troops on the Kanawha River to Louisville in 1862 and then dismantled.

The Katie Frisbee

The Katie Frisbee was a sternwheel packet with a wood hull, built in 1853 at California, Pennsylvania. She was 456 tons, 203 feet long, 32 feet wide, and 7.3 feet from bottom timbers to the main deck floor timbers in the body of the hull about midships. With Capt. Frisbee, she ran Memphis to Napoleon route on the

– 333 –

White River carrying U.S. Mail. She was the first at the scene when the steamboat Pennsylvania exploded at Ship Island on June 13, 1858. When the Katie Frisbee was dismantled in 1861, her engines went to The Louisville steamboat.

STEAMBOATS USED WOOD FOR FUEL

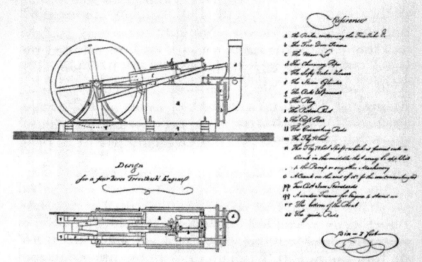

Fig. 24. Rastrick's design of a diagonal Trevithick engine for a steamboat, *c.* 1813. From the *Goodrich Papers*

Wood was burned below a boiler full of water, at an average rate of 4 cords of wood an hour. When the water boiled the steam it released powered a piston, which then turned the paddle wheel at the stern (rear) of the boat to move the water craft forward.

Van Hawkins, in *Smoke up the River: Steamboats and the Arkansas Delta*, page 36, writes:

> "When a vessel's fuel supply dwindled, its pilot pulled into the first woodyard he reached, generally located four to five miles apart along rivers. Sometimes fuel appeared at a plantation landing, cut and stacked there, but often fuel came from isolated sites.
>
> ...a boat reached the bank, tied up and dropped gang-

ways, crewmen and deck passengers, who were required to help load wood to pay for their passage, dashed ashore...

According to Huddleston, those who owned wood did not have to be present. If his wood was picked up, the owner went to a convenient landing when the boat was due and presented his bill. Theft of cordwood stacked along Delta rivers was 'almost unknown.'

...If a steamer became dangerously low of fuel... crews disembarked and chopped down trees."

The first practical steamboat was built by American inventor Robert Fulton in 1807. The most important advantage of a paddlewheel-powered boat Fulton designed is the low draught, so the boats could go far up the rivers, even when the water level was very low. This was a very important feature for opening up the frontier for pioneers and settlers.

Eventually oil and coal replaced wood for fuel. A few years later diesel engines would replace coal and oil engines.

Steamboat "Wooding Up" on the Mississippi River

Steamboat on the White River, circa 1863

View of San Francisco, 1852

San Francisco, 1850.
Nsansome Street At The Beginning Of The California Gold Rush.

CHAPTER SIX
Exhibit of Bob Crossman's
Butterfield Postal History Collection

Exhibit Purpose: To show covers carried by Butterfield's Overland Mail between September 1858 and March 1861. Also, to include some additional information on, and artifacts from, overland mail carried immediately before and immediately after the existence of Butterfield's Overland Mail Company.

Background: The population of California tripled in size in less than a decade in large part due to the discovery of gold and the Gold Rush that resulted. In response to that growth, on March 3, 1857, Congress authorized Aaron V. Brown, U.S. Postmaster General, to contract for delivery of the U.S. mail overland to California. The mail was to be carried overland in four-horse stagecoaches from St. Louis and Memphis to San Francisco in twenty-five days or less. The contract was awarded to the Overland Mail Company, John Butterfield, president.

Butterfield's Overland Mail Company stagecoach service operated from mid September 1858 to mid March 1861, carrying U.S. Mail and passengers between the Mississippi River and California to fulfill the U.S. postal contract.

Simultaneously the Overland Mail left San Francisco, St. Louis and Memphis. Stations were built every 15 to 20 miles for a change of horses for this day and night, almost non-stop 23 day transcontinental journey.

The two eastern terminus, Memphis and St. Louis began the westward journey by train. From St. Louis the train traveled 168 miles to tracks end at Tipton, Missouri. From Memphis, the train traveled 24 miles to tracks end 12 miles east of Madison, Arkansas. Transferring from the trains, the two stagecoaches traveled westward from Tipton, Missouri and Madison, Arkansas merge at Fort Smith. From Fort Smith the Overland continued as a single stagecoach westward toward the terminus at San Francisco.

From San Francisco, the stagecoach headed east to Fort Smith, where the mail and passengers were divided, based on destination.

Image Source: Western Cover Society

1850 Pre-Butterfield's Overland Mail

Before the existence of Butterfield's Overland Mail route, mail was still carried to California, however it traveled slower. This letter traveled 529 miles in 40 days. Eight years later, the Butterfield stages, in contrast, would cover some of the same roads, but travel the 2,700 miles in only 23 days.

Postmarked
June 26, 1850
Jackson, TN
eighty miles due
east of Memphis.

Note on Reverse:
*"Rec'd this letter,
Tuesday, Aug. 6th,
1850."*

This cover was purchased at the 2018 Portland, Oregon Stamp Show from John F. Ullmann Collectibles of Edmonds, Washington.

Contents of this Folded Letter Sheet

Jackson Tenn. June 25th 1850
Tuesday

D'r Robert

 I am anxious to hear from Texas and to know how you are pleased with prospects. I have seated myself to draft you a few lines. I wrote to Thomas some time ago asking information on various subjects relative to my contemplated move to your part of the country, but his reply was not of such a flattering character as to cause me to sacrifice my property here to go to a new country Thomas has done very well, all things considered, he would not see me suffer I believe, but in the event that I sold my property on credit here. I wanted some assurance for that assistance that I could depend on.

 That part of my letter he has passed unnoticed. This I regret as it has frustrated all my hopes of moving and being able to engage in business to my satisfaction. I certainly expected nothing, only as a loan and feel sorry that I mentioned it at all.

 I would not borrow a dollar from any man without giving him ample security. I have offered my property for sale, but have not had but one offer yet for it, viz 10 annual payments each $225.00 bearing that this is what I gain, and have spent besides about $700.00 for improvements, I can not sell on such credit and have anything to start business with to carry it on successfully. Therefore for the present I am not deciding what will be my future course about that matter.

 Thomas arrived at Reynoldsburg on Tennessee River a few days ago on his way to Ireland. He says he can not come to see us until he returns.

 Amelia has been very unwell for about 3 months. She has the Dyspepsia, I think. I think her general health has some what improved in a few days and I hope she will continue to improve. She exercises very much. The children are well. Your children are all well and getting a long about as usual.

 Mrs. Henderson and Mary are well also. Susan is here. ____, she borrowed Mr. Smith's buggy & John drove. I met them on Thursday. Susan was quite unwell with she left home with chills, but exercises good water and a scatterment of her ideas by the trip, all combined, have made her look much better and knocked the chills out of sight. She has been here 10 days and has improved in health daily. Recollect you owe me a big Doctor bill for the trip too, but this we will settle in Texas. We go today to Mr. Barns for dinner tonight to Mrs. McWilliams, tomorrow to Mr. Davisons for dinner then home again.

 Susan speaks of starting some again next week, so you may rest satisfied that the Bairns at home are well attended to as Susan & John are in good health here. Susan has had a great many Ladies to see her, and has returned a good many visits. Her trip has added to her health and I hope will be remembered with pleasure and as it will cost only her trouble, she will not sustain any loss Indeed I am satisfied she has escaped a spell of chills by ____ing at this time.

 After you see your way pretty clear about business prospects & c I want to hear from you how you like the country, how business compares with your expectations, what amount you sell each month & what is the amount of your profit monthly.

 Business with me is dull. I am not making expenses, however this is the dullest time of the year.

 Crops are very bad generally in this country owing to incessant rains and frost.

 The last letter received from you was written at Houston. Susan is expecting one from you daily. I wrote to Mary and told her to forward all letters up to the 27th to his place.

 Say to John, that he must not for the present buy any cattle or anything for me, as I can't come to any decision about moving as I can't sell my town property, but may have an opportunity after a while. Give our united love to John & Margaret. Let us know Eliza has got.

 We shall be glad to hear from you to know how you are pleased & c. Susan and all unite in love to you and best wishes your good health & that you may be able to realize all your expectations and get into a prosperous business is the wish.

Yours Truly, James P. Co

1858 Ocean Steam Ship Cover to Maine

The sender used a US postal stationary envelope, embossed with a green U16 on buff paper. The letter was written on September 20, 1858 and was canceled at the San Francisco, California Post Office the following day, September 21, 1858.

This cover was mailed one week after the beginning of Butterfield's Overland Mail Co. route. The sender could have, for no additional postage, requested for this letter to be carried *"overland via Los Angeles"* by stagecoach. In 1858 and 1859, the default route for all transcontinental mail was by ocean going ship to the Isthmus of Panama or by ship around the southern tip of South America.

Postmarked:
    September 21, 1858
    San Francisco,
    California

Addressed to:
    J. W. Webb Esq.
Care of Farris & Webb
    Bangor, Main

*This cover was purchased at the 2014 APS Little Rock Show
from Roger Gutzman, R. G. Stamps of Bigg, California.*

1850 Cruchley Map, with Postal/Passenger sailing routes added.

1858 Westbound Ocean Steam Ship Cover to San Francisco

Based on the postmark, this cover was mailed from either Carmichael or Carbondale, Pennsylvania. Postmarked August 4, this 1858 letter from Pennsylvania was carried by oceangoing steamship. Since the letter was in transit only 5 to 6 weeks, arriving September 17-19, 1858 it must have crossed at the Panama Isthmus on its way to San Francisco. If it had been carried further south past the tip of South America, it could not have made that longer journey in only 44 to 46 days.

Traveling over 3,000 miles, it carried the correct postage paid with a ten cent stamp.

Purchased at the 2021 APS show in Chicago
from Mark C. Reasoner of Prospect Heights, Illinois.

1861 Eastbound Ocean Steam Ship Cover to New York

In late December 1860, Butterfield's Overland Mail Co. became the defaul carrier of all transcontinental mail. This particular letter would have traveled b stagecoach on the Butterfield, except that the sender specifically wanted this lette to travel by ocean steam ship, and marked on the cover "Via Panama."

Postmarked January 10, 1861 in Sacramento, California and addressed t Robert McCaull, Cayuga Bridge, Cayuga County, New York, traveling over 3,00 miles, it carried the correct postage paid with a ten cent Scott #35 stamp.

Purchased at the 2021 APS show in Chicago
from Paul and Becky Huber of Beaufort, North Carolina.

Butterfield Mail On The Memphis Route

This letter was mailed from Quincy, California on February 26, addressed to Fort Valley, Georgia - a distance of over 3,000 miles requiring postage of 10¢. The Quincy postmaster wrote "Paid 10^{c}" in the upper right to indicate that the sender had paid the postage at the Quincy Post Office.

John Birkinbine, of American Philatelic Brokerage in Tucson, Arizona believes there is a 95% probability that this letter, with a Georgia destination, traveled the Memphis leg of the Butterfield route instead of the St. Louis route.

Postmarked:
Feb 26 Quincy, Cal.
Addressed to:
  Rev. Whitman C. Hill
  Fort Valley,
    Houston Co. Georgia

The Rev. Hill was born 1790, admitted as a Methodist minister in 1809, and died 1861.

This cover was purchased on ebay from
Mark Baker, Pollock Pines, California, mbcovers@directcon.net

This is one of just a handful of Memphis route covers that have survived.
From the Quincy, California post office, this letter would have traveled
February 26 or 27th by horseback or wagon south to catch
the 8 a.m. Monday or Thursday Butterfield Stage out of San Francisco.
From San Francisco via Los Angeles, Fort Yuma then to Gila River, Arizona.
Then from Gila River to Tucson, and to Soldier's Farewell, Texas.
Then to ElPaso, Pecos River Crossing, Fort Chadbourne, to Fort Belknap.
Then to Sherman, Texas to Fort Smith, Arkansas, then to
Little Rock and by stage or steamboat to Memphis.
At Memphis a train would have completed the journey to Georgia.

If this letter was mailed in 1859, it would have traveled from Little Rock to Memphis, on the March 22nd Steamboat *"Jennie Whipple"* that was owned by John Butterfield.

If this letter was mailed in 1860 or 1861, the *"Jennie Whipple"* was unavailable – grounded above Little Rock due to low water. So then, the letter would have then traveled by stagecoach all the way from Fort Smith across Arkansas.

© 2022 Robert O. Crossman

1859 Memphis Route - Butterfield's Overland Mail Cover to Mississippi

The sender of this cover (envelope) paid the 10¢ postage for a ½ ounce letter traveling more than 3,000 miles. The sender wrote instructions to the postmaster in the upper left of the envelope: *"Overland via Los Angeles."*

Arriving in Little Rock, this letter departed on John Butterfield's Arkansas River steamboat "Jennie Whipple," on May 6, arriving at Memphis May 9, 1859.

Postmarked:
San Francisco,
April 8, 1859

Designated:
"Overland via Los Angeles"

Addressed to:
Miss Zoe LaCrozer
Nactchez,
Mississippi

This cover was purchased at the
Little Rock Pinnacle Club Stamp Show in 2018.   ex Allen

November 1858 Butterfield's Overland Mail Cover to Kentucky

The first eastbound batch of Butterfield's Overland Mail left San Francisco on September 16, 1858. Just sixty days later, this cover was postmarked in November of 1858 in San Francisco. While most of the transcontinental mail in 1858 was carried by ship to the Isthmus of Panama, transported over the Isthmus, then boarded onto a second ship for the trip north to the states. This sender, however, preferred that the letter travel my stagecoach so the sender wrote instructions to the postmaster in the lower left: *"via Overland Mail Los Angeles."*

This particular letter may have been carried over the Memphis route instead of St. Louis route since this letter's destination was due east of Memphis, just north of Nashville across the Kentucky state line

Postmarked:
November of 1858
San Francisco,
California.

US postal stationary
envelope: Scott #U15

Addressed to:
Miss Mary Ann Stewar
Columbus,
Adair County,
Kentucky.

This cover was purchased at the 2018 Little Rock Pinnacle Stamp Show.

© 2022 Robert O. Crossman

1859 Memphis Route - Butterfield's Overland Mail Cover to East Tennessee

This is one of just a handful of Memphis route covers that have survived.

This cover was mailed from Iowa City, California, postmarked July 14, 1859. The Iowa City postmaster stamped a circular "PAID 10" to indicate the sender paid the 10¢ postage due for letters traveling 3,000 miles or more.

Leaving Iowa City, California and traveling about 140 miles south to San Francisco this cover boarded Butterfield's Overland Mail Co. stagecoach to Fort Smith, then on to Little Rock. Arriving in Little Rock, Arkansas about August 1 or 2, 1859, this letter departed on John Butterfield's Arkansas River steamboat *"Jennie Whipple,"* arriving at Memphis August 5, 1859. From Memphis this cover travelled another 400 miles due east to Philadelphia, Monroe County, Tennessee.

This letter was probably sent by Robert R. Cleveland to his wife, Sydney G. Nelson Cleveland (born July 15, 1811 - died October 23, 1884). Robert R. Cleveland's ancestors moved from Virginia to Blount County, Tennessee after the Revolutionary War, and the Cleveland children scattered through Eastern Tennessee.

Postmarked:
 Iowa City, Cal.
  JUL 14, 1859

Butterfield's steamboat, the
*Jennie Whipple, carried this letter
from Little Rock to Memphis.*

6 Horse illustrated cover:
 "Overland Mail, from San Francisco via Los Angeles"

Addressed to:
 Mrs Sydney G.
  Cleavland,
  Philadelphia,
  Monroe County,
  East Tennessee

This cover was purchased on ebay from andrew2u, November 28, 2021

This envelope was printed by "Hutchings & Rosenfield, No. 146 Montgomery Street, San Francisco." The same company also printed the engraving below of San Francisco in 1858.

SAN FRANCISCO, 1858.

Butterfield Mail On The St. Louis Route

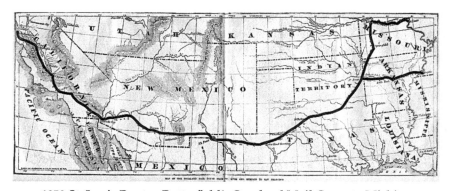

1859 St. Louis Route - Butterfield's Overland Mail Cover to Michigan

This letter was mailed from Green Springs, California on February 22, 1859, addressed to Richland, Michigan - a distance of over 3,000 miles requiring postage of 10¢. The stamp that was affixed to this envelope either fell off in transit, or was removed at some point by a postage stamp collector.

The original letter is missing, but it does contain a note that was sent with the letter:

Reil Mountain, Feb. 21st, 1859

Friend James
Will you please hand the enclosed to your sister and oblige.

Yours Truly
G. Thompson

James Rowley, Esq.

Mr. Thompson was most likely one of the Gold Rush "49 ers" - men who rushed to California seeking gold. The Gold Rush began on Jan 24, 1848 when gold was found by James W. Marshall at Sutter's Mill in Coloma, California. The news of the gold rush brought approximately 300,000 people to California from the rest of the United States and abroad. These men were anxious to write home to their sweethearts and wives, and to receive return mail from them with love and news from home.

Mailed from:
Green Springs, California on Feb. 22nd
Designated in the lower left corner: *"Overland mail via Los Angeles"*
Addressed to: James Rowley Richland, Macomber Co Michigan

This cover and enclosed letter was purchased from
Labron Harris, P.O. Box 739, Glen Echo, Maryland

December 1860 Butterfield's Overland Mail Cover to Kentucky

Alex Norman mailed this letter from San Pablo, California on December 20, 1860 in a printed cover, addressed to Mr. James McNaughton, Owensville, Bath County, Kentucky. San Pablo is just a few miles north of San Francisco, across the bay. On top of the red of the stagecoach and printed in black below the team of horses are the words *"Overland Via Los Angeles."* With a Kentucky destination, this cover may have traveled the Memphis Route.

The 10¢ postage stamp that was attached either fell off in transit, or was removed later by a postage stamp collector.

Purchased at the 2021 APS show in Chicago
from Phillip Sager, Geezer's Tweezers, of Pikesville, Maryland.

1858 St. Louis Route - Butterfield's Overland Mail Cover to Ohio

This letter was postmarked August 7, 1859 in San Francisco, addressed to owell & Van Deman, Atty's at Law, Delaware, Del. Co., Ohio. Postage paid ith a Scott #31 ten cent stamp since destination was over 3,000 miles.

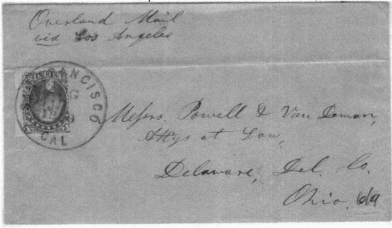

Purchased at the 2021 APS show in Chicago
from Don Tocher, U.S. Classics, of Sunapee, New Hampshire.

1858 St. Louis Route - Butterfield's Overland Mail Cover to Wisconsin

The sender of this cover (envelope) paid the 10¢ postage for a ½ ounce letter traveling more than 3,000 miles with a Scott #32 stamp, type II first issued in 1857. The sender wrote instructions to the postmaster across the upper edge of the envelope: *"Overland via Los Angeles."*

Postmarked with a pen cancel - two strokes with black ink

Addressed to:
 Miss Jennie Brown,
  Fond du lac,
  Wisconsin

This cover was purchased on ebay from
"Postal 38", Mount Kisco, New York on November 21, 2020.

1859 St. Louis Route - Butterfield's Overland Mail Cover to Massachusetts

This letter was mailed from San Francisco, California on May 22, 1859, addressed to Framingham, Massachusetts - a distance of over 3,000 miles requiring postage of 10¢. The original stamp that was affixed to this envelope either fell off in transit, or was removed at some point by a postage stamp collector. Shown here in it's place is a 10¢ Scott #33 postage stamp, with flaws, that has been attached to this cover to give the reader a better idea of what the cover once looked like.

The recipient, Ezra Dyer, was born Nov. 11, 1770 and died June 28, 1870. His wife was named Anne, and they had a daughter Elizabeth W. on April 5, 1818. Ezra was the son of Asa and Ruth Whitmarsh Dyer, grandson of Joseph Dyer, great grandson of William, and great great grandson of Christopher.

Postmark:
 San Francisco
 May 22, 1859

Preprinted Envelope
 by Hutchings &
  Rosenfield:
 "From San Francisco
 via Los Angeles"

Addressed to:
 Ezra Dyer Esq.
  Framingham
  Massachusetts

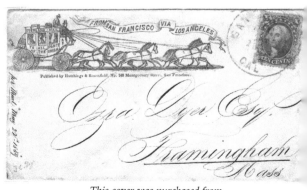

This cover was purchased from
Gary Kunzer of Webster, New York

1859 St. Louis Route - Butterfield's Overland Mail Cover to Massachusetts

This letter was mailed from San Francisco, California on June 27, 1859, addressed to Boston, Massachusetts - a distance of over 3,000 miles requiring postage of 10¢. Mailed June 27, 1859, travelling east by stagecoach for about 23 days, it would have arrived in St. Louis on Thursday, July 21, 1859. It then took 14 days to travel through the postal system by train from St. Louis to Boston, arriving in George Simmon's hands on August 4, 1859, 38 days in transit from San Francisco.

Postmark: San Francisco, California, June 27, 1859, *"Pr O. L. Mail via Los Angeles"*
US postal stationary envelope: Scott #U17, Die 2, Pale green on white
Addressed to: George A. Simmons Esq., 21 Long Wharf, Boston, Massachusetts

George A. Simmons was a manufacturer of sperm, whale and lard oil and sperm candles, oil works on Newton St., counting room, No. 21 Long Wharf, Boston.

1860 St. Louis Route - Butterfield's Overland Mail Cover to California

This letter was mailed from Pigeon Cove, Massachusetts on November 20, 1860, addressed to Benicia, California - a distance of over 3,000 miles requiring postage of 10¢.

According to John Birkibine of Tucson, Arizona, it is highly likely that Mr. Roscoe Wheeler moved to Benica, California as part of the gold rush.

According to the records of John Birkinbine: Leaving Gloucester, Massachusetts on November 21, 1860 it would have arrived at St. Louis by train at 8 am on Thursday, November 22, 1860. The cover was then carried by train to Tipton, Missouri where it continued west on Butterfield's mail stagecoaches. The route west involved these stations:

Tipton, Missouri, departing at 6 pm for a 10 hour trip covering 160 miles to
Springfield, Missouri, departing at 7:45 am for a 37 ¾ hour trip covering 143 miles to
Fayetteville, Arkansas, departing at 10:15 am for a 26 ½ hour trip covering 100 miles to
Fort Smith, Arkansas, departing at 3:30 am for a 17 ½ hour trip covering 65 miles to
Sherman, Texas, departing at 12:30 am for a 45 hour trip covering 205 miles to
Fort Belknap, Texas, departing at 9:00 am for a 32 ½ hour trip covering 146 ½ miles to
Fort Chadbourne, Texas departing at 3:15 pm for a 30 ¼ hour trip covering 136 miles to
Pecos River Crossing, Texas departing at 3:45 am for a 36 ½ trip covering 165 miles to
El Paso, Texas, departing at 11:00 am for a 55 ¼ hour trip covering 248 ½ miles to
Soldier's Farewell, Texas, departing at 8:30 pm for a 33 ½ hour trip covering 150 miles to
Tucson, Arizona, departing at 1:30 pm for a 41 hour trip covering 184 ½ miles to
Gila River, Arizona, departing at 9:00 pm for a 31 ½ miles trip covering 141 miles to
Fort Yuma, California, departing at 3:00 am for a 30 hour trip covering 135 miles to
Los Angeles, California, departing at 8:30 am for a 52 ½ hour trip covering 254 miles to
Fort Tejou, California, departing at 7:30 am for a 23 hour trip covering 96 miles to
Visalia, California, departing at 11;30 am for a 28 hour trip covering 127 miles to
Firebaugh's Ferry, California, departing at 5:30 am for an 18 hour trip covering 82 miles to
San Francisco, California, arriving on December 16, 1860.
After arriving in San Francisco on December 16, 1860
it was carried 36 miles north to Benica, California by horseback or wagon
and delivered to Mr. Roscoe Wheeler.

The original letter has been removed, but this cover still contains a handwritten note: *"Contained letter from Mother to Papa dated Nov. 20, 1860 written just before leaving Pigeon cove for California."*

Postmark:
  Gloucester,
  Massachusetts
  November 20, 1860

Directions in upper left
  "Overland"
Postage:
  10¢ Washington,
  Scott #35, Type V

Addressed to:
  Mr Roscoe Wheeler
  Benicia
  California

This cover was purchased from Rainer Gerlach of Sooner Stamps in Tulsa, Oklahoma.

1860 St. Louis Route - Butterfield's Overland Mail Cover to California

This letter was mailed from Hallowell, Maine on December 18, 1860, addressed to Nevada City, California. The 10¢ postage is for a distance of over 3,000 miles.

Postmark:
Hallowell, Maine
December 18, 1860

Designated in the
lower left:
  "Over Land"

Addressed to:
Thomas F. Dingley Esq.
  Nevada City,
    California

This cover was purchased from
Bill (William Stewart) Langs of New Jersey

Bean's 1867 *History of Nevada County* records that the recipient, T. F. Dingley was a large stockholder and superintendent of the Providence Mine from its beginning. The Providence Mine is an extension of the Soggs, or Nevada Company's ledge, being situated on the south side of Deer Creek. It was located by T. F. Dingley, and the next year a six-stamp mill was erected and the ledge opened under his superintendency, having associated with some parties in San Francisco, when the company was incorporated. In 1861, the capacity of the mill was increased by the addition of six stamps, and it now has three Williams and five Knox pans. The

ledge is opened by means of tunnels, starting in above the mill, and running south. The pay rock is taken from large chimneys, situated at unequal distances, while the ledge between the chimneys is quite small, in places running down to a mere seam. The mill is run by a steam engine, and is situated on the opposite side of the creek, and a little below, the mill of the Nevada Company.

Nevada City was born amid wild excitements and fostered by men from every state across the country, who chose to ignore many of the customs and laws of civilized society. Nevada City was almost abandoned at times for the allurements of other and over-praised localities. Man came and went, made few acquaintances, were absorbed in the pursuit of wealth, and paid little attention to other matters.

© 2022 Robert O. Crossman

1860 St. Louis Route - Butterfield's Overland Mail Cover to Texas
WESTBOUND

This letter was mailed from St. Louis, Missouri on March 7, 1860 to Jacksboro in north central Texas. Jacksboro was located on one route of the Butterfield Overland Mail. Regular postal service began at Jacksboro in 1859. Since this letter was traveling less than 3,000 miles, only 3¢ postage was required. The envelope was roughly opened along the right edge, but the tear did not affect the stamp affixed. The sender used a Lynde Bushnell Bookseller and Stationer advertizing cover.

There is a contemporaneous manuscript notation at the bottom left requesting it be carried *"Via Overland Mail."* This envelope is addressed to the early Jack County pioneer, D. B. J. Sterrets, Esq. in Jacksboro, Texas.

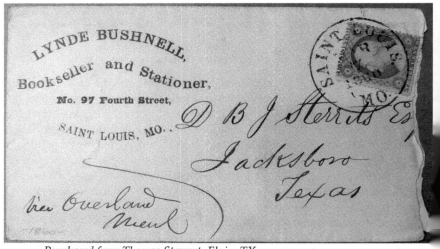

Purchased from Thomas Stewart, Elgin, TX
Hipstamp.com November 14, 2021

Notation on reverse side:
Bushnel March 6, 60

Jacksboro was first settled in the 1850's, with newcomers attracted b land offers from the Texas Emigration and Land Office. Originally calle "Mesquiteville," the community grew up along the banks of Lost Cree and spread out over the pasture land between Lost Creek and the wa

ters of the West Fork of Keechi Creek. It was renamed "Jacksboro" in 1858, when it became the county seat, in honor of brothers William and Patrick Jack, veterans of the Texas Revolution. The county was one of the few in Texas to vote against secession before the Civil War.

BUTTERFIELD MAIL NOT MARKED
"Overland via Los Angeles"

On December 17, 1859, the postmaster General ordered that unless otherwise directed, the default method for transporting transcontinental mail would be by Butterfield's Overland Mail Co. instead of by ocean ship. Prior to this, only letters specifically directed on the face of the envelope: *"overland"* or *"via Los Angeles"* were carried by the Butterfield Overland stagecoaches.

1860 St. Louis Route - Butterfield's Overland Mail Cover to Ireland

This letter was mailed from San Francisco, California on May 5, 1860 and headed east on a 23 day stagecoach ride to St. Louis. From there it traveled by train to New York City where it transferred to a ship to reach J.O. Flaherty in Enniscorthy, Wexford County, Ireland.

Postmark:
San Francisco
May 5, 1860

Addressed to:
O. Flaherty Esq.
Attorney at Law
Enniscorthy
County Wexford,
Ireland

1860 St. Louis Route - Butterfield's Overland Mail Cover to California

This letter was mailed from Adrain, Michigan on January 25, 1860 to Mrs. Henry B. Potter of San Francisco. The ocean route was no longer the default method of transporting transcontinental mail – therefore this cover was carried by Butterfield's Overland Mail between St. Louis, Fort Smith and to San Francisco.

Postmark:
Adrain, Michigan
January 25, 1860

Addressed to:
Mrs. Henry B. Potter
San Francisco
California

1860 Honolulu Hawaii to Boston via Butterfield's Overland Mail
Eastbound

This letter was postmarked on Monday, November 26, 1860 in Honolulu, Hawaii, addressed to Mr. Judson Shute of Boston, Massachusetts. This letter was carried by ship to the USA, arriving at San Francisco on Friday, December 21, 1860.

Following the December 17, 1859 order of the Postmaster General that the default carrier of transcontinental mail would be Butterfield's Overland Mail Co (instead of by Ocean Steamer), this letter would have been held at the San Francisco Post Office over the weekend, and placed in a mailbag departing on Butterfield's Overland Mail stage Christmas Day, Monday, December 24, 1860 for a 24 day trip to St. Louis, scheduled to arrive on Thursday, January 17, 1861.

This letter would have continued eastbound on a train for delivery to the Boston, Massachusetts post office to await for Judson Shute to call for his mail.

According to the Honolulu paper, *The Pacific Commercial*, the only mail ship departing for San Francisco between Nov. 26 and Dec. 20th was the *Francis Palmer*, departing on Dec. 8th. Typically it took about 12 days to sail to San Francisco.

The large "12" in the San Francisco postmark indicates that the recipient needs to pay the 12¢ due - 10¢ for the transcontinental rate, and 2¢ for the ship fee.

This cover was purchased October 21, 2021 on ebay from larrysellcovers of Hornell, New York

Judson Shute was born in Montgomery, Alabama, on August 20, 1837 to William M. Shute (1804-1870) and Martha Chaplin (1806-1882). He passed away December 29, 1911 in Boston, Suffolk County, Massachusetts.

Judson Shute had 2 children: Katherine Hamer Shute (1862-1939) and M Chaplain Shute (1871-1954).

BUTTERFIELD MAIL NOT MARKED
"Overland via Los Angeles"

1860 St. Louis Route - Butterfield's Overland Mail Cover to Maine

This letter was postmarked at the gold rush town of Camptonville, California on December 12, 1860 and headed east on a 23 day stagecoach ride to St. Louis. From there it traveled by train to Miss Eliza A. Berry of Brunham Village, Maine. No designation of "via overland" or "via Los Angeles" was needed since Butterfield's Overland Mail Co. was the default carrier of all transcontinental mail in all of 1860.

Purchased at the 2021 APS show in Chicago
from Labron Harris of Glen Echo, Maryland

Camptonville, California is about 170 miles north east of San Francisco

Gold was discovered at that location in 1850, and the place first became known as Gold Ridge. In 1854, when the community received its first post office, the name Gold Ridge was changed to Camptonville, honoring the town blacksmith Robert Campton.

During the gold rush years, Camptonville was a frequent stop for travelers and freight wagons since it was on the Henness Pass Road, a major route over the Sierra Nevada via Henness Passs. There is a plaque in Camptonville revealing that the town had over 50 saloons had brothels and even a bowling alley once upon a time. By 1863 William . Brewer passed through Camptonville and described it in his journal as follows:

"September 10 we started on our way--first to Nevada [City], a few miles, a fine town in a ch mining region, then to San Juan North (there are several other San Juans in the state), then Camptonville, a miserable, dilapidated town, but very picturesquely located, with immense hy- aulic diggings about. The amount of soil sluiced away in this way seems incredible. Bluffs sixty a hundred feet thick have been washed away for hundreds of acres together. But they were not h, the gold has 'stopped,' the town is dilapidated--but we had to pay big prices nevertheless."

When the gold mining in the area diminished, the local economy turned to the timber indus- . When Sierra Mountain Mills closed in 1994 it put 75 people out of work, and the population Camptonville plummeted. Today the is only businesses in town are the Lost Nugget gas station/ venience store, post office, elementary school, Burgee Dave's bar and restaurant in the old yo Saloon building, and the district office of the Yuba River Rangers and fire crew.

Butterfield's Mail Route Ends

In March of 1861, primarily due to increasing conflict along the route due to southern secessionists, the Post Master General closed the southern 'Oxbow' Overland Mail Co. route. Transcontinental mail was redirected north, avoiding the southern states, to the Central Overland Mail Route. The last Butterfield Overland mailbag left St. Louis on March 18, 1861 and arrived at San Francisco on April 13, 1861.

The Central Overland Mail Route
1861 to 1869

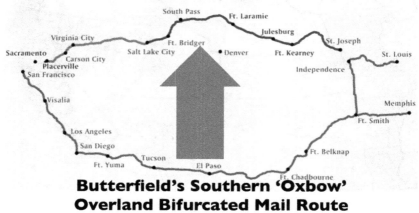

Butterfield's Southern 'Oxbow'
Overland Bifurcated Mail Route
1858-1861

1864 Central Overland Mail Cover to Tennessee

This letter was mailed from San Francisco, California on May 3, 1864 to Mr. C. W. Christy of Memphis, Tennessee.

At the time of this letter, the Sanitary Commission reports that Mr. Christy was the Superintendent and Relief Agent of *"Soldier's Lodge."* In a letter from Mr. Christy printed in the 1864 issue of *The Sanitary Reporter*, he reported that in April, 1864 the Soldier's Lodge in Memphis serviced 1,420 soldiers, serving

4,802 meals, and furnished 1,324 night lodging. They also furnished transportation to 127 soldiers, clothing to 6, added in correcting paper to 9, aided in drawing pay to 13, gave money to 5, and sent 13 to the hospital.

This cover was purchased on ebay from Richard Quining, 3207 Peace Rose St., Bakerfield, California 93311-2990

1863 Central Overland Mail Cover to Nevada Territory

This letter was mailed by C & A Ives Company from Detroit, Michigan on June 16, 1863 to Butler Ives at Carson City, Nevada Territory. The ten cent overland postage rate for letters carried over 3,000 miles was paid with three 3¢ and a 1¢ postage stamp.

This cover was purchased from Kurt Harding, of Boerne, Texas, at the October 2021 Pinpex Stamp Show in Jacksonville, Arkansas

The senders, C & A Ives Company were bankers. The Ives family purchased the lot in 1850, with a 28 year lease for $15,916 under the condition that they would construct a brick building on the lot within one year, with one store facing Jefferson Ave., and two stores facing Griswold Street. The bank office faced Jefferson, and Albert Ives owned the grocery story facing Griswold. By 1863, S. H. had retired, and turned the bank over to Calab and Albert. Soon Butler Ives was added to the firm, and the name changed to A. Ives & sons.

The letter was mailed to Butler Ives. Butler Ives was hired by the Nevada Territorial Surveyor General on July 15, 1861. He would run a guide meridian northward, the backbone for all surveys of the Public Lands in that area.

From Carson City, in November of 1861, Butler Ives wrote to his brother William, "...I have taken my present contract for subdividing 6 1/2 townships at $12.00 per mile."

Butler Ives wrote to William in the summer of 1863, "I am tired enough to go to bed. Have 200 men at work on the road divided into four gangs and all have 50 more this week....I have 10 to 30 miles horseback riding every day."

In the mean time, confusion and unrest over the location of the boundary between the Nevada Territory and the State of California continued.

Butler Ives died December 27, 1871 while he was engaged in surveying the proposed railroad from the Summit to Sausalito.

Butler Ives, Jr.
Jan. 31, 1830 to Dec. 27, 1871

1864 Westbound Central Overland Mail Cover to California

Henry Coe Sr.

Edward (abbreviated Edw) Huntington mailed this letter from Rome, New York on November 2, 1860 to Henry W. Coe of San Jose, California. The distance was over 3,000 miles and required ten cents postage, paid here with three 3¢ and one 1¢ stamp.

San Jose is about 50 miles south of San Francisco. San Jose was officially founded as California's first civilian settlement on November 29, 1777, as the Pueblo de San José de Guadalupe

The November 2, 1860 letter is not enclosed, but two other letters between these correspondents are still enclosed in the envelope below: April 4, 1859 and December 3, 1858.

Henry W. Coe, Sr. was born February 6, 1820 in Northwood, N. H, and died June 17, 1896. He moved into California in 1848. He settled in San Jose, where he purchased 150 acres in the section known as The Willows. Here he established a beautiful country residence, the hospitality of which was nowhere surpassed. He cleared his tract, and was the first man to plant fruit trees and hops. Mr. Coe was the first extensive shipper of hops to New York, Liverpool and Australia, and he grew the first tobacco in California, from which he made cigars, and the first silk grown and manufactured from the native product of the United States. His experimental crop demonstrated the possibility of silk culture in Santa Clara Valley, both soil and climate being admirably adapted to the mulberry and cocoon.

He was exceptionally well read, with a memory that was remarkable, and he retained his faculties up to within an hour of his death. He remembered perfectly General LaFayette's visit to this country. He and his brother Eben had stood watching on the banks of the Hudson when Fulton first ran his steamer on its waters. He knew San Francisco when it contained only a population of five hundred.

Henry W. Coe acquired the San Felipe Ranch and had his two sons, Henry Coe Junior and Charles Coe. In 1892, the brothers vastly expanded the property owned by their family by acquiring 6,000 additional acres within the bodies of water and hills of the Diablo Valley. In 1958 the deed of the ranches were deeded to California which allowed the state to convert the property to a state park, named The Henry Coe Sr. State Park.

1863/4 Westbound Central Overland Mail Cover to California

This letter was postmarked October 1 in New York, and addressed to Stephen S. Smith of San Francisco, California.

The postal rate for ½ ounce letters from March 3, 1863 until September 31, 1883 was 3¢. This particular letter weighed 1 ounce, so the postmaster marked on the front upper right "Due 3" to signify that double rate needed to be charged, and 3¢ was to be collected from Stephen S. Smith when he picked up his letter in San Francisco..

Purchased at the 2021 APS show in Chicago
from Mark C. Reasoner of Prospect Heights, Illinois.

This letter was carried by train from New York to St. Jo Missouri. ~~om~~ there a stagecoach, similar to the one below, carried the letter west~~ard~~ toward its destination.

Stagecoach on the Overland Trail near Laramie, Wyoming.

1863 Central Overland Stage Mail to France

This rare surviving cover travelled from San Francisco to St. Joseph, Missouri via the Central Overland Stage. There, it was transferred to a train for New York, where it boarded the British passenger liner, Scotia for Europe on January 27, 1864. It arrived at Liverpool on February 5, 1864. Then on to Paris, back stamped February 7, 1864. Then it arrived in Bourdoux and there received a red Calais transit stamp on front, and back stamped on February 8, 1864.

H. Y. Schroder & Co. mailed this folded envelope to Veillon Frerez in Bourdoux, France. It is postmarked at San Francisco on December 30, 1863. The sender paid the 15¢ unpaid treaty rate. Then a 3¢ debit was marked on the front. A hand written 8 pence debit was marked on the front at Liverpool.

The ship Scotia was operated by the Cunard Line that won the Blue Ribbon in 1863 for the fastest westbound transatlantic voyage. Scotia was the last oceangoing paddle steamer, and as late as 1874 she made Cunnard's second fastest voyage. Laid up on

The Scotia

1876, Scotia was converted to a twin-screw cable layer in 1879. She served in her new role for twenty-five years until she was wrecked off of Guam in March of 1904.

Recipient wrote on reverse:
H. F. Schrider, San Francisco, 29 Dec. 1863
Received 8 Feb 1864   Replied 24 Feb 1864

This cover was purchased at the Pinnacle Stamp Club Show in Little Rock from
Bill Burdick, Bill's Stamps & Postcards of Mountain Home, Arkansas   Ex Noel, Walske 3

1864/1865 Central Overland Mail Cover to Washington D.C.

This letter was mailed from San Francisco, California on April 2, addressed to Doctor Charles Sutherland, Medical Purveyor, Washington D.C.

Postage at this point had been reduced to 3¢ even for mail traveling over 3,000 miles. The sender affixed a 3¢ Scott #65 stamp.

In the spring of 1864, Dr. Charles Sutherland was appointed chief purveyor of the medical supply depot in Washington D.C., and was promoted to lieutenant colonel. He only held this position for a portion of 1864 and 1865, when he was then appointed chief purveyor of the New York City medical supply depot. He remained in that position until 1876.

In June of 1876, Sutherland was promoted to colonel and assigned as medical director of the Division of the Pacific. He held that position until 1884, when he was assigned as medical director for the Division of the Atlantic. Sutherland was promoted to brigadier general in December of 1890 and appointed as Surgeon General of the United States Army. In 1893, he retired and was succeeded by George Miller Sternberg as Surgeon General.

General Charles Sutherland

This cover was purchased on ebay from the E-Commerce Store, Charlotte, North Carolina on June 27, 2021.

Some of the Last Pieces of Mail
Carried by the Central Overland Stagecoach
EASTBOUND
1868/1869 Central Overland Mail Covers to Connecticut

About five months before the end of the Central Overland Mail these four covers from the same sender in Alton, New Hampshire were mailed to Allyn Stanley Kellogg of Vernon, Connecticut.

The recipient of these covers was Allyn Stanley Kellogg (1824-1893), Vernon Connecticut's first true historian. He was born on October 15, 1824 to Deacon Allyn Kellogg (1794-1873) and Eliza White (1807-1876). Deacon Allyn was the son of Ebenezer Kellogg, Jr (1764-1812) and the grandson of Rev. Ebenezer Kellogg (1737-1817), the first pastor of the Congregational Church in Vernon. Allyn Stanley chose to go into ministry rather than industry and graduated from Williams College in 1846 with high honors. A.S. went on to Yale Theological Seminary and graduated in 1850 at age 26. In the late 1880's a number of articles written by Allyn Stanley were published in the new Rockville Journal as he continued writing. Other publishers of genealogies and town histories often credited him as he was generous with his support.

Allyn Stanley Kellogg

These covers were purchased from PostalStationary.com of Alton, New Hampshire in February and June of 2021.

The 1st cover was mailed May 16, 1868 and was received 21 days later on June 6, 1868.
The 2nd cover was mailed Dec. 17, 1868 and was received 19 days later on Jan. 5, 1869.
The 3rd cover was mailed Jan. 6, 1869 and was received 17 days later on Jan. 23, 1869.
The 4th cover was mailed Jan. 16, 1869 and was received 17 days later on Feb. 2, 1869.

Some of the Last Pieces of Mail
Carried by the Central Overland Stagecoach
WESTBOUND
1869 Central Overland Mail Covers to California

These two covers were mailed at Saco, Maine and addressed to Mr. William Pierce at the firm of H & W Pierce in San Francisco, California with a 3¢ Scott #65 stamps affixed.

In *California Ranchos*, by Burgess Mc Shumway, chapter XXV San Francisco, an 1865 record is found of Wm. Pierce obtaining a 942 acre ranch: "Canada de Guadalupe La Vistacion y Rodeo Viejo, #152, San Francisco, San Mateo Cos.. Grant of 2 sq. leagues (including Canada de Guadalupe La Vistacion y Rodeo Viejo, #151) made in 1841 by Gov. Alvarado to Jabob P. Leese. Patent for 942.93 acres issued in 1865 to Wm. Piece. In T 3S. R 5W, MDM."

In 1885, Henry Pierce and W & W Pierce exhibited cattle at the San Francisco Fair: Class IV Holstein Bulls, in the one year old category four bulls named Edmund 5th, Edgar S., Dugald S. and Donatus S., in the category of cows, three years old and over: Annie. Several of their cattle won "best bull of show" and "best cow of show."

The receiver mark on reverse:
H & W. Pierce
S.F. Mar 29 1869
REVEALS THAT DELIVERY TOOK 42 DAYS TO COMPLETE.

The top cover is postmarked:
Saco, Maine
Feb 15

The bottom cover is postmarked:
Saco, Maine
January 3

Purchased from Michael Patkin, 10 Attitash Ave., Merrimac, Massachusetts

1958 Reenactment of
Butterfield's Overland Mail

On the 100th Anniversary of the first trip of Butterfield's Overland Mail, many re-enactments were held across the old "southern oxbow" route from San Francisco to the Mississippi River towns of Memphis and St. Louis.

The WESTBOUND cover below was postmarked at St. Louis on September 16, 1958 and addressed to Mountain View, California.

ThE EASTBOUND re-enactment cover, shown below, was postmarked at San Francisco, California on October 10, 1958 on the first day a new US postage stamp was available for sale The new 4¢ stamp commemorate *"Overland Mail • 1858 • 1958"*.

Butterfield's Overland Mail
Is Not Forgotten by the Post Office

In 1994, the US Post Office printed a sheet of postage stamps, with each stamp in the sheet commemorating a different person or *"Legend of the West."* One of the stamps, was a 29¢ stamp shown on this cover commemorating the Overland Mail. The stamp is affixed to a Collins Hand Painted First Day Cover.

The US Post Office expanded the Legends of the West series by also printing a two sided postcard for each of the persons or events in the series. The postcard below commemorates the Overland Mail. Both sides of the postcard are shown below.

Purchased August 2021 on ebay from Asset Auctions, Indianapolis, Indiana.

The postal rate to send a letter during the Butterfield's Overland Mail Co. time was 10¢ for any distance over 3,000 miles, and only 3¢ for any distance less than 3,000 miles. During the last month of Butterfield's ox bow southern route operation, starting February 27, 1861 the rates changed to require 10¢ prepaid postal rate on letters from any point east of the Rocky Mountains to any point on the Pacific side of the Rocky Mountains and vice versa.

Unclaimed Letters 1865

During the years of the Butterfield Overland Mail Co. the post office did not deliver door to door. Rather, individuals went to the Post Office on a regular basis and asked for their mail. If a letter sat uncalled for, the postmaster would print a list of names, asking that they come to pick up their mail. The list shown here is from the Saint Louis paper, The Daily Missouri Republican, June 18, 1865.

Home delivery, as we know it today, did not begin until about 1910 to 1915.

LIST OF LETTERS
Remaining Unclaimed in the Post-office at St. Louis, State of Missouri, June 17, 1865.

Officially Published in the Missouri Republican having the Largest Circulation.

——To obtain any of these letters, the applicants must call for "*advertised letters*," give the date of this list, and pay one cent for advertising.

——"If not called for within one *month*, they will be sent o the Dead Letter Office.

"*Free delivery* of letters by *carriers*, at the residence of the owners, may be *secured* by observing the following *rules*:

"*Direct* letters plainly to the street and number, as well as the Postoffice and State.

"*Head* letters with the writer's *Postoffice* and *State*, *street* and *number*, sign them plainly with full name, and request that answers may be directed accordingly.

"Letters to strangers or transient visitors in a town or city, whose special address may be unknown, should be marked in the lower left hand corner, with the word 'Transient.'

"*Place* the postage *stamp* on the *upper right-hand* corner, and *leave space* between the stamp and direction for *post marking* without interfering with the writing.

"N. B.—*A Request* for the *Return* of a letter to the writer, if unclaimed within 30 days or less, written or printed with the writer's *name, Postoffice* and *State*, across the left hand end of the envelope, on the face side, will be complied with the usual prepaid rate of postage, payable when the letter is delivered to the writer.—Sec. 28, Law of 1863."

——The office will be open at 7 A. M., and close at 7 P. M.—Sundays from 12 to 1 P. M. PETER L. FOY, Postmaster.

LADIES' LIST.

ADAMS MISS L A
Adams Mary J

Alexander Mary
Allington Melissa

A Postal Joke from 1861

In the March 1, 1861 issue of *The Constitutional Union*, Des Arc, Arkansas the following article appears:

"NOVEL USE FOR POSTOFFICE STAMPS. — A correspondent of The New York Times, writing from California gives an amusing story, the particulars of which happened at Fort Yuma, in Arizona. He says:

An officer was telling me the other day how he lost his postage stamps. He haq sent up here for some twenty dollars' worth, and had left them on his table. Now, the habits, manners and customs thereabouts are considerably on the free and easy style, and the [civilians] are allowed to run around the garrison at libitum, if they behave themselves.

On this occasion a young [civilian,] who had run of the quarters, and was very much at home anywhere and everywhere, happened to stray into my friend's room, and seeing the postage stamps, began to examine them with much curiosity. She discovered that they would stick, if wet, and forthwith a happy idea struck her. Now, the fashionable dress of the ladies in that warm climate is of the briefest description. She was ambitious to dress up and excite the envy of the other [young women.]

So she put on the postal currency, and much to the astonishment of the garrison, made her appearance on the parade ground presently entirely covered over with postage stamps. She was stuck all over with Benjamin Franklin, and the Father of his Country was placarded all over her ladyship's glossy skin indiscriminately, regardless of dignity and decency.

The roar that greeted her, from the commander down to the drummer boy, was loud enough to be heard nearly at headquarters in San Francisco, but [...] she preserved her equanimity, and did not seem at all disconcerted, but sailed off with the step and air of a princess, while my friend rushed into his quarters to discover himself minus of his twenty dollars' worth of postage stamps, and that was intended for the mail had been appropriated to the female.

She might have been put in the Overland coach and gone through — she certainly could not have been stopped for want of being prepaid."

Postal Rates

The postal rate to send a letter during the Butterfield's Overland Mail Co. time was 10¢ for any distance over 3,000 miles, and only 3¢ for any distance less than 3,000 miles.

During the last month of Butterfield's ox bow southern route operation, starting February 27, 1861 the rates changed to require 10¢ prepaid postal rate on letters from any point east of the Rocky Mountains to any point on the Pacific side of the Rocky Mountains and vice versa.

Apr 1, 1855	to 3,000 miles	3 cents	prepayment compulsory
	over 3,000 miles	10 cents	
Feb 27, 1861	over the Rockies	10 cents	1855 Act modified to require 10 cent prepaid postal rate on letters from any point east of the Rocky Mountains to any point on the Pacific side and vice versa Ship rate: 2 cent fee added to inland postage if transmitted by mail; 5 cents due if delivered at post of entry (any weight)

Source: Mails of the Westward Expansion, 1803 - 1861
by Steve Walske and Richard Frajola, Appendix G: Postal Rates

Post Office, San Francisco, California (ca. 1850)
William Endicott (1816–1851) *Source: Library of Congress*

The U.S. Post Office opened its first San Francisco branch in 1848. No ma[...] was delivered to the gold fields, so miners waited each morning for the post offi[...] to open. This lithograph, made after a drawing by H. F. Cox, depicts four lin[...] at the post office, for Spanish-language service, general delivery, parcel delive[...] and newspaper pickup.

Concerning Enterprising Mail Carriers in San Francisco, California

The California gold rush miners, after spending up to six or eight months traveling to arrive in the gold fields were anxious to receive mail from home. Alden Woodruff in a letter written on February 4, 1850 writes,

Dear Father –

It is now almost ten months since I heard from home. On my arrival in California, I was certain of getting a letter – but have not yet received a single one. What is the reason you do not write?

Two days later Alden Woodruff, writes in a second letter:

I received your letter of 22nd October, 1849, on yesterday, per the express. It only cost me $2 postage to get it; but that's nothing, for I was glad to get it at any cost. It is the first time I have heard from home since I left Fort Smith.

The "express" Woodruff refers to were the enterprising mail carriers who picked up mail from the Post Office in San Francisco, and delivered them to the miners at the various camps out in the wilderness and mountains for fees upwards of $2 of gold per letter delivered. [*Arkansas in the Gold Rush*, by Priscilla McArthur, 1986, page 126.]

Stephen Chapman Davis, arriving at the gold fields, ran an express carrying mail into the gold fields. He had the names of 300 miners who requested him to obtain any letters at Sacramento or San Francisco. He writes in his journal:

I just returned from below bringing some 50 letters... The postage on letters is 40¢ but we get $1.50 each... As soon as I come in sight... the miners drop their tools and run to meet me, in haste to get letters from their dear friends at home. And those who are so unfortunate as to receive no letters... look upon their fellow miners who are reading epistles... penned in fine hand of a female, frequently a tear comes... to the eye, while the heart grieves at being thus forgotten by loved ones at home."

[*Arkansas in the Gold Rush*, by Priscilla McArthur, 1986, page 127]

An Arkansan named J. Rankin Pyeatte, travelling to California seeking gold, wrote home on December 9, 1849 wondering why he had received no letters from home. He engaged an express merchant to carry his mail to him in the gold fields 200 miles from San Francisco for $1 extra for each letter:

Dear Companion, Children and Friends,

Having not heard a word from you since I left home, I have become very anxious to receive something from you. It would do me more good than anything I could think of... You may think you know how anxious I a to get a letter from you, but you know nothing about it, nor cannot know unless you were in the same situation that I am in, having been absent about 8 months and not having heard a word from you. I have no doubt but you have heard from us several times, for I have written six letters to you from different points. Why have I not gotten a letter I cannot tell unless they are directed to San Francisco. This place is so far distant, 200 miles, from that, we can't get letters there.

We made arrangements with a merchant to lift our letters out of the post office there and bring the to Sacramento City for one dollar extra on the letter."

[Arkansas in the Gold Rush, by Priscilla McArthur, 1986, page 188-189]

California Gold Rush

This first day cover's postage is was paid with a U.S. Scott #3316 33¢ California Gold Rush stamp celebrating the 150th Anniversary. The first day of issue for this stamp was June 18, 1999.

The Pony Express

The Pony Express is often confused with Butterfield's Overland Mail Co. In reality, they were two completely different operations . When the Butterfield southern route was cancelled, the revised postal contract also included a Pony Express:

March 12, 1861.– Route No. 12578, California, St. Louis, and Memphis to San Francisco semi-weekly, four-horse coaches. Overland Mail Company, E. S. Alvord, Superintendent. – $625,00.

Ordered: Pursuant to act of Congress, approved 2d of March 1861, and the acceptance of the terms thereof by the Overland Mail Company, Modify the present contract with that company for route No. 12578, executed 16th of September, 1857, to take effect 16th of September, 1858, so as to discontinue service on the present route and to provide for the transportation of the entire letter-mail six times a week on the Central Route: said letter-mail to be carried through in twenty days' time, eight months of the year, and in twenty-three days the remaining four months of the year, from St. Joseph, Missouri, (or Atchison, in Kansas,) to Placerville, in California, and also for the delivery of the entire mail, three times a week each way, to Denver City and Great Salt Lake City; and incase the mail does not amount to six hundred pounds per trip, then other mail matter to make up that weight per trip to be conveyed; but in any event the entire Denver City and Salt Lake City mails, and the entire letter-mail for California, to be conveyed.

The contractors also to be required to convey the residue of all mail matter in period not exceeding the thirty-five days, with a privilege of sending the latter semi-monthly from New York to San Francisco in twenty-five days by sea and the public documents in thirty-five days. **And to be required also, during the continuance of their contract, or until the completion of the overland telegraph, to run a pony express semi-weekly at a schedule time of ten days, eight months of the year, and twelve days four months of the year, and to convey for the Government free of charge, five pounds of mail matter, with liberty of charging the public for transportation of letters by said express not to exceed $1 per half ounce.** *The compensation for the whole service to be ,000,000 per annum, to take effect on or before the 1st of July, 1861, and to expire 1st of July, 1864. The number of the route to be changed to 10773 and the service to be recorded in the route register for Missouri.*

Note at bottom of this order: 'In behalf of the Overland Mail Company the undersigned accept above modification of their contract. 12th of March, 1861.'

W. B. Dinsmore, President. E. S. Alvord, Supt, O. M. Co.

This 1966 postcard was purchased from RKA Covers. It was postmarked in 1966 with a circular red ink handstamp: *"Pony Express, April 3, St. Joseph"*

Pony Express Local Stamps 1861 to 1883

The Central Overland, California and Pikes Peak Express Company, inaugurated in 1860, was the pioneer Pony Express system and was developed to bring about quicker communication between the extreme portions of the United States. Delivery via the water route was 28 to 30 days, with two monthly sailings, and by the overland route the time was 28 days. In 1860 the pioneer Pony Express carried letters only, reducing the time for the 2,100 miles (from St. Joseph, Missouri to San Francisco) to about 12 days. The postage rate was originally $5 the half-ounce. About April 1, 1861, Wells, Fargo & company became agents for the Central Overland, California and Pikes Peak Express Company and issued $2 red and $4 green stamps. The rates were cut in half about July 1, 1861, and new stamps were issued. the $1 red, $2 green and $4 black, and the $1 garter design.

This is the Pony Express stamp collection of Bob Crossman.

*The first four stamps in the second row are all forgeries
that were made in an attempt to deceive stamp collectors.*

– 370 –

Express Companies

In the early 1800's the idea of establishing an express company began to flourish. Their primary focus was to provide speedy delivery of parcels or merchandise.

During the steamboat years, express companies would help transport goods from the steamboat inland to mercantile stores some distance from any river port.

© 2022 Robert O. Crossman

Langton's Pioneer Express
(1855 - 1865)

Samuel W. Langton and N. W. Williams formed Langton's Pioneer Express in March 1855 following the collapse of Adams Express in February. Langton had already been in the express business on his own or with partners since 1850. When started his extensive routes from the mining areas included steamboat service from Marysville and Sacramento to San Francisco. He began connecting with Wells, Fargo at Marysville in 1857 and quit the steamboat route. In early 1865, after the death of Sam Langton in 1864, the firm was sold to Lamping & Co's Express.

Pacific Union Express
(1868 - 1869)

This California express company was formed by Lloyd Tevis, Charles Crocker, Darius O. Mills and Henry Bacon, the owners of the Central Pacific Railroad, which operated between San Francisco, Sacramento and Reno in Nevada Territory. Pacific Union Express was created under exclusive contract to carry mail and gold for the C.P.R. in direct competition with Wells Fargo & Co., whose stagecoach line was already faltering due to the expansion of both the C.P.R. and the Union Pacific Railroad. Their objective to compete against Wells, Fargo & Co. was aggressively pursued, but in December 1869 the company sold out to the larger, better-capitalized firm. The company only lasted from July 1, 1868 till December 1869 when it was sold to Wells Fargo for $5 million, a princely sum at that time.

United States Express
(1854 -   )

The United States Express Company was organized in 1854, with the view of doing a western business over the N.Y. & Erie Railroad. It's capital stock was $500,000, with D.N. Barney, president; H. Kip, superintendent, and Theo. B. Marsh, treasurer. This express had about 200 agencies, and many employees worthy of particular mention for their fidelity and untiring service. Its field of operations includes the most remote settlements in the western country. *(History of the Express Companies, by Alexander Lovett Stimson, p. 78.)*

These are images of Bob Crossman's Express stamp collection.

CHAPTER 7
Steamboat
Photo Album

On the following pages there are photographs of steamboats from the Arkansas River, White River, and Lower Mississippi River.

"Whipple Steamboat"
Sketch by David Garrison, Conte Crayon, Nov. 19, 2010
utheastern Community College, 1500 West Agency Rd., West Burlington, Iowa

– 373 –

Steamboat at Wharf at Commerce Street, Little Rock, Arkansas, ca. 1884
Image courtesy of the U.S. Army Corps of Engineers office, Little Rock, Arkansas

Steamboat Eagle, the first steamboat to arrive at Little Rock, Arkansas, 1822

On March 16, 1822, Captain Morris piloted the steamboat The Eagle to Little Rock, seventeen days after departing New Orleans. The Eagle was the first steamboat to reach Little Rock. Arriving at Little Rock early in the morning, Captain Morris, fired a salute of several guns in order to arouse the town.

From Little Rock, the Eagle headed upriver toward the community of Dwight Mission, founded by Presbyterians in what is now Pope County at the mouth the Illinois Creek. Due to low water on the Arkansas, it was unable to make it upstream to Dwight Mission. On March 19, 1822, the Eagle returned to Little Rock then headed back to New Orleans.

Steamboat Wichita, a snag boat, at Little Rock, Arkansas
Image courtesy of the U.S. Army Corps of Engineers office, Little Rock, Arkansas

The Arkansas Belle, 1870 - 1880 -
lt for the Memphis and Arkansas River trade by Captain Woodburn. She sold
870 to the Evansville and Cairo Line and did not end up on the Arkansas River.

Steamboat Jesse Blair at Engle's Bluff near Sylamore on the White River, ca 1901.
She was a small gasoline sternwheeler that operated on upper the White River.
Source: Huddleston Steamboat Photograph Collection (UALR.PH.0070)

Steamboat U.S.S. Snag Boat Henry Sheldon shown anchored at Sylamore,
on the upper White River, June 22, 1900
Source: Huddleston Steamboat Photograph Collection (UALR.PH.0070)

Steamboat Des Arc at De Vall's Bluff on the White River during the Civil War
Source: Huddleston Steamboat Photograph Collection (UALR.PH.0070)

Steamboat Osage on the White River.
eamboat Osage was one of the largest boats to go up the river as far as Warsaw
Source: History of Benton County, Missouri, vol. II (White & Miles, 1969)."
Source: Huddleston Steamboat Photograph Collection (UALR.PH.0070)

Steamboat Quapaw
Dismantled at Batesville, Arkansas in the spring of 1988
Source: Huddleston Steamboat Photograph Collection (UALR.PH.0070)

Steamboat Black Hawk was at the Battle of Arkansas Post during the Civil W
Source: Huddleston Steamboat Photograph Collection (UALR.PH.0070)

Steamboat Harben at Arkansas Post, Deck Hands are Loading, June 2, 1900
Image courtesy of the U.S. Army Corps of Engineers office, Little Rock, Arkansas

Steamboat Big Rock at Little Rock, ca. 1938
Image courtesy of the U.S. Army Corps of Engineers office, Little Rock, Arkansas

Steamboat mail packet on the White River, Arkansas
Image courtesy of the U.S. Army Corps of Engineers office, Little Rock, Arkansas

Steamboat Ozark Queen
The Ozark Queen was 133′ long and 25 ft. wide.
Launched in 1896. Last voyage was in 1903.
Captain Woodbury unloading merchandise for the general stores at Calico., Arkansas.

Steamboat Rex with a full passenger load, ca. 1894/5 at DeVall's Bluff
Source: Huddleston Steamboat Photograph Collection (UALR.PH.0070)

Steamboat R. P. Walt was a lavish steamboat that traveled the White River, boasting fine carpets, furniture, and a piano
Source: Huddleston Steamboat Photograph Collection (UALR.PH.0070)

Steamboat "City of Muskogee" on the Arkansas River

Steamboat Joe Peters, Docked on the White River
TSource: Huddleston Steamboat Photograph Collection (UALR.PH.0070)

Steamboat Cleveland
Image courtesy of the U.S. Army Corps of Engineers office, Little Rock, Arkansas

Steamboat Myrtle B, ca. 1899
Image courtesy of the U.S. Army Corps of Engineers office, Little Rock, Arkansas

Steam Snagboat C. B. Reese at Little Rock, Arkansas, Jan. 1900
Source: Huddleston Steamboat Photograph Collection (UALR.PH.0070)

Steamboat General Pierson passing by Hopefield, Arkansas on the Mississip
Source: Hopefield, Arkansas: Important River-Rail Terminal, James R. Fair
Arkansas Historical Quarterly, Vol. 57, No. 2, Summer 1998, page 202

Steamboat Moark
The Moark, a gasoline-fueled sidewheeler, operated on the upper White River.
She made regular runs from Forsyth to Branson, MO, from about 1905 to 1911.

Steamboat Arkansas Belle
Source: Huddleston Steamboat Photograph Collection (UALR.PH.0070)

Steamboat Sheldon at Sylamore, Arkansas, June 22, 1900
Image courtesy of the U.S. Army Corps of Engineers office, Little Rock, Arkansas

Steamboat Arabia, Arabia Museum in Kansas City
Arabia sank September 5, 1856 on the Missouri River, carrying 200 tons of carg

Steamboat A. D. Allen at Batesville, Arkansas
Image courtesy of the U.S. Army Corps of Engineers office, Little Rock, Arkansas

Steamboat A. D. Allen, view of stern at Batesville, Arkansas
Image courtesy of the U.S. Army Corps of Engineers office, Little Rock, Arkansas

Steamboat Charles Morgan landing during high water at Mound City on the north side of Hopefield, Arkansas, right across the Mississippi from Memphis
Source: *Library of Congress, Copyright Dec. 31, 1910*

Close up of the above photo, showing the upper-class "Cabin Passengers" watching the deck hands below unloading freight for the shore.

Steamboat Alice Dean, docked in Memphis, Tennessee
Source: Huddleston Steamboat Photograph Collection (UALR.PH.0070)

A Mississippi River Landing at Memphis, Tennessee, ca. 1906
Source: Wikipedia "History of Memphis, Tennessee"

Steamboat Eugene, Based in Memphis, Tennessee
Source: Huddleston Steamboat Photograph Collection (UALR.PH.0070)

Steamboat Charles T. Campbell pushing Barges, Memphis, Tennessee in 193
Image courtesy of the U.S. Army Corps of Engineers office, Little Rock, Arkansas

"Sternwheel Steamboats on Mississippi, 1895"
These narrow steamboats were designed for travel on the Mississippi tributaries.
Image from Mississippi Sternwheelers

Steamboat 'City St. Joseph' loading cotton on the Memphis waterfront.
Source: Library Collection, Drawer 26, Folder 33, 4981,
Tennessee State Library and Archives.

Steamboat Silver Cloud - a 'Tinclad' River Gunboat

This steamboat had iron armor added for protection during the Civil War. This 186-photo was taken while she was on patrol duties at Helena, Arkansas. The 236 to USS Silver Cloud was built in 1862 at Brownsville, Penn., for commercial use. Sh was acquired by the Navy in April 1863 and commissioned a month later. Silve Cloud was assigned to patrol the Tennessee River interdicting Confederate transpo ration, convoying Union steamers, protecting Federal positions and raiding enemy held locations. Sold in August, 1865 she was converted to a side-wheel steamer fc civilian employment and was lost in 1866 after striking a snag in Buffalo Bayo Texas. *Source: Huddleston Steamboat Photograph Collection, UALR Center for Arkans History and Culture*

Steamboat Marmora (U.S.S. Tinclad No. 2)
Source: Huddleston Steamboat Photograph Collection (UALR.PH.0070)

Steamboat U.S.S. Tinclad No. 9
Source: Huddleston Steamboat Photograph Collection (UALR.PH.0070)

Steamboat Cricket (U.S.S. Tinclad No. 6)
Source: Huddleston Steamboat Photograph Collection (UALR.PH.0070)

Steamboat sidewheeler Ben Campbel

Steamboats Graham, Harry Lee and James Lee
Memphis wharf as seen from the ferry crossing the Mississippi River
from Hopefield, Arkansas about 1908.

Steamboat Explorer with a Load of Cotton
Source: Huddleston Steamboat Photograph Collection (UALR.PH.0070)

Steamboat Josie Harry
A painting of the Steamboat Josie Harry owned by Captain Milt R. Harry of
Jacksonport, named for his wife Josie Hamblet from Augusta, Arkansas.
Built at a cost of $55,000, this luxury steamboat was carpeted with silk velvet,
sterling silver service, 1,800 lbs roof bell, and
a 5 tone chime whistle that could be heard 50 miles away.
Burned Dec. 7, 1883, 12 miles below Memphis.
Source: Huddleston Steamboat Photograph Collection (UALR.PH.0070)

Steamboat Rees Pritchard
Source: Huddleston Steamboat Photograph Collection (UALR.PH.0070)

Steamboat Ora Lee
Source: Huddleston Steamboat Photograph Collection (UALR.PH.0070)

Steamboat Missouri
Source: Huddleston Steamboat Photograph Collection (UALR.PH.0070)

Steamboat Gem
No photo is known of the sternwheel packet 130' X 30' the *Jennie Whipple*.
However, it was similar to this Mississippi 135' X 21' X 3' sternwheel packet, the Gem, shown here docked at New Orleans.

Steamboat Alton, Mural in Alton, Illinois
Alton's historic past as a thriving river community at one time rivaled
nearby St. Louis as an important river port. Thi mural greets visitors to
the city as they cross the Clark Bridge from Missouri.

"Steamboat Frontenac"
The Mississippi River steamboat Frontenac (1896-1918) was 138 ft. x 38 ft.,
just slightly larger than the Jennie Whipple at 130 ft. x 30 ft.

Steamboat Belle Memphis, 1880
This 267 ft. x 42 ft. boat was built at Jeffersonville, Indiana in 1880.
Her wheelhouse is pictured below in a newspaper engraving from 1883.

**"Life on a Mississippi Steamboat -
The Story Teller in the Wheelhouse of the Belle Memphis"**
Source: Frank Leslie's Illustrated Newspaper, November 10, 1883

© 2022 Robert O. Crossman

Steamboat Annie P.

We do not have an image of the 135 ft. x 30 ft. Jennie Whipple, built 1857, Brownsville, PA. She was, however, a sternwheel steamboat like the Annie shown above and below. The 98 ft. x 23 ft. Annie P. was built in 1906 Shrevepor La. for W. M. Porter and named for his wife, Annie. Pictured here arriving at Den son on the Red River. *Source: Photos possibly by Jack Hendricks.*

Summary

In 1858 John Butterfield was misled to believe that the Arkansas River was navigable year round by boats with a drought under twelve inches. As a result, in September of 1858 the Arkansas River levels were so low that John Butterfield was forced to hastily sub-contract the Memphis to Fort Smith route to John T. Chidester's stagecoach line.

On only 8 occasions John Butterfield's steamboat, *Jennie Whipple*, was able to fulfill his original plan of carrying Overland passengers and mail between Memphis and Fort Smith.

On 73 additional occasions *Jennie Whipple* was able to complete the Little Rock to Memphis leg of the route.

On 4 additional occasions the *Jennie Whipple* made a run between Little Rock and Fort Smith, with stagecoaches completing the Little Rock to Memphis portion of the Overland Mail route.

In 1860 and 1861, the *Jennie Whipple* was stranded for more than a year in Indian Territory (Oklahoma) because of record low water levels in the Arkansas River.

During the Civil War, the *Jennie Whipple* transported Union troops and arms on numerous occasions.

The financial records of Butterfield's Overland Mail Co. have not survived. So, we are unable to determine if operating the *Jennie Whipple* was more profitable than sub-contracting John T. Chidester's stagecoach line.

With two Overland Mail Co. stages headed east each week, and two Overland Mail Co. stages headed west each week, the swing and home stations would have to prepare for four visits each week. The Overland was in operation from mid September 1858 to early April 1861, for a total of 81 weeks. With four stages arriving at each swing station weekly, that would come to 324 times the station would hear the stage conductor's horn blow and would have to quickly prepare to switch out the teams with fresh horses.

The number of 324 arrivals holds true for all of the Butterfield's Overland route except for the Memphis to Fort Smith portion where, when the river water was favorable, steamboats were utilized and the swing stations were completely bypassed.

Based on the records currently available, the stations between Little Rock and Fort Smith would have greeted 312 stages, with steamboats carrying mail and passengers the remaining 12 times. [8 times as part of a Memphis to Fort Smith trip, and 4 times as part of a Little Rock to Fort Smith trip.]

The stations between Little Rock and Memphis would have greeted as many as 243 stages, with steamboats carrying the mail and passengers the remaining 81 times. [73 times a part of a Little Rock to Memphis trip, and 8 times as part of a Fort Smith to Memphis trip.]

The official schedule required the Overland Mail to depart Memphis westbound at precisely 8 am every Monday and Thursday, and to depart Fort Smith eastbound at precisely 1 pm every Sunday and Wednesday. However, fluctuations in river water levels, fog, snags, and sandbars kept John Butterfield's steamboat *Jennie Whipple* from keeping precisely to the official Overland Mail Co. schedule. On numerous occasions, the *Jennie Whipple* delayed the Overland Mail by several days

In contrast, according to the Report of the Postmaster General to the 2nd Session of the 35th Congress, dated March 3 1859 [his listing of 1858 arrivals and departures are reprinted in the early pages of this book] – in spite of the land route difficulties of mud, sand, fording creeks, floods, ice and snow – Butterfield's sub-contractor John T. Chidester was able to keep far closer to the official schedule of arrivals and departures, than the *Jennie Whipple*, when using his stagecoaches to carry the Overland Mail and passengers between Memphis and Fort Smith.

Appendix One

1874 Asher & Adams Map of Arkansas and Indian Territory
This map indicates location of Steamboat Landings along the river banks.
Source: An 1874 Printing of this map is in the possession of the author.
On the following seven pages, overlapping close ups of this map are shown giving greater detail of the various steamboat landing sites.

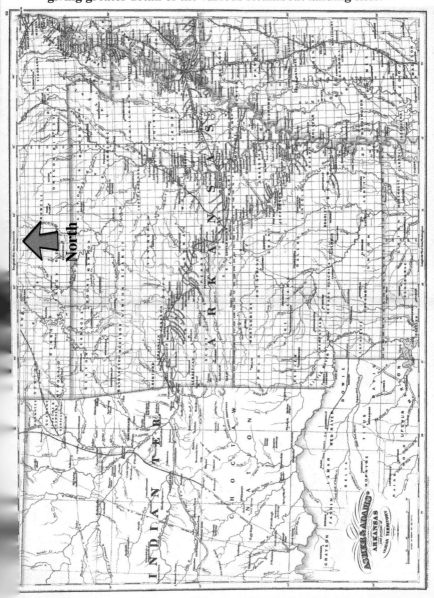

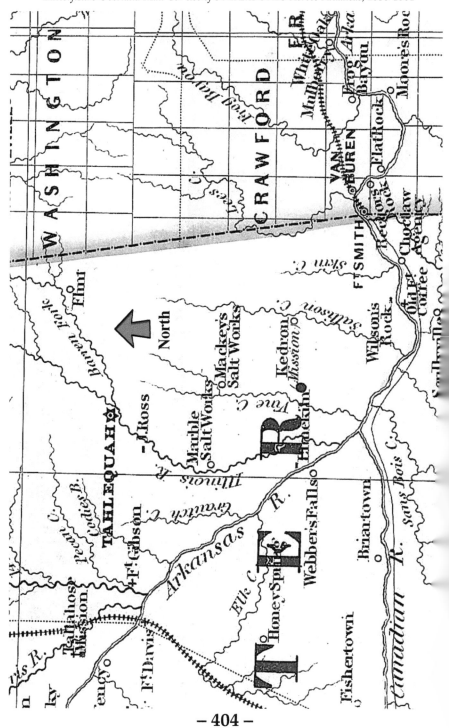

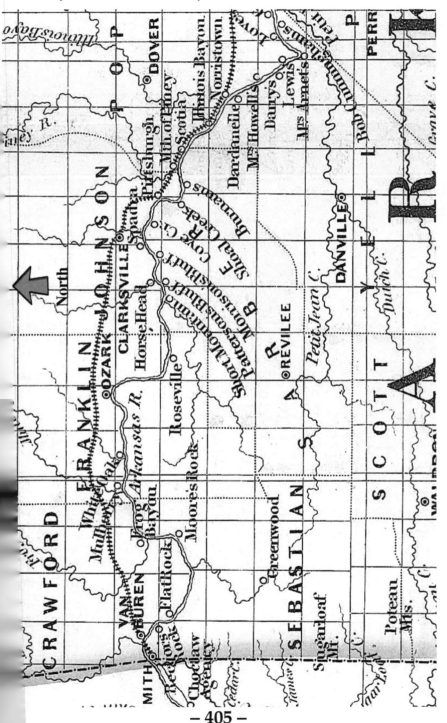

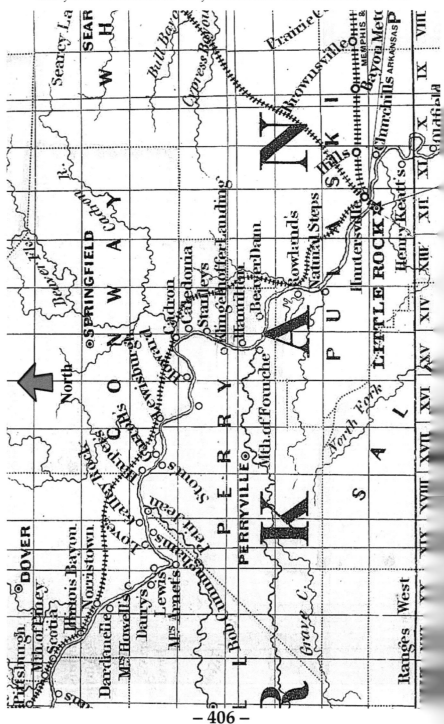

© 2022 Robert O. Crossman

Butterfield's Overland Mail Co. Use of STEAMBOATS Across Arkansas, 1858-1861

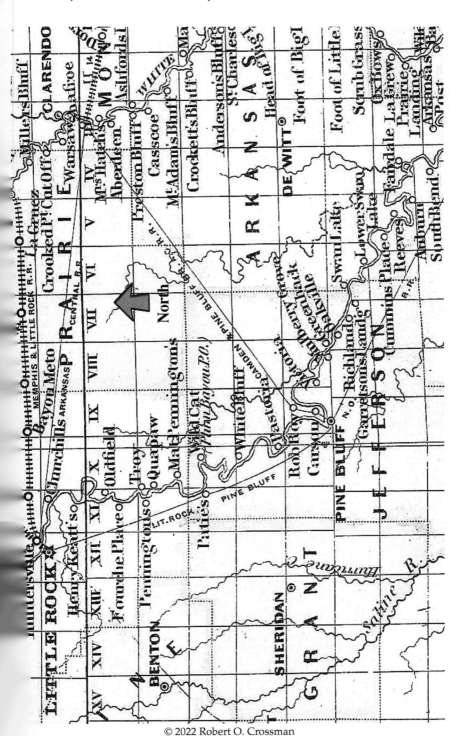

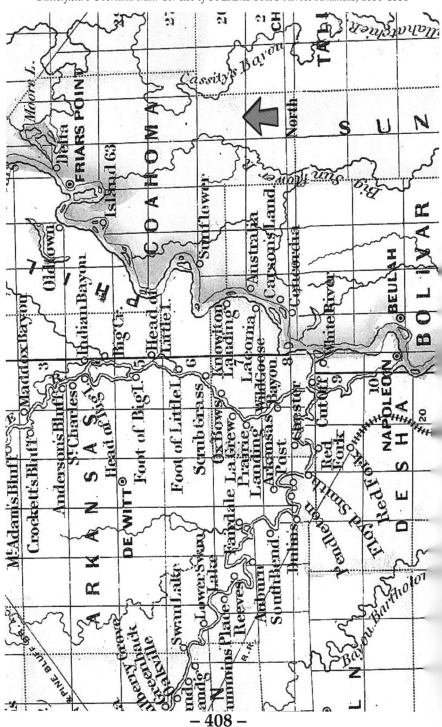

© 2022 Robert O. Crossman

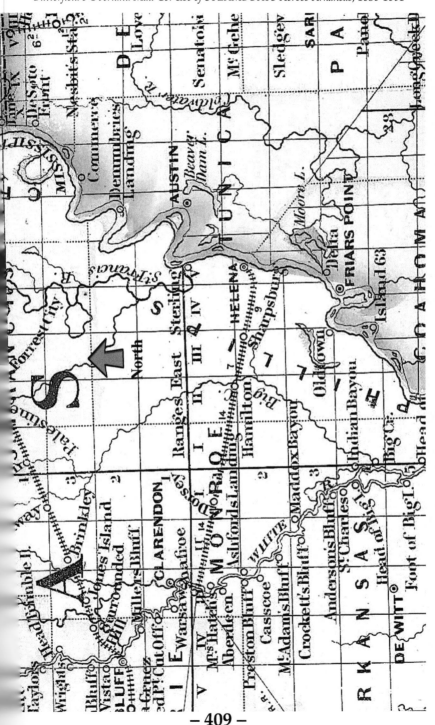

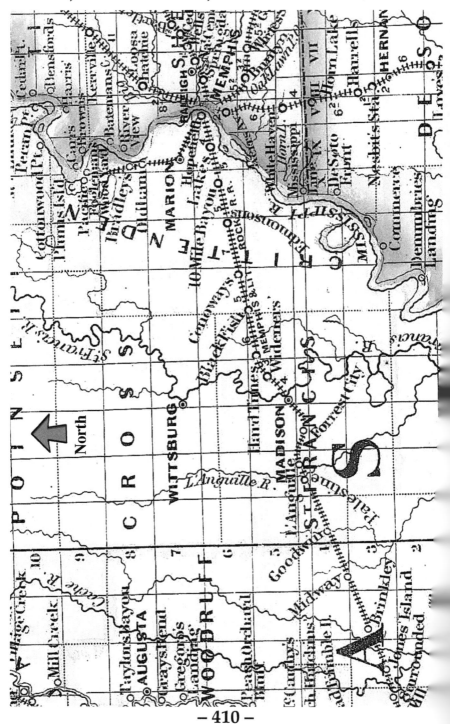

© 2022 Robert O. Crossman

Appendix Two
Map of the Arkansas River, Fort Smith to Little Rock, circa 1869
Showing Detail Along the Arkansas River Bank
Source: Courtesy of the Faulkner County Museum
Lynita Langley-Ware, M.A., R.P.A. Director

On the following 14 pages, a twenty foot map on the wall of the Faulkner County Museum is broken into 23 different photographs below. Numbers have been added to each side of each page to help the reader to visually reconstruct this twenty foot long map. Arrows have been added to highlight 12 significant landings.

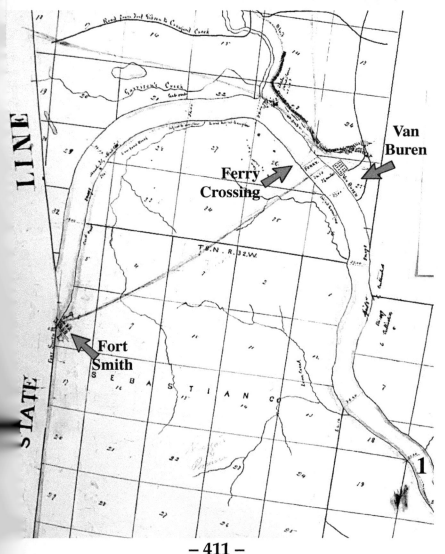

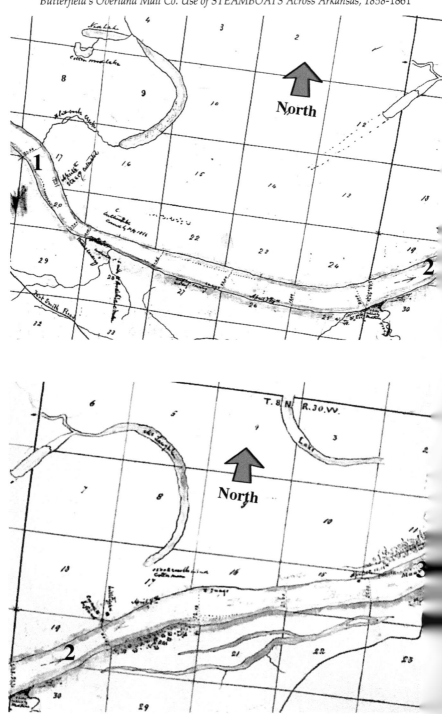

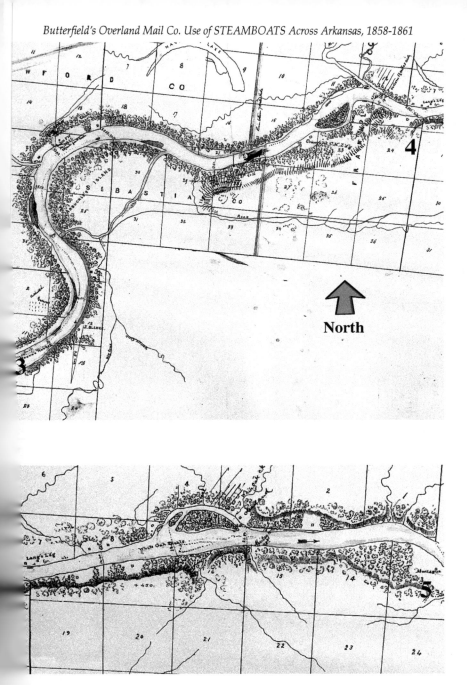

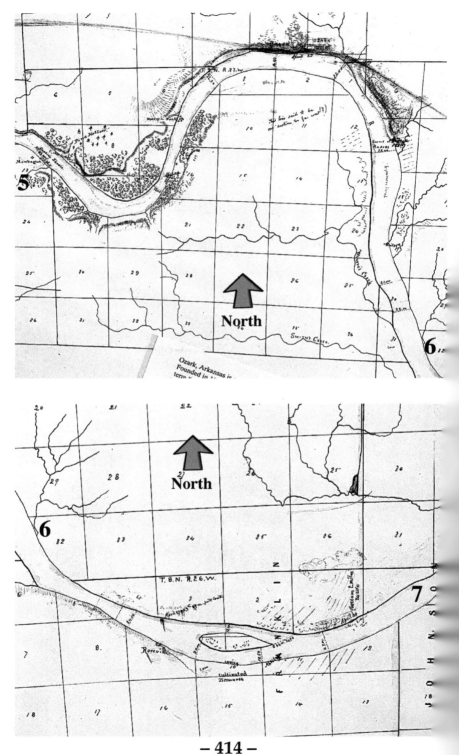

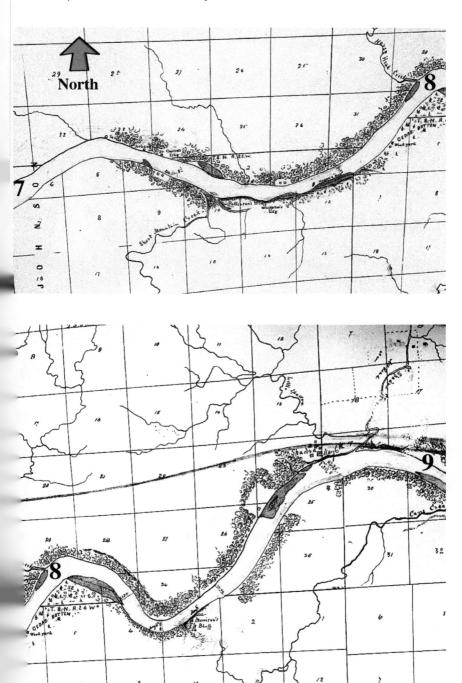

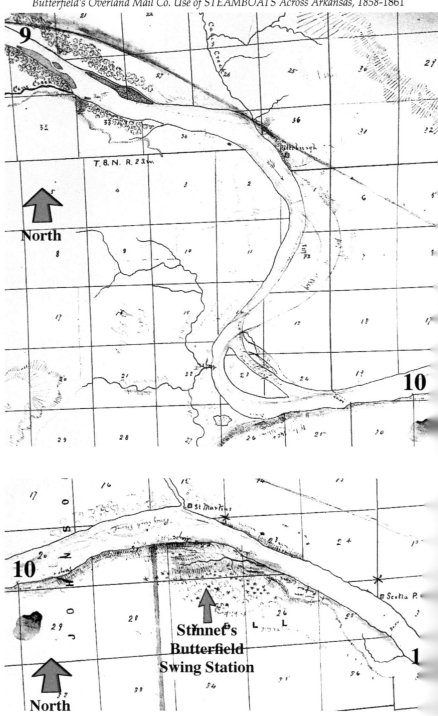

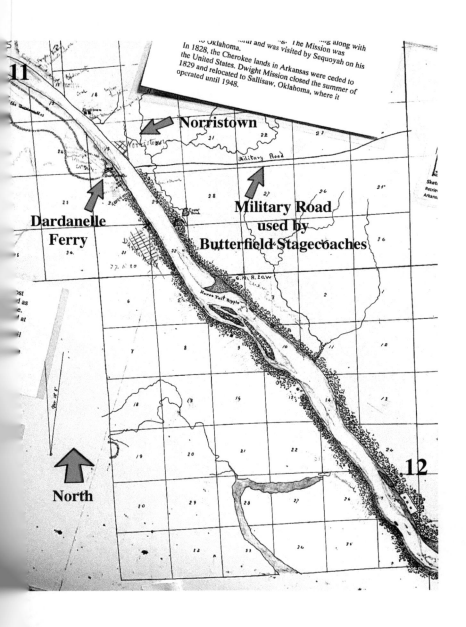

In 1828, the Cherokee lands in Arkansas were ceded to the United States. Dwight Mission closed the summer of 1829 and relocated to Sallisaw, Oklahoma, where it operated until 1948.

Norristown

Military Road
used by
Butterfield Stagecoaches

Dardanelle Ferry

North

11

12

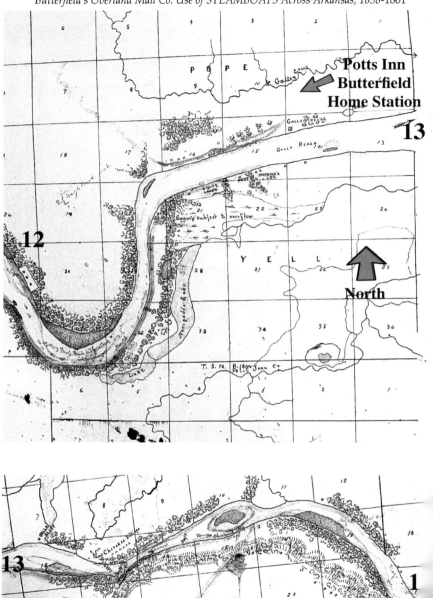

© 2022 Robert O. Crossman

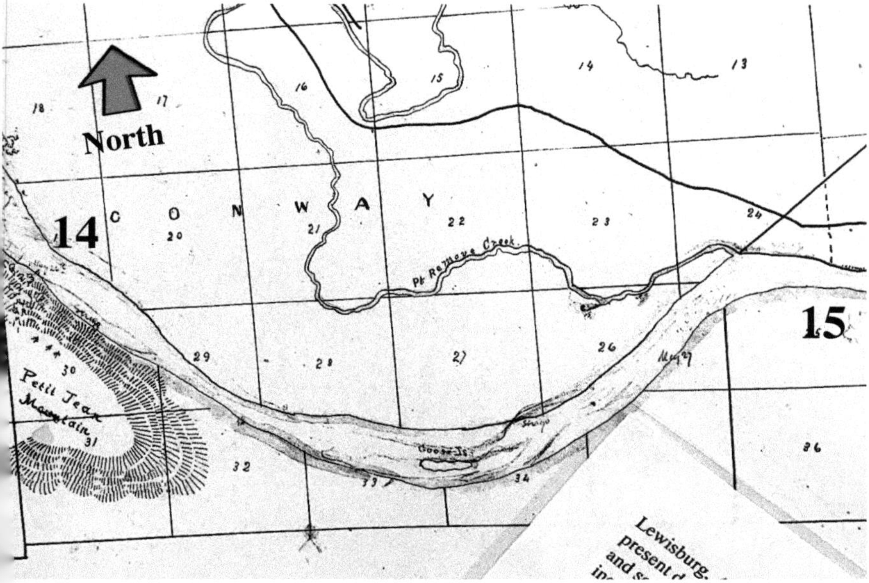

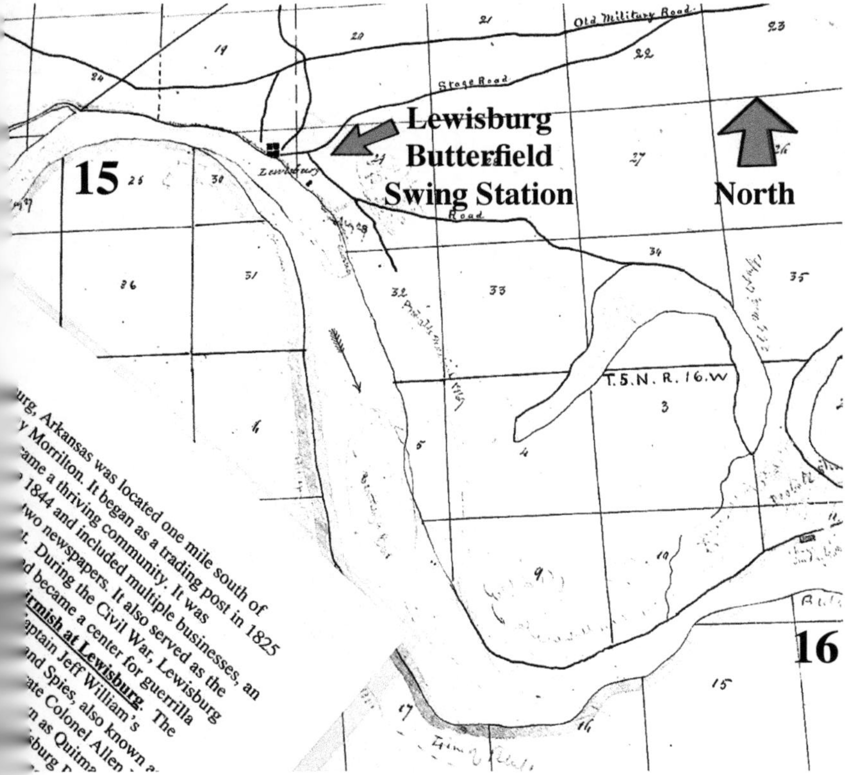

North

14

C O N W A Y

Petit Jean Mountain

15

Lewisburg
**Butterfield
Swing Station**

North

15

16

Old Military Road

T. 5. N. R. 16. W.

...burg, Arkansas was located one mile south of
...y Morrilton. It began as a trading post in 1825
...came a thriving community. It was
...1844 and included multiple businesses, an
...wo newspapers. It also served as the
.... During the Civil War, Lewisburg
...d became a center for guerrilla
...rmish at Lewisburg. The
...aptain Jeff William's
...and Spies, also known
...ate Colonel Allen
...n as Quitm...
...sburg...

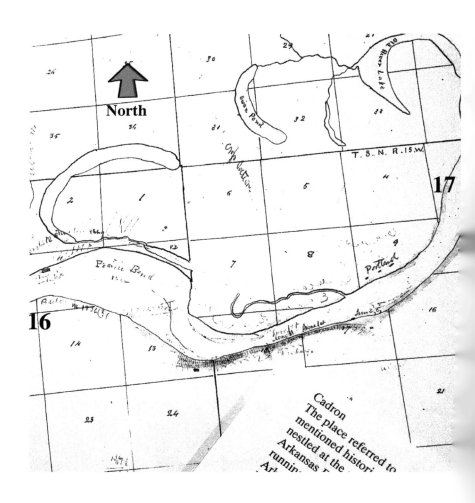

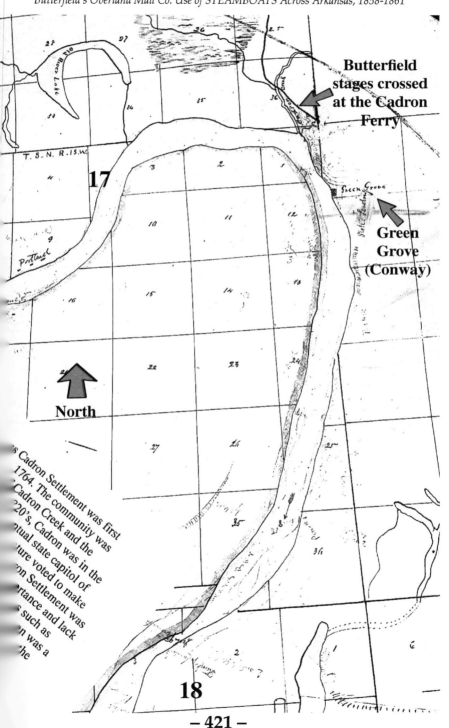

Butterfield stages crossed at the Cadron Ferry

Green Grove (Conway)

North

s Cadron Settlement was first
1764. The community was
Cadron Creek and the
'20's, Cadron was in the
tual state capitol of
ure voted to make
on Settlement was
rtance and lack
s such as
n was a
he

18

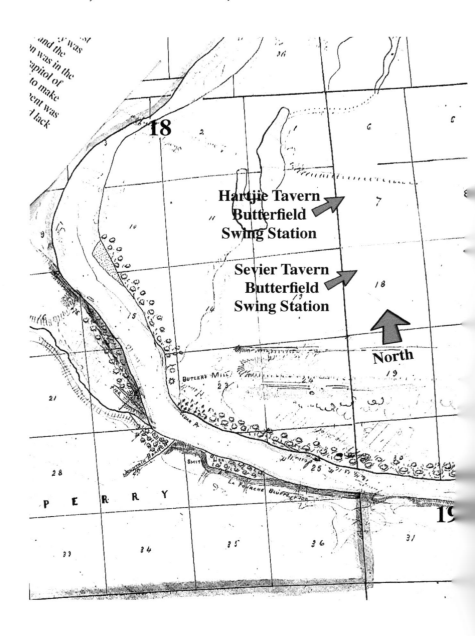

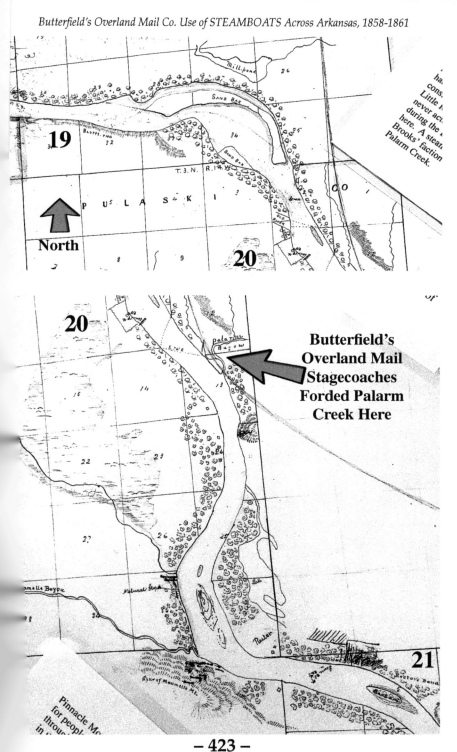

Butterfield's Overland Mail Stagecoaches Forded Palarm Creek Here

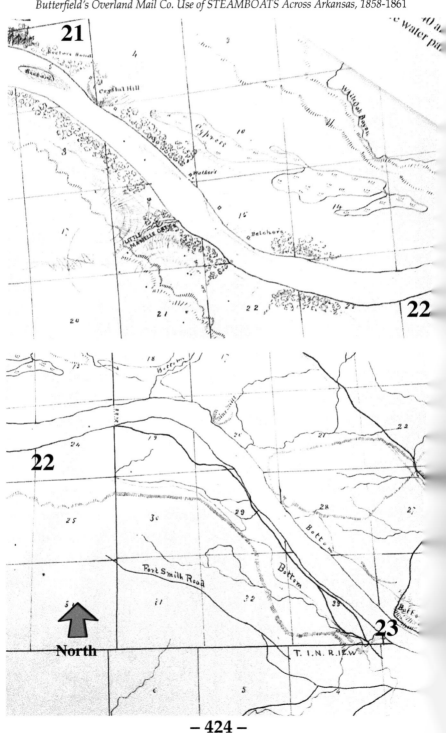

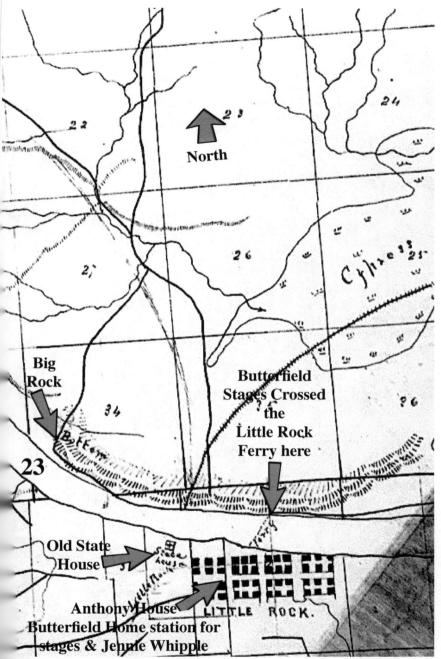

North

Big Rock

Butterfield Stages Crossed the Little Rock Ferry here

23

Old State House

Anthony House
Butterfield Home station for stages & Jennie Whipple

LITTLE ROCK.

te in the lower right corner of the 20 foot +/- map: *"Tracing seems to have ___ by Ass't Eng. Abert making his survey Ark River in 69"*

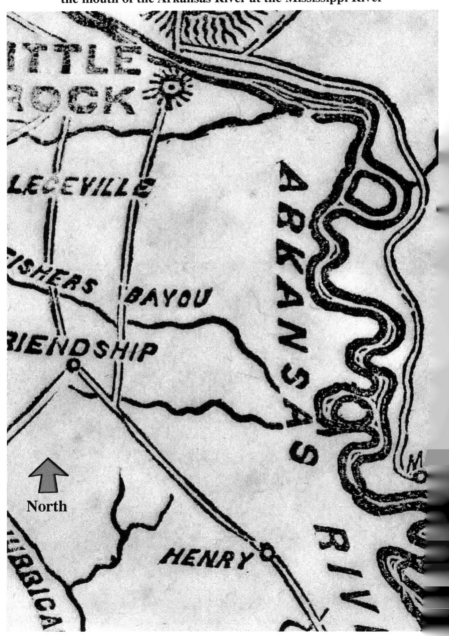

Butterfield's Overland Mail Co. Use of STEAMBOATS Across Arkansas, 1858-1861

Appendix Three
1863 Map of Arkansas River from Little Rock to
the mouth of the Arkansas River at the Mississippi River

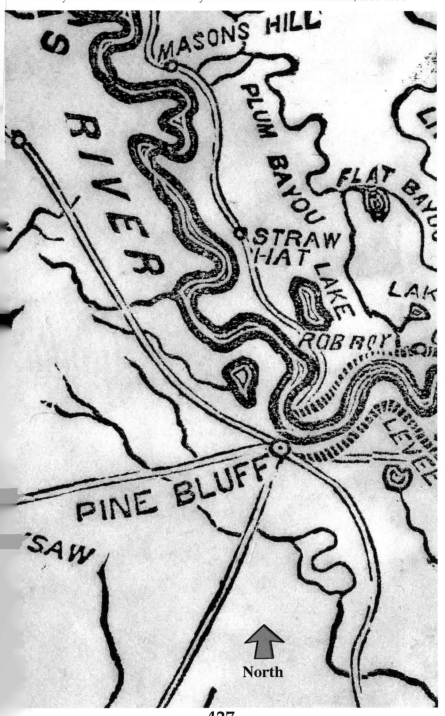

North

© 2022 Robert O. Crossman

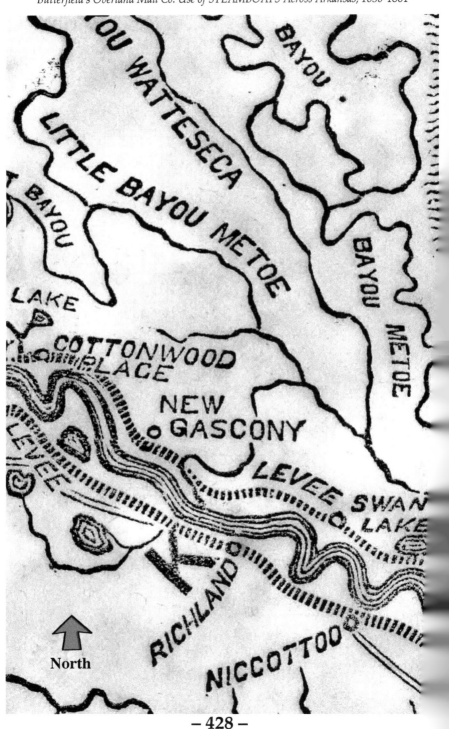

© 2022 Robert O. Crossman

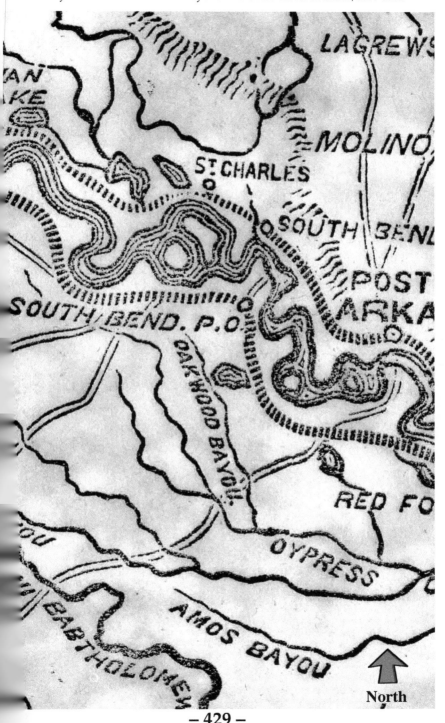

North

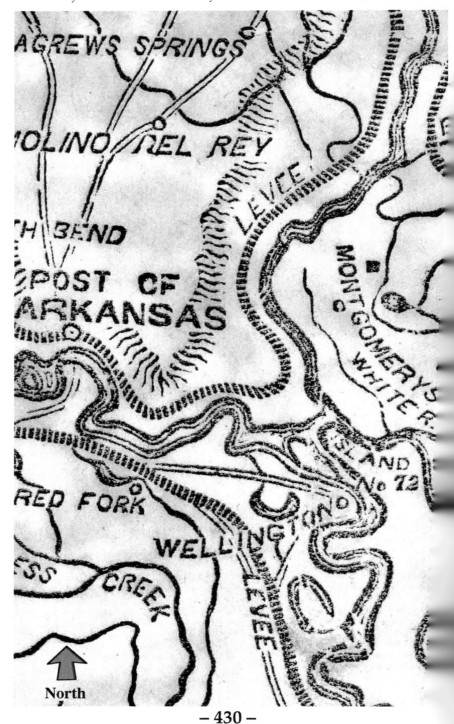

North

© 2022 Robert O. Crossman

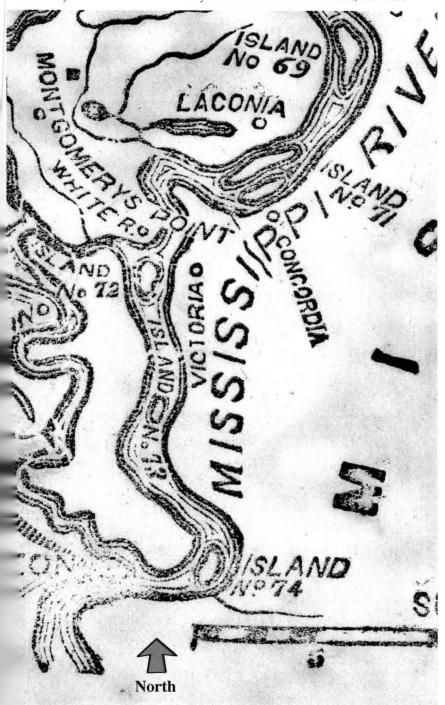

North

Appendix Four
1888 Map of the White River, Des Arc to its Mouth at the Mississippi
Butterfield's sub-contractor, John T. Chidester, carried the Overland Mail Co. mail and passengers from Des Arc to Clarendon for six months,

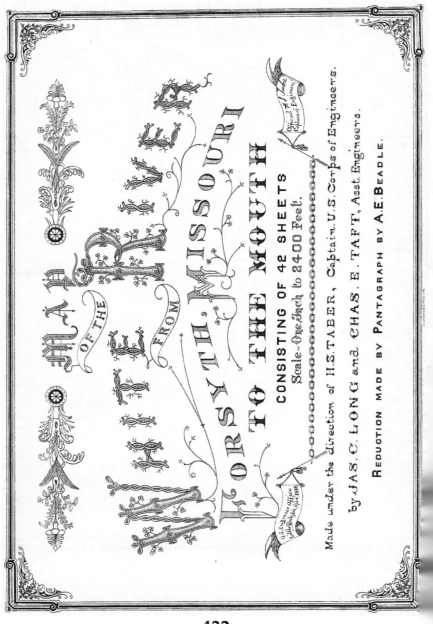

© 2022 Robert O. Crossman

Map images courtesy of The U. S. Corps of Engineers
https://usace.contentdm.oclc.org/digital/collection/p16021coll10/id/10496/rec/1

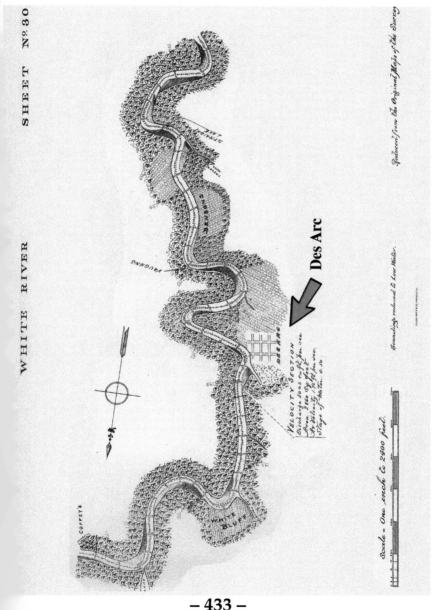

© 2022 Robert O. Crossman

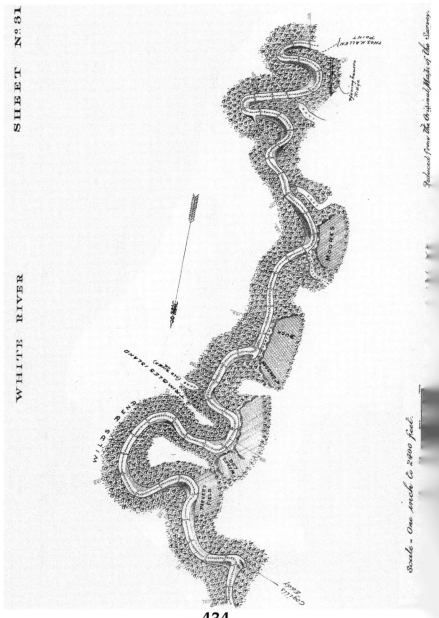

SHEET N.º 81

WHITE RIVER

Reduced from the Original Maps of the Survey.

Scale - One inch to 2400 feet.

**The author has added an arrow and text below
to highlight the maps' location of a shipwreck.**

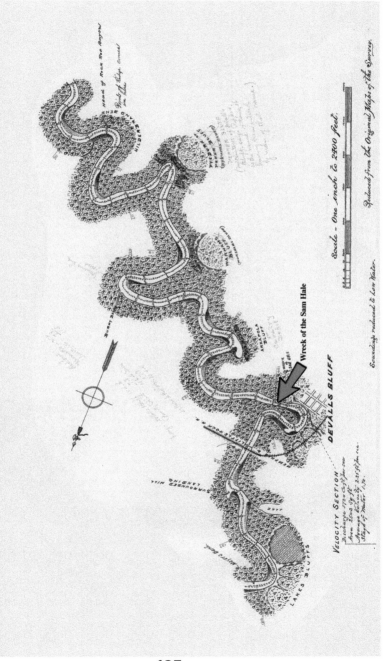

**The author has added two arrows and text below
to highlight the maps' location of two shipwrecks.**

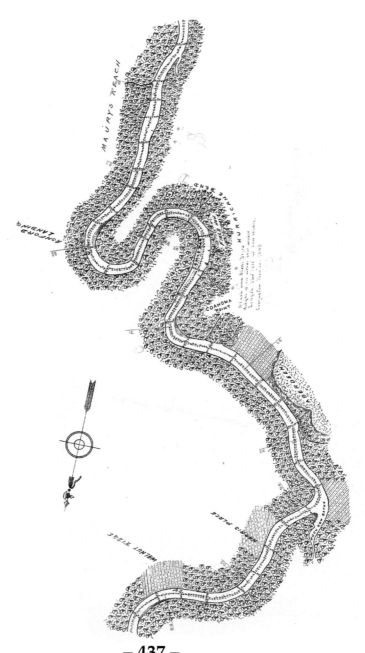

© 2022 Robert O. Crossman

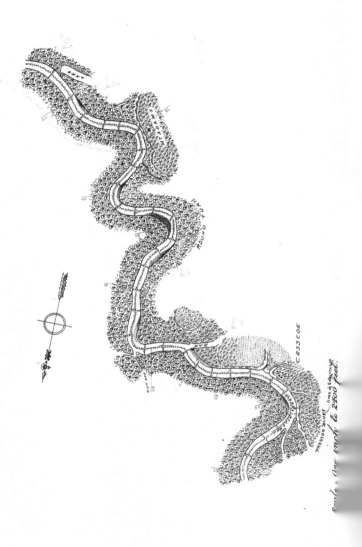

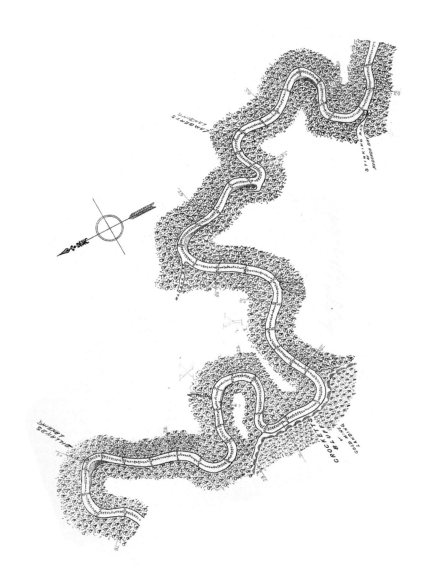

SHEET Nº 87

WHITE RIVER

The author has added three
arrows and text below
to highlight the maps' location
of three shipwrecks
in this portion of the
White River.

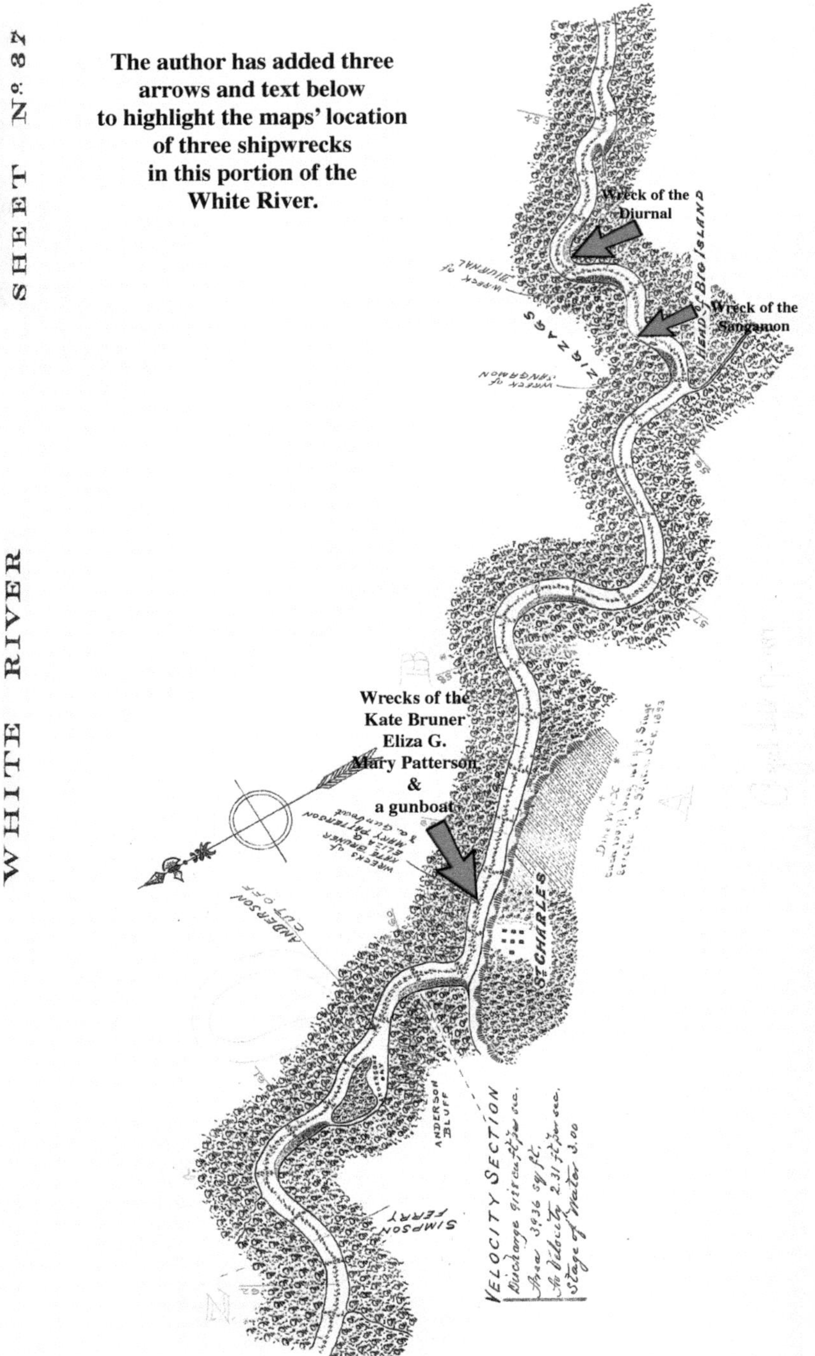

Wreck of the
Diurnal

Wreck of the
Sangamon

Wrecks of the
Kate Bruner
Eliza G.
Mary Patterson
&
a gunboat

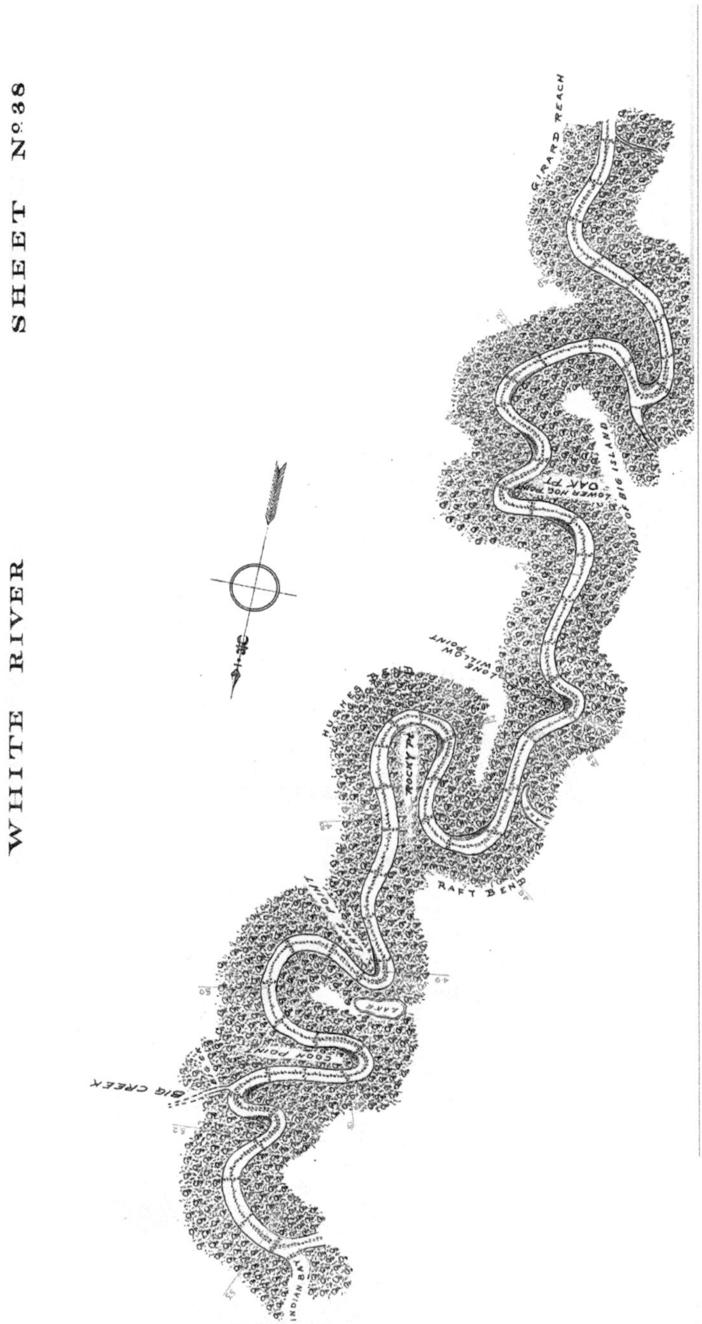
WHITE RIVER SHEET No. 38
GIRARD REACH
LOWER HOG POND
OAK PT
FOOT OF BIG ISLAND
LONE WILLOW POINT
HUGHES BEND
ROCKY PT
RAFT BEND
LAKE POINT
COON POINT
BIG CREEK
INDIAN BAY

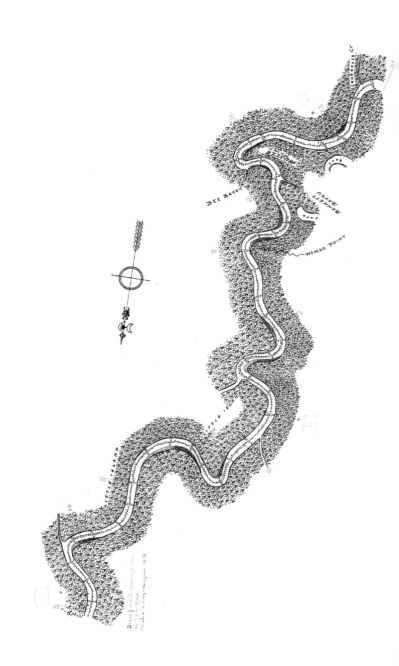

WHITE RIVER   SHEET N⁰. 39

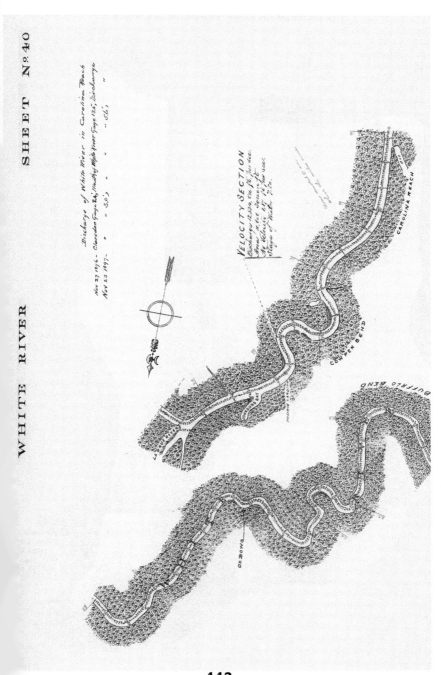

**The author has added an arrow and text below
to highlight the maps' location of shipwreck.**

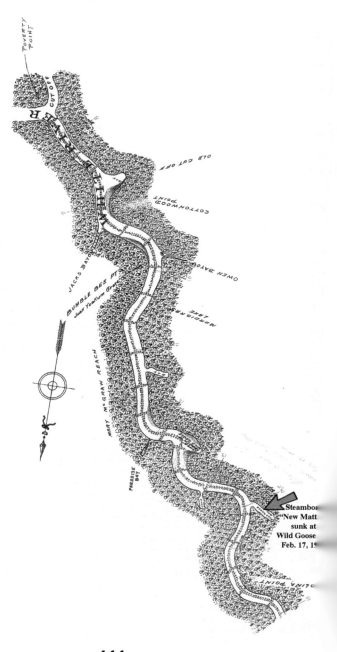

Steamboa
"New Matt
sunk at
Wild Goose
Feb. 17, 1

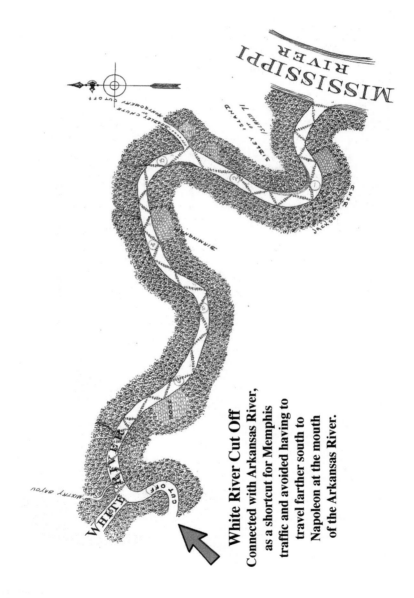

White River Cut Off
Connected with Arkansas River, as a shortcut for Memphis traffic and avoided having to travel farther south to Napoleon at the mouth of the Arkansas River.

MISSISSIPPI RIVER

SIGHT MONSTER TURTLE ON WHITE RIVER BOTTOM

Cotter, Dec. 17.—Parties arriving here from Branson, Mo., a point above here on White River, report the sighting of an enormous turtle in White River near the Maine Club by raftsmen bringing in cedar. The turtle was sighted on the bottom of the river, and when the men first saw it they supposed it was a boulder on the bottom. They estimated its weight at 300 pounds. The report of the big river monster created quite a sensation among the sportsmen of Branson, and Tom Brainard, one of the local anglers, organized a party to go out and capture it. As it will be impossible to gig the turtle they took a number of strong ropes which they will endeavor to loop over it and land it in that manner.

Arkansas Democrat (Little Rock, Arkansas) · 17 Dec 1912, Tue · Page 14

THE WHITE RIVER MONSTER

The Arkansas Game and Fish Commission has a problem to solve, first the identification of a reputed monster said to be a resident at the present time of an eddy in White River near Newport and second, to accomplish its capture or destruction. The secretary of the commission has invited Dr. S. C. Bellinger, zoologist of the University of Arkansas, to head an expedition to White River with the hope held out of adding a monstrosity of some sort to the university's museum.

"The White River monster," according to reports received by the Game and Fish Commission, "is supposed to rise to the surface in the late afternoons and float or swim around for periods of from five to fifteen minutes, with its head under water. No one has seen its head. It was described as being about the width of an automobile and as long as three autos. The back is supposed to look 'like a wet elephant.'"

Negro tenants on a nearby plantation were the first to sight the monster, but they have not been the only ones. The plantation owner for one has since seen it and has vouched for the monster's existence.

For the Fish and Game Commission the presence in White River of the monster is a matter of more than curiosity of the everyman kind. An element of an official interest enters into the problem. The great eddy in which the monster is credited with having taken up an abode has become famous for its stock of catfish, and there is some evidence to indicate that the monster has been making free with the catfish, contrary to the commission's conservation plans. In times past the eddy has been a favorite fishing place for the plantation tenants. They could set their trotlines in it with a reasonable certainty of a good mess of catfish the next morning. Fishing in the eddy is all to the bad now and the monster is blamed.

White River rises in the Ozarks and finally reaches the Mississippi after a long journey, much of it through swampy forest lands. The eddy which now emerges into the news to contest with Loch Ness for public interest in Twentieth Century monsters of an unidentified type is supposed to be 65 feet or so in depth, deep enough to accommodate any sort of varment and catfish of a size to satisfy its appetite.

Nashville Banner (Nashville, Tennessee)

AS THE EDITOR SEES IT

The Public Believes In "Monsters"

Someone has said that "a lie will travel half-way around the world while the truth is getting started." This statement itself may be an exaggeration, but it bears considerable truth. Perhaps a lie is believed more readily that the truth because it is usually more sensational. This accounts for the numerous false reports and stories of local, state and national government. Every community has its individuals who create and spread false rumors, some of which have an element of truth sufficient to make them seem convincing. These persons see "monsters" like the famed White River monster of Newport, Ark., the story of which has been recently disclosed as follows from the St. Louis Star-Times:

Loyal citizens of this little river town are indignant, for the state game and fish commissioner has declared the famous White River "monster" which terrorized the countryside for weeks was only the invention of an opportunist farmer.

According to D. C. Graves, Arkansas game and fish commissioner, the "monster" was created by Bramlett J. Bateman, a farmer who wished to be let alone so he could reap profits of a discovery.

Here is the story of the "monster's" invention as related by Graves:

Bateman discovered a large bed of valuable white sand mussel shells on a bar near his White River plantation. He began digging the shells out of the shallow water and selling them at a shel'boat at a profit of about $100 a day.

Soon, however, three Negroes stumbled upon the bed of shells and began to make inroads into Bateman's harvest. This set the farmer to thinking how he might regain his monoply of the shell digging.

Late one night he dragged a water-logged scow to the deep eddy which swirled darkly about the edge of the shell bar. Turning the ancient boat over, he sank it and anchored it with stones.

Next morning the Negroes resumed their work. When they were digging, the old boat rose from the depths with a mouthful gurgle. At sight of the moss-covered bottom of the scow emerging from the yellow waters the Negroes dropped their shovels and fled.

Bateman then resumed his solitary digging and while profited the Negroes spread the story of the monster. By the time the tale reached surrounding counties the monster had come a fire-snorting creature with huge warts on its back.

Swarms of fearful but curious sight-seers came for miles around to try to catch a glimpse of the monster thresh into foam the previously tranquil waters of the White River.

Never being one to pass up a money-making opportunity Bateman then fenced off his farm and posted signs: "25 cents to see the White River monster."

The monster received so much publicity after that a professional diver came here to walk the river bottom in search the creature's lair.

That's Commissioner Graves' version of the excitement but loyal Newport citizens still insist the monster was the real thing.

The Pineville Democrat (Pineville, Missouri) Mar 30, 1939, page 2

Appendix Five
Ribbon map of the Father of Waters by Coloney & Fairchild.
Published at St. Louis, Mo. : Coloney & Fairchild, 1866
Image Courtesy of the Library of Congress https://www.loc.gov/item/86691596/

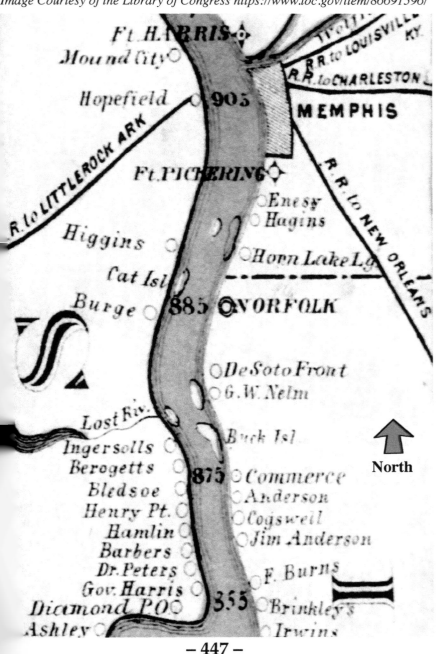

North

© 2022 Robert O. Crossman

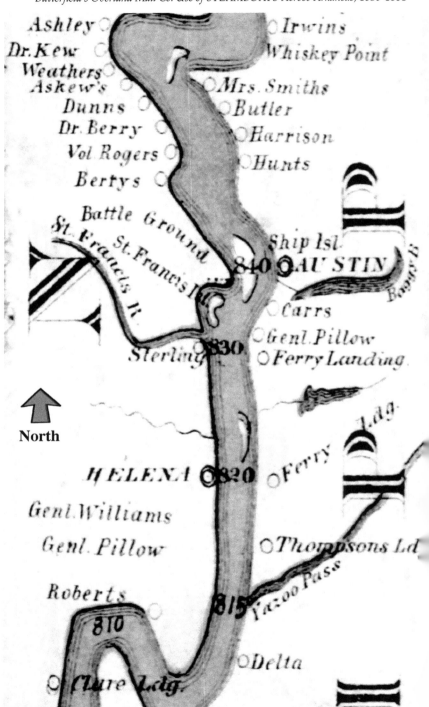

Ashley

Dr. Kew

Weathers

Askew's

Dunns

Dr. Berry

Vol. Rogers

Bertys

Irwins

Whiskey Point

Mrs. Smiths

Butler

Harrison

Hunts

Battle Ground

St. Francis R.

St. Francis R.

Ship Isl.

840 AUSTIN

Bogus B.

Carrs

Genl. Pillow

Ferry Landing

Sterling 830

North

HELENA 820

Ferry

Genl. Williams

Genl. Pillow

Roberts

810

815 Yazoo Pass

Thompsons Ld

Delta

Clure Ldg.

Delta

Clare Ldg.

Mrs. Wilkinson 805 Friars Point

Old Town Ldg.

Isl. Ledbetters

No.62. Isl. No.63.

Dekers 135 Burk

Websters

Holstead Bairds

L. B. Shoat

Isl. No.64

Jones Robsons Ldg.

Dermonts Ensleys

Barneys Donaldson

Peaks Parker

Isl. No.65 Vandervorts

SqGillins **North**

Mrs. Offit 105 Isl. No.66.

Maryposi L. Chambers

Rosal Sunflower

Isl. No. 67 Spears

Isl. No.68 Grove L.

Johnson Australia

Isl. No. 69 Spears

Laconia 745 Whitworth

Marlor Farrar

Dr. Henrys McGhee

White

North

© 2022 Robert O. Crossman

Appendix Six
Arkansas River and Tributaries Flood Control Plan June 10, 1932
U.S. Engineer Office, Memphis, Tennessee
Images Courtesy of the Arkansas Historic Preservation Program
1100 North Street, Little Rock, AR 72201

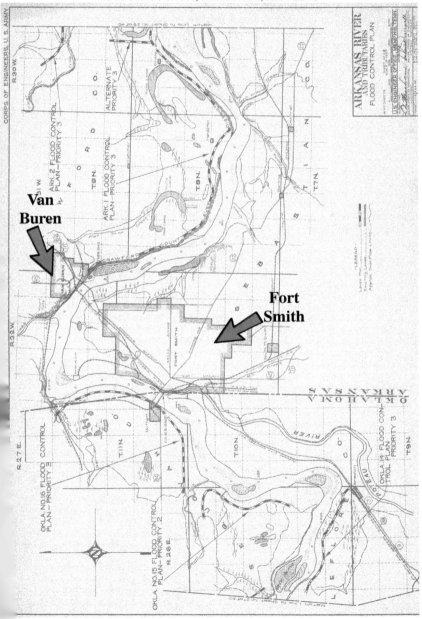

© 2022 Robert O. Crossman

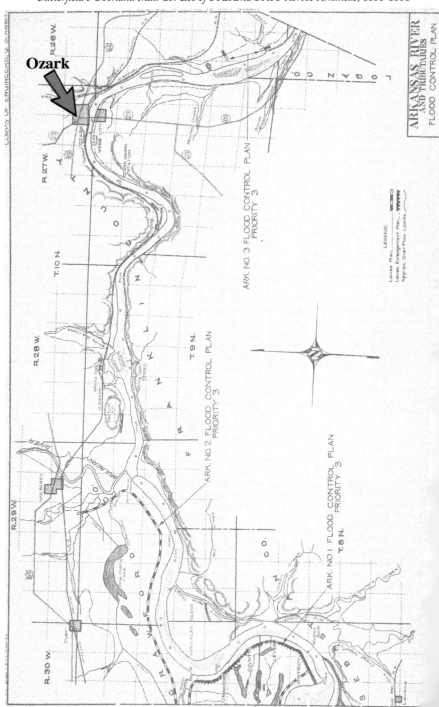

Ozark

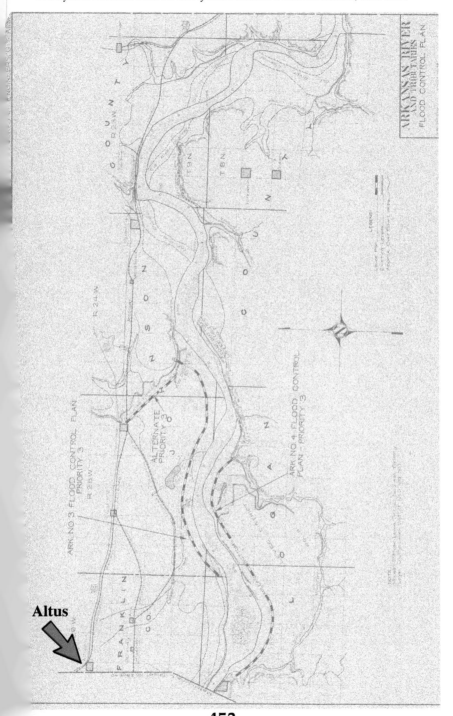

Altus

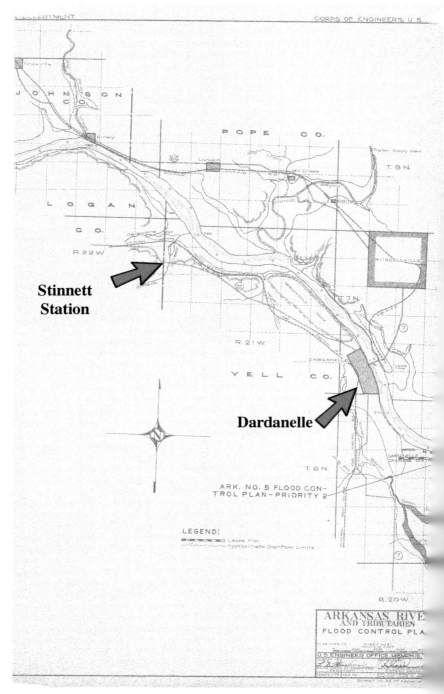

Stinnett Station

Dardanelle

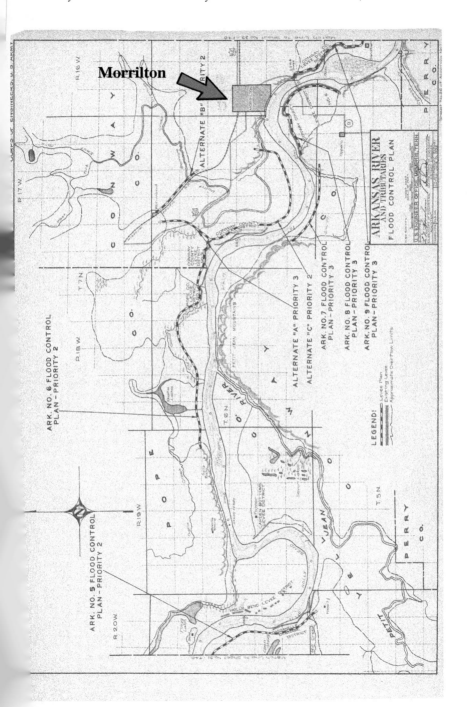

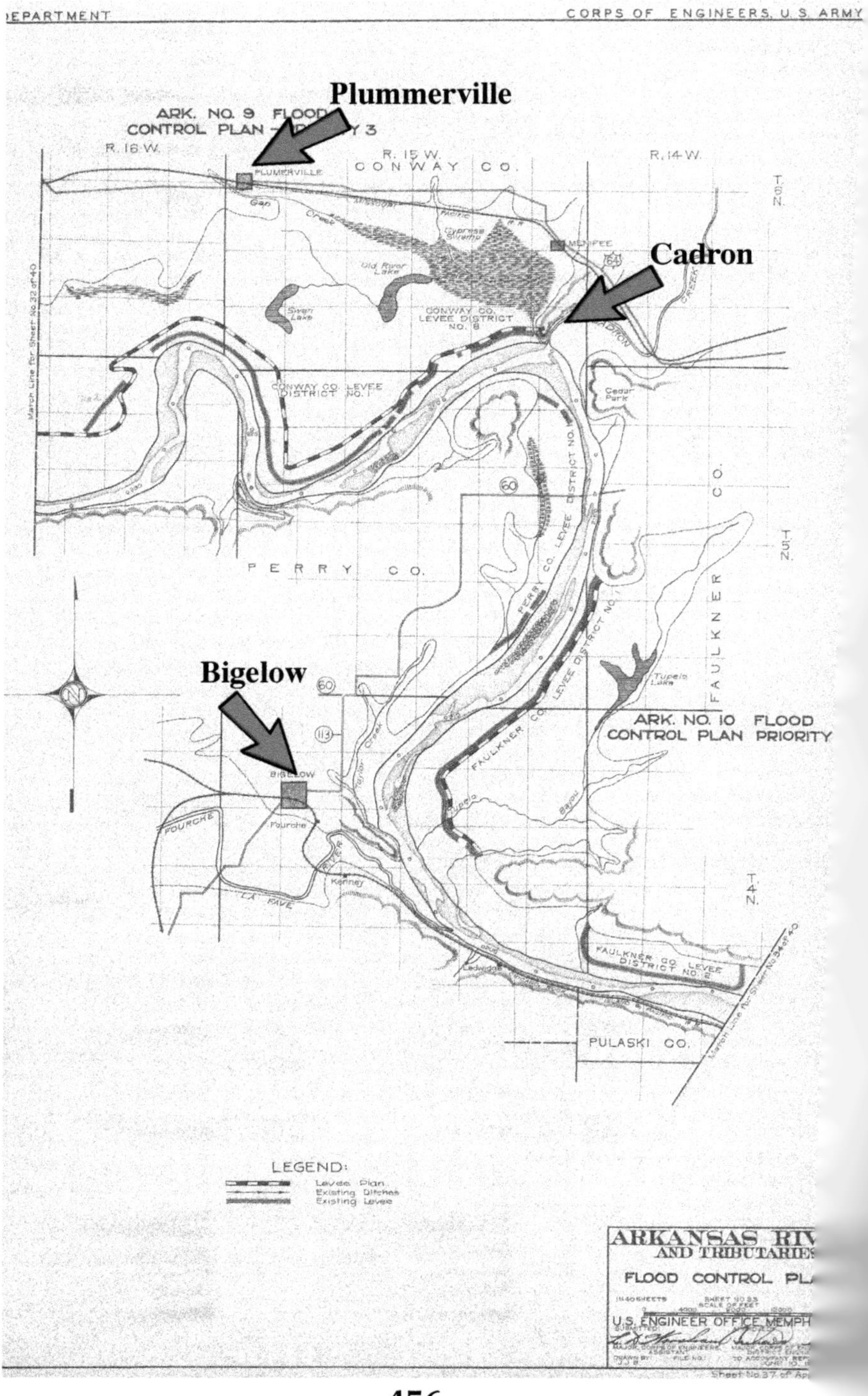
DEPARTMENT
CORPS OF ENGINEERS, U.S. ARMY
Plummerville
ARK. NO. 9 FLOOD CONTROL PLAN
R. 16 W.
R. 15 W.
R. 14 W.
CONWAY CO.
PLUMERVILLE
MENIFEE
Cadron
Cypress Swamp
Old River Lake
Swan Lake
CONWAY CO. LEVEE DISTRICT NO. 8
CONWAY CO. LEVEE DISTRICT NO. 1
Cedar Park
PERRY CO.
PERRY CO. LEVEE DISTRICT NO. 1
FAULKNER CO. LEVEE DISTRICT NO. 1
FAULKNER CO.
Tupelo Lake
Bigelow
ARK. NO. 10 FLOOD CONTROL PLAN PRIORITY
BIGELOW
Fourche
FOURCHE
LA FAVE
Kenney
Ledwidge
FAULKNER CO. LEVEE DISTRICT NO. 2
PULASKI CO.
LEGEND:
Levee Plan
Existing Ditches
Existing Levee
ARKANSAS RIV
AND TRIBUTARIES
FLOOD CONTROL PL
U.S. ENGINEER OFFICE, MEMPH

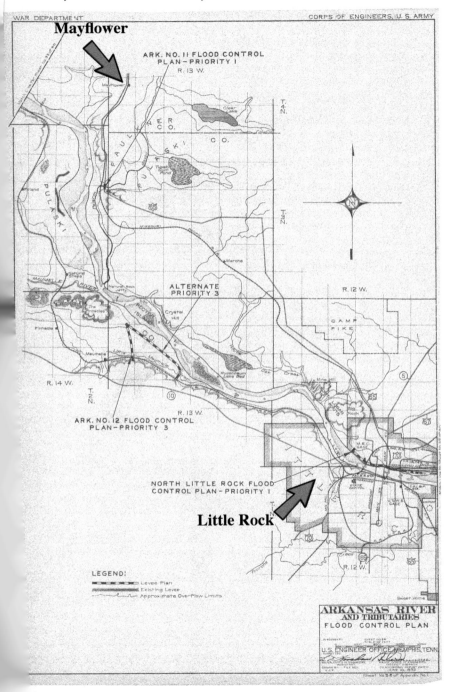

© 2022 Robert O. Crossman

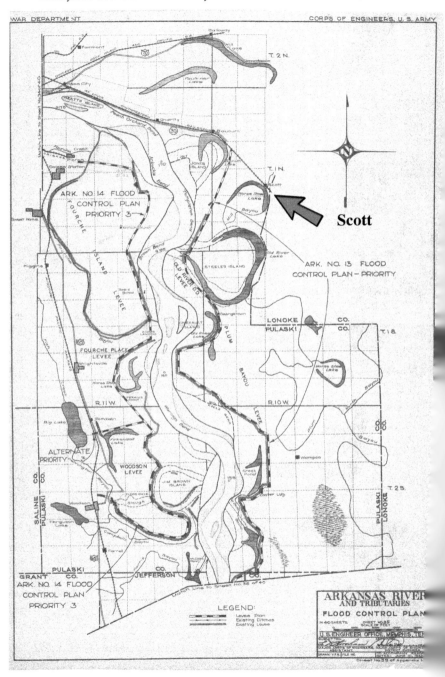

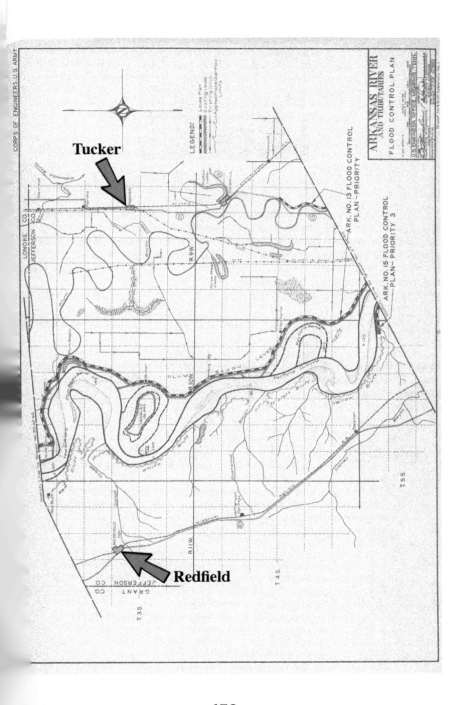

Dr. Bob Crossman has lived within a few hundred feet of Butterfield's Over land Mail Co. stage route across Arkansas most of his adult life in Russellville Morrilton, Brightwater, North Little Rock, Pottsville, and since 1988 in Conway.

He is a member of the Southern Trails Chapter of the Oregon-California Trail Association, Faulkner County Historical Society, Arkansas Historical Association the Shiloh Museum of Ozark History, and numerous postal history organization:

After graduating from Russellville High School, Bob received a B.A. fror Hendrix College in Conway, Arkansas, and received graduate and post-graduat degrees from SMU in Dallas, Texas.

He is the author of the 2021 book, *"Butterfield's Overland Mail Co. STAGI COACH TRAIL Across Arkansas 1858-1861,"* Ingram Spark Press, and the 20: book, *"Butterfield's Overland Mail Co. Use of STEAMBOATS Across Arkansas 185 1861,"* Ingram Spark Press.

He has also authored several articles including: *"Fort Smith's Connection to f Butterfield's Overland Mail Co.: Stations Between Memphis and Fort Smith"* in the Fc Smith Historical Society Journal, Fall 2021, p. 25-43; *"The Butterfield Overland M Company: Faulkner County Connection"* in the Faulkner County Facts & Fiddlin; Fall 2021, p. 24-32; and *"Dardanelle's Connection to Butterfield's Overland Mail Co."* the Yell County Historical Society Journal, Fall 2021.

His postal history published articles include: *"Walter Arndt Elected Postmas General of McDonald Territory"* The American Philatelist, Dec. 2008

Before retiring as a national and state staff member of The United Methoc Church, he wrote several additional books including:

Living Generously / Giving Generously, Ingram Spark Press, 2020

Preach Grace: 480 Sermons from a New Church in Conway, Arkansas, 2020

New Church Handbook: Planting New Churches in the Wesleyan Tradition, 2018

Committed to Christ: Six Steps to a Generous Life, Abingdon Press, 2012

Six Steps to a Generous Life: Living Your Commitment to Christ, Abingdon Press, 20

He also wrote the following articles for the United Methodist Church:

Why Are Wesleyans Starting New Churches? Seedbed Publishing, 2016

50 Ways to Missionally Engage The Mission Field Around Your Church, 2013

50 Ways to Increase Worship Attendance, 2011

50 Ways to Welcome a New Pastor or Associate Pastor, 2011

Dr. Bob Crossman
bcrossman@arumc.org
8 Sternwheel Drive, Conway, AR 72034-9391

© 2022 Robert O. Crossman

CPSIA information can be obtained
at www.ICGtesting.com
Printed in the USA
LVHW012307161221
706400LV00015B/367